C.H.VOGT, LITH.MILWAUKEE.   PRINTED BY J.KNAUBER & CO.

FALL RIVER, MASS.

THE TRIAL

of

LIZZIE

BORDEN

a true story

CARA ROBERTSON

Simon & Schuster
New York London Toronto Sydney New Delhi

Simon & Schuster
1230 Avenue of the Americas
New York, NY 10020

First Simon & Schuster hardcover edition March 2019

SIMON & SCHUSTER and colophon are registered
trademarks of Simon & Schuster, Inc.

For information about special discounts for bulk purchases,
please contact Simon & Schuster Special Sales at 1-866-506-1949
or business@simonandschuster.com.

The Simon & Schuster Speakers Bureau can bring authors to
your live event. For more information or to book an event, contact
the Simon & Schuster Speakers Bureau at 1-866-248-3049
or visit our website at www.simonspeakers.com.

Interior design by Lewelin Polanco

Manufactured in the United States of America

1   3   5   7   9   10   8   6   4   2

Library of Congress Cataloging-in-Publication Data is available.

ISBN 978-1-5011-6837-6
ISBN 978-1-5011-6838-3 (ebook)

For Mom and Dad

It is many a year since a criminal case in this country has excited such universal interest and been the subject of so much discussion as the Borden murder. It has all the fascination of a mystery about which there may be a thousand theories and upon which opinions may differ as variously as the idiosyncrasies of those who form them. There is so little absolute evidence that everybody can interpret the probabilities and circumstantial indications to suit himself, and much will depend upon his general view of human nature and its capabilities. There seems to be little prospect that the mystery will be cleared up by the trial . . . The verdict, if there shall be a verdict, will make little difference.

"Will It Remain a Mystery?"
New York Times, June 17, 1893

Contents

Part 1
MURDER

Part 2
TRIAL

Part 3

VERDICT

List of Illustrations

Persons of Interest

Rev. Edwin A. Buck, missionary of Central Congregational Church
Marienne Chagnon, neighbor, second wife of Dr. Chagnon
Marthe Chagnon, neighbor, daughter of Dr. Chagnon
Dr. Weneslas Chagnon, neighbor
Adelaide Churchill, next-door neighbor of the Bordens
Hannah Gifford, dressmaker
Jane Gray, stepmother of Abby Borden; mother of Sarah Whitehead
John Grouard, painter
Dr. Benjamin Handy, physician and owner of holiday cottage at
    which Lizzie was expected
Hiram C. Harrington, brother-in-law of Andrew Borden, married to
    Andrew's sister Lurana
Charles J. Holmes, Borden family friend and adviser, president of the
    Fall River Five Cents Savings Bank, and deacon of Central Con-
    gregational Church
Marianna Holmes, Borden family friend, wife of Charles J. Holmes
Elizabeth Johnston, friend of Lizzie, schoolteacher
Rev. William Walker Jubb, pastor of the Central Congregational Church
Hymon Lubinsky, ice cream peddler
Mary Raymond, dressmaker
Alice Russell, friend and former neighbor of Emma and Lizzie
Charles Sawyer, ornamental painter
Augusta Tripp, friend and former schoolmate of Lizzie Borden
Sarah Whitehead, half sister of Abby Borden, daughter of Jane Gray

FALL RIVER OFFICIALS

Officer George Allen
Mayor John Coughlin
Captain Dennis Desmond
Officer Patrick H. Doherty
Lieutenant Francis Edson
Assistant Marshal John Fleet
Officer Phil Harrington

City Marshal Rufus Hilliard
Officer Joseph Hyde
Officer William Medley
Officer Michael Mullaly
Matron Hannah Reagan
State Detective George Seaver
Deputy Sheriff Francis Wixon

LAWYERS

Melvin O. Adams, Lizzie Borden's defense lawyer

Andrew J. Jennings, Borden family lawyer

Hosea M. Knowlton, district attorney for the Southern District of Massachusetts

William H. Moody, district attorney for Essex County

Arthur S. Phillips, associate of Andrew Jennings

Albert E. Pillsbury, attorney general of Massachusetts

George D. Robinson, former governor of Massachusetts and Lizzie Borden's defense lawyer

JUDGES

Josiah Blaisdell, inquest and preliminary hearing, district court judge

Caleb Blodgett, trial judge, superior court

Justin Dewey, trial judge, superior court

Albert Mason, chief trial judge, superior court

MEDICAL EXPERTS

Dr. David Cheever, professor of surgery, Harvard

Dr. Albert Dedrick, physician

Dr. William Dolan, Bristol County medical examiner

Dr. Frank Draper, Suffolk County medical examiner, professor of legal medicine, Harvard

Professor Edward Wood, professor of chemistry, Harvard

REPORTERS AND COLUMNISTS

Joe Howard, Jr., *Boston Globe*

Elizabeth Jordan, *New York World*

John Manning, *Fall River Daily Herald*

Kate McGuirk, *New York Recorder*

E. H. Porter, *Fall River Daily Globe*, author of *Fall River Tragedy*
Julian Ralph, *New York Sun*
Amy Robsart, *Boston Post*
Walter P. Stevens, *Fall River Daily Evening News*
Henry Trickey, *Boston Globe*

Part 1

MURDER

Chapter 1

SOMEBODY
WILL DO SOMETHING

View of Fall River block, including D. R. Smith's drugstore, *courtesy of Fall River Historical Society*

On the morning of August 3, 1892, Eli Bence was working at D. R. Smith's drugstore on South Main Street in Fall River, Massachusetts, when a woman entered the store to ask for ten cents' worth of prussic acid. Prussic acid is a diluted form of hydrocyanic acid, a quick-acting poison—transparent, colorless, and volatile. As the *New Bedford Evening Standard* later reported, "If a person wished to kill and avoid detection, and that person were wise, hydrocyanic acid would be the first choice among all deadly drugs." The woman, however, volunteered that she needed the prussic acid "to put on the edge of a sealskin cape." Bence refused her request, explaining

Lizzie Andrew Borden,
*courtesy of Fall River
Historical Society*

that prussic acid was sold only on doctor's orders. Although he recognized her as "Miss Borden," it was not until another man whispered "This is Andrew J. Borden's daughter" that he looked at her "more closely" and noticed what he would later term "her peculiar expression around the eyes." She insisted that she had purchased the poison on prior occasions, but he stood firm. She departed unsatisfied. It was not the end of the story.

Lizzie Borden lived on Second Street near the bustling commercial center of Fall River, Massachusetts. In 1892, the Borden household at 92 Second Street consisted of Andrew Borden; his second wife, Abby; his grown daughters, Emma and Lizzie; and the family's domestic servant, Bridget Sullivan. An occasional houseguest, John V. Morse— the brother of Andrew Borden's first wife—rounded out the ménage. Neither of the Borden daughters, each past thirty, appeared likely to marry. Because their father was a man of consequence, their material comfort seemed assured. Yet it was not a happy home. The Bordens "did not parade their difficulties," but, as many commented, "things were not as pleasant at the Borden house as they might be."

A tall, gaunt, and severe-looking man, Andrew Borden was a walking advertisement for the then-popular "science" of physiognomy: his

Andrew Jackson
Borden, *courtesy of Fall
River Historical Society*

character was an exact match for his appearance. As the Bordens' former neighbor Alice Russell put it, "He was a plain-living man with
rigid ideas, and very set." His brother-in-law Hiram Harrington remarked, "He was too hard for me." In some respects, this was not
surprising. Andrew Borden was a self-made man. He had earned his
more than quarter-million-dollar fortune through a combination of
financial acumen and hard work, but he had maintained that position
through a determined frugality. As one newspaper reported, "He was
what is called close-fisted, but square and just in his dealings." He liked
to boast that in his years of business he had never borrowed a cent.
Andrew Borden had begun his career as a cabinetmaker, providing furniture for the dead as well as the living. An 1859 advertisement in the
Fall River Daily Evening News read: "Keep constantly on hand, Burial
Cases and Coffins, Ready-made of all kinds now in use in this section
of the country." Borden and his partner William Almy sold furniture
"at lower prices than can be bought elsewhere in this city." Andrew par-
layed his interest into more diverse commercial endeavors, ultimately
serving as president of the Union Savings Bank, a member of its board
of trustees, a director of the Merchants Manufacturing Company, the
B.M.C. Durfee Safe Deposit and Trust Company, the Globe Yarn Mill
Company, and the Troy Cotton and Woolen Manufactory. But his
most significant holdings were in real estate, and "he never made a

A. J. Borden building,
*courtesy of Fall River
Historical Society*

purchase of land for which he was not ready to pay cash down." He owned farmland across the Taunton River in Swansea, and in 1890 he built what was described as "one of the finest business blocks in the city located at the corner of South Main and Anawan streets." It was to this, the A. J. Borden building, a physical manifestation of his standing in Fall River, that he directed his steps every morning.

His own domestic arrangements were much more modest. In 1871, the Bordens moved from 12 Ferry Street, Andrew's father's home, to the house on Second Street. It was a step over, not a step up. Andrew Borden turned the former two-family house with separate floors for each family into a two-story residence for his family. During this renovation, he removed the upstairs faucet, leaving only the large soapstone sinks in the kitchen and cellar serviced by a cold-water tank. The following year, he connected the house to the city water supply, giving the occupants a flushable water closet in the cellar. But that was the extent of the house's luxuries. Everyone in the Borden household, as the reporter Julian Ralph later put it, "was his or her own chambermaid."

Andrew Borden married twice. His first wife, Sarah Morse Borden, had grown up on a farm. They married on Christmas evening in 1845. She brought him no dowry but bore him three daughters, two of whom—Emma and Lizzie—survived infancy. She herself died

Borden house on
Second Street, *courtesy of*
Fall River Historical Society

of "uterine congestion" and "disease of spine" in March 1863. Two years after Sarah's death, Andrew married Abby Gray. As a couple, they resembled the fairy-tale Spratts—Andrew long and lean, Abby short and plump. Andrew Borden needed a housekeeper and a mother for his children. Abby's feelings for Andrew were never recorded, but his offer must have been tempting to a thirty-seven-year-old spinster from a family continually skirting financial distress. Or perhaps it was her own father's remarriage to a comely widow and the subsequent birth of a daughter that prompted her decision to leave the increasingly crowded family home.

If she imagined a new life as the matriarch ensconced in a fond family circle, Abby made a poor bargain. Emma, fourteen at the time of her father's remarriage, resisted any maternal overtures: she always referred to Abby by her first name and never as "Mother." Perhaps her grief foreclosed a warmer relationship with the woman she viewed as her mother's replacement. Mary Ashton Rice Livermore, a friend of the first Mrs. Borden and later a pioneering suffragist, believed that Emma "had never ceased to regard Abby D. Borden as in some sense a usurper in the household in which at least one member cherished with jealous regard the sweet memories of a sanctified mother." Emma may have felt she served as mother to Lizzie and resented Abby's intrusion. Much later, Emma explained: "When my darling mother was

Abby Borden, *courtesy of Fall River Historical Society*

on her deathbed she summoned me, and exacted a promise that I would always watch over 'Baby Lizzie.'"

Abby may have hoped for more from her younger stepdaughter, but there, too, she experienced a certain froideur. Lizzie did call Abby "Mother," but she confided only in her older sister, Emma. As Lizzie herself put it, she "always went to Emma." Lizzie also had a special rapport with her father. Andrew Borden wore no ring to commemorate his marriage to Abby, but when his favorite daughter, Lizzie, gave him a thin gold ring, he promptly put it on his finger and wore it until his death. Lizzie was Andrew's namesake—christened Lizzie Andrew Borden—and it suited her. Like her father, she was forthright—a friend called her "a monument of straightforwardness"—and resolute. Lizzie later said that Andrew may have been "close in money matters, but I never asked him for anything that I wanted very much that I didn't get, though sometimes I had to ask two or three times."

Having perhaps married without affection, Abby also lacked the consolations of authority. Her husband retained tight control over the finances and her grown stepdaughters appeared to prefer their own company, receiving occasional visitors in the upstairs guest room. As family friend and former neighbor Alice Russell would later remark, "Mrs. Borden did not control the house; the whole summing up of it, was that." When John Grouard arrived to paint the Borden house in May 1892, Andrew told him that Lizzie "was to select the color, and I better not go on with it until the color was determined." (Lizzie did not approve of the tubs he had mixed; she supervised the remixing to the perfect shade of "dark drab.") In another sign of Abby's lesser status, her stepdaughters received the same allowance as she did. For Lizzie and Emma, it was pin money for whatever extras they might enjoy; Abby's allowance went toward household expenses. Yet, she seemed to accept her lot. According to her own stepmother, Abby was a "closed-mouth woman" who could "bear a great deal and say nothing."

Abby's attempt to help her half sister transformed her stepdaughters' chilly tolerance to open animosity. Abby's father left his house to his wife Jane Gray and their daughter Sarah Whitehead. Abby's stepmother wanted to sell her half of the property but Sarah did not have the funds to buy her share. At Abby's request in 1887, Andrew purchased Mrs. Gray's half interest and put it in Abby's name to allow Sarah and her husband to live there rent-free. His daughters objected to his spousal solicitude. What he did for Abby, Lizzie and Emma believed, he should do for his own flesh and blood. Andrew sought to appease his daughters by transferring property of equal value into their names. This effort at equalization was not a success. Instead, Andrew's purchase of the Whitehead house raised the tension in the Borden household to the surface. Thereafter, Bridget served two sittings of each meal because the daughters refused to eat with their parents and neither daughter would speak to Abby except in response to a direct question. "We always spoke," Emma later explained. Lizzie pointedly began referring to Abby as Mrs. Borden, her *stepmother*, and expressed her hostility toward Abby to anyone who asked. In March 1892, Lizzie chastised her dressmaker for referring to Abby as her mother. She said: "Don't say that to me, for she is a mean good-for-nothing thing."

Emma Borden, *courtesy of Fall River Historical Society*

Augusta Tripp, Lizzie's friend and former classmate, said: "Lizzie told me she thought her stepmother was deceitful, being one thing to her face, and another to her back." As Abby's own stepmother, Jane Gray, succinctly put it: "I told Mrs. Borden I would not change places with her for all her money."

Money was the source of other dissatisfactions in the household. Andrew Borden's miserly habits—in particular, his refusal to live on the Hill, the neighborhood of choice for the Fall River elite—placed his daughters in virtual social quarantine. Lizzie, in particular, did not appreciate her father's determined economies, and she freely indicated her unhappiness with her living conditions. As Alice Russell astutely explained, "He was a very plain living man; he did not care for anything different. It always seemed to me as if he did not see why they should care for anything different." She elaborated: "They had quite refined ideas, and they would like to have been cultured girls." Lizzie's estranged uncle, Hiram Harrington, was less charitable: "She thought she should entertain as others did, and felt that with her father's wealth she was expected to hold her end up with the other members of her set. Her father's constant refusal to entertain lavishly angered her."

In 1890, just prior to her thirtieth birthday, Lizzie Borden briefly experienced an unwonted measure of freedom when her father sent her on a Grand Tour of Europe in the company of other unmarried women of her acquaintance. In their shared cabin during the return voyage, Lizzie confided to her distant cousin Anna Borden her unwillingness to return to the house on Second Street with sufficient vehemence that Anna was able to recount the conversation three years later. Yet, return she did, at which point her father gave her a sealskin cape. The motivation for such extravagant gifts is unclear: Andrew Borden was a man who calculated the probable returns on his investments carefully, and the record discloses no other comparable generosity toward his daughters. After all, their weekly allowance remained set at four dollars—less than the weekly wage of a female spinner in the local mills.

Less than a year after Lizzie's return from Europe, at the end of

June 1891, the Borden household was the scene of a mysterious crime. Captain Dennis Desmond reported to 92 Second Street to learn the odd particulars: Abby's jewelry drawer had been rifled and some trinkets—most notably, a gold watch and chain of particular sentimental value—were missing. Andrew's desk had also been denuded of about $80 in cash, $25 to $30 in gold, and several commemorative streetcar tickets. Although the theft occurred in the middle of the day, none of the women in the house—neither Bridget, nor Emma, nor Lizzie—claimed to have heard a sound. When the police arrived, Lizzie Borden excitedly led them on a tour of the house and showed them the lock on the downstairs cellar door, which had apparently been forced open with a "6 or 8 penny nail." She suggested: "Someone might have come in that way." Desmond was stunned by the interloper's good fortune: the thief had broken in and discovered the Bordens' bedroom without attracting the attention of the women in the house. Andrew Borden noticed that the thief could only have entered through Lizzie's bedroom, and three times told Desmond: "I am afraid the police will not be able to find the real thief." The police were baffled or, at least, thought better of voicing their suspicions; Andrew Borden called off the investigation and attempted to keep word of the theft out of the papers.

Though the incident was officially forgotten—or suppressed—by the police and by the Bordens, Andrew Borden left the household with a daily reminder of his suspicion. He locked his bedroom every day and then left the key in the sitting room in plain sight. Because the house had no central halls, the upstairs bedrooms opened onto each other. The elder Bordens also securely locked their connecting door, which opened into Lizzie's room. (Emma's room was only accessible through Lizzie's room.) For her part, Lizzie moved furniture to block her side of the connecting doors. As a result, the Borden house may have been the most elaborately secured domicile in town, for the front door was triple-locked and family members elaborately locked and unlocked their bedrooms and bureaus throughout the day.

Abby was acutely aware of her stepdaughters' feelings, but it was not until August 2, 1892, two days before her death, that she considered them life-threatening. Despite the oppressive heat of summer, the Bordens ate leftover swordfish. That evening, the elder Bordens spent a nauseated, sleepless night and Bridget and Lizzie experienced a milder form of the same malady. Emma was not at home; she had been away for nearly two weeks visiting friends in Fairhaven. Though such incidents were common in Fall River—they were colloquially known as "the summer complaint"—Abby did not view her distress as typical. Instead, on the following morning, she went across the street to her doctor's house and confided that she thought she had been poisoned. Learning of their fish dinner, Dr. Seabury Bowen was not alarmed, but he did accompany Abby back across the street to examine Andrew, who refused his medical expertise. In fact, the Borden patriarch stood angrily on the threshold, blocking Dr. Bowen's entrance and shouting that he would not pay the doctor for the visit.

The subject might have remained closed, but the household—with the exception of Lizzie—fell ill again that evening after a meal of mutton stew. The prosecutor would later argue that the happenstance of food poisoning "was an illness suggestive of an opportunity to a person desiring to procure the deaths of one or other of those people." That same evening, Lizzie paid a call on her friend and former neighbor Alice Russell and confided her fears. She believed the milk had been poisoned and alluded to nebulous threats against her father by unnamed men. Alice Russell was a sensible woman and she pointed out the absurdity of Lizzie's fears. Despite Miss Russell's reassurance, Lizzie spoke of her uneasiness and sense of foreboding, remarking: "I feel as if something was hanging over me that I cannot throw off, and it comes over me at times, no matter where I am." She added: "I don't know but somebody will do something."

Chapter 2

AN INCREDIBLE CRIME

Front of Borden house on Second Street, *courtesy of Fall River Historical Society*

On the morning of August 4, 1892, Adelaide Churchill looked out her kitchen window and saw her next-door neighbor Lizzie Borden standing just inside the Bordens' screen door. The daughter of a former mayor, now reduced to taking in boarders, she kept a sharp eye trained on the neighborhood. Concerned, she opened her window and called out, "What is the matter?"

Lizzie Borden replied, "Oh, Mrs. Churchill, do come over. Someone has killed father."

Side steps of Borden
house, *courtesy of Fall
River Historical Society*

HORRIBLE BUTCHERY

It was an inconvenient day for any crime; the bulk of the police force
was off at Rocky Point near Providence, Rhode Island, enjoying their
annual picnic. Chief Marshal Rufus Hilliard, however, was on duty. A
large, handsome man with a commanding presence, Hilliard was just
the person for the crisis. But when he received the telephone call alert-
ing him to "trouble at the Borden house," he had no idea that he was
dealing with anything special. Serious violent crime was rare in Fall
River. At most, he expected some kind of disturbance. Drawing from
his depleted reserve, he sent a single officer to the house. Patrolman
George Allen ran part of the way and made the trip in less than four
minutes. What he found was both horrible and bizarre: Andrew Borden had been, as a local newspaper would report, "hacked to pieces."
Yet, for all the carnage, there were no signs of disturbance in the house,
nor was the murder weapon anywhere in sight. Though the house was
on a busy thoroughfare within earshot of the center of town, no one—
including the surviving members of the household—had seen or heard
anything out of the ordinary. Allen pressed a nosy passerby, an ornamental painter named Charles Sawyer, into service as a guard and ran
back to the station house for assistance. Sawyer would regret his prying
after spending a full seven hours on sentry duty, all the while in fear of

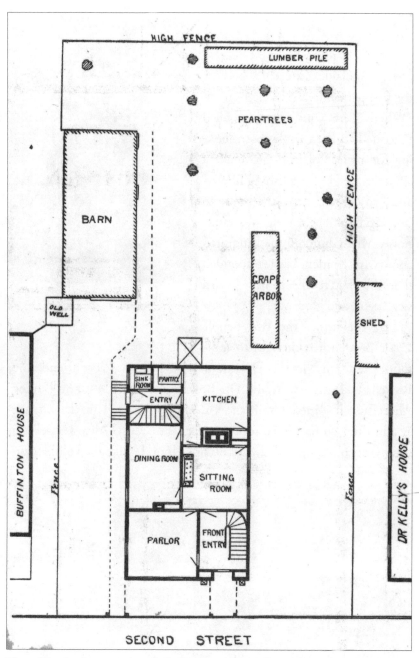

Plan of Borden house and yard, E. H. Porter, *The Fall River Tragedy*, 1893, *collection of the author*

the murderer's return to the scene of the crime.

While waiting for the police to arrive, Adelaide Churchill became the first person to ask Lizzie Borden: "Where were you?" Lizzie replied that she had been in the barn looking for a piece of iron—to make a sinker (a weight for a fishing line)—and had come back to the house to investigate after hearing a strange noise. Mrs. Churchill then inquired about Mrs. Borden. Lizzie responded that Abby had received a note from a sick friend and gone out.

Marshal Rufus Hilliard, *courtesy of Fall River Historical Society*

By this time, the two people Lizzie Borden had thought to summon, the family doctor, Dr. Seabury Bowen, and close friend Alice Russell, had arrived. While Dr. Bowen examined Andrew Borden, Alice Russell joined Lizzie and Adelaide Churchill in the kitchen. A tall, thin woman once reckoned a great beauty, Alice Russell was forty years old, unmarried, and no one's fool. Unlike the voluble Mrs.

Body of Andrew Borden on sofa, *courtesy of Fall River Historical Society*

Churchill, Miss Russell set to work fanning Lizzie. Emerging shaken from the living room, Dr. Bowen left to wire Emma Borden who was visiting friends in Fairhaven, some thirty miles away. Lizzie asked him not to reveal the full horror lest he alarm the elderly woman with whom Emma was staying.

Bridget Sullivan, *courtesy of Fall River Historical Society*

Bridget Sullivan, unlike the others, had not forgotten about the absent Abby Borden. Increasingly agitated, she suggested asking Mrs. Whitehead, Abby's half sister and closest friend, of her whereabouts. Lizzie then volunteered that she thought Abby had returned and gone upstairs. If the women present retained the capacity to be shocked, this was startling information. Abby, Lizzie had said, had gone out. She had made no mention of her return. Someone had to look for her. Mrs. Churchill agreed to accompany the reluctant Bridget upstairs. Mrs. Churchill only ascended high enough "to clear [her] eyes above the second floor." But it was enough to see the body of Abby Borden in the guest bedroom. Mrs. Churchill rushed back to relay her gruesome discovery. Alice Russell asked, "Is there another?" Mrs. Churchill's response: "Yes." Lizzie said, "O, I shall have to go to the cemetery myself."

Upon his return, Dr. Bowen examined the remains of another Borden. His first thought was that Abby had died of fright. Barely five feet tall, Abby Borden weighed over two hundred pounds, and Dr. Bowen did not initially attempt to move her. Her body was face-down, surrounded by coagulated blood rather than the fresh oozing liquid covering Andrew Borden's clothes. This left little doubt as to the order of deaths and suggested that Abby had been slain sometime before her husband. Yet, it was not until officers Michael Mullaly and Patrick H. Doherty arrived on the scene that her body was turned over, revealing the extent of her injuries, and permitting Dr. Bowen to ascertain the real cause of her death. Referring to both murders, Dr. Bowen later remarked, "Physician that I am and accustomed to all sorts of horrible sights, it sickened me."

By the time Dr. Bowen finished his preliminary examination of Abby Borden, "the cry of murder swept through the city of Fall River like a typhoon." Indeed the brutality of the murders led one newspaper to speculate that Jack the Ripper had come to America. Police officers arrived in force and their numbers attracted an even greater contingent of passersby and concerned citizens. Hundreds of people gathered in front of the Borden house. The next morning, there would be over fifteen hundred spectators.

As the residents of Fall River watched and waited, the police, led by the assistant marshal, John Fleet, "a dyed-in-the-wool policeman," constructed a timeline of the morning of the murders. Abby and Andrew Borden, still suffering from apparent food poisoning, ate breakfast about 7:00 a.m. with their houseguest John V. Morse, Andrew's brother-in-law. The breakfast consisted of cold mutton, mutton soup, johnnycakes, coffee, and tea. Morse departed at 8:45 a.m. to visit relatives who lived on Weybosset Street. At 8:50 a.m., Lizzie Borden ate a

Body of Abby Borden in guest bedroom, *courtesy of Fall River Historical Society*

light breakfast of cookies and coffee by herself. Emma, the older sister, had been out of town for two weeks visiting friends in Fairhaven. Prior to her departure, Andrew Borden had insisted on establishing where she could be reached by telegraph, leading one paper to ask, "Did He Have a Presentiment?" At 9:15 a.m., Andrew Borden left the house to attend to business downtown, and Abby asked Bridget to wash the outside windows. By 9:30 a.m., Abby went up to the guest bedroom to make the guest bed and was struck down by nineteen blows. The force of the blows shattered her skull and separated a flap of skin from her back.

At 10:45 a.m., Andrew Borden returned home, but stood on the doorstep fumbling with the lock, unaware that the door had been bolted from the inside. As she struggled to unlock the door, Bridget uttered an exclamation that evoked laughter from Lizzie Borden, who was apparently descending from the front landing—directly opposite the open door of the guest bedroom where her stepmother lay dead. After entering the hallway, Andrew removed his bedroom key from the mantel in the sitting room, its location during the day, and went up the back stairs to his bedroom. When he came downstairs, Lizzie greeted her father and inquired about the mail. In turn, he asked about Abby and was told that she had gone out after receiving a note. Andrew took off his coat and settled down on the sofa for a nap. Whether or not this was his usual practice, this decision to take a late-morning nap on a Thursday elicited no particular comment from either Bridget or Lizzie. But sometime between 10:45 a.m. and 11:45 a.m., this nap became his final slumber. His assassin struck ten times and departed.

The timeline was straightforward but presented one obvious question: How did the assassin manage to commit his crimes without attracting the attention of either Lizzie Borden or Bridget Sullivan? If the murderer was not a member of the household, then he would have had to elude both women for over an hour and a half between the murders. A cramped clothes closet next to the upstairs guest bedroom where Abby was slain could have provided a refuge, but the bedroom door itself remained open, advertising rather than hiding the crime. The cellar door and front door were locked throughout the morning and the screen door at the side of the house was usually in sight of Bridget Sullivan as she went about her household tasks. Moreover, while Andrew's napping figure presented a convenient target for the assassin, Abby was upstairs making the bed in the guest bedroom when she was struck down. And no one had heard a sound. The *Fall River Daily Herald* observed that the two-hundred-pound Abby must have jarred the house when she fell.

As they searched for clues, the police also looked closely at the victims. They wondered how a quiet elderly couple could have provoked such murderous hatred. What they would find would be almost as unsettling as the crime itself.

SPINDLE CITY

In 1892, Fall River was the third-largest city in Massachusetts and its most important center for textile production. Connected to New York and Boston by regular shipping lines, Fall River benefited from its communication with these major urban centers of commerce. But, at its core, "the Manchester of America" remained a mill town. Like many such towns, Fall River was divided into restrictive social groups

Fall River as seen from Mt. Hope Bay, circa 1891, *courtesy of Fall River Historical Society*

based upon class, ethnicity, and religion. The elite derived their status from their Yankee heritage, their Congregationalism or other Protestantism, and their ownership of the mills. Foremost among the Protestant elite were the Bordens, the Durfees, and the Braytons. In fact, until 1813, the members of the Borden family owned the water power of the Quequechan River flowing into and under the city, a title particularly important in a mill town. Through marriages and business arrangements, the leading families of Fall River preserved their control and cemented their status. That status, in turn, contributed to a self-regarding provincialism that proved difficult to dislodge. Outsiders who married into the local elite struggled with the unwritten sumptuary rules: for example, Detroit heiress Mary Newcomb learned to her chagrin that her Paris trousseau was "much too dressy for Fall River" and, on the advice of a helpful matron, put her dresses à la mode into storage to "age."

Large influxes of immigrants into Fall River—mostly Irish Catholics, French Canadians, and Portuguese—altered the composition of the city in the course of the nineteenth century. These recent arrivals in Fall River found employment in the textile mills or in allied industries. Although native-born Americans had toiled in the mills early in the century, by the 1890s nearly all the men and women who worked there were immigrants. At the beginning of the century, mill work was not considered demeaning to native-born workers, especially women who wanted to earn extra money for a dowry. In fact, in 1817, Hannah Borden, the daughter of a mill stockholder, was singled out as a particularly valued employee. With the arrival of foreign labor and the rise of more restrictive attitudes about the proper role of women— so long as they were middle-class and native-born—earning extra pin money in this fashion ceased to be an option. Under the immigration law of July 1864, corporations could literally import workers and withhold a percentage of their wages for the first year in order to defray the costs of their passage. Even before such legislation was enacted, Irish-Catholic and English immigrants made up the majority of workers in the textile mills by 1850. By 1885, French Canadians were the most important single ethnic group employed in the region's textile industry. Other immigrants, particularly Irish women like the twenty-six-year-old Bridget Sullivan, entered domestic service. But in exchange for better housing (and a wage of between two dollars and six dollars per week), Bridget suffered a galling trade-off: the Bordens (with the exception of Abby) called her "Maggie," the name of their previous domestic servant, rather than learning her name.

Each of the city's social groups inhabited distinct geographic sectors. The segmentation into ethnic ghettos paralleled the pattern of settlement in other industrial New England towns of the same period. But, unlike such towns, the odd topography of the waterfront town mirrored its elaborate hierarchy and gradations of influence. Located at the mouth of the Taunton River, where it is joined by the Quequechan River before emptying into Mount Hope Bay, Fall River rises sharply in increments from sea level. South Main Street, less than one-half mile from shore and on the same level as the Borden house, is 119 feet above the mean high-water mark of the Taunton River. In contrast, Highland Avenue, which marks the upper boundary of the city's elite Hill district, runs from 254 feet to 355 feet above the river. Many of the newly arrived immigrants lived closest to the water and

View of Second Street looking south (Borden house is the second house on the left), *courtesy of Fall River Historical Society*

View of Second Street looking north (Borden house is the second house on the right), *courtesy of Fall River Historical Society*

the mills. Slightly higher in altitude were the more established Irish and lesser Protestants who lived in the flats on roughly the same level as South Main Street. Their homes ranged from tenements to modest single-family houses like the Bordens' home on Second Street. Lizzie Borden lived on the same plane as the middle-class Irish of the "flats" around the business district, far beneath her Borden cousins who lived on "the Hill." The location, like the house, suited Andrew, but his daughters would have preferred a more fashionable address.

Though the Yankee mill and banking families effectively owned Fall River through the early twentieth century, the newer arrivals constituted an important political force when they voted as a bloc— composing a voting majority by the 1890s—and an important economic power when they organized into unions. For over two-thirds of the nineteenth century, only prominent Yankees, like Adelaide Churchill's father, were elected to public office in Fall River. However, in the late 1880s, the first Catholic mayor, John W. Cummings, was elected and a Catholic physician, John W. Coughlin, held the office from 1890 to 1894, and therefore had the unenviable task of informing Lizzie Borden of the police department's suspicion about her story. His sister Annie's marriage to Hugo Dubuque, a leader of the French Canadian community, helped join the Irish and French Canadians into an effective Democratic voting bloc. Significantly, the Irish Democratic political ascendancy did not change the unwritten social rules. Although Lizzie Borden received the condolences of the Catholic physician and mayor, John W. Coughlin, none of her family had ever interacted socially with their Catholic neighbors, Dr. and Mrs. Kelly or Dr. and Mrs. Chagnon and daughter Marthe. Upon discovering her father's body, Lizzie Borden sent Bridget to find Dr. Bowen, who was not at home. Bridget left word with Dr. Bowen's wife that he was needed urgently at the Borden house. It apparently never occurred to either of the women to summon the neighboring Dr. Kelly or Dr. Chagnon. Instead, Lizzie Borden waited inside the screen door for the uncertain arrival of Protestant medical assistance.

But despite her good Yankee name, Lizzie Borden stood in peculiar relationship to the social structure of Fall River. The most prominent Borden in Fall River assured the public: "No true Borden has ever placed a stumbling block in the way of the law and no member of my family will in any way hamper the police in their investigation." Lizzie Borden may have been a Borden but she was a lesser Borden. Lizzie Borden's great-grandfather, Richard Borden, inherited less money than his brother Thomas and his line did not thrive. The descendants of Thomas Borden distinguished themselves as entrepreneurs and established themselves in the elite; Richard Borden left a mere four hundred dollars to his son Abraham, Lizzie Borden's grandfather. Abraham Borden improved his lot by peddling fish, earning enough to support his family. But his only legacy to his son was the freehold in a house on Ferry Street. And while much was made of Andrew Borden's fortune at his death, his wealth paled beside that of his cousin Colonel Richard Borden, whose heirs inherited stock worth between three and four million dollars. Richard Borden's son Matthew Chaloner Durfee Borden was even richer and grander, consolidating his own business empire with print- and ironworks in Fall River and his place in New York society with a private box in "the Golden Horseshoe" at the Metropolitan Opera. At his death, he had more than doubled his father's fortune.

Andrew Borden was, as he liked to remark, a self-made man. As a result, he was temperamentally unsuited to assume "his rightful place" in the social life of Fall River. He was far more interested in accumulating money than spending it, preferring to accrue interest rather than gain social recognition. A journalist described his pleasure as confined to "piling up dollars." His daughters, particularly Lizzie, may have wanted more—to live, as Alice Russell had remarked, "as other people lived." Lizzie and Emma chose, for example, to attend the "society church," the Central Congregational Church, rather than patronize the more modest house of worship where Andrew Borden rented a pew. Andrew had once belonged to the Central Congregational Church but left following a dispute over a real estate transaction. The church did not agree to his price for a tract of land he owned; he showed his displeasure by voting with his feet. By contrast, Lizzie and Emma continued to worship there. Lizzie sought to ingratiate herself among the Central Congregational Church leadership, even volunteering to teach the children of Chinese immigrants at Sunday school.

Lizzie Borden threw herself into such charitable works to improve her social position and because they were the only culturally sanctioned activities for women of her class. In addition to teaching Sunday school, she was secretary-treasurer of the local Christian Endeavor Society, a member of the Women's Christian Temperance Union (WCTU), and a dabbler in the Ladies Fruit and Flower Mission. But there is little evidence that she found these activities satisfying. Too old to attend one of the new women's colleges and too wealthy for the mills, Lizzie Borden, like other middle-class women of her generation, was relegated to unproductive marginality, free to enjoy her leisure in the presumed comforts of her home. Unlike most other women of her generation, however, Lizzie Borden never married. The average age of marriage in the 1890s was twenty-two; at thirty-two, Lizzie Borden was a spinster. While her parents lived, she would always be a houseguest in her father's home. And who would own the house after he died? Insecure about her place in Fall River society, Lizzie Borden remained equally unsure about her position in the family. In the words of a contemporary journalist, Julian Ralph, her situation exemplified "a peculiar phase of life in New England—a wretched phase" suffered by "the daughters of a class of well-to-do New England men who seem never to have money enough no matter how rich they become, whose houses are little more cheerful than jails, and whose women folk had, from a human point of view, better be dead than to be born to these fortunes." "Crime," he said, "seems to attend that phase and point it out as relentlessly as the knife of a surgeon is aimed at a cancerous growth."

EVERY MAN TURNED DETECTIVE

In this era, America derived its vision of the criminal classes from European models in criminology, especially those of Cesare Lombroso, the leading proponent of the Italian school of criminology. Lombroso had challenged earlier assumptions—linking criminality with a simple inability to resist temptation—in favor of a model of difference. Criminals, he believed, were born, not made. He characterized the criminal as a primitive throwback, an atavistic specimen born for evil deeds. Drawing upon contemporary anthropological studies of "other races," he believed the physical structures of their bodies displayed their criminal natures—ranging from asymmetrical physiognomy to other bodily stigmata. In all cases, the born criminal's physical traits were seen as less evolved, more apelike. In a series of reviews of criminological literature published in the *American Journal of Psychology*, Dr. Arthur MacDonald summarized the latest thinking: "The true criminal has something of the incompleteness of the beast; he is like a man who has remained animalized."

Americans found independent confirmation of Lombroso's theories in their own criminal classes. Richard L. Dugdale, for example, famously described a series of blood relatives, the "Juke" family, languishing in a New York prison for assorted offenses and concluded that eugenics, intended to eliminate further generations of such degenerate specimens, offered the best solution. The larger environment merely triggered their underlying atavistic criminal nature. By contrast, the reform-minded Charles Loring Brace, author of *The Dangerous Classes of New York and Twenty Years' Work Among Them*, used explicitly evolutionary language in his theory of the inherited degeneracy. Though he lamented the likely transmission to future generations of the dangerous classes' appetite for liquor, sexual licentiousness, and laziness, he hoped to mold them in the image of his more moral and fortunate class. For many, it was clear that the "dangerous classes" largely arrived from foreign shores. In one of her popular lectures, the prominent suffragist and temperance advocate Mary Ashton Rice Livermore contended: "An invasion of migrating peoples, outnumbering the Goths and Vandals that overran the south of Europe, has brought to our shores a host of undesirable aliens . . . Unlike the earlier and desirable immigrants, who have helped the republic retain its present greatness, these hinder its developments. They are discharged convicts, paupers, lunatics, imbeciles, peoples suffering from loathsome and contagious diseases, incapables, illiterates, defectives, contract laborers, who are smuggled hither to work for reduced wages, and who crowd out our native working men and women. Our jails, houses of corrections, prisons, poor-houses, and insane asylums are crowded with these aliens."

The Fall River Police Department, headed by Marshal Rufus Hilliard, began its investigation by immediately rounding up the usual suspects. In keeping with prevailing attitudes about criminality, the Fall River police expected to find a depraved outsider with a foreign accent. That year, as in the prior years, more than two-thirds of those arrested were born abroad. (The Report of the City Marshal helpfully listed the national origin of all those arrested.) Stories circulated that "a Swede or a Portuguese" in Borden's employ had come to the Borden house demanding money on the morning of the murders. Lizzie herself vouched for Alfred Johnson, the Swede. The police eliminated Johnson and Portuguese laborers from Borden's Swansea farm as well as several other immigrant suspects. Peleg Brightman reported that he had seen a bloody axe owned by Joseph Silvia. When the police investigated, they found children with "dirty dresses on, which were caked with blood." This alarming sight had an apparently innocent explanation: their mother explained that the children were "very subject to the nose bleed." The police concluded that the axe itself was too "old, dull, and . . . worn" to have caused the wounds on the Bordens. The police were also called to the New Bedford Savings Bank to pick up "a Portuguese" who was attempting to cash out his savings of "sixty odd dollars." He, like the others, gave "a satisfactory account of himself" and was released. Another line of thought hinged on the nature of the crimes, that there was something "effeminate" about the hacking and, therefore, according to racial theories of the day, pointed to a "Chinaman."

Many contemporary commentators envisaged the murderer through the lens of Lombroso's theories—a brutish throwback, more monster than man. One newspaper conceived of the guilty party as a "human fiend," for no ordinary criminal could repeatedly axe two elderly people. After the murders, Rev. William Walker Jubb, pastor of the Central Congregational Church, the society church favored by Lizzie and her sister, Emma, asked his congregation not to allow rumor to blight the lives of the innocent, which he contrasted with the necessary character of the true murderer. He asked, "What must have been the person who could have been guilty of such a revolting crime? One to commit such a murder must have been without heart, without soul, a fiend incarnate, the very vilest of degraded humanity, or he must have been a maniac."

The idea of a maniac as the murderer provided an explanation for the shocking brutality of the murders: the skulls of the Bordens had been so shattered by the force of multiple blows that the victims were virtually unrecognizable. One witness described Andrew's face as "a mass of raw meat." The prominent attorney and former mayor Milton Reed also advised: "Look for the maniac." He explained: "We who have had some experience with criminals, and some knowledge of crime, know that murderers do not stand over the victims delivering blow after blow when they know the victims are dead . . . In every detail it shows the stubborn and dogged brutality of the insane."

Dr. Benjamin Handy, a respected local physician and Borden

family friend, claimed to have seen a pale young man, eyes fixed on the sidewalk, walking nervously on Second Street the morning of the murders. Transformed by newspaper accounts into "Dr. Handy's wild-eyed man," the Fall River police identified him as "Mike the Soldier," the sobriquet of a local dipsomaniac who had been seen in the area around the same time. They ruled him out and, over Dr. Handy's objections that he was not the same man, they turned their attention to other strangers. The officers became suspicious of Dr. Handy's sighting when he seemed reluctant to go to Boston to identify another possible suspect and then "readily pronounced him not the man" even though "his face was very much shaded." Dr. Handy, it was noted, owned the holiday cottage in the seaside village of Marion, Massachusetts, where Lizzie had planned to join a group of friends.

Unsolicited advice came from a variety of sources. Among the "multitude of crank communications" sent to the police and the prosecutors were suggestions about where to search—the kitchen stove, the attic, a well, and the piano (if, the writer acknowledged, the Bordens owned a piano)—on the theory that all would make excellent hiding places. An infallible clue to the murderer's identity, some insisted, could be found in the eyes of the victims, for the retinas retained the last image seen: "Dark mysteries have been brought to light in this manner by means of photography." Still others imagined a secret society, perhaps anarchists, taking revenge on the Borden household. Most had more conventional ideas, offering leads on suspicious characters or enjoining the police to arrest someone closer to home. A few even confessed, including a man who claimed to be the illegitimate son of Andrew Borden and a woman he had committed to an insane asylum. One man, Charles Peckham, actually turned himself in. He, like the others, was quickly ruled out. Marshal Hilliard explained, "I have devoted attention to many stories that were foolish just because of the enormity of the crime, and in order that I might leave no stone unturned to solve it."

Even those beyond the veil of this life weighed in. A medium claimed to have had word from the late Andrew Borden, but the

famously reticent Mr. Borden refused to divulge his murderer's identity. "Trance Medium and Physician" J. Burns Strand recounted his
vision of the murders. He offered to "come at once" to Fall River and,
in the interim, enjoined the authorities to "arrest Morse, Lizzie and
the man at West Port." Yet it seemed "there was a diversity of opinion
in the spirit world as to the identity of the person who murdered Mr.
and Mrs. Borden." One medium explained: "Spirits don't know everything . . . And if they didn't happen to be looking just at the moment
when the murder was committed they couldn't be expected to know
about it."

Popular opinion among the living favored John V. Morse, Andrew's
brother-in-law, because he was an outsider whose visit coincided with
the murders. One newspaper profile of Morse termed him "The Suspected Man." With his ragged beard and shallow gray bloodshot eyes,
Morse looked the part of the shifty Western horse trader, a "long, lanky,
hard-featured fellow, who dressed like a scarecrow and ate like a cormorant." He did not appear to improve upon acquaintance, for he was
"regarded by his neighbors as a very eccentric and peculiar man." Like
his brother-in-law, he was reserved and "close, almost to the point of
penuriousness." The Fall River police had to rescue him from an angry
mob that followed him around in the days after the murders. But as
if in a detective novel, Morse appeared to have an airtight alibi. He
had memorized the number of the streetcar on which he was riding
at the time of Andrew Borden's death and even recalled the number
on the streetcar conductor's cap. As it happens, the conductor did not
remember him but did recall the six priests Morse named as his fellow
passengers. Mrs. Daniel Emery, the relative he visited on Weybosset
Street, confirmed his departure time and, in an uncanny coincidence,
Dr. Bowen arrived to attend Mrs. Emery's daughter just as Morse was
leaving the house at 11:20 a.m. The *Fall River Daily Herald* reported
a possible motive, based on a tip from an unnamed member of the
Borden family, that Lizzie "regarded Mr. Morse with more tenderness
than most nieces feel for their uncles." According to the source, Andrew
Borden was well aware of her attachment and "he was constantly on

the alert to see the breath of scandal did not reach his home." But there was nothing to support that tantalizing rumor. If anything, Lizzie seemed to view her uncle with hostility or, at best, indifference. Even though she was aware of his presence on Wednesday, she did not see Morse until after the murders on Thursday afternoon. She later said she was annoyed by the sounds of her uncle, father, and stepmother conversing downstairs and had shut her bedroom door.

Dr. Bowen also faced suspicion—not as a serious suspect, but as a possible paramour of Lizzie Borden's. Jane Gray, Abby's stepmother, re-

John V. Morse, *courtesy of Fall River Historical Society*

layed four-year-old gossip about Lizzie's relationship with her doctor. While the rest of the family was at the Borden farm during that summer, Lizzie stayed in Fall River. Dr. Bowen escorted her to church one Sunday evening, an act of gallantry that launched a thousand wagging tongues. According to Mrs. Gray, "Some remarked how courageous she was to remain in the house alone; but others replied in a very knowing way, perhaps she has acceptable company."

Dr. Bowen's actions on the day of the murders also seemed questionable. First, he provided the medical explanation for a pail of small towels "covered with blood" found soaking in the wash cellar. Officer William Medley asked Lizzie about the contents. Rather than explain the towels were menstrual cloths, she referred him to Dr. Bowen, who vouched for her, declaring "it had been explained to him, and was alright." Bridget, however, said that "she had not noticed the pail until that day, and it could not have been there two days before [as Lizzie claimed], or she would have seen it, and put the contents in the wash." Second, he acted as a gatekeeper, closing Lizzie's door on the police and insisting that she be given a few moments to compose herself. Finally, Officer Harrington saw Dr. Bowen in the Bordens' kitchen looking at scraps of paper that he appeared to be trying to assemble. When challenged by Harrington, Bowen said, "It does not amount to anything," adding that it was a note about his daughter's proposed visit. He then tossed the scraps onto the kitchen stove. Harrington saw the name Emma as it burned. Bowen's daughter's name was Florence. Was Dr. Bowen acting in good faith as the trusted family physician or was he trying to protect someone in the house?

After exhausting the suspects outside the immediate family, the police turned their attention to the two women at the scene of the crime. If the murderer was not a member of the household, then he, or she, would have had to avoid both women for the hour and a half between the murders. The housemaid Bridget Sullivan was considered a plausible suspect. Irish immigrants alone composed over a third of those arrested between 1889 and 1893. One of Marshal Hilliard's civic-minded correspondents told him to arrest Bridget Sullivan, who "carried out the orders of her priest," adding that "true Americans will learn in time never to imploy [*sic*] a catholic." Another warned that servants were "a sly and lying class." Although an axe was a "man's" weapon because of the physical strength and proximity required, working-class Irish women were known to be perfectly capable of swinging one, for domestic service often included chopping wood and slaughtering animals. Bridget Sullivan did not need to perform such duties because cords of wood arrived regularly from the Borden farm in Swansea. Nonetheless, she knew enough to be petrified. She

Dr. Seabury Bowen, *courtesy of Fall River Historical Society*

was saved by Lizzie Borden's version of events that placed Bridget outside during Abby's murder and upstairs in her attic bedroom when Andrew was killed. Yet, despite the dearth of evidence linking her to the crime and the absence of any discernable motive, the president of the board of aldermen wondered out loud why she had not been arrested. Andrew Jennings, the Borden family lawyer, seconded these sentiments, asking pointedly, "In the natural course of things who would be the party to be suspected?"

Puzzled by the inconsistencies in Lizzie's account of her movements at the time of the murders, the police began to suspect the bereaved daughter of having had a hand—or two—in the murders. In his notes from his interview with Lizzie Borden on the evening of August 4, Officer Phil Harrington struggled to voice this horrifying suspicion: "Lizzie stood by the foot of the bed, and talked in the most calm and collected manner; her whole bearing was most remarkable under the circumstances. There was not the least indication of agitation, no sign of sorrow or grief, no lamentation of heart, no comment on the horror of the crime, and no expression of a wish that the criminal be caught. All this, and something that, to me, is indescribable, gave birth to a thought that was most revolting. I thought, at least, she knew more than she wished to tell." When he joined Assistant Marshal Fleet and the other officers in a search of the barn, where Lizzie claimed to have been at the time of her father's death, he told Fleet: "I don't like that girl." After a comprehensive search of the barn and its loft, Harrington said to Fleet: "If any girl can show you or me, or anybody else what could interest her up here for twenty minutes, I would like to have her do it." Shaking his head, the stolid Lancashireman Fleet could only mutter that it was "incredible."

There were other oddities. For example, there was the missing note. Lizzie said that her stepmother received a note from a sick friend and had gone out. Abby's presumed absence from home was given as the reason for Lizzie's failure to search for Abby after discovering her father's body. Yet, no note was found at the house and no one came forward to identify herself as the author. Even if, for reasons of her own, the mysterious sender did not wish to declare herself, it seemed "strange," as the reporter Edwin Porter observed, "that the boy who delivered the note has not made himself known."

Lizzie's estranged uncle Hiram Harrington all but accused her directly. He told the police and the *Fall River Daily Globe*: "When the perpetrator of this foul deed is found, it will be one of the household." He left little doubt about which member of the household he suspected. "I had a long talk with Lizzie yesterday, Thursday, the day of the murder, and I am not at all satisfied with [her] . . . demeanor." He also remarked: "She is very strong-willed, and will fight for what she considers her rights." Abby's brother-in-law George Fish went further. He directly accused Lizzie (and Morse) of hiring an assassin to kill the Bordens "simply to get them out of the way."

The day after the murders, Emma and Lizzie offered a five-thousand-dollar reward "to any one who may secure the arrest and conviction of the person or persons who occasioned the death of Andrew J. Borden and his wife." No one came forward. They also hired Superintendent O. M. Hanscom of the Pinkerton Detective Agency to supplement the police investigation. Hanscom had been a celebrated Boston police detective, fired for running afoul of high-ranking and corrupt members of his own police department. Speculation that he was really in place to safeguard the family interests was given credence by his visits to Andrew Jennings's office. But, after only two days on the job, Hanscom "disappeared as mysteriously as he came." Meanwhile, Fall River seethed with tension. In the view of Edwin Porter of the *Fall River Daily Globe*, the town believed "it must clear up the mystery or go insane."

Chapter 3

DONE WITH THEORIES

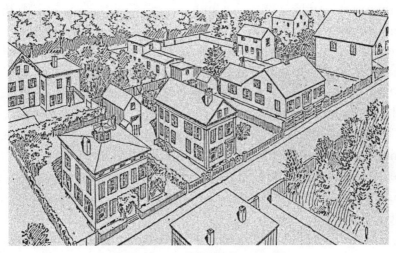

Second Street neighborhood, *Boston Globe*

ndrew and Abby Borden's funeral took place on Saturday, August 6. As Lizzie had specifically requested on the day of the murders, the firm of James Ellis Winward handled the arrangements. At 11:00 a.m., the elderly pastor of First Congregational Church, Rev. W. W. Adams, assisted by Rev. Edwin A. Buck, began the private service at 92 Second Street. It was a snug affair. About seventy-five people—relatives, business associates, and neighbors—crowded into the sitting room. The service itself was as simple as the black cloth-draped cedar coffins containing the bodies of Andrew and Abby Borden: "There was no singing and no remarks."

Few of the mourners continued to the interment; it was for

immediate family only. But the funeral cortege was well attended. According to the *Boston Globe*, 2,500 people waited outside on Second Street. The *New York Times* put the number between 3,000 and 4,000. The front door slowly opened, and Lizzie Borden left the house leaning on the undertaker's arm. Emma emerged with John Morse, the clergymen, and the gentlemen pallbearers, Andrew Borden's friends and business peers. They entered the waiting carriages and followed the hearse to Oak Grove Cemetery. Andrew Borden's final route took him past the Andrew J. Borden building on South Main Street: "As the procession wended its way along North Main Street many old associates of Mr. Borden were seen to raise their hats." Once the carriages had departed, Marshal Hilliard and his deputies began their search of the house. It was, as the the *New York Herald* observed, "their first chance to work undisturbed by the presence of the Borden girls . . . They ransacked the house from attic to cellar." Over the course of their investigation into the murders, the police pulled up pieces of carpet, removed wall trim, and counted blood spots. Fingerprint analysis, as a standard method of police procedure, would not be used in the United States for another decade.

A smaller but still sizable crowd of several hundred people awaited the funeral party at the gates of Oak Grove Cemetery, the traditional resting place of Fall River's Protestant elite. Here, as at the house, more than a dozen policemen kept the spectators in order. At the grave site, Andrew's cousins and business associates, Richard A. Borden and Jerome Cook Borden, served as two of his pallbearers. Frank Lawton Almy, one of the owners of the *Fall River Daily Evening News*, captained Abby's pallbearers. Except for John Morse, the family members remained in their carriages. One uninvited mourner, "an elderly lady in plain dress," approached the grave. It was thought that she had been "employed long ago by the Bordens." The police quickly hustled her back behind the barricade.

But that was not the biggest surprise of the morning. After the pallbearers unburdened themselves, the family members departed. Then, after a discreet "pause of perhaps five minutes," the policemen returned the caskets to the hearses; they had been ordered not to bury the bodies. The bodies were placed in the receiving vault to await further indignities. Dr. William Dolan, the county medical examiner, assisted by Dr. Frank W. Draper, his Suffolk County counterpart, performed autopsies in the Oak Grove Cemetery's ladies' lounge on Thursday, August 11, a week after the murders.

LIZZIE ON THE RACK

By Tuesday, August 9, "the intense excitement in Fall River" grew to a "fever heat." News broke that an inquest was to be held at the police station, presided over by the Second District Court's Judge Josiah C. Blaisdell. Blaisdell, a long-serving judge of "remarkable vitality" and a former mayor, was a fitting choice. An inquest is a judicial inquiry, required by state law in cases of violent or unexplained death. It was a secret proceeding, open to neither the public nor the press. But that did not prevent reporters and ordinary citizens from following the comings and goings of likely participants. At 10:00 a.m., "a hack, containing Marshal Hilliard and Officer Harrington, had gone to the Borden house to convey Miss Lizzie and a friend" to the inquest. So acute was the public's interest that "business was partially suspended in the center of the city as it had been on Thursday noon, when the story of the tragedy was first made known." Those who lingered at the Borden house had their patience rewarded. Officer Patrick Doherty appeared at the house to bring Bridget Sullivan to the police station. Doherty was a handsome man with a sympathetic manner, one day shy of his thirty-third birthday. Bridget cried and insisted that she had already told all she knew. Doherty, however, managed to elicit some additional information: "[Bridget] remarked that things didn't go in the house as they should, and that she wanted to leave and had threatened to do so several times." She also claimed that she had remained out of loyalty to Abby Borden, whom she termed "a lovely woman."

Inside the courtroom on the second floor of the police station, Judge Blaisdell, City Marshal Hilliard, the medical examiner, several officers, the stenographer, Annie White, and District Attorney Hosea Knowlton awaited Bridget Sullivan's entrance. Judging by Bridget's "deep distress," it might as well have been a firing squad.

District Attorney Hosea Knowlton, tasked with the investigation and eventual prosecution of the murders, dominated the room. He was a man prefiguring a Teddy Roosevelt guide to masculinity, a large man who seemed the incarnation of solidity, powerful in body

City Marshal Hilliard standing in front of the Central Police Station, *courtesy of Fall River Historical Society*

as well as mind. As one reporter later rhapsodized, he had "a head as hard as iron set on a neck that is a tower for strength. His shoulders are a yard apart. His legs are the foundation of a bridge. He is by nature combative, and he snorts like a war horse." Later, a colleague remembered him as a "manly man" with "no trace of anything artificial, either in his manner, his language, or his nature." The son of an itinerant minister who ultimately led the Universalist Church in New Bedford, Knowlton had risen by his own conspicuous merit. After graduating from Harvard Law School, he established a thriving practice in New Bedford before entering public service. There, too, he met with success as a state representative and state senator before taking on the job as district attorney for the Southern District of Massachusetts. Within two years of the inquest, he would be sworn as Massachusetts attorney general. In that capacity, he recommended "exempting minors and women from the death penalty," minors as a matter of sound public policy and women for "mostly sentimental" reasons. Later, he went further, arguing against capital punishment for any defendant: "That the punishment of murder by death does not tend to diminish or prevent that crime; that a man who is so far lost to reason as to conceive the commission of murder with deliberate and premeditated malice aforethought does not enter into a discussion with himself of the consequences of the crime; that the infliction of the death penalty is not in accord with the present advance of civilization, and that it is a relic of barbarism, which the community must surely outgrow, as it has already outgrown the rack, the whipping post, and the stake." Whatever reservations he may have had about capital punishment, he thoroughly investigated the murders and conducted a searching inquest.

Bridget Sullivan seemed to be a cooperative witness; she answered Knowlton's questions comprehensively. Her story was straightforward. After cleaning the breakfast dishes, she washed the outside windows, chatting with the neighbors' housemaid, and then moved inside. She felt so tired that she decided to lie down. (Bridget had Thursday afternoons and Sundays off and may have simply been getting a head start on her half day.) Lizzie called for her, told her Andrew was dead, and sent her for Dr. Bowen. Although she had seen Lizzie pass through the kitchen in the early morning, she could give no additional information about Lizzie's whereabouts that morning.

Hosea M. Knowlton, *courtesy of Fall River Historical Society*

After she testified, Bridget recovered in the matron's apartment. Later, Officer Doherty escorted her back to the Borden home. But that was only a brief stop on her journey. After retrieving her belongings, she left for her cousin's house on Division Street, never to return to the Second Street house.

Knowlton intended to call Lizzie Borden to testify next. As the only other person besides Bridget Sullivan known to be in the house at the time of the murders, she was a crucial witness. But more than that, she was now the main suspect. Mindful of her legal peril, Borden family lawyer Andrew Jennings sought permission to "look after her interests" at the inquest. Jennings was a Fall River native with an established law practice. Like Knowlton, whom he would succeed as district attorney, Jennings served in the state legislature, first in the House of Representatives and then in the Senate. Knowlton saw no reason to allow Jennings to interfere with his questioning. He insisted that he was merely investigating the crime, as required by Massachusetts law, not conducting an adversarial proceeding. Jennings was a diminutive man, much smaller than Knowlton, but he was "a hard fighter" and retained the vigor that carried him to athletic success as the pitcher on the Varsity Nine at Brown. He was also reckoned to be "a splendid dancer." "His eyes," said one reporter, "fairly snap when he is in motion" and he had the remarkable "ability to be everywhere and see everything at once." He also had an "admirable voice, which he use[d] to great effect" in his argument against being excluded, "but the Court would not yield and he was compelled to withdraw."

Lizzie Borden took the stand at

Andrew Jennings, *courtesy of Fall River Historical Society*

about 2:00 p.m. It would be a long afternoon for both the witness and the district attorney. Knowlton's main objectives were to look for motive and opportunity. Knowlton began with the background to the murders. He asked whether Andrew or Abby Borden had any enemies: "Do you know of anybody that your father was on bad terms with?" Lizzie mentioned a man who had threatened her father because of his refusal to rent the man one of his properties. But she did not know the man's name. The only name she could conjure was her uncle Hiram Harrington, married to her paternal aunt Lurana. That dispensed with Andrew Borden's enemy list. No one, according to Lizzie, was on bad terms with her stepmother. She admitted, however, that she had herself had "words" with her stepmother about five years before.

Knowlton tried to clarify the extent of the discord. But Lizzie was cagey. When asked if she had been on cordial terms, she said, "It depends upon one's idea of cordiality perhaps."

Knowlton tried again: "According to your idea of cordiality?"

Lizzie allowed that they "were friendly."

In frustration, Knowlton acquiesced to her formulation: "Cordial, according to your idea of cordiality?"

Lizzie agreed: "Quite so . . . I do not mean the dearest of friends in the world, but very kindly feelings and pleasant. I do not know how to answer you any better than that."

Knowlton tried another tack: "Were your relations toward her that of daughter and mother?"

Lizzie answered: "In some ways it was and in some it was not." She declined to elaborate, because, she said, "I don't know how to answer it." She admitted that she had once called Abby "Mother" but switched her form of address to "Mrs. Borden." Knowlton established that this change in title occurred at the time of the "difference of opinion" five years previously.

In contrast to the evident intergenerational tension, the Borden marriage appeared harmonious. Nonetheless, Lizzie seemed taken aback when Knowlton asked if the elder Bordens were "happily united." Marriages are inscrutable, even to those who inhabit the same living space. Perhaps she had not considered the question, simply accepting the existence of the relationship as a central fact in her life. She hedged, assenting with the caveat so far as she knew. Knowlton demanded: "Why do you hesitate?"

"Because," she said, "I did not know how to answer you any better than what came into my mind. I was trying to think if I was telling it as I should, that's all."

Knowlton pounced: "Do you have any difficulty in telling it as you should?"

Lizzie explained: "Some of your questions I have difficulty answering because I don't know just how you mean them."

In the simplest way possible, he asked: "Did you ever know of any difficulty between her and your father?" Lizzie admitted she knew of none.

Knowlton then switched tacks again. He asked Lizzie what she was wearing on the day of the murders. Lizzie explained that, in the morning, she had been wearing "a navy blue, sort of a Bengaline silk skirt with a navy blue blouse" but in the afternoon she had changed into a "pink wrapper." He asked if that was her only change of dress that day. After receiving an affirmative answer, he let the matter drop.

Dispensing with textiles for the time being, Knowlton pulled on the loose thread in the Borden household: John V. Morse. Was his visit a coincidence—mere bad timing and nothing more—or did his presence bear some important relationship to the murders? So Knowlton asked Lizzie about Morse's prior visits. Lizzie professed to find the question difficult to understand. Morse, she explained, had been in the East for almost a year. The implication seemed to be that she counted the entire year as "a visit." But Knowlton was after something more particular, specifically whether Morse had visited "before he came east."

"Yes," Lizzie said, "if you remember the winter that the river was frozen once . . . he was here that winter, some fourteen years ago, was it not?"

Knowlton replied with irritation: "I am not answering questions but asking them." He tried again, asking how often Morse had visited between that visit of fourteen years ago and this current one.

Lizzie said that he had visited "once" since then but added, oddly, that she did not know "whether he has or not since."

To narrow down the number of visits, Knowlton asked, "How many times this last year has he been at your house?"

Lizzie did not answer the question: "None at all to speak of. Nothing more than a night or two at a time."

Knowlton pursued the overnight visits, seeking perhaps to arrive at a number: "How often does he come to spend a night or two?"

Lizzie purported to be unable to produce the required answer: "Really, I don't know. I am away so much myself." Knowlton could not quite believe what he was hearing.

He repeated: "Your last answer is that you don't know how much he had been here because you had been away yourself so much?" Then he added: "That is true the last year or since he has been east?"

Lizzie admitted: "I have not been away the last year so much but other times I have been away when he has been here." After some prodding, Lizzie finally agreed that he had made one other visit in the intervening period, perhaps five or six years earlier. Knowlton returned to the recent past and asked about Morse's presence at the house during the last year. Again Lizzie claimed to know little of his visits, as she was "away a great deal in the daytime; occasionally at night." As for his current visit, Lizzie would not speculate about when Morse arrived before the murders. She said she knew he was there on Wednesday because she heard his voice during the day, but she did not see him at any point that day. She went out to visit Alice Russell in the evening. When she came back from her visit about 9:00 p.m., she went straight up to her room. Moreover, she did not see him the next morning, and she also failed to ask about him. It seemed unfathomable that she should display a complete dearth of curiosity about the uncle in the bedroom next to hers, a point Knowlton specifically pursued. (Morse himself explained that he had visited in 1865, 1876, 1878, and 1885—once for an entire year.)

Whether or not Morse's presence at the house was directly connected to the murders, it revealed the extent of Lizzie's estrangement from her parents. Despite sharing a house, they conducted their lives separately. Even Lizzie's own biological uncle seemed to fall into the category of Andrew and Abby's visitor and therefore did not merit a greeting. Nor did John Morse think to knock on the door of his niece to inquire after her health. Was this typical of their lack of interest in each other? Or had something fundamentally changed in their relationship? And did this particular visit have a special significance that accounted for their studied avoidance of each other? It was decidedly odd.

Another coincidence prompted Knowlton to make one final inquiry before turning to the details of Thursday morning: She had planned to join a group of friends who left for Marion earlier in the week. Had she departed as scheduled, she would have been away on August 4. Why had Lizzie postponed her trip? Lizzie said that she had decided to wait until Monday because, as secretary-treasurer of the Christian Endeavor Society, she had to attend a meeting on Sunday. Knowlton accepted the answer for the time being but the matter did not rest there.

Lizzie had written to one of the group early in the week of the murders, presumably to explain her decision. The recipient had burned the missive, fearing that it might be misconstrued in light of the murders. On September 14, the *Fall River Daily Herald* would report that Lizzie had volunteered to chop the firewood for the kitchen stove at the cottage, as she had a "very sharp hatchet" in her possession. Officer Phil Harrington had passed along the story to Knowlton the previous week but had discounted its authenticity. Summarizing the story in a letter to Attorney General Pillsbury, Knowlton added: "If this is so, it means insanity."

Officers questioned Elizabeth Johnston about the letter but she refused to discuss it, stating "I have said all I think I should about that letter." She then consulted Andrew Jennings, "who told her that she need not tell the contents of the letter if she did not want to; and best position not only to see any theoretical intruder but also to observe Abby's movements or lack thereof. If she was alone downstairs between her father's departure and return, then, as Knowlton commented, "it would have been extremely difficult for anybody to have gone through the kitchen and dining room and front hall without your seeing them." But there was another problem with that story. Bridget Sullivan said she had been inside washing the windows downstairs when Andrew Borden returned. She had, after all, unbolted the front door to admit him. Knowlton asked: "Do you think she might have gone to work and washed all the windows in the dining room and you not know it?" Lizzie persisted in her denial. Knowlton declared: "It is certain beyond reasonable doubt she was engaged in washing the windows in the dining room or sitting room when your father came home. Do you mean to say you knew nothing of either of those operations?"

Even more surprising was Lizzie's account of her actions during the second critical period of that morning, the interval between her father's return at about 10:45 a.m. and the discovery of his body about an hour later. Shortly after Andrew's return to the house, Lizzie said she decided to go to the barn for a sinker in advance of her trip to Marion on Monday. Incredulous, Knowlton asked: "It occurred to you after your father came in it would be a good time to go to the barn after sinkers?" Knowlton pressed her about her expedition: Did she have a hook or fishing line? If, as she explained, there was fishing line at the family farm, did she not expect to find sinkers there as well?

She insisted that she had said there were lines and "perhaps hooks" at the farm but "I did not say I thought there were sinkers on my lines." She said she knew there was lead in the barn and had thought it might be fashioned into sinkers. On her way to the barn, she stopped under the pear tree for some pears. She then went to the upper story of the barn for the lead.

Knowlton summarized sarcastically: "[You] went to the second story of the barn to look for sinkers for lines you had at the farm, as you supposed, as you had seen them there five years before that time?"

she did not want to." None of the other women in the Marion party (Anna C. Holmes, Mary L. Holmes, Isabel Fraser, Louise Remington, or Mabel Remington) would speak to the police.

Knowlton then moved on to the timeline of events, turning to questions of opportunity. Where exactly was Lizzie Borden throughout the morning of August 4? There were two short windows in which the murders of Abby and Andrew must have occurred and for which Lizzie and Bridget were the only other surviving occupants of the house. Morse left immediately after breakfast. Andrew Borden left the house at 9:15 a.m. and returned at about 10:45 a.m. By then, Abby was dead. Andrew Borden himself was dead by 11:45 a.m.

Knowlton turned his attention to the first part of the morning. Lizzie explained that she decided to iron handkerchiefs. Because the "flats" were not yet hot enough, she passed the time reading an old *Harper's* magazine. She said: "I sprinkled my handkerchiefs . . . and took them in the dining room. I took the ironing board in the dining room and left the handkerchiefs in the kitchen on the table and whether I ate any cookies or not, I don't remember. Then I sat down looking at the magazine, waiting for the flats to heat. Then I went in the sitting room and got the *Providence Journal* and took that into the kitchen." She also said she had not seen her stepmother since Abby had gone up to freshen up the guest room around the time Andrew left the house. Abby had told her that she had already changed the bedsheets and only needed to put new covers on the shams. According to Lizzie, Abby also intended "to close the room because she was going to have company Monday and she wanted everything in order."

Knowlton inquired, "What explanation . . . can you suggest, as to what she was doing from the time she said she had got the work all done in the spare room, until 11 o'clock?"

Lizzie appeared stumped. She suggested that Abby might have made her own bed. But that, given the Bordens' system of locks and bolts, would have required Abby to come down the front stairs, retrieve the key from the sitting room shelf, and go up the back stairs to the bedroom she and Andrew shared. Lizzie, however, said she had not seen her pass even though she claimed to be downstairs during Andrew's absence. Later she speculated Abby might have been using the sewing machine in the guest room but she admitted she had not heard the noisy machine.

Contrary to Bridget's statement after the murders and at the inquest, Lizzie testified that she was downstairs when her father came home. A few minutes later, she said she was upstairs when her father came home but she had only been there a few minutes.

Knowlton delicately pointed out the discrepancy: "You remember, Miss Borden, I will call your attention to it so as to see if I have any misunderstanding, not for the purpose of confusing you, you remember that you told me several times that you were downstairs and not upstairs when your father came home."

Nonplussed, Lizzie replied: "I don't know what I have said. I have answered so many questions and I am so confused I don't know one thing from the other."

Knowlton ignored the outburst: "Calling your attention to what you said about that a few minutes ago . . . you have said you were upstairs when the bell rang and were on the stairs when Maggie [Bridget Sullivan] let your father in, which now is your recollection . . . That you were downstairs when the bell rang and your father came?" Lizzie again said she thought she was downstairs.

At times it seemed that Lizzie was deliberately tormenting Knowlton with a Yankee version of the rope-a-dope. He was forced to repeat questions or ask slightly rephrased versions about every subject covered. She answered questions as tersely as possible and, when caught in a contradiction, wiggled out of the bind by suggesting she had misunderstood the question. Or she digressed, answering in an elliptical and unresponsive manner. All in all, it was an infuriating performance. But by the end of the afternoon, Lizzie Borden herself seemed exhausted and even disoriented. Her stories were contradictory; she might have frustrated her interlocutor but her answers were on the record. She had also revealed a great deal about the background tension in the Borden household, information that Knowlton was sure to put to use.

Knowlton, however, revealed nothing for the time being. Instead, he issued a brief press bulletin indicating only that two witnesses testified.

The next day, when the inquest resumed, Lizzie Borden returned to the witness stand and Knowlton returned to the timeline. First, he sought to pin down Lizzie's version of the early-morning period, in particular, when exactly she had seen Abby and her father on Thursday. Lizzie said that before her father left that morning, she had seen Abby in the dining room and her father in the sitting room. Alluding to the family's gastric distress of the previous day, Abby had asked her how she was feeling. Abby then told her that she was going out and would get their dinner. Knowlton paused this line of questioning to ask if it was "usual" for Abby to go out and to be gone for dinner. Lizzie again appeared stumped and had recourse to an awkward formulation: "More than once in three months, perhaps." Put in a more normal syntax, her answer meant that Abby rarely was out for dinner—at most, every other month or so. Returning to the timeline, Lizzie said she had gone into the kitchen and down into the cellar for clean clothes. When she walked through the main floor, she had seen her father reading the paper.

With one important exception, Lizzie hewed to her prior day's testimony about being downstairs all morning. She volunteered that she had gone upstairs and "basted a piece of tape" on a dress.

Knowlton exploded: "Do you remember you did not say that yesterday?"

Unmoved, Lizzie replied, "I don't think you asked me. I told you yesterday I went upstairs directly after I came up from down cellar, with the clean clothes."

In exasperation, Knowlton said, "Miss Borden, I am trying in good faith to get all the doings that morning of yourself and Miss Sullivan and I have not succeeded in doing it. Do you desire to give me any information or not?"

Now flustered herself, Lizzie replied that she could not give him information she did not have, adding "I don't know what your name is!"

Significantly, Lizzie placed herself at the center of the house, in the

Lizzie retorted: "I did not intend to go to the farm for lines. I was going to buy some lines here."

Knowlton could not believe his ears: "What was the use of telling me a while ago you had no sinkers on your line at the farm?"

After more sparring about the fishing apparatus, Knowlton sought to reel in his catch. He inquired minutely about how exactly she spent the claimed fifteen to twenty minutes in the barn. He insisted that her search for the lead could only have taken a few minutes. Lizzie volunteered that she went over to the west window, straightened a curtain, and ate her pears. Knowlton asked: "Do you mean to say you stopped your work and . . . sat still and ate some pears?" Recalling Lizzie's earlier testimony that she told Abby she would not eat dinner, he added sarcastically: "You were feeling better than you did in the morning . . . Well enough to eat pears, but not well enough to eat anything for dinner?" Knowlton concluded his questions about the barn, observing, "You have put yourself in the only place, perhaps, where it would be impossible for you to see a person going into the house?"

Knowlton's incredulity may have arisen, in part, from a lack of understanding of the life of leisured women. Lizzie's account of her activities seemed unfathomable to a man accustomed to a life of purpose. It was hard to imagine Knowlton tarrying to eat a pear while on the hunt for some object he needed. But was Lizzie's progress around the house and out to the barn any more dilatory than that of other women of her station? One day was much like another. Would other women like Lizzie Borden be able to account for their time minutely even if their lives were of manufactured and restless activity?

Knowlton explored Lizzie's knowledge of the Borden arsenal. (He helpfully mansplained the differences between a hatchet, "a short handled, wide bladed instrument," and an axe, "longer handled and smaller bladed.")

Lizzie said she "knew there was an old axe down [in the] cellar," but disavowed knowledge of any hatchets. Knowlton then asked, "Can you give any occasion for there being blood on them?" Lizzie said that her father "killed some pigeons in the barn last May or June." She thought "he wrung their necks." But when she saw the dead pigeons in the house, she noticed a few were "headless." She could not say whether the heads "were twisted off" or severed. She did recall that she had asked, "Why are these heads off?"

Before ending the day's ordeal, Knowlton returned to the source of the discord in the Borden household. He sought "the particulars of that trouble that you had with your mother four or five years ago" about the Fourth Street house, formerly owned by Abby Borden's father.

Lizzie gave an uncharacteristically loquacious response: "The stepmother, Mrs. Oliver Gray, wanted to sell it and my father bought out the Widow Gray's share. She did not tell me and he did not tell me, but some outsiders said he gave it to her; put it in her name. I said if he gave that to her, he ought to give us something. Told Mrs. Borden so. She did not care anything about the house herself. She wanted it so this half-sister could have a home . . . And we always thought she persuaded father to buy it. At any rate, he did buy it and I am quite sure she did persuade him. I said what he did for her, he ought to do for his own children. So, he gave us grandfather's house. That was all the trouble we ever had." Knowlton replied mildly that she had still not explained the trouble between them. Perhaps he, the devout son of an itinerant minister, could not imagine that Andrew's conveying a half interest in a modest house to his wife could cause the rift in the household, a rift that persisted until Andrew's and Abby's deaths. Lizzie replied, as if it were obvious, that "I said there was feeling four or five years ago when I stopped calling her mother." And, she added tartly, "I told you that yesterday." She then explained that her father bought the Ferry Street house "back from us some weeks ago. I don't know just how many."

Perplexed, Knowlton asked, "What do you mean by 'bought it back'?"

Lizzie replied: "He gave us money for it." Knowlton let the point drop.

Lizzie's second day of testimony revealed how much the property dispute still rankled. In contrast to her terse answers to Knowlton's other questions, she lost her verbal self-control when discussing the transfer. Moreover, the timing of Andrew's repurchase of the Ferry Street house from his daughters was suggestive. He had transferred his interest in the house five years earlier. Could it be a coincidence that he would decide to buy it back from them a few weeks before he died? Might the cash have been intended to mollify his daughters in advance of changes to his will?

Later that day, the significance of that property dispute was confirmed by the inquest testimony of Emma Borden and Hiram Harrington. Emma reluctantly agreed that her father's equalizing gift of property to the girls "did not entirely heal the feelings." Emma insisted, however, that she—not Lizzie—bore the real grudge against Abby. Emma also called Morse "a very dear uncle of ours, of mine." Like Lizzie, she named her uncle Hiram Harrington as the only person known to be on bad terms with her father. Harrington, for his part, admitted that he and Andrew did not speak to each other but, except for that, the households were on good terms. He also said that Lizzie spoke of her stepmother in "an unfriendly way."

In the course of their testimony, Dr. Bowen and Adelaide Churchill confirmed the timeline, Lizzie's change of dress, and that Lizzie told them Abby had received a note and gone out. Adelaide Churchill also testified that Lizzie had later asked her to look for Abby. Adelaide said: "She said she wished somebody would try to find Mrs. Borden because she thought she had heard her come in."

But the most intriguing piece of information came from John V. Morse. He testified that Andrew had spoken to him of making a will in the last year. On the Monday after the murders, Charles Cook, Andrew Borden's business manager, told Officer William Medley that Andrew had spoken to him of making a will—though he would later disavow the comment. At the time, he refused to comment on the Borden family relations "on account of my position . . . as I do not know what my relations may be with the family, when this thing is settled." The police searched for a will, employing "an expert operator under police surveillance" who labored for eight hours to open Andrew Borden's safe. The safe contained "quite a sum of money and many valuable papers" but no will. At the end of the day, Knowlton issued a bulletin for the press that listed the witnesses examined but gave no hint of the drama within the courtroom: "Inquest continued at 10 to-day . . . Nothing developed for publication."

On August 11, the inquest resumed and Knowlton again questioned Lizzie Borden. But this time he was more concerned with what she might have done outside the home than in it. After hearing news of the murders, a clerk at a local drugstore told officers that Lizzie had tried to buy prussic acid before the murders, ostensibly to "put an edge on" a sealskin cape. Knowlton began: "Your attention has already been called to the circumstance of going into the drugstore of Smith's on the corner of Columbia and Main Streets, by some officer, has it not, on the day before the tragedy?" Lizzie allowed that "somebody has spoken of it to me," but she claimed she did not know that drugstore. Knowlton asked if she had gone into "any drugstore" to ask for prussic acid. "No," she declared, saying that she was home all day on Wednesday, August 3. Later, he asked whether she had any "sealskin sacks." She acknowledged that she did and that the sealskins were "hanging in [a] large white bag in the attic." Knowlton asked if she ever put prussic acid on them. Lizzie insisted: "I don't use anything on them."

Knowlton accepted the impasse. He had what he needed. Three witnesses would testify to Lizzie's visit to the drugstore. Later, in a letter to Attorney General Albert Pillsbury, he would describe Lizzie Borden's inquest testimony as her "confession." So he could afford to be magnanimous. He said: "You can appreciate the anxiety that everybody has to find the author of this tragedy, and the questions that I put to you have been in that direction. I now ask you if you can furnish any other fact, or give any other, even suspicion, that will assist the officers in any way in this matter." Lizzie helpfully produced another dubious character. She had seen a shadowy figure around 9:00 p.m. lurking outside the house. She explained: "I came home from Miss Russell's one night and as I came up, I always glanced towards the side door. As I came along by the carriage-way, I saw a shadow on the side steps. I did not stop walking, but I walked slower. Somebody ran down the steps . . . I thought it was a man because I saw no skirts . . . I hurried in the front door as fast as I could and locked it." Unfortunately, she could be certain of neither the time nor the date. She said that she had seen the figure after her sister's departure for Fairhaven two weeks before the murders. And, as if suddenly wakened to its apparent significance, she also reported yet another suspicious character skulking around the house the previous winter. She knew that she had seen him on a Thursday because she was coming home from church and she could say that he "was not a very tall person." But that was all—except, of course, for the prospective renter ordered out by her father. That man, however, remained elusive. In essence, those were Lizzie Borden's final words about the murders. She never uttered another word under oath.

Unlike Lizzie Borden, Knowlton had more information to disclose. In addition to the three drugstore employees, Knowlton called five more witnesses. Two witnesses, Charles Sawyer and Alice Russell, had firsthand knowledge of events after the murders were discovered. Charles Sawyer, an ornamental painter pressed into guard service at the Borden house, described the comings and goings to the Borden house. As a close friend, Alice Russell had more intimate knowledge of the household and was one of the first people to speak to Lizzie after the murders were discovered. She recalled Lizzie telling her that she had gone into the barn for some tin or lead to fix a window screen. Oddly, she could not remember any information about Lizzie Borden's morning dress before she changed into a pink wrapper.

Alice Russell proved more astute in her comments on relations in the Borden family. She testified that she had never seen any "wrangling" in the family but admitted that she did not think they were "congenial" because "their tastes differed in every way." This view was given further support by Abby's half sister Sarah Whitehead, Borden friend Augusta Tripp, and the seamstress Hannah Gifford. In their telling, however, the daughters' animus was directed squarely at Abby. Sarah Whitehead described Abby as "a woman who kept everything to herself." But Lizzie, according to Augusta Tripp, considered Abby "deceitful." Indeed, Gifford recalled an incident a few months earlier in which she had been shocked by Lizzie's vehemence. In the course of a fitting, she asked Lizzie what sort of dress she thought would be becoming for Abby, who was a "fleshy" woman. Lizzie responded that Abby was "a mean old thing . . . and we don't have anything to do with her, only what we are obliged to." She added: "[W]e stay up stairs most of the time . . . we don't always eat with . . . them; sometimes we wait until they are through."

All in all, the inquest presented a damning picture. It revealed a household divided between the elder and younger Bordens, the surface calm a sign of intractable hostility rather than brokered peace. And it seemed impossible that any outsider could have entered the house the morning of August 4. Even if someone had slipped in undetected, it was hard to imagine where an intruder might have secreted himself. Bridget Sullivan had a plausible account of her morning activities, corroborated in part by Lizzie Borden herself. Lizzie Borden, however, had given more than one version of her own movements and none of them was favorable. She said she was downstairs waiting for an iron flat to heat while her stepmother was murdered in the upstairs guest room directly above. Yet, when Andrew returned, Bridget Sullivan had been downstairs washing windows and had seen Lizzie descending the stairs. After her father came home, Lizzie went to the upper story of the barn in search of a sinker for a yet-to-be-obtained fishing tackle. When she found her father's body, she made no effort to inform or locate Abby. But after Dr. Bowen had left to wire her sister about Andrew's death, she said she thought she had heard Abby return. A druggist recounted her attempt to buy prussic acid. If she had indeed wanted to use the poison to clean a sealskin cape, why had she not acknowledged the attempt at the inquest? The Bordens had not been poisoned, but an unsuccessful effort to procure prussic acid might explain the use of a readily available household implement like a hatchet. For the investigators, it all pointed inexorably to Lizzie's guilt.

ARREST

After consultation with Knowlton, Marshal Hilliard was ready to serve an arrest warrant. Despite his successful effort to keep Jennings out of the inquest proceedings, Knowlton agreed that Hilliard should notify the defense counsel first. Hilliard went to Jennings's house so that the lawyer could support and advise his client. When Jennings arrived at the courthouse, he "found her reclining upon a lounge in the matron's room, and Emma and Mrs. Brigham seated near her." The *New York Times* reported: "She took the announcement of her arrest with surprising calmness." The *New York Herald*, by contrast, relayed a dubious report that "she fell into a fit of abject and pitiable terror." Whatever her state of mind, she was compos mentis enough to execute a power of attorney granting her sister, Emma, the right to collect any rents and pay any bills arising from their joint real estate holdings. The Fall River police department arrest book recorded her description: "Height: 5'4"; Complexion: Light; Hair: Light; Eyes: Gray." Her arrest was one of three for murder in Fall River that year and the only woman. One oddity escaped much of the press coverage: the warrant only mentioned Andrew Borden's murder.

Afterward, she was transported to the county jail in Taunton. According to the *Boston Daily Advertiser*, her journey "took the form of a public ceremonial." It seemed as if the whole town had assembled to meet her train. There, she discovered that her keeper was the mother of a childhood friend. Mrs. Wright, the matron, was reduced to tears at the change in circumstances since their last encounter. It was, according to the *New York Herald*, "an affecting scene." She was taken to her cell, a room nine and a half feet long and seven and a half feet wide, furnished with a bed, chair, and washbowl. Though forced to suffer the indignity of incarceration, Lizzie Borden enjoyed special privileges: Mrs. Wright substituted one of her own soft pillows for the standard prison issue. The *Fall River Daily Herald* reported that "some bright bits of color and other things calculated to soften the abrupt contrast with the unhappy girl's own room . . . have found their way into the prison cell." Lizzie also ordered dinners from the local hotel, supplementing the spartan prison fare. But otherwise, according to the *Fall River Daily Herald*, little was known of her daily life; "Outside of visits by her sister, her minister and counsel and one friend, Miss Borden has been virtually dead to the world."

Yet she was not forgotten. As she waited, Lizzie Borden became a popular cause. The local chapter of the Young Person's Society of Christian Endeavor, based at Lizzie Borden's own church, adopted a resolution expressing its "sincere sympathy . . . and confident belief that she will soon be restored to her former place of usefulness among us." Chapters of the Women's Christian Temperance Union sent telegrams of support. The Massachusetts WCTU president, Susan Fessenden, circulated a petition demanding Lizzie's release on bail, arguing that "thirty years of virtuous living should count for much in such a doubtful case." At the annual convention of the state WCTU, Fessenden conveyed her outrage: "Should Miss Borden . . . die under the treatment to which she has been subjected, no one would hang for her forfeited life. It would be a legal murder." The redoubtable Mary Ashton Rice Livermore visited Lizzie in jail. Livermore, a former Fall River resident acquainted with the first Mrs. Borden, told the *Boston Post*: "She talked to me freely of the whole case, but very calmly and sadly . . . You can see that the girl feels her position keenly." Anna Katharine Green, whose novel *The Leavenworth Case* featured an innocent woman ensnared by circumstantial evidence, declared: "I Believe Her Innocent."

Still others accused the police of persecution: they penned indignant letters to Marshal Hilliard and the papers. For example, Taunton resident Dr. S. P. Hubbard wrote: "I think the whole lot of you fellows better put your heads in soak . . . The idea of trying to fasten the Butchery of Mr. Borden on his daughter and letting the fellow escape . . . is outrageous in the extreme. He has had time to get to California." Mr. Edward Parkhurst went further: "It is high time some one should inform you what an asinine servant of the law you are making of yourself. A coat of tar and feathers would be your just desserts [*sic*]." Hilliard defended himself against the suspicions of bias toward Lizzie Borden, urging the public to "suspend judgment": "I have chased down more than 100 outside clews in 10 days . . . it was not until all the evidence was in that action was taken . . . she has not been imprisoned in haste nor without a full understanding of what her arrest means."

Some in Fall River shared the outrage of Lizzie Borden's far-flung supporters; others took a more jaundiced view, discerning the unstated prejudice in the concern about arresting "a lady." When the bodies were discovered, the immediate and universal reaction was horror. But once the initial shock had passed, the local reactions revealed the discontent and division in Fall River. An anonymous correspondent berated the police: "You do not show much energy or interest in investigating the Borden murder—probably if the suspected parties were poor mill hands you would not stand on ceremony with them." Indeed, as the *Fall River Daily Herald* reported, "A remark that is going the rounds is that if the parties at present suspected were poor people they would have been locked up before now." For the Irish-Catholic paper of choice, the *Fall River Daily Globe*, and its readers, the contrasting treatment of Lizzie Borden and Bridget Sullivan was especially galling. While other newspapers praised Lizzie Borden for her "calm" and "self-possession," the paper wondered at her coolness, describing her as "wearing a mask of stoical indifference that fit her like a glove." It waited impatiently for the mask to slip.

she did not want to." None of the other women in the Marion party (Anna C. Holmes, Mary L. Holmes, Isabel Fraser, Louise Remington, or Mabel Remington) would speak to the police.

Knowlton then moved on to the timeline of events, turning to questions of opportunity. Where exactly was Lizzie Borden throughout the morning of August 4? There were two short windows in which the murders of Abby and Andrew must have occurred and for which Lizzie and Bridget were the only other surviving occupants of the house. Morse left immediately after breakfast. Andrew Borden left the house at 9:15 a.m. and returned at about 10:45 a.m. By then, Abby was dead. Andrew Borden himself was dead by 11:45 a.m.

Knowlton turned his attention to the first part of the morning. Lizzie explained that she decided to iron handkerchiefs. Because the "flats" were not yet hot enough, she passed the time reading an old *Harper's* magazine. She said: "I sprinkled my handkerchiefs . . . and took them in the dining room. I took the ironing board in the dining room and left the handkerchiefs in the kitchen on the table and whether I ate any cookies or not, I don't remember. Then I sat down looking at the magazine, waiting for the flats to heat. Then I went in the sitting room and got the *Providence Journal* and took that into the kitchen." She also said she had not seen her stepmother since Abby had gone up to freshen up the guest room around the time Andrew left the house. Abby had told her that she had already changed the bedsheets and only needed to put new covers on the shams. According to Lizzie, Abby also intended "to close the room because she was going to have company Monday and she wanted everything in order."

Knowlton inquired, "What explanation . . . can you suggest, as to what she was doing from the time she said she had got the work all done in the spare room, until 11 o'clock?"

Lizzie appeared stumped. She suggested that Abby might have made her own bed. But that, given the Bordens' system of locks and bolts, would have required Abby to come down the front stairs, retrieve the key from the sitting room shelf, and go up the back stairs to the bedroom she and Andrew shared. Lizzie, however, said she had not seen her pass even though she claimed to be downstairs during Andrew's absence. Later she speculated Abby might have been using the sewing machine in the guest room but she admitted she had not heard the noisy machine.

Contrary to Bridget's statement after the murders and at the inquest, Lizzie testified that she was downstairs when her father came home. A few minutes later, she said she was upstairs when her father came home but she had only been there a few minutes.

Knowlton delicately pointed out the discrepancy: "You remember, Miss Borden, I will call your attention to it so as to see if I have any misunderstanding, not for the purpose of confusing you, you remember that you told me several times that you were downstairs and not upstairs when your father came home."

Nonplussed, Lizzie replied: "I don't know what I have said. I have answered so many questions and I am so confused I don't know one thing from the other."

Knowlton ignored the outburst: "Calling your attention to what you said about that a few minutes ago . . . you have said you were upstairs when the bell rang and were on the stairs when Maggie [Bridget Sullivan] let your father in, which now is your recollection . . . That you were downstairs when the bell rang and your father came?" Lizzie again said she thought she was downstairs.

At times it seemed that Lizzie was deliberately tormenting Knowlton with a Yankee version of the rope-a-dope. He was forced to repeat questions or ask slightly rephrased versions about every subject covered. She answered questions as tersely as possible and, when caught in a contradiction, wiggled out of the bind by suggesting she had misunderstood the question. Or she digressed, answering in an elliptical and unresponsive manner. All in all, it was an infuriating performance. But by the end of the afternoon, Lizzie Borden herself seemed exhausted and even disoriented. Her stories were contradictory; she might have frustrated her interlocutor but her answers were on the record. She had also revealed a great deal about the background tension in the Borden household, information that Knowlton was sure to put to use.

Knowlton, however, revealed nothing for the time being. Instead, he issued a brief press bulletin indicating only that two witnesses testified.

The next day, when the inquest resumed, Lizzie Borden returned to the witness stand and Knowlton returned to the timeline. First, he sought to pin down Lizzie's version of the early-morning period, in particular, when exactly she had seen Abby and her father on Thursday. Lizzie said that before her father left that morning, she had seen Abby in the dining room and her father in the sitting room. Alluding to the family's gastric distress of the previous day, Abby had asked her how she was feeling. Abby then told her that she was going out and would get their dinner. Knowlton paused this line of questioning to ask if it was "usual" for Abby to go out and to be gone for dinner. Lizzie again appeared stumped and had recourse to an awkward formulation: "More than once in three months, perhaps." Put in a more normal syntax, her answer meant that Abby rarely was out for dinner—at most, every other month or so. Returning to the timeline, Lizzie said she had gone into the kitchen and down into the cellar for clean clothes. When she walked through the main floor, she had seen her father reading the paper.

With one important exception, Lizzie hewed to her prior day's testimony about being downstairs all morning. She volunteered that she had gone upstairs and "basted a piece of tape" on a dress.

Knowlton exploded: "Do you remember you did not say that yesterday?"

Unmoved, Lizzie replied, "I don't think you asked me. I told you yesterday I went upstairs directly after I came up from down cellar, with the clean clothes."

In exasperation, Knowlton said, "Miss Borden, I am trying in good faith to get all the doings that morning of yourself and Miss Sullivan and I have not succeeded in doing it. Do you desire to give me any information or not?"

Now flustered herself, Lizzie replied that she could not give him information she did not have, adding "I don't know what your name is!"

Significantly, Lizzie placed herself at the center of the house, in the best position not only to see any theoretical intruder but also to observe Abby's movements or lack thereof. If she was alone downstairs between her father's departure and return, then, as Knowlton commented, "it would have been extremely difficult for anybody to have gone through the kitchen and dining room and front hall without your seeing them." But there was another problem with that story. Bridget Sullivan said she had been inside washing the windows downstairs when Andrew Borden returned. She had, after all, unbolted the front door to admit him. Knowlton asked: "Do you think she might have gone to work and washed all the windows in the dining room and you not know it?" Lizzie persisted in her denial. Knowlton declared: "It is certain beyond reasonable doubt she was engaged in washing the windows in the dining room or sitting room when your father came home. Do you mean to say you knew nothing of either of those operations?"

Even more surprising was Lizzie's account of her actions during the second critical period of that morning, the interval between her father's return at about 10:45 a.m. and the discovery of his body about an hour later. Shortly after Andrew's return to the house, Lizzie said she decided to go to the barn for a sinker in advance of her trip to Marion on Monday. Incredulous, Knowlton asked: "It occurred to you after your father came in it would be a good time to go to the barn after sinkers?" Knowlton pressed her about her expedition: Did she have a hook or fishing line? If, as she explained, there was fishing line at the family farm, did she not expect to find sinkers there as well?

She insisted that she had said there were lines and "perhaps hooks" at the farm but "I did not say I thought there were sinkers on my lines." She said she knew there was lead in the barn and had thought it might be fashioned into sinkers. On her way to the barn, she stopped under the pear tree for some pears. She then went to the upper story of the barn for the lead.

Knowlton summarized sarcastically: "[You] went to the second story of the barn to look for sinkers for lines you had at the farm, as you supposed, as you had seen them there five years before that time?"

Lizzie retorted: "I did not intend to go to the farm for lines. I was going to buy some lines here."

Knowlton could not believe his ears: "What was the use of telling me a while ago you had no sinkers on your line at the farm?"

After more sparring about the fishing apparatus, Knowlton sought to reel in his catch. He inquired minutely about how exactly she spent the claimed fifteen to twenty minutes in the barn. He insisted that her search for the lead could only have taken a few minutes. Lizzie volunteered that she went over to the west window, straightened a curtain, and ate her pears. Knowlton asked: "Do you mean to say you stopped your work and . . . sat still and ate some pears?" Recalling Lizzie's earlier testimony that she told Abby she would not eat dinner, he added sarcastically: "You were feeling better than you did in the morning . . . Well enough to eat pears, but not well enough to eat anything for dinner?" Knowlton concluded his questions about the barn, observing, "You have put yourself in the only place, perhaps, where it would be impossible for you to see a person going into the house?"

Knowlton's incredulity may have arisen, in part, from a lack of understanding of the life of leisured women. Lizzie's account of her activities seemed unfathomable to a man accustomed to a life of purpose. It was hard to imagine Knowlton tarrying to eat a pear while on the hunt for some object he needed. But was Lizzie's progress around the house and out to the barn any more dilatory than that of other women of her station? One day was much like another. Would other women like Lizzie Borden be able to account for their time minutely even if their lives were of manufactured and restless activity?

Knowlton explored Lizzie's knowledge of the Borden arsenal. (He helpfully mansplained the differences between a hatchet, "a short handled, wide bladed instrument," and an axe, "longer handled and smaller bladed.")

Lizzie said she "knew there was an old axe down [in the] cellar," but disavowed knowledge of any hatchets. Knowlton then asked, "Can you give any occasion for there being blood on them?" Lizzie said that her father "killed some pigeons in the barn last May or June." She thought "he wrung their necks." But when she saw the dead pigeons in the house, she noticed a few were "headless." She could not say whether the heads "were twisted off" or severed. She did recall that she had asked, "Why are these heads off?"

Before ending the day's ordeal, Knowlton returned to the source of the discord in the Borden household. He sought "the particulars of that trouble that you had with your mother four or five years ago" about the Fourth Street house, formerly owned by Abby Borden's father.

Lizzie gave an uncharacteristically loquacious response: "The stepmother, Mrs. Oliver Gray, wanted to sell it and my father bought out the Widow Gray's share. She did not tell me and he did not tell me, but some outsiders said he gave it to her; put it in her name. I said if he gave that to her, he ought to give us something. Told Mrs. Borden so. She did not care anything about the house herself. She wanted it so this half-sister could have a home . . . And we always thought she persuaded father to buy it. At any rate, he did buy it and I am quite sure she did persuade him. I said what he did for her, he ought to do for his own children. So, he gave us grandfather's house. That was all the trouble we ever had." Knowlton replied mildly that she had still not explained the trouble between them. Perhaps he, the devout son of an itinerant minister, could not imagine that Andrew's conveying a half interest in a modest house to his wife could cause the rift in the household, a rift that persisted until Andrew's and Abby's deaths. Lizzie replied, as if it were obvious, that "I said there was feeling four or five years ago when I stopped calling her mother." And, she added tartly, "I told you that yesterday." She then explained that her father bought the Ferry Street house "back from us some weeks ago. I don't know just how many."

Perplexed, Knowlton asked, "What do you mean by 'bought it back'?"

Lizzie replied: "He gave us money for it." Knowlton let the point drop.

Lizzie's second day of testimony revealed how much the property dispute still rankled. In contrast to her terse answers to Knowlton's other questions, she lost her verbal self-control when discussing the transfer. Moreover, the timing of Andrew's repurchase of the Ferry Street house from his daughters was suggestive. He had transferred his interest in the house five years earlier. Could it be a coincidence that he would decide to buy it back from them a few weeks before he died? Might the cash have been intended to mollify his daughters in advance of changes to his will?

Later that day, the significance of that property dispute was confirmed by the inquest testimony of Emma Borden and Hiram Harrington. Emma reluctantly agreed that her father's equalizing gift of property to the girls "did not entirely heal the feelings." Emma insisted, however, that she—not Lizzie—bore the real grudge against Abby. Emma also called Morse "a very dear uncle of ours, of mine." Like Lizzie, she named her uncle Hiram Harrington as the only person known to be on bad terms with her father. Harrington, for his part, admitted that he and Andrew did not speak to each other but, except for that, the households were on good terms. He also said that Lizzie spoke of her stepmother in "an unfriendly way."

In the course of their testimony, Dr. Bowen and Adelaide Churchill confirmed the timeline, Lizzie's change of dress, and that Lizzie told them Abby had received a note and gone out. Adelaide Churchill also testified that Lizzie had later asked her to look for Abby. Adelaide said: "She said she wished somebody would try to find Mrs. Borden because she thought she had heard her come in."

But the most intriguing piece of information came from John V. Morse. He testified that Andrew had spoken to him of making a will in the last year. On the Monday after the murders, Charles Cook, Andrew Borden's business manager, told Officer William Medley that Andrew had spoken to him of making a will—though he would later disavow the comment. At the time, he refused to comment on the Borden family relations "on account of my position . . . as I do not know what my relations may be with the family, when this thing is settled." The police searched for a will, employing "an expert operator under police surveillance" who labored for eight hours to open Andrew Borden's safe. The safe contained "quite a sum of money and many valuable papers" but no will. At the end of the day, Knowlton issued a bulletin for the press that listed the witnesses examined but gave no hint of the drama within the courtroom: "Inquest continued at 10 to-day . . . Nothing developed for publication."

On August 11, the inquest resumed and Knowlton again questioned Lizzie Borden. But this time he was more concerned with what she might have done outside the home than in it. After hearing news of the murders, a clerk at a local drugstore told officers that Lizzie had tried to buy prussic acid before the murders, ostensibly to "put an edge on" a sealskin cape. Knowlton began: "Your attention has already been called to the circumstance of going into the drugstore of Smith's on the corner of Columbia and Main Streets, by some officer, has it not, on the day before the tragedy?" Lizzie allowed that "somebody has spoken of it to me," but she claimed she did not know that drugstore. Knowlton asked if she had gone into "any drugstore" to ask for prussic acid. "No," she declared, saying that she was home all day on Wednesday, August 3. Later, he asked whether she had any "sealskin sacks." She acknowledged that she did and that the sealskins were "hanging in [a] large white bag in the attic." Knowlton asked if she ever put prussic acid on them. Lizzie insisted: "I don't use anything on them."

Knowlton accepted the impasse. He had what he needed. Three witnesses would testify to Lizzie's visit to the drugstore. Later, in a letter to Attorney General Albert Pillsbury, he would describe Lizzie Borden's inquest testimony as her "confession." So he could afford to be magnanimous. He said: "You can appreciate the anxiety that everybody has to find the author of this tragedy, and the questions that I put to you have been in that direction. I now ask you if you can furnish any other fact, or give any other, even suspicion, that will assist the officers in any way in this matter." Lizzie helpfully produced another dubious character. She had seen a shadowy figure around 9:00 p.m. lurking outside the house. She explained: "I came home from Miss Russell's one night and as I came up, I always glanced towards the side door. As I came along by the carriage-way, I saw a shadow on the side steps. I did not stop walking, but I walked slower. Somebody ran down the steps . . . I thought it was a man because I saw no skirts . . . I hurried in the front door as fast as I could and locked it." Unfortunately, she could be certain of neither the time nor the date. She said that she had seen the figure after her sister's departure for Fairhaven two weeks before the murders. And, as if suddenly wakened to its apparent significance, she also reported yet another suspicious character skulking around the house the previous winter. She knew that she had seen him on a Thursday because she was coming home from church and she could say that he "was not a very tall person." But that was all—except, of course, for the prospective renter ordered out by her father. That man, however, remained elusive. In essence, those were Lizzie Borden's final words about the murders. She never uttered another word under oath.

Unlike Lizzie Borden, Knowlton had more information to disclose. In addition to the three drugstore employees, Knowlton called five more witnesses. Two witnesses, Charles Sawyer and Alice Russell, had firsthand knowledge of events after the murders were discovered. Charles Sawyer, an ornamental painter pressed into guard service at the Borden house, described the comings and goings to the Borden house. As a close friend, Alice Russell had more intimate knowledge of the household and was one of the first people to speak to Lizzie after the murders were discovered. She recalled Lizzie telling her that she had gone into the barn for some tin or lead to fix a window screen. Oddly, she could not remember any information about Lizzie Borden's morning dress before she changed into a pink wrapper.

Alice Russell proved more astute in her comments on relations in the Borden family. She testified that she had never seen any "wrangling" in the family but admitted that she did not think they were "congenial" because "their tastes differed in every way." This view was given further support by Abby's half sister Sarah Whitehead, Borden friend Augusta Tripp, and the seamstress Hannah Gifford. In their telling, however, the daughters' animus was directed squarely at Abby. Sarah Whitehead described Abby as "a woman who kept everything to herself." But Lizzie, according to Augusta Tripp, considered Abby "deceitful." Indeed, Gifford recalled an incident a few months earlier in which she had been shocked by Lizzie's vehemence. In the course of a fitting, she asked Lizzie what sort of dress she thought would be becoming for Abby, who was a "fleshy" woman. Lizzie responded that Abby was "a mean old thing . . . and we don't have anything to do with her, only what we are obliged to." She added: "[W]e stay up stairs most of the time . . . we don't always eat with . . . them; sometimes we wait until they are through."

All in all, the inquest presented a damning picture. It revealed a household divided between the elder and younger Bordens, the surface calm a sign of intractable hostility rather than brokered peace. And it seemed impossible that any outsider could have entered the house the morning of August 4. Even if someone had slipped in undetected, it was hard to imagine where an intruder might have secreted himself. Bridget Sullivan had a plausible account of her morning activities, corroborated in part by Lizzie Borden herself. Lizzie Borden, however, had given more than one version of her own movements and none of them was favorable. She said she was downstairs waiting for an iron flat to heat while her stepmother was murdered in the upstairs guest room directly above. Yet, when Andrew returned, Bridget Sullivan had been downstairs washing windows and had seen Lizzie descending the stairs. After her father came home, Lizzie went to the upper story of the barn in search of a sinker for a yet-to-be-obtained fishing tackle. When she found her father's body, she made no effort to inform or locate Abby. But after Dr. Bowen had left to wire her sister about Andrew's death, she said she thought she had heard Abby return. A druggist recounted her attempt to buy prussic acid. If she had indeed wanted to use the poison to clean a sealskin cape, why had she not acknowledged the attempt at the inquest? The Bordens had not been poisoned, but an unsuccessful effort to procure prussic acid might explain the use of a readily available household implement like a hatchet. For the investigators, it all pointed inexorably to Lizzie's guilt.

ARREST

After consultation with Knowlton, Marshal Hilliard was ready to serve an arrest warrant. Despite his successful effort to keep Jennings out of the inquest proceedings, Knowlton agreed that Hilliard should notify the defense counsel first. Hilliard went to Jennings's house so that the lawyer could support and advise his client. When Jennings arrived at the courthouse, he "found her reclining upon a lounge in the matron's room, and Emma and Mrs. Brigham seated near her." The *New York Times* reported: "She took the announcement of her arrest with surprising calmness." The *New York Herald*, by contrast, relayed a dubious report that "she fell into a fit of abject and pitiable terror." Whatever her state of mind, she was compos mentis enough to execute a power of attorney granting her sister, Emma, the right to collect any rents and pay any bills arising from their joint real estate holdings. The Fall River police department arrest book recorded her description: "Height: 5'4"; Complexion: Light; Hair: Light; Eyes: Gray." Her arrest was one of three for murder in Fall River that year and the only woman. One oddity escaped much of the press coverage: the warrant only mentioned Andrew Borden's murder.

Afterward, she was transported to the county jail in Taunton. According to the *Boston Daily Advertiser*, her journey "took the form of a public ceremonial." It seemed as if the whole town had assembled to meet her train. There, she discovered that her keeper was the mother of a childhood friend. Mrs. Wright, the matron, was reduced to tears at the change in circumstances since their last encounter. It was, according to the *New York Herald*, "an affecting scene." She was taken to her cell, a room nine and a half feet long and seven and a half feet wide, furnished with a bed, chair, and washbowl. Though forced to suffer the indignity of incarceration, Lizzie Borden enjoyed special privileges: Mrs. Wright substituted one of her own soft pillows for the standard prison issue. The *Fall River Daily Herald* reported that "some bright bits of color and other things calculated to soften the abrupt contrast with the unhappy girl's own room . . . have found their way into the prison cell." Lizzie also ordered dinners from the local hotel, supplementing the spartan prison fare. But otherwise, according to the *Fall River Daily Herald*, little was known of her daily life; "Outside of visits by her sister, her minister and counsel and one friend, Miss Borden has been virtually dead to the world."

Yet she was not forgotten. As she waited, Lizzie Borden became a popular cause. The local chapter of the Young Person's Society of Christian Endeavor, based at Lizzie Borden's own church, adopted a resolution expressing its "sincere sympathy . . . and confident belief that she will soon be restored to her former place of usefulness among us." Chapters of the Women's Christian Temperance Union sent telegrams of support. The Massachusetts WCTU president, Susan Fessenden, circulated a petition demanding Lizzie's release on bail, arguing that "thirty years of virtuous living should count for much in such a doubtful case." At the annual convention of the state WCTU, Fessenden conveyed her outrage: "Should Miss Borden . . . die under the treatment to which she has been subjected, no one would hang for her forfeited life. It would be a legal murder." The redoubtable Mary Ashton Rice Livermore visited Lizzie in jail. Livermore, a former Fall River resident acquainted with the first Mrs. Borden, told the *Boston Post*: "She talked to me freely of the whole case, but very calmly and sadly . . . You can see that the girl feels her position keenly." Anna Katharine Green, whose novel *The Leavenworth Case* featured an innocent woman ensnared by circumstantial evidence, declared: "I Believe Her Innocent."

Still others accused the police of persecution: they penned indignant letters to Marshal Hilliard and the papers. For example, Taunton resident Dr. S. P. Hubbard wrote: "I think the whole lot of you fellows better put your heads in soak . . . The idea of trying to fasten the Butchery of Mr. Borden on his daughter and letting the fellow escape . . . is outrageous in the extreme. He has had time to get to California." Mr. Edward Parkhurst went further: "It is high time some one should inform you what an asinine servant of the law you are making of yourself. A coat of tar and feathers would be your just desserts [*sic*]." Hilliard defended himself against the suspicions of bias toward Lizzie Borden, urging the public to "suspend judgment": "I have chased down more than 100 outside clews in 10 days . . . it was not until all the evidence was in that action was taken . . . she has not been imprisoned in haste nor without a full understanding of what her arrest means."

Some in Fall River shared the outrage of Lizzie Borden's far-flung supporters; others took a more jaundiced view, discerning the unstated prejudice in the concern about arresting "a lady." When the bodies were discovered, the immediate and universal reaction was horror. But once the initial shock had passed, the local reactions revealed the discontent and division in Fall River. An anonymous correspondent berated the police: "You do not show much energy or interest in investigating the Borden murder—probably if the suspected parties were poor mill hands you would not stand on ceremony with them." Indeed, as the *Fall River Daily Herald* reported, "A remark that is going the rounds is that if the parties at present suspected were poor people they would have been locked up before now." For the Irish-Catholic paper of choice, the *Fall River Daily Globe*, and its readers, the contrasting treatment of Lizzie Borden and Bridget Sullivan was especially galling. While other newspapers praised Lizzie Borden for her "calm" and "self-possession," the paper wondered at her coolness, describing her as "wearing a mask of stoical indifference that fit her like a glove." It waited impatiently for the mask to slip.

Chapter 4

A MOST
REMARKABLE WOMAN

Taunton Jail, showing the garden, 1892, *courtesy of Fall River Historical Society*

As defense counsel, Andrew Jennings worked to serve Lizzie's interests inside and outside the courtroom. According to the *New Bedford Evening Standard*, Jennings lay "awake nights forming plans" for Lizzie Borden's defense. He assumed the mantle of Lizzie's protector and spokesman, directing his client and her friends not to talk to newspapers. In one instance, he even stood in for her dead father. When Curtis Piece, whom Lizzie Borden had previously met at Westport and who the police briefly and mistakenly suspected was her mystery lover, importuned Lizzie for permission to visit her in jail, Jennings sent a strongly worded rebuke. "Dear Sir," he wrote, "For your sympathy . . . she is grateful but she is at a loss to understand why you should presume upon her unfortunate position to open correspondence with her, or write to Sheriff Wright asking for an interview. She does not wish to see you, nor to receive letters from you. She has not, 'tis true, a father to appeal to, or family to compel you to cease your attempts to force yourself upon her notice; but there are others who can and will supply his place."

SUPPOSE A MAN

Jennings knew he had a formidable adversary in District Attorney Hosea Knowlton. Jennings had already lost his bid to represent Lizzie at the inquest. Their next clash came with the announcement that Judge Blaisdell—the judge who had presided over the inquest (and who had denied Jennings's request to assist his client at that proceeding)— would also preside over Borden's preliminary hearing. A preliminary hearing, under Massachusetts law, was held to determine that the prosecution had sufficient evidence of a serious crime to try the defendant in superior court. The rationale for the hearing was essentially jurisdictional. The district court tried only minor crimes, misdemeanors, or felonies punishable with little to no jail time. Serious crimes—almost all felonies—required the judge to "bind over" the accused person for a trial in superior court. But, unlike the inquest, this was not a secret, one-sided proceeding. The prosecution did not need to prove guilt beyond a reasonable doubt, as at a trial, but it did need to show "probable cause." Whether or not Knowlton chose to reveal his entire hand, it provided the defense with its first meaningful look at the evidence against Lizzie Borden and an opportunity to contest it.

At Judge Blaisdell's announcement, Jennings "jumped to his feet." He exclaimed: "The difference between this proceeding and the inquest is apparent and glaring." Jennings said that the judge must be prejudiced against the defendant because of his prior knowledge of the evidence

"Suspense," according to Porter, "was momentarily broken, however, by a threatened fight between a New Bedford newspaper man and a violently disposed individual past middle age." Finally, the lawyers entered the courtroom: Andrew Jennings, "dressed in a steel gray suit with frock coat and white tie," arrived first, followed by Knowlton, wearing "a pepper and salt suit" and an incongruously "jaunty white straw hat." He had just returned from his summer vacation cottage in Marion, Massachusetts, and he looked "sunbronzed" and rested. (He facetiously told Attorney General Pillsbury that his vacation had been "killed with the Bordens.") But it was Melvin O. Adams who cut the most impressive figure. This was Adams's first outing as Lizzie Borden's champion, and he did not disappoint. "Dressed in a suit of navy blue," Adams, "despite the heat, looked as cool and placid as if victory had been won by his client and the mercury was at freezing." The mercury was far from freezing inside the courtroom. Rather, "The air was stale, the heat very oppressive, and those within were almost as anxious to get out as those outside were to get in." Those who persevered were not rewarded for their endurance. After all the anticipation, Hosea Knowlton informed the court that the medical experts were not ready to testify and requested a continuance until Thursday.

The crowds returned to their homes but Lizzie Borden remained in the Fall River Police Station, billeted at Matron Reagan's jail apartment. It was an amicable arrangement. Instead of being escorted back and forth under police guard to Taunton, she received visits from her sister and a small circle of local friends. On Wednesday, Emma arrived early for her normal visit; however, Matron Reagan said she soon overheard "loud voices." Glancing into the room, she saw Lizzie lying on the bed and heard her declare: "Emma, you've given me away." Emma then replied: "I only told Mr. Jennings what I thought he ought to know." Lizzie responded: "You have and I will let you see I won't give in one inch." She then turned onto her left side, faced out the window, and did not speak again until Jennings arrived later that morning.

This, Jennings knew, was trouble. He drew up a statement for the matron to sign, denying the quarrel occurred. But when Matron Reagan was presented with the statement, she refused to sign, stating that she needed to consult Marshal Hilliard. A motley delegation of Borden's lawyers, friends, and newspapermen followed Matron Reagan on her trek through the building to Hilliard's office. Upon hearing of the Jennings plan, Hilliard told her not to sign any statement and advised her to "remain silent until she was called upon to testify to what she had heard." Jennings was furious. Brandishing the statement, he addressed the assembled newspapermen, charging that Hilliard had refused to let the matron sign the denial-of-the-quarrel story. According to Porter, "An excited scene followed in which there was much animated talk." Most papers reported the quarrel but, the *Boston Globe* complained, "some other jealous papers, exasperated at being 'beaten' on such a development in this remarkable case, saw fit to throw doubt on the *Globe's* exclusive."

On Thursday, August 25, the preliminary hearing resumed. Crowds formed early and the reporters, nearly fifty in all, "touched elbows all around as they wrote." Despite the importance of the occasion, regular business consumed the first part of the morning: "The entrance of Bridget Sullivan at ten minutes before 10 o'clock transferred the interest of the spectators from the trial of a Sunday liquor seller." The alleged liquor merchant argued that "he had purchased many hogsheads of beer to celebrate the accession of Gladstone to power, and had no intention of selling the stuff." The man's creative excuse that he was toasting the fourth premiership of British Liberal stalwart William Gladstone was amusing but the audience eagerly awaited the entrance of the prisoner, the sight denied them on Monday.

Accompanied by a few select friends, Lizzie Borden arrived in court "calm and self possessed, with less apparent agitation than the throng of men and women who were watching her." Indeed, one reporter observed: "If the prisoner had been a spectator idly drawn by curiosity to the scene, she could not have been more self-controlled." He continued: "As she came in from the outer corridor and passed through the doorway on the right of the judge's bench she straightened her back, assumed an air of haughty concern, and with nerves steeled for the encounter, came before the throng." The actual spectators, "a majority of whom were women . . . dressed in holiday attire," seemed unfazed by the gravity of the occasion, chattering away in the audience. By the afternoon, the temperature in the packed courtroom became "almost unbearable."

To prove Lizzie Borden "probably guilty," Knowlton intended to show that only Lizzie Borden had the motive and opportunity to commit the murders. He opened his case, calling the Bristol County medical examiner, Dr. William Dolan. Barely thirty-five years old and "somewhat inclined to be stout," Dr. Dolan was in his first year as medical examiner; the Borden murders were his baptism by fire. He described the sight of Andrew's head as "ghastly." All in all, the direct examination went well: "Possessing a very gentlemanly manner, a clear voice and excellent command of English, he gave his testimony on the direct examination with confidence and distinctness." He explained that he had examined both Andrew's and Abby's bodies on August 4.

Dr. William Dolan, *courtesy of Fall River Historical Society*

As he began to read a description of the wounds from his notes, he was halted by Jennings's objection. So he recited the wounds from memory.

Knowlton then asked him what was, for him, the essential point: Had Abby been dead for at least two hours before the examination? This time Adams objected. Knowlton insisted he had asked such a question in every case he had tried. Displaying his sardonic wit, Adams retorted: "There were a number of bad habits the District Attorney had acquired which could be corrected." But Judge Blaisdell permitted the question. Before Dr. Dolan could answer, Jennings objected, leading Knowlton to point out that "the habit of arguing after a decision was not one of his bad ones, and Mr. Adams objected to Mr. Knowlton's hitting him over Mr. Jennings' shoulder." As a reporter summarized the testy exchange: "Frequent wrangles took place between the lawyers, in which the court occasionally took a hand . . . Col. Adams' audacious retorts brought smiles to the face of the prisoner, who then appeared more comfortable than at any time during the day."

Dolan's unflustered demeanor withered under Adams's "scathing attack" during his cross-examination. Adams questioned the manner in which the autopsy was first conducted, and lacerated Dolan for the lack of a full report in an attempt to make the medical investigation appear inadequate and "bungling." According to the *Boston Globe*, "Mr. Adams was at times very severe in his manner of questioning, and made Dr. Dolan apparently very uncomfortable." Another observer characterized the lawyers' differing styles: "District Attorney Knowlton takes it easily, as is his custom; Mr. Jennings scowls, as is his custom; and Mr. Adams shoots queries as though he had an inexhaustible supply of them."

But the sensation of the day had little to do with the legal case. In response to a question from Mr. Adams, Dr. Dolan revealed that the Bordens' heads had been removed, the skulls "cleaned" and "in his possession." The *Fall River Daily Herald* summarized: "This announcement created a mild sensation in the court. Everybody's eyes turned toward the sisters to see how they took the announcement that their father's body had been buried headless. Emma's eyes filled with tears and her head sank upon her hand. Lizzie appeared for an instant startled and quickly looked toward her sister . . . A moment afterward there was the same unmoved interest in the case as might have been expected of a spectator in the benches a dozen feet away."

The following morning, Dr. Dolan returned to the witness stand, but his tenure was mercifully brief. Most of the morning revolved around a flurry of witnesses testifying to Andrew Borden's last morning walk and fixed the time of his return to Second Street. John V.

Morse, the houseguest whose bedchamber had been the site of Abby's slaughter, also gave his account of events. Morse explained that he had arrived after lunch on Wednesday, August 3, left about 3:00 p.m. to visit Andrew Borden's Swansea farm, and returned that evening. On cross-examination, he said that everyone in the house was sick and volunteered that "Mr. Borden said the milk might have been poisoned."

Bridget Sullivan was the key witness of the day. Pale and frightened, she reluctantly took the stand. The *Boston Globe* declared: "Her face was very white and her eyes downcast." She did not make eye contact with Lizzie Borden; she did not even look up as Lizzie entered. When Knowlton questioned her, she replied in a low tone "inaudible at the distance of ten feet from the witness stand." Nonetheless, she had the full attention of everyone in the room: "The crowd in the court room began to show a decided interest, which increased in her testimony." Most notably, "Emma Borden sat with her gloved hand shading her eyes" and Lizzie's face betrayed a slight "flush . . . which those who have studied her features have learned to know as an indication of emotion, and she carefully listened to every sentence as it was presented."

What Bridget had to say was of critical importance to Knowlton's strategy. Dr. Dolan had established, at the very least, that Abby was killed before Andrew. Bridget was the only other person known to be in the house with Lizzie between Andrew's departure and the discovery of his body. She alone could rule out the possibility of an intruder happening upon an unlocked house and awaiting his opportunity to strike in the day. To that end, Bridget testified she had locked the screen door and the wooden door at the back of the house before she went to bed and found them still locked in the morning. Like the other members of the household, she, too, was ill the next morning and vomited in the backyard shortly after breakfast. She could not be certain that she had locked the screen door after her return to the house. Mrs. Borden had asked her to wash the windows, inside and out. Later in the morning, she heard Mr. Borden attempt to open the locked front door. As she opened the door for him, she heard Lizzie laugh at the top of the stairs. Lizzie asked her father about the mail and told him that Abby had gone out. While Andrew went into the sitting room for a nap, Lizzie ironed handkerchiefs in the dining room. She also told Bridget about a sale of dry goods at Sargent's, advising her to go out and avail herself of the bargain.

Bridget's testimony supported the prosecution's argument that Lizzie was the only person with the opportunity to kill first Abby and then Andrew on August 4. Knowlton also wanted to emphasize that Lizzie had lied about the note Abby had received. Knowlton asked whether it was Abby's "habit to notify you when she went out." (It was.) Adams jumped up to object. Knowlton asked a different question to make a similar point: "Then the only thing you know about her going out was what Lizzie told you?" This time Jennings objected. Knowlton decided that was enough for the day. When the hearing resumed, Knowlton elicited two final pieces of information from Bridget. First, she testified that Lizzie had said she had heard a groan before coming back into the house to discover her father's body. Second, she revealed that she had not seen Lizzie crying at any point on Thursday. The first provided an example of Lizzie's shifting account of her actions on August 4; the second afforded Knowlton an opportunity to suggest Lizzie's composure had sinister import.

Adams responded with a vigorous cross-examination, "directing the questions at the young woman with unprecedented rapidity." Bridget Sullivan, however, "stood the ordeal very well and her stereotyped answers were 'Yes, Sir.' and 'No, Sir.'" He did not succeed in undermining her testimony, but Lizzie seemed to enjoy the performance, even emitting a "hearty laugh" when Adams compared Abby's size to Knowlton's bulk. Emma, however, was not amused: "She was decidedly nervous, shifting about in her seat and keeping her fan going." From time to time, she whispered questions into Jennings's ear.

After Bridget Sullivan's testimony, court was adjourned for the weekend. The prosecution's decision was strategic. The *New York Times* quoted police sources who emphasized the significance of Bridget's testimony: "These officers say that the story of the servant shows how manifestly impossible it was for any one to enter or leave the house while Lizzie was alone with first her mother and then her father." Adams nonetheless insisted that he was not worried: "He has also given it as his opinion, and he is one of the shrewdest criminal lawyers in the Bay State, that something far stronger than has yet been presented will have to be made public before the presiding Justice will be justified in holding Lizzie Borden for the Grand Jury." John Milne, the owner of the *Fall River Daily Evening News*, the organ of the Fall River establishment, concurred: "There has been, up to the present, not a single item of evidence that can have weight against the defendant . . . [T]he only thing proved is what has been admitted by Miss Lizzie's adherents from the first. She was alone at the time Mr. Borden was murdered and has no one to support her statement that she was not alone . . . the Government stands absolutely without a motive."

Knowlton had not forgotten about the motive. But first he offered something far more explosive: Lizzie Borden's attempt to buy poison the day before the murders. First, Eli Bence, the druggist at D. R. Smith's, identified Lizzie as the woman who had attempted to buy prussic acid on August 3. When asked if he was certain, Eli Bence testified: "It was the first time I was ever asked for prussic acid in that manner." Adams treated the witness to a full measure of disdain. He ridiculed Bence's inability to recall what color dress the woman wore, whether she carried "a purse or bag," and if she wore a veil or hat. Having purported to recognize Lizzie, in part, from her voice, he asked: "Do you make any pretensions to vocal culture?" and "Do you claim to have a particularly sensitive or educated ear for sounds?" Bence demurred. Adams asked, "What was the peculiarity about this voice?"

Bence said: "She spoke in a tremulous voice."

At this point, Lizzie was overheard to say: "I never was in that man's store in my life."

As if he had heard his client, Adams said, "I suppose you are reasonably sure of the people you see . . . [D]id you ever mistake one person for another, find you had made a mistake in identification?"

Bence admitted that such a thing was "a matter of common experience," yet he could not himself recall doing so.

Jennings's subsequent investigation turned up two instances that could call into question Bence's certainty about his identification: According to one Jas. Taussiq, "Bence once made a bet that this Taussiq was killed in an accident he witnessed." When he next saw Taussiq, Bence reportedly told him: "I was never so much surprised at seeing you come in here." A druggist at a different pharmacy recounted another story Bence had told him: Bence "mistook a person in Boston & hit him & like to got arrested for it." There were also two other instances of women seeking prussic acid on the Monday before the murders: Hypolyte Martel reported turning away a woman seeking first arsenic, then prussic acid. According to the *Fall River Daily Herald*, "A woman also called at Corneau & Latourneau's drugstore on Pleasant street on the same date, but it was found out afterward that it was the wife of Inspector McCaffrey who was then on a crusade against the drug stores." Better still for the defense, "[s]he is said to resemble Miss Borden."

Nonetheless, two others in the store, Frank Kilroy and Frederick B. Hart, also testified that Lizzie Borden had asked for poison. Frederick B. Hart, another drug clerk at D. R. Smith's, confirmed Bence's account. Under cross-examination, Kilroy, a medical student, contradicted part of Bence's testimony but supported his identification of Lizzie as the woman who had asked for the prussic acid. He thought she spoke in a "loud tone" and he did not notice any "tremulous tones." Although he had not been taken to the house to identify Lizzie Borden's voice, he had seen her several times on the street before he encountered her in the store. Like Bence, he could not describe her dress or even if she had worn a veil. Aside from that cavil, the identification stood. Lizzie betrayed the strain: "The prisoner herself has been more uneasy than has been her wont, and though her undemonstrative nature still asserts itself, the constant biting of the lips and the restless movements of the hands indicate that there is a limit even to the wonderful power of self-control which she seems to possess."

After that blow, the defense needed good news. Medical expert and

Harvard chemist Professor Edward Stickney Wood unexpectedly provided a break from the prosecution's relentless success. First, he declared the Bordens' stomachs free of poison. Second, he could not identify the murder weapon. He found no blood or human hair on any of the hatchets or axes taken from the Borden house. But any defense jubilation was short-lived. Knowlton next read Lizzie Borden's inquest testimony into the record for two hours. Even her supporters found "it was very painful . . . to hear the recital she had given of her visit to the barn and her purpose in going." With that coup, the government rested its case.

The defense was brief and to the point. The prosecution had not produced the murder weapon and no blood had been found on Lizzie. Neighbors reported strange noises in the night and had seen odd men about the neighborhood. Although the courtroom was uncomfortably warm, Lizzie needed a woolen shawl, embodying her special ability "to keep cool when other people are warm or excited."

All that remained were closing arguments. For the occasion, Borden wore a dark blue gown with a black lace hat "adorned with a few red berries," and black gloves. Andrew Jennings spoke for Lizzie Borden. He spoke of his friendship with Andrew Borden, effectively vouching for his late client's daughter. It had its intended effect. When Jennings "drew his pathetic pictures of her youth and relations with her murdered father, she broke completely down and burst into tears, sitting with her hands in her eyes." He explained away her inconsistent answers as a function of the inquisition conducted against her. In his telling, she was "on the rack" at the inquest. He minimized the disagreement over the property and emphasized the lack of a credible motive. Comparing the two women in the house at the time of the murders, he asked: "In the natural course of things who would be the party to be suspected? Whose clothing would be examined, and who would have to account for every moment of her time? Would it be the stranger, or would it be the one bound to the murdered man by ties of love? And . . . what does it mean when we say the youngest daughter? The last one whose baby fingers have been lovingly entwined about her father's head. Is there nothing in the ties of love and affection?" He dismissed the notion that Lizzie could have, as a matter of her physical capacity, committed the murders: "Every blow showed that the person who wielded that hatchet was a person of experience with the instrument . . . [N]o hand could strike those blows that had not a powerful wrist and experience in handling a hatchet." And, if she were guilty, where was the blood?

The prosecutor's closing argument was short and to the point. Knowlton lamented the painful duty that had befallen him. He reminded the judge that Professor Wood, the chemist, and Dr. Dolan, the medical examiner, agreed that both victims were killed by a hatchet or some other sharp implement and that Abby died more than an hour and a half before Andrew. "Who could have done it?" Knowlton answered his own question: "No man could have struck them. You are struck with the thought that it was an irresolute, imperfect feminine hand." He continued: "The first obvious inquiry is who is benefitted by that removal?" The defendant. And who had the only opportunity of committing both murders? Again, the defendant. As for Lizzie's attempt to buy prussic acid, Knowlton argued: "The crime was done as a matter of deliberate preparation." Finally, he alluded to Lizzie's "singular" demeanor: "While everyone is dazed, there is but one person, who . . . has not been seen to express emotion." In closing, he summarized his case: "She has been dealing in poisonous things; . . . her story is absurd; and . . . hers and hers alone has been the opportunity for commission of the crime." As Knowlton concluded, "a deathly silence" permeated the room, a mood of dread made manifest as "the sun, which had been streaming into the room during the early afternoon, went under a cloud . . . and a chilling draught at the same moment came in at the open window."

The anticipation was brief. "Paler than usual," Judge Blaisdell "allowed his keen eyes to wander about the courtroom." After jotting a note on "the large piece of legal paper which the officers . . . could see was the murder complaint," Judge Blaisdell began to speak. Then he paused. Continuing in a "husky voice, almost inaudible," he slowly and deliberately rendered his judgment, "its impressiveness enhanced by the palpable reluctance with which it was uttered": "Suppose for a single moment that *a man* was standing there. He was found close by that guestchamber which to Mrs. Borden was a chamber of death. Suppose that a man had been found in the vicinity of Mr. Borden and the only account he could give of himself was the unreasonable one that he was out in the barn looking for sinkers, that he was in the yard, that he was looking for something else. Would there be any question in the minds of men what should be done with such a man?" He continued, his voice now "almost a whisper": "So there is only one thing to do—painful as it may be—the judgment of the court is that you are probably guilty and you are ordered to wait the action of the Superior Court."

During his speech, Lizzie "sat calm and apparently unmoved." By contrast, "strong men lowered their heads. Weaker men wiped tears from their eyes. Every woman in the courtroom sobbed and wept except one." But as she rose, Lizzie seemed to falter. Once standing, "she was as resolute, as composed, and as self-possessed as at any time during the entire hearing." She assured her stalwart supporter Reverend Buck: "Don't be afraid. I am all right. I feel quite composed." She added as she left the courtroom for Taunton jail: "It is for the best, I think. It is better that I get my exoneration in a higher court, for then it will be complete." Lizzie's lawyer Jennings was far less sanguine. He told reporters: "I am all tired out and want to go home. I don't see what I can add to what I have already said." Nonetheless, he gamely continued: "The government has not the slightest evidence in support of their claim of a motive excepting the fact of some little difficulty six years ago with the stepmother . . . The government has not by any means established the improbability of the murder being committed by some one outside the family."

LIZZIE BORDEN'S SECRET

On Monday, October 10, the *Boston Globe* published a bombshell— its headline: "Lizzie Borden's Secret." The secret was threefold: she was pregnant, her father knew, and Andrew threatened to turn her out of the house if she did not reveal "the name of the man who got [her] into trouble." According to the *Boston Globe*, Andrew Borden issued his ultimatum on August 3, telling Lizzie: "You can make your own choice and do it tonight. Either let us know what his name is or take the door on Saturday, and when you go fishing fish for some other place to live." There was more. The article also named twenty-five prosecution witnesses—some present at the decisive family quarrel, others who had seen a hooded Lizzie Borden in the guest room at the time of her stepmother's murder. The list included familiar names with new revelations: Bridget Sullivan, according to the article, had over-heard an ominous discussion between Morse and Lizzie. Morse said: "Quarreling will not fix the thing. Something else has got to be done." Lizzie, for her part, tried to buy Bridget's silence: "Are you a fool or a knave?" she demanded. From farther afield, another witness claimed Lizzie had offered to sell her Abby's gold watch for $10. This watch had been stolen during the unsolved burglary the previous year. Yet another declared Lizzie Borden had consulted a lawyer to inquire how the order of deaths—if, say, a wife were to die before her husband—would affect the other beneficiaries in a given will. It was compelling, it was damning, and it was "the most gigantic 'fake' ever laid before the reading public."

How did such an elaborate hoax find its way into print? Henry Trickey, the *Globe*'s star crime reporter, bought what he thought was the government's case from a private detective named Edwin McHenry for $500. McHenry owned a Providence, Rhode Island detective bureau; he and his wife, Nellie, assisted the Fall River police during the Borden investigation. He also had a history with Trickey: they had been on opposing sides of another murder case—the trial of Dr. Graves in Denver, Colorado—the previous year. (Pinkerton detective O. M. Hanscom was another alumnus of that case.) McHenry was, to put it charitably, unscrupulous and he apparently relished the opportunity of doing Trickey a bad turn. Later McHenry described the sequence of events: "After Mr. Trickey had made the proposition to buy the State's case from me, I lay in bed that day and thought the matter over, and formed some idea of the story which I could give out . . . He wrote and I dictated. We were at it until three o'clock in the morning." Before he was duped, Trickey was reckoned one of the best reporters in Massachusetts. In retrospect, Trickey's initial credulity was understandable. A colleague later noted that his enthusiasm for his job and his "loyalty" to the paper "sometimes outran his caution." McHenry's fake also had clever verisimilitude in its chosen details—Andrew's reference to Lizzie's stated plan of fishing in Marion (presented as the reason for her trip to the barn); the many Fall River surnames on the fictitious list of witnesses (including Chace with two *c*'s); the illicit affair (with resulting pregnancy) as the motive for the murders. That said, even a cursory investigation would have shown that most of the claimed witnesses did not exist.

Fearing a scoop by a rival paper, Trickey's superiors at the *Boston Globe* also chose not to conduct any investigation and rushed the tale into print. Within ten hours, the editors knew it was a hoax. On October 12, the *Boston Globe* retracted the story and offered a "heartfelt apology" to Lizzie Borden "for this inhuman reflection upon her honor as a woman, and for any injustice the publication of Monday inflicted upon her." Trickey left Boston to confront McHenry, declaring that there would be a "funeral in Providence if he ever laid his eyes on him." But less than two months later, it was he who was dead. Having fled to Canada to escape an indictment for his role in the affair, Trickey fell under the wheels of a westbound train near Hamilton, Ontario. Attorney General Pillsbury did not trust the initial report of his death. He instructed an officer to make sure "that it is actually Trickey who was killed." He had known the reporter "pretty well" and considered Trickey "to be capable of a number of things."

Though viewed widely as the "moving spirit" in the affair, McHenry found support from Marshal Hilliard, who "found McHenry a capable, reliable, and trustworthy officer." McHenry, though, had been responsible for unearthing other sensational tidbits that were perhaps too good to be true. He reported that, according to two milliners on Fourth Street, Lizzie Borden had been "practicing in a gymnasium for a long time and . . . boasted of the strength she possessed." He did, however, track down the source of an intriguing statement purportedly made by Adelaide Churchill "that there was one thing she saw in the house the day of the murder, that she would never repeat, even if they tore her tongue out." Unhelpfully, the source was "one George Wiley, a clerk in the Troy Mill," who was passing along second- or thirdhand gossip. McHenry claimed he was never properly compensated for all of his hard work on the Borden case: "I plodded through in silence, and where is my reward?" he lamented to a fellow journalist.

As to the substance of the Trickey-McHenry Affair, newspapers of all persuasions took a collective vow of silence. As Porter put it, "So delicate in fact has the matter become that no newspaper has attempted to publish anything more than an occasional reference to it; although more than one great daily is in possession of the main facts." Despite the day of turmoil for the Borden team, the hoax made Lizzie Borden a figure of sympathy, especially in the pages of a chastened *Boston Globe*.

A TRUE BILL

The legal machinery ground on: the grand jury of twenty-three men drawn from the county voting rolls commenced its investigation on November 15. The preliminary hearing had determined there was sufficient evidence to try the defendant in superior court; the grand jury's role was to decide whether or not to indict, or formally charge, the defendant with a particular crime. As one jurist explained, "In Massachusetts the grand jury is, and always was, merely an informing and accusatory body: it does not hear criminal cases on the merits; it does *not* determine guilt or innocence." In the normal procedure, the prosecutor presents evidence to support an indictment; the defense plays

Governor George D. Robinson, *courtesy of Fall River Historical Society*

no role in the proceedings. But Knowlton, in a departure from the standard practice, offered Jennings an opportunity to present evidence for the defense. Perhaps he hoped he would be relieved of the responsibility to prosecute Lizzie Borden. Nonetheless, on December 2, 1892, the Grand Jury indicted Lizzie Borden for the murders of Andrew and Abby Borden, one of fourteen indictments for murder in Massachusetts that year. In legal parlance, it returned a "true bill" on three different indictments: one for the murder of Andrew Borden, a second for the murder of Abby Borden, and a third for the murder of both Andrew and Abby Borden. Knowlton reported to Pillsbury that the jury's vote to indict had been "substantial but not unanimous." In keeping with the secrecy of the procedure, he did "not even know how any man voted."

Jennings may have failed to influence the grand jury, but he was not idle. He hired another legal luminary, George D. Robinson, a former Republican congressman and former governor of Massachusetts. Robinson's name, the *Boston Sunday Herald* would observe, "is almost a household word . . . and he can well be termed one of the most popular men in the state." Another newspaper described him as "an old fashioned type": "His build shows that he loves the good things of life, and his face shows that he thinks and works hard." A large, distinguished-looking man, Robinson, like the dapper Melvin Adams, displayed his figure to advantage in well-tailored suits. But, for all his sartorial finery, he had the common touch, renowned for standing before the jury in a relaxed posture as if he had dropped by to chat. It came naturally to him. Robinson may have been a Harvard man but he had not been born to an easy life. As a boy, he worked on his father's farm. After college, he spent nine years as a teacher, holding the position of principal of Chicopee High School before he became a lawyer. His habit of unpretentious clarity and "calm cheerfulness" served him well. In addition to his fame and legal skill, he was credited with "an extended knowledge of human nature possessed by but few professional men." Paraphrasing Shakespeare's Antony, Senator Henry Cabot Lodge declared in tribute: "He was the plain, blunt man who spoke right on; and he was a master of this most difficult and telling kind of oratory. He was no phrase-maker, no rounder of periods, no seeker for metaphors; but he was one of the most effective and convincing speakers, whether to Congress, to a great popular audience, or to a jury, that I ever listened to . . . He used simple language and clear sentences. . . . He had, above all, the rare and most precious faculty of making his hearers feel that he was putting into words just what they had always thought, but had never been able to express quite so well." He also knew his own worth. His purported $25,000 fee belied his folksy manner. (Jennings and Adams were each rumored to earn $15,000 apiece.)

Meanwhile, Lizzie Borden languished in jail with little comfort from her legal team. Robinson's hiring had raised her spirits temporarily—he had insisted on meeting her before undertaking her defense and, after two hours of discussion with her, declared his belief in her innocence. But she lamented to her old friend Annie Lindsey that her lawyers "gave her no hope of anything *soon*, or ever of an *acquittal*." Her spirits were buoyed by simple comforts permitted in her cell: a few plants, candy sent by Annie, and a male cat named Daisy. Cats keep their own counsel. And Daisy, she said, was "the quietest boy I ever saw but is lots of company for me." She won second place in a readers' contest in the *Boston Journal*—the prize, a complete set of William Thackeray's works. She would have preferred Dickens. During the preliminary hearing, she had been unable to make her way through Thackeray's *Pendennis*. But the confinement wore on her. In

May she wrote: "My spirits are at ebb tide. I see no ray of light amid the gloom. I try to fill up the waiting time as well as I can, but every day is longer and longer . . . My heart is heavy and the burden laid upon me seems greater than I can bear."

AN ASYLUM MAY BE HER LOT

While Borden waited, newspapers openly speculated about her sanity. One headline read: "An Asylum May Be Her Lot." But she seemed so very normal. At school, the former principal of her grammar school recalled her as "an average scholar, neither being exceptionally smart, nor noticeably dull." At home, she was a moody child, apparently of a melancholy disposition. A high school friend described her as "rather blue" on more than one occasion. Later, in her prophetic conversation with Alice Russell the night before the murders, Lizzie described her own pensiveness: "When I was at the table the other day . . . the girls were laughing and talking and having a good time, and this feeling came over me, and one of them spoke and said, 'Lizzie, why don't you talk.'"

Whether or not she was inclined to depressive moods, Lizzie appeared normal to those around her. As the Pinkerton detective O. M. Hanscom observed, "the murder[s] looked like the work of a lunatic, while Lizzie appeared to be a level-headed self-possessed woman." The journalist Elizabeth Jordan concurred: "No jury will believe that woman, with her firm face and steady intelligent eyes, ever did any important thing she had not subjected to the unobscured light of . . . reason." For some, including the *Boston Herald*, Lizzie Borden's apparent normality and "impassive coolness" during the investigation paradoxically provided the best evidence of her insanity: "There is nothing that tends more to induce the belief in insanity in this case than this most extraordinary exhibition." An unnamed "official" source explained: "It is a well-known fact that one may be comparatively sound on all matters but one. That is the way I think it is with Lizzie."

Nonetheless, the *Boston Advertiser* declared: "It is an open secret in police circles that the government officers believe that Miss Borden was insane at the time of the murders." In this instance, the *Advertiser* was right. At the very least, the prosecutors thought the matter worth serious inquiry. First, they consulted experts. Attorney General Pillsbury wrote to Dr. George Jelly, the former superintendent of the McLean Asylum for the Insane and later chairman of the Massachusetts State Board of Insanity, asking for an opinion about Lizzie's sanity. Though he was often called upon to examine prominent individuals and pronounce upon their mental fitness, Jelly declined to do so, writing: "I do not think that the indications of insanity which you mention, are sufficiently strong or tangible enough to enable me to express an opinion." Pillsbury then wrote to Jelly's successor at McLean, Dr. Edward Cowles, to inquire if the "mechanical aspects of the case" indicated "that it was the work of a maniac." Cowles replied that he did not know enough about "the mechanical aspects" to venture an opinion, but said that his "inferences have been *against* a theory of insanity in the person charged with the crime, from anything I have so far read concerning *her conduct* before or after the event."

Both Knowlton and Pillsbury tried to persuade Andrew Jennings to permit a doctor to examine Lizzie Borden. Knowlton reported: "I could do nothing whatever with Jennings. He took exactly the position I feared he would, and seemed to regard it as some sort of surrender if he consented to anything." After meeting Jennings in person on August 22, Pillsbury thought he had made some progress in convincing him to permit the prosecution's expert to examine Lizzie Borden; however, Jennings "went away saying that he must see Adams" first. Adams's advice was clear: "We could not do anything which suggested a doubt of her innocence." Knowlton lamented: "We can make some investigations into family matters without him, but it will not be so thorough as it would be if we had his assistance."

The police investigation into possible insanity in the Borden family, conducted by Moulton Batchelder of the Massachusetts state police force, turned up nothing of great interest. Most agreed that the

Morse and Borden family tree had some odd apples but none could point to any rumors of insanity. Captain James C. Stafford declared that Lizzie Borden's mother had been "a peculiar woman. She had a *very bad temper.*" Anna Howland averred, "I always heard that they were somewhat peculiar and odd." Moulton Batchelder underlined the report of Sarah Morse's temper as well as the following comment from neighbor Rescom Case: "We never heard that any one of them is or ever was insane but *I think some of them are worse then [sic] insane.*" The former city marshal, David S. Brigham, passed along the opinion that Lizzie was a "woman of bad disposition if they tell all what they know." (Brigham was the manager of the B.M.C. Durfee Safe Deposit and Trust Company, on whose board Andrew Borden served, but it is not clear how he had gleaned his information.) George A. Pettey, who had lived at the Second Street house before it was converted into a single residence, said that Lizzie was known to be "ugly." By contrast, Lizzie's friend Mary Brigham (David Brigham's daughter-in-law) told the *Fall River Daily Herald*: "She was a girl of very even temper. She never became excited . . . Her conduct since the murder has been just what anyone who knew her would expect." Dr. Handy (who owned the Marion cottage where Lizzie had been expected to join her friends) denied that he had ever seen "any indications of insanity." "Although hysteria is common to that sex," he continued, "she never showed any signs of it."

Hysteria was the most common explanation for the transgressive acts of middle-class women. By the end of the nineteenth century, women's nature was seen as fundamentally different from male models of physiology. On balance, women were seen as more prone to ailments, both biological and psychological. A female pathological condition, hysteria (as opposed to neurasthenia, an ailment associated with men undone by the stresses of capitalism) dominated medical discussions related to women. Noting the prevalence of the disease in young unmarried women, doctors initially claimed that hysterical symptoms resulted from a wandering womb, and later, with greater research into brain function, assigned neurological causes. In the last two decades of the century, however, researchers could find little evidence for hysteria's organic etiology. Yet, women remained uniquely vulnerable to the disorder and their biology or their biologically ordained role seemed somehow central to the puzzle. In large part, the extreme importance accorded to their reproductive systems relative to the rest of their physiological functions created this perception. These gendered anatomical and physiological models resulted from, and in turn justified, contemporary attitudes about women's essential capabilities and psychology. Physicians attributed women's illnesses to underlying nervous and moral disorders. As the innovator of the notorious "rest cure" for female hysterics, Dr. S. Weir Mitchell, explained, "Women warp morally if long nervously ill."

These psychological and physiological understandings of women's nature necessarily converged in criminal trials, for the state of mind of the accused was essential in determining not only guilt or innocence but also their ultimate responsibility. By far the most important factor in evaluating responsibility was evidence of menstruation. Menstruation encapsulated the entire problem of female physiology, psychology, and behavior. The onset of menses was viewed as a time of great danger, a systemic shock repeated monthly with varying intensity. Experts like the influential Austrian criminal psychologist Hans Gross contended that menstruation lowered women's resistance to forbidden impulses, opening the floodgates to a range of criminal behaviors. Although such transgressions usually resulted in theft rather than more serious crimes, some warned of women's potential for violence. As Gross argued, "Menstruation may bring women to the most terrible crimes. Various authors cite numerous examples of sensible women driven to do the most inconceivable things—in many cases to murder." In the interests of "mercy" and "justice," Dr. Henry MacNaughton-Jones, a prominent English physician, argued that "the relation of . . . a disorder of menstruation to any criminal act ought to be taken into consideration in determining the responsibility of the woman."

Lizzie herself had testified at the inquest that she had "fleas," a local euphemism for menstruation, in the days before the murders. On its face, this provided an innocent explanation for bloody towels soaking in a pail and a spot of blood found by police on an inner skirt. But her lawyers were aware of the potential significance of her menstruation. Arthur Phillips, Jennings's young associate, later wrote: "There was no evidence that she was ever hysterical or abnormal in these periods, nor was there evidence of any unusual mental condition."

Quietly, Jennings ran down some disturbing rumors. His notebook contains the entry "Ask Emma if she took cat out which scratched her, put it on chopping block & cut head off." There were several versions of this story making the rounds. For example, an anonymous correspondent advised Marshal Hilliard "to look up the cat story in which Lizzie Borden killed some time ago." Another anonymous correspondent wrote to Knowlton that the Bordens' milkman "knew for a *fact* that Miss Lizzie decapitated a kitten which belonged to her stepmother." There seemed to be no foundation for the stories, though one "unwilling" writer, a Mrs. Apthorp of Boston, helpfully suggested that the animal hair found on one of the hatchets "which Professor Wood said looked like a cow's hair, may have come from this cat." The cat rumor later resurfaced during the trial. Elizabeth Jordan, correspondent for the *New York World*, wrote: "Nobody would be authority for this story; everybody had heard it from somebody else. But it went the rounds all day long and there was more blood with a sharper axe every time it was told."

On behalf of the defense, Andrew Jennings flatly rejected the notion of insanity and promised the trial would vindicate his client. Lizzie Borden, however, was less confident, writing to her friend Annie Lindsey in January 1893, "I cannot for the life of me see how you and the rest of my friends can be so full of hope over the case." Less than a month before the trial, she wrote to Annie again, wondering if "the tangled threads would *never* be smoothed out." Her own doubts were mirrored in the private correspondence of Knowlton and Attorney General Pillsbury. Because Knowlton and Pillsbury agreed that "neither of us can escape the conclusion that she must have had some knowledge of the occurrence," they were obligated to proceed with the prosecution. "Personally I would like very much to get rid of the trial of the case," Knowlton wrote to Pillsbury, "however, I cannot see my way clear to any disposition of the case other than a trial." "The case," he continued, "has proceeded so far and an indictment has been found by the grand jury of the county that it does not seem to me that we ought to take the responsibility of discharging her without trial, even though there is every reasonable expectation of a verdict of not guilty . . . I think it may well be that the jury might disagree upon the case. But even in my most sanguine moments I have scarcely expected a verdict of guilty."

As attorney general, Albert Pillsbury was expected to prosecute the capital case personally. Newspaper accounts speculated on a rift among prosecutors, hypothesizing that, unlike Knowlton, Pillsbury wavered about proceeding against Lizzie Borden. But, unbeknownst to the public, he was a sick man, recovering from a sudden incapacitating illness in late December. Although he expressed hopes that he would be able to participate, he took no chances: he recruited the promising young district attorney of Essex County, William Moody, to help Knowlton prosecute the case. Pillsbury told him: "I do not feel sure that we shall have to draw upon you, but we may. I am, at present, under strict orders not to undertake more than a certain amount of work, nor anything of an unusually trying character." Because of the sensitivity of the case, Moody was sworn to secrecy. He wrote to Pillsbury: "I will of course heed your

William H. Moody, *courtesy of Fall River Historical Society*

injunction as to silence, knowing as I do the uncertainty of the course you may adopt, and remembering your caution."

Still in his thirties, District Attorney William Moody had "as high a reputation as any public prosecutor in the state." He cut a dashing figure: he was blond, blue-eyed, and dressed like a New Yorker. And he was "as bright and alert as he is handsome." The Borden trial was merely an early step in a glittering career. He was touted as a likely candidate to succeed Pillsbury as Massachusetts attorney general, assuming he could beat the other likely candidate, Hosea Knowlton. But he opted to ascend to the national stage. After serving in Congress, Moody was appointed by his former Harvard classmate Theodore Roosevelt as secretary of the navy and then attorney general of the United States. The handsome bachelor also played the role of the avuncular escort to Roosevelt's high-spirited daughter Alice. After selecting Oliver Wendell Holmes, Jr. and William R. Day, Roosevelt chose Moody as his final appointment to the Supreme Court in 1906. His tenure, however, was short-lived: ill health forced his retirement three years later.

With Moody pegged as an alternate, the trial preparations continued. Knowlton and Pillsbury conferred in person on Wednesday, April 26. After a flurry of scheduling telegrams, the prosecutors and defense attorneys agreed to meet on Saturday, April 29. On May 2, Pillsbury informed Robinson: "Chief Judge Mason says they conclude to have the trial begin Monday not later than eleven. He evidently still regards New Bedford as the place. He suggests that Miss Borden should be arraigned and plead."

Lizzie Borden's arraignment required a complex ruse to avoid a press stampede. On Monday, May 8, 1893, Sheriff Wright traveled to New Bedford alone and then doubled back to retrieve his prisoner. Lizzie herself was "not in sight more than two seconds" before being hustled to a waiting cab and taken to court. As she entered the courtroom, "she faltered." According to the *New Bedford Evening Standard*, "It was but an instant, however, for she seemed to brace herself and then walked steadily to the dock." Mrs. Wright, the sheriff's wife, by contrast seemed "nervous and agitated." When it was time to plead, Lizzie Borden did not hesitate: "In a voice firm, clear, and resonant, she replied, 'I am not guilty.'" Outside the courthouse, a crowd gathered, "spectators paced anxiously up and down the sidewalks, determined to catch a glimpse of her as she emerged." They were largely foiled by another "blind"—empty hacks waited outside both entrances, front and rear. Lizzie Borden was eventually spirited away on the 5:50 train for Taunton. It had been a short excursion: portal to portal in less than four hours.

By the end of the week, Pillsbury concluded he could not participate and designated Moody as his successor. On Sunday, May 13, 1893, Knowlton and Moody spent six hours conferring about the case. Moody agreed to interview every witness and to "prepare the case thoroughly." Knowlton offered to let Moody take the lead, "tender[ing] him the stroke oar," but Moody "prefer[red] to take the junior part." The following day, a relieved Knowlton told Pillsbury: "He is going into the case *con amore*." Nonetheless, he continued: "I regret more than I can express, not only on my account, but on yours, that the final decision is that you cannot be with us. You were entirely right in your remark that no possible course we could take in the case would relieve us from criticism, more or less offensive."

On the Sunday before the trial, the *Fall River Daily Globe* reported: "The preliminaries are completed, and this morning the curtain ascends on the most notorious chapter of the Borden murder mystery . . . About it all there is the atmosphere of suppressed excitement—the longing for the opening of the act, and the ending of the suspense."

Part 2

TRIAL

Chapter 5

THE CURTAIN ASCENDS

Exterior of Bristol County courthouse, New Bedford, Massachusetts, *courtesy of Fall River Historical Society*

On May 30, 1893, another axe murder roiled Fall River. Twenty-two-year-old Bertha Manchester suffered "twenty-three distinct and separate axe wounds on the back of the skull and its base." The papers were quick to note the similarity to the Borden murders: the weapon in each case appeared to be an axe, all three victims were killed during the day, and each suffered many more wounds than were necessary to kill. The *Providence Journal* went further. "The Man with the Axe," declared its June 2, 1893, headline, "Has Once Again Come to the Front in Fall River." Elizabeth Jordan of the *New York World* agreed, remarking, "So it seems there is in Fall River some Jack the Chopper, who has the knack of hacking people to pieces, with strikingly similar evidence of senseless brutality in each instance, and of slipping cleverly through the hands of the police just as did the Whitechapel murderer or murderers in London." Marshal Hilliard, however, dismissed any "parallel with the Borden case." The *New Bedford Evening Standard* expanded on the critical differences: "Everything about the Borden mystery points to a well-concocted plan to kill, while the evidence in the Manchester case points to a struggle and sudden impulse to kill." When Jose Correa deMello (spelled Correiro in news accounts), a disgruntled farmhand from the Azores, was arrested on June 4, he seemed designed by central casting for the murderer's role. The Manchester case was the stuff of nativist nightmares: a young woman—said to be "modest, retiring, self-sacrificing"— brutally murdered on her father's farm by an insane Portuguese immigrant with a grievance about his wages. Correa deMello had arrived only a few months earlier. He could not, therefore, have committed the Borden murders. He had also confessed to the Manchester murder, removing the slim possibility that a still unknown third party had committed both the Manchester killing and the Borden murders. Yet, would the men selected as Borden jurors have this information before deciding Lizzie Borden's fate? Headlines announcing Correa deMello's arrest on June 5, 1893, shared newspaper space with coverage of the first day of Lizzie Borden's trial in New Bedford, a day devoted to selecting a jury.

New Bedford, Massachusetts, had not been a consensus choice for the trial venue. Fall River papers lobbied for a local trial, given that all the witnesses resided there. The *Fall River Daily Evening News* argued that "convenience and expense are in favor of this city." Civic leaders were also keen to realize the financial benefits of hosting the Borden trial. The defense preferred Taunton, the Bristol County seat, where Lizzie Borden had been housed since her preliminary hearing. On December 12, 1892, Jennings wrote to Attorney General Pillsbury:

"My client is very anxious to have the case tried at Taunton as she very much prefers to stay at her present quarters." But when the trial date was finally set for June 5, the starting date of New Bedford's regular criminal court term, journalists correctly guessed that New Bedford would be the venue.

New Bedford was fifteen miles east of Fall River, and at least thirty minutes by the trolley train. It was known for its prominence as a whaling port for much of the nineteenth century. As a result of this history, New Bedford had once been the richest city per capita in America, the fortunes of its "blubber aristocracy" extending beyond whaling and into textile mills. Considered "one of the most beautiful towns in New England," its central residential district boasted "grand elms, gorgeous gardens, and green lawns." Within a few blocks of some of the earliest mansions stood the Bristol County courthouse. The Bristol County courthouse in New Bedford was built in 1831 in Greek Revival style. One observer declared it "one of the most picturesque buildings in this very picturesque old city." It boasted four classical pillars in the front and a bell tower, but, though set off by a large green lawn, "it was completely eclipsed in architectural and material appearances" by its surrounding "pretentious residences." Its second-floor courtroom had nothing like the capacity for the audience of spectators and journalists expected for the Borden trial. Despite its limitations, the New Bedford court prepared for the press siege.

The trial of Lizzie Borden, according to the *Providence Journal*, would be "one of the greatest murder trials in the world's history." The *New York World* more modestly declared it "the trial of the most extraordinary criminal case in the history of New England." Regardless, the *Boston Globe* proclaimed "It will be impossible to exaggerate the interest felt and manifested by intelligent readers throughout the country in the outcome of this trial of a comparatively young woman for the murder of her father and stepmother." The *Boston Globe* estimated that, among its own readership, "there are at this moment 100,000 persons devoting what they are pleased to call their minds to

Interior of courtroom, *courtesy of Fall River Historical Society*

a hopeless analysis of this tremendous case." To satisfy this demand, so many correspondents and reporters converged on New Bedford that the *New Bedford Evening Standard* questioned whether a more distinguished collection of newspaper writers were ever detailed to cover a murder trial. To accommodate the journalists, the second-floor courtroom was modified to include five extra tables in the space usually reserved for witnesses. Each table would accommodate five reporters seated on high cane-back stools. In use, the arrangement brought to mind a schoolhouse invigilation, reporters silently scribbling away with the high sheriff keeping charge. The Associated Press was allotted four places, with the remainder to representatives of Massachusetts papers. The Fall River and New Bedford papers were given priority. But the New York papers rebelled; Joseph Pulitzer's paper the *New York World* asked for the chief justice's intercession. The New York petition granted, Sheriff Wright partitioned the prisoner's dock, installing another long table behind a temporary rail to make room for the New York papers. The wire services, by contrast, were relegated to a horse shed at the rear of the courthouse. To make the accommodations marginally less grim, a floor was laid and the structure was divided into three compartments with the west and east ends dedicated to the Postal Telegraph and the Standard and Associated Press, respectively.

Eight lesser wire services were crammed together in the middle. The *Boston Globe* had its own dedicated wire service in a separate structure tucked around the corner. So many wires traveled out from those buildings, one wag noted, "you could hang all the washings of all Bristol County on them."

Julian Ralph of the *New York Sun* and Joseph Howard, Jr., who covered the trial for the *Boston Globe* and the *New York Recorder*, were the best known of the group. Both were exemplars of the story rather than information model of the news, "narrat[ing] the news with an eye toward character, plot, setting, dialogue, dramatic pacing, and other literary elements," a style termed the "new journalism." By 1893, Joseph Pulitzer's *New York World* had surpassed the *Sun* in circulation (150,000 daily readers) and, despite its earned reputation for pioneering yellow journalism, practiced a mix of the informational and story-based journalism that owed less to tabloid journalism than the *Sun*. The *Sun* remained the least expensive and the most accessible. It is perhaps best remembered for its 1897 editorial with the immortal line "Yes, Virginia, there is a Santa Claus."

Julian Ralph had already covered momentous stories of the day, including Henry Ward Beecher's adultery trial in 1875, before joining the *Sun*, then the New York paper with the largest circulation. He worked hard at his craft: turning events into stories required, in his words, "know[ing] what to write and what to leave out, what to make the most of, what is worth a paragraph, and what is worth a whole page of a newspaper." In 1893, he was at the height of his powers: he

Julian Ralph, *public domain, from Google Books scan of Frank M. O'Brien,* The Story of the Sun *(New York: George H. Doran Company, 1918)*

covered Grover Cleveland's inauguration as president in March, the opening of the World's Columbian Fair in Chicago in May, and the legislative debates on free silver in Washington, DC. In addition to his work at the *Sun*, between 1890 and 1895, he published nearly 150 articles in major magazines like *Harper's*. He had turned forty at the end of May, looked every inch of his six-foot height, and radiated good health. Crediting his constitution for his physical endurance and his innate disposition for his "unconquerable persistence"—both, in his view, essential for a newspaperman—he would ultimately travel to Russia, China, and South Africa during the Boer War. He later explained: "The life of every journalist is as hard as nails; that of the special correspondents is even harder." Yet a certain fastidiousness seemed at odds with his swashbuckling adventures: he wore his thinning hair neatly parted and his handlebar moustache narrowed to a precisely waxed point.

As a general matter, he disliked covering crime, but took special pride in having saved an innocent young man from the gallows. In his autobiography, *The Making of a Journalist*, Ralph wrote: "It was a case of pitting cold logic against detective stupidity; for what milder term can I give to that too common habit with some police of making an arrest and then twisting and distorting evidence to fit the bird in hand, rather than . . . set themselves the more difficult task of finding the real culprit." He had his own remarkable near miss as well. In 1883, he covered the murder of a young woman in New Jersey. Wary of all strangers showing an interest in the case, the dead woman's brothers began to suspect the journalist who wrote so movingly of their sister's death. The brothers tried to force Ralph to touch their dead sister's body "according to an age-old superstition which holds that such dumb mouths will accuse a murderer." (Ten years later, he recalled the incident, wondering if the skull of Andrew Borden might accuse or clear his daughter.)

Joe Howard, Jr., a veteran of over thirty years of murder trials, including that of President Garfield's assassin Charles J. Guiteau, arrived in New Bedford at the apogee of a long career. A former reporter for the *New York Times* and founding member of the New York

Press Club, he graduated from daily journalism to a more comfortable life of sought-after columnist and lecturer. Examples of his most popular speeches give a sense of life as a bon vivant and boldface name: "Journalism," "Cranks," and "People I Have Met." His columns appeared in the *Boston Globe*, Boston's most widely circulated paper, with a readership nearly double that of the business-minded *Boston Record* and ten thousand subscribers greater than its closest competitor, the *Boston Herald*. (The columns also appeared in the *New York Recorder* and were reprinted in other papers as well.) Nearly sixty at the time of the Borden trial, Howard

Joe Howard, Jr., *Boston Globe*

looked like the celebrated columnist he was—the highest-paid newspaperman in the country. He had a bald pate, bushy moustache, and a pointed red beard. He seemed to enjoy defying conventions: it was whispered that he traveled everywhere with an attractive blond stenographer. And he alone among all the many men in the courtroom flouted propriety and wore comfortable summer clothes. Howard was what his colleague Julian Ralph termed one of the "Bohemians" of the press, survivors of a less professional era, when it was "a haphazard, unmethodical business," who now "wear clean linen, live comfortably, and are only called 'Bohemians' because they do not take life as seriously as most persons." Howard was fond of noting incidents that allowed his readers to feel as if they, too, were inside the courtroom witnessing the spectacle. For example, later that day, Howard mentioned "a most demonstrative cow, whose mooing was almost continuous, frequently interrupting the learned judge, often drowning the responses of mild-mannered witnesses, and causing as far as the eye could see the one and only smile that changed the impassiveness of the Borden countenance." The cow became such a regular feature of the reports that the *Boston Globe*'s editorial section opined: "The irreverent cow that moos beneath the windows of the courthouse in New Bedford will go down into fame with the historic cow that kicked over Mrs. O'Leary's kerosene lamp and was thus the great first cause of the big Chicago fire in 1871."

Female reporters—including Elizabeth Jordan and Anna Page Scott of the *New York World* and Amy Robsart of the *Boston Post*—were also on hand to cover the trial. They were considered noteworthy enough to warrant illustrations in rival papers of unusual and interesting persons attending the trial. They were not exactly novelties: the number of women journalists more than doubled in the 1890s (from "888 in 1890 to 2,193 at the turn of the century"—still less than

Elizabeth Jordan, *public domain from Google Books scan of Elizabeth Garver Jordan,* Tales of the Cloister, *vol. 4 (New York: Harper & Brothers, 1901)*

10 percent of the total number of journalists), but a few had full-time jobs as reporters. As Jordan herself put it, women reporters in the 1890s were "more numerous, and they are further in [than in the earlier part of the century]; but their tenure of office is distinctly open to discussion."

The contrast between Julian Ralph and Joe Howard, Jr., on the one hand, and Elizabeth Jordan on the other could not have been more noteworthy. Elizabeth Jordan was a convent-educated woman from Milwaukee who decided to make her mark as a journalist in New York City. Her first important opportunity was in the summer of

1890, shortly after her twenty-fifth birthday. Her editor sent her to the seaside town of Cape May, New Jersey, for a feature on the daily life of President Harrison's family, including their much-discussed five-year-old grandson. Many seasoned journalists had failed to penetrate the Harrisons' retreat. Dressed in a "fresh white linen tailor made suit," Jordan brazenly called upon the household, turning a chance encounter with Mrs. Harrison in the front hall into an extended interview while they both played with the little boy on the beach.

Jordan had a gift for more difficult stories as well. She followed her light interview, featuring the Harrisons' cosseted grandson, with a tragic story called "The Death of Number Nine." One of the nuns who taught her encouraged Jordan to let the readers shed their own tears. She took the advice to heart when dealing with this heartrending material. According to Jordan's later summary, "This was the simple tale of a sick baby, carried three miles through New York streets one night in its mother's arms, only to have her discover at Bellevue Hospital that the child was dead." The mother, lacking funds for a proper burial, left her child there to be buried anonymously as "Number Nine" at Potter's Field. As a result of her piece, enough money was raised not only to bury the child "with dignified simplicity" but also to give his mother and siblings a chance for "a happier life." That and other pieces won her the respect of her colleagues—though they jokingly begged her "to drop the damned formality and convent polish." Within a decade she had become editor of *Harper's Bazaar*, a successful fiction writer, and an intimate of cultural and literary figures ranging from the actor Otis Skinner to the writer Frances Hodgson Burnett. It was even rumored that she and Henry James shared a "warmer emotion than a pleasant friendship." She denied "the silly gossip" but counted him among her close friends, marveling at "the strange power of Henry James's eyes. They made me feel in those instants as if he had read me to the soul." Later in her life, she edited Sinclair Lewis's first two novels. But, long before those happy milestones, she attracted notoriety with her first short story, "Ruth Herrick's Assignment," published in *Cosmopolitan* magazine, which told the story of a woman on trial for murder who confessed her guilt to a sympathetic female reporter. As a result, Jordan was widely thought to have heard and then suppressed Lizzie Borden's confession out of a sisterly solidarity. Jordan disavowed any connection but admitted she, like many of her colleagues, was a Borden partisan. In her memoir *Three Rousing Cheers*, named for the customary greeting inaugurated in her circle, she declared: "The reporters around me were for Miss Borden as one man—convinced of her innocence, showing the conviction between the lines of their reports, and burning with sympathy for her."

MONDAY, JUNE 5, 1893

No spectators were allowed on the first day but crowds lingered around the courthouse nonetheless. Around 11:00 a.m., a ripple of excitement announced Lizzie Borden's arrival: "a modest little carryall stopped at the door, from which alighted the heroine of the day." She might have been arriving to Central Congregational Church, striding quickly to her seat in the dock as if it were her regular pew. For the occasion, she wore a black wool dress with a new black lace hat, accented by two blue rosettes and a small blue feather, and black gloves that were to be her unvarying accessory throughout the trial. The dress, trimmed with purple velvet at the cuffs and hem, "fitted her as perfectly as if she had been measured for it in Paris." The hat alone was "a model for theatregoers." Despite her new finery, the elegance of the ensemble was undercut by a large, "rather loud" enamel pansy pin at her throat.

Lizzie Borden herself was a bit of a disappointment. As Julian Ralph observed with apparent surprise: "She is, in truth, a very plain-looking old maid. She may be likened to a typical school marm, plain, practical and with a face that shows the deep lines of either care or habitual low spirits . . . There is nothing wicked [or] criminal, or hard in her features."

"Every picture which has been made of this woman," wrote Elizabeth Jordan, "either absurdly flatters her or grossly maligns her." She explained: "Viewed fully in the face Lizzie Borden is plain to the point of homeliness . . . Viewed in profile, much of the unpleasantness of the woman's face disappears. It becomes then rather a refined and sensitive face, which is not without womanly gentleness." Popular reports transformed her into "a brawny, big, muscular, hard-faced, coarse-looking girl." Ralph declared: "She is, in fact, neither large nor small, nor tall nor short, but is of the average build, and in demeanor is quiet, modest, and well bred." More than that, there was, Ralph concluded, "about her that indefinable quality which we call ladyhood." He admitted she was "far from good looking" and observed delicately that the "lower part of her countenance" was "greatly overweighted," but he also rhapsodized about Lizzie's "beautiful, fine, nut-brown hair, soft and glossy to a degree." Elizabeth Jordan noticed that she tended her hair carefully, with a perfect curl in her bangs. Others were less kind, emphasizing the broadness of her face and her masculine jaw. One even noted her awkward gait, adding, "I could not be sure, but I strongly suspect she toes in." All of the descriptions grappled with the disjuncture between the relative ordinariness of her physical appearance and the horror of the crime for which she was on trial.

But what was most striking was her extraordinary self-possession. Despite the scrutiny, she remained unruffled, the still center of the spectacle unfolding around her. At the direction of her counsel, Lizzie received no visitors the day before the trial so that she could rest before her impending ordeal. Whether or not she required this intervention, she walked confidently before the press gauntlet. "A most interesting study is this young lady from Fall River," observed Joe Howard. "Lizzie Borden has a remarkable temperament and her control over herself is always voluntary; seldom does she lose the strong grasp she has upon the muscles of her entire person." Julian Ralph concurred: "She behaved like a self-possessed girl, with all the grit that comes of American blood . . . She was modest, calm, and quiet and it was plain to see that she had complete mastery of herself, and could make her sensations and emotions invisible to an impertinent public." Elizabeth Jordan questioned whether her self-possession arose from the "sheer force of an iron resolution or by a hopeless resignation to a malign fate." Regardless, she characterized Lizzie Borden as "aloof as a Buddha in a temple." Lizzie Borden herself objected to the popular image of her stoicism in an earlier interview. She explained to Kate McGuirk of the *New York Recorder*: "I never did reveal my feelings, and I cannot change my nature now . . . I have tried hard . . . to be brave and womanly through it all. I know I am innocent, and I have made up my mind that no matter what comes to me I will try to bear it bravely and make the best of it."

Shortly afterward, she was joined by her legal team led by the Borden family lawyer and Fall River counselor, Andrew Jennings. Jennings, thought Julian Ralph, had "more energy than all the rest of the people in the courtroom." He was followed by the expert trial lawyers he had recruited to bolster the defense: the urbane Boston lawyer Melvin O. Adams and the former governor George D. Robinson. Together, they were, as the *Providence Journal* put it, "a powerful triumvirate."

Because of Pillsbury's illness, Knowlton headed the prosecution. Perhaps it was only fitting that the task had fallen to Knowlton, the man who would succeed Pillsbury as attorney general. Knowlton threw himself into the task: "If he were a witch burner, or, possessed the spirit of one . . . he could not be more firm and unyielding than he is in his regard, and he has behind him the strong pressure of his big and powerful personality." Indeed, Julian Ralph described him as "a veritable Cromwell, a round-headed powerful and bustling big man, built like a bull." His impatience to begin was manifest immediately: he had come in and out of the courtroom several times before the arrival of the Borden team. His colleague District Attorney William Moody, whose appearance for the prosecution would be formally entered that day, was calmer but vigilant. They were not quite a Mutt and Jeff pairing: Knowlton did not tower over Moody but his muscular solidity seemed to dwarf his lithe colleague.

After what may have seemed like an age but was only ten minutes, the crier announced the arrival of the court. In Massachusetts, capital cases (cases in which conviction could result in the imposition of the death penalty) were heard by a panel of three superior court judges, selected by the chief judge. The three judges were Chief Justice Albert Mason, Associate Justice Caleb Blodgett, and Associate Justice Justin Dewey. All had practiced law more than twenty years before ascending to their judicial offices; each had been admitted to the bar the year Lizzie Borden was born. At first glance, the bearded judges composed an "imposing bench . . . with the suggestion of unrelenting Puritan sternness about it, calculated to chill an evildoer to his very marrow." Chief Justice Albert Mason was, in the words of one reporter, "a dignified old gentleman, with a benignant expression of countenance, silvered hair and beard, so cut as to emphasize his square built and significant under jaw." His "large brown eyes," thought Elizabeth Jordan, betrayed a "searching melancholy." In Jordan's view, Mason's entire aspect radiated thoughtfulness. Like Judge Mason, Judge Justin Dewey was a silver-headed and gray-bearded eminence, "a scholarly looking man with a large head," and a "massive face, lighted by kindly eyes." Most thought him a "tender-hearted man." Most important for the defense, he had been appointed to the bench by Lizzie Borden's counsel, Governor George Robinson, yet he had a "reputation for wisdom and impartiality." He took careful notes of the proceedings. Judge Caleb Blodgett, by contrast to the others, was a bit of a dandy. Though he was, in fact, the eldest of the three, he appeared to be "a younger and of a more modern type of individual, scrupulously careful as to the cut of his hair and beard, with an intellectual forehead, a piercing eye, a noticeably neat habit of attire, clad indeed à la mode from his white necktie to his well-polished boots." Nonetheless, he oozed good nature. He was considered, if anything, "too merciful, even lenient." All were married men with children; Mason had daughters Lizzie's age. Judging by their countenances alone, the judges were, according to Joe Howard, "precisely the kind of trio an innocent man would like to be tried by."

At the beginning of May, Chief Judge Mason met with his fellow judges Blodgett and Dewey to discuss procedural matters. Mason

Chief Judge Albert Mason, Judge Caleb Blodgett, and Judge Justin Dewey, 1892, *Boston Globe*

was concerned that one of the judges might fall ill during the trial; there was no precedent for determining whether the trial could continue with the remaining two. Prior to 1891, the Supreme Judicial Court of Massachusetts had jurisdiction over capital cases and the issue had simply not come up in superior court. In a letter to Pillsbury on the subject, he referred to Pillsbury's own illness as "an illustration of the danger." He questioned whether a legislative fix might be preferable, for "[t]o enter a trial of this character at the end of a hard years [*sic*] work and in hot weather is attended with considerable risk of a large expense coming to nought from disability of a single judge." After thinking the matter over, however, Mason concluded that "the objections to attempting legislation at the present time outweigh the risk of going on with the statutes as they are. When the matter is considered it should be without haste and with no reference to any particular case."

The Reverend Julien of New Bedford, "a preacher of intense vitality and great aplomb," offered a prayer, and jury selection began. Jurors were to be chosen from a panel of prospective jurors drawn from the county voting registers and summoned to appear at the courthouse on that day. The judges had determined that because of "the intense prejudice for and against the prisoner" in Fall River, the potential jurors would be drawn from other areas of the county. The 150 prospective jurors, all men, were solid New England characters, many of whom appeared anxious to resume their normal activities. (Women did not have the right to serve until 1950 and would not become jurors until 1951 in Massachusetts.) One newspaper speculated that it would be hard to find young men for the jury who had not already formed an opinion on the case. There was at least one African American among the prospective jurors—African American jurors had served on Massachusetts juries since 1860.

One by one, the men stood in front of the jury box to be questioned by Judge Mason. As Joe Howard explained: "The examination of jurors in a Massachusetts court is no joke. Instead of occupying a comfortable chair on the witness stand . . . the juror stands in an open space in front of the jury box exposed to the view of all concerned." Unlike other jurisdictions in which lawyers ask questions, in Massachusetts "the judge does all the talking." Chief Justice Mason handled the examinations gracefully: "He spoke very carefully, firmly, and distinctly, enunciating each syllable separately, and rolling his r's a little." His questions were "incisive, yet there is something so suave and reassuring in his manner" that he put the prospective jurors at ease.

The men were asked: Were they related to the prisoner or to the victims? One was an uncle by marriage; he was excused. This unexpected family reunion permitted a small moment of levity in the tense atmosphere. Uncle and niece smiled and saluted each other. Had they

Selecting a jury, *Boston Globe*

formed or expressed an opinion in relation to the case and were they aware of any bias or prejudice? Yes, said Mr. Baker, the first but not the last to do so. Thirty-five men had formed an unshakable conclusion about the case. Did they have an objection to the death penalty? Nineteen proclaimed scruples and were dismissed. Joe Howard observed that "this sentiment is spreading with noticeable strength throughout New England." Ten were excused for other reasons. Those that the judge pronounced fit to serve (or "indifferent" in formal parlance) were still subject to challenge by the prosecution and defense. The defense challenged seventeen, the commonwealth fifteen.

Knowlton and Moody conferred and decided whether or not to challenge jurors. Knowlton, the *Fall River Daily Herald* declared, "possesses the faculty of making a rapid and accurate judgment of human nature. His powers of reading character in the countenance are strongly developed." But he did not leave anything to chance. Each of the men in the pool were investigated. The *New Bedford Evening Standard* reported: "It is said that so thorough has the work been that each side knows the opinion of almost every man summoned." For example, Knowlton's notes reveal the following entry about the forty-fifth prospect (and ultimate juror number six), William Westcott: "American. Farmer. Independent in Politics. Comes to Congregational church. Not interested in religion. Married and *second wife*. Has not talked about the case." The conclusion: "Good practical man."

On the defense side, Jennings took charge. He sized up each man, looked at his notes, and indicated via a quick shake of his head whether Lizzie Borden should announce her acceptance or rejection of the prospect. (Julian Ralph thought they looked like "schoolgirls holding a pantomime conversation.") Lizzie used the railing to haul herself upright, moistened her lips, and spoke when required. Otherwise, she observed the action silently, wiping the perspiration from her face. Her black Japanese fan served a dual purpose: when she was not fanning herself, she chewed on the handle, apparently heedless of her observers. Initially, it seemed that the defense would challenge all prospective jurors of Irish descent. But ultimately John C. Flynn of Taunton was seated. Knowlton was pleased: his investigators had pronounced him a "good man: a very intelligent Irishman." After nine hours and 101 names, a jury emerged. Joe Howard said: "Every one of them wears a mustache, a majority of them are very tall with sunburned necks and not over *intelligent* in expression." He added: "They are not a jolly looking set of men." The judges chose white-maned real estate owner Charles I. Richards of North Attleborough as foreman to preside over a jury of six farmers, three mechanics, and two manufacturers. Richards, "a kindly featured man with a full head of hair," had been considered "*doubtful*" by the prosecution's investigators.

The jurors were permitted to send telegrams to their families to inform them of their likely extended service. In addition to Mr. Richards, the jurors were George Potter (Westport), William F. Dean (Taunton), Frederick C. Wilbar (Raynham), Lemuel K. Wilbur (Easton), John Wilbur (Somerset), William Westcott (Seekonk), Louis Hodges (Taunton), Augustus Swift (New Bedford), Frank G. Cole (Attleborough), John C. Flynn (Taunton), and Allen H. Wordell (Dartmouth). Flynn was the youngest at thirty-five and Hodges the eldest at fifty-nine. These were the twelve men who, as Elizabeth Jordan wrote, "under the legal guidance of three judges and the misguidance of six lawyers," would decide Lizzie Borden's fate. All were solid citizens. One paper declared it as good a jury "as could be desired or obtained." The *New Bedford Evening Journal* commented on "their strong and typical New England faces." Joseph Howard imagined them "unaccustomed . . . to metropolitan experiences of any nature." But they had one salient experience in common: like the judges, they were married men, heads of households. Most were fathers.

After swearing their oaths, the jurors were taken to the Parker House hotel, their home for the duration of the trial. Their meals, like their accommodation, was paid for by the county; each would earn $3 a day for his service. They were assigned rooms in the north section of the third floor, specially partitioned for their exclusive use. The partition included a door secured with a Yale lock, its single key in the custody of the deputy sheriff. The attorneys were housed on the second floor at opposite ends of the corridor; the judges' rooms separated the adversaries. Lizzie Borden's own housing continued to pose difficulties. She contracted bronchitis after her arraignment in May. She had recovered by the start of the trial but was nonetheless housed in the central jail rather than the county prison. The *Fall River Daily Herald* explained: "It is not considered to be decent, however, to lock up at night any prisoner who has been passing the daylight hours under the terribly nervous strain which will naturally accompany the coming one in a cell room where her next door neighbor is likely to be a howling drunkard, full of remorse and the vision of things uncanny."

TUESDAY, JUNE 6, 1893

Perhaps discouraged by the rigorous crowd control of the opening day, fewer spectators gathered for the second day of the trial. But those who came were a determined bunch; a small queue had already formed at 6:00 a.m. The spectators had a long wait. The jury arrived at 8:30 a.m., escorted by Deputy Sheriff Nickerson and Deputy Sheriff Arnold in the rear. Sheriff Wright entered with Lizzie Borden at three minutes before 9:00 a.m.

As the clerk read the long indictment, Lizzie Borden looked at the ground: "Every word seeming to fall like an additional weight upon [her] shoulders." But once Moody rose to give the opening statement, he had her full attention. Moody laid out the facts of the murders, the setting of the Borden house and its location in town, and the inescapable conclusion that Lizzie Borden must be responsible. Moody, in Howard's view, had "the rare gift of common sense, and without attempts at vocal gymnastics tells a clean cut, well-matured history of the crime, adroitly weaving therein his theory of the guilt of the prisoner and its whys and wherefores."

Moody began by baldly acknowledging the seeming impossibility of the crime and the perpetrator: "Upon the fourth day of August of the last year, an old man and woman . . . each without a known enemy in the world, in their own home, upon a frequented street in the most populous city in this County, under the light of day and in the midst of its activities, were . . . killed by unlawful human agency. Today a woman of good social position, of hitherto unquestioned character, a member of a Christian church and active in its good works, the own daughter of one of the victims, is at the bar of this Court, accused . . . of these crimes." He admitted that he could not improve on this simple statement of fact: "There is no language . . . at my command which can better measure the solemn importance of the inquiry."

Andrew Borden was, he said, a man of considerable property who chose to live upon "a narrow scale." About five years before the murders, "Some controversy had arisen about some property, not important in itself." But that controversy created "an unkindly feeling" between Lizzie and her stepmother. Moody acknowledged: "[I]t will be impossible for us to get anything more than suggestive glimpses of that feeling." He offered two telling examples: Lizzie no longer called her stepmother "Mother" and she not only referred to Mrs. Borden as her stepmother, but she also sharply corrected those who gave her the more familial appellation. "I know of nothing that will appear in this case more significant of the feeling that existed between Mrs. Borden and the prisoner," Moody continued, than her correction of the police officer who asked when she had last seen her mother. Lizzie said: "She is not my mother. She is my stepmother. My mother is dead." He also noted the daughters' habit of avoiding meals with Andrew and Abby and drew the jury's attention to Mr. Borden's habit of locking and bolting doors inside the house as well as to the exterior. As Moody put it, "Although they occupied the same household, there was built up between them by locks and bolts and bars, an impassable wall."

Moody then set the temporal scene of the crime and noted four unusual facts in the lead-up to the murders: First, John Morse, Lizzie's uncle, was visiting. Second, the household developed food poisoning. Third, Lizzie Borden, he alleged, went to the drugstore in search of prussic acid purportedly to clean a sealskin cape. Finally, she visited her former neighbor and intimate friend, Alice Russell, to confide her fears that they would be poisoned. During Moody's recitation of these central facts, Lizzie Borden looked straight at her accuser, attentive yet apparently unconcerned. That is, until Moody mentioned her former intimate Alice Russell. Ever so slightly, Lizzie shifted her foot.

Yet, at this moment of heightened suspense, Moody stepped out of his narrative to describe the house, both its location in the neighborhood and its odd interior layout. It was a house on a busy street within a short distance of City Hall: "It may fairly be called a thoroughfare . . . for foot passengers as for carriages." He reminded the jury that the house had three exterior doors: the front door

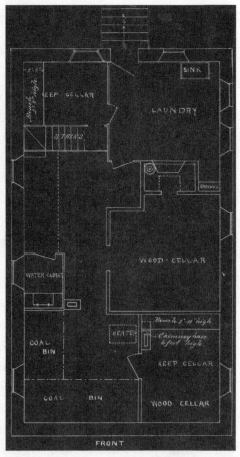

Plan of cellar, *courtesy of Fall River Historical Society*

with steps down to the sidewalk, the side door on the north adjacent to Mrs. Churchill's house, and the rear door of the cellar with steps up to the backyard.

Moody then took the jury on a virtual tour of the Borden home. The front door opened onto a front hall. Inside the hall, there were two doors and a stairway leading upstairs, along the right wall. Door number one led to the parlor on the left. Door number two, opposite the front door, led to the sitting (or living) room. In the sitting room, immediately to the left, was the door to the dining room. The dining room led to the kitchen, which was also accessible through a door at

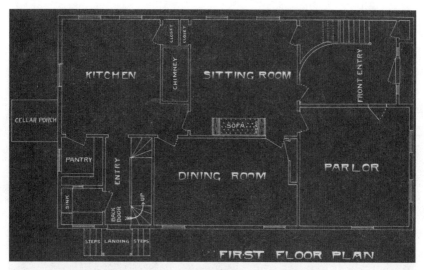

Plan of first floor, *courtesy of Fall River Historical Society*

the far end of the sitting room. The kitchen also opened onto a narrow back hall. The back hall led to the back staircase (providing access to the elder Bordens' bedroom on the second floor and Bridget Sullivan's bedroom on the third) and also to the exterior side door (where Lizzie was spotted by Adelaide Churchill).

The second floor had essentially the same floor plan. From the upstairs landing, there were three doors: a door leading to a clothes closet, another to the guest room in which Mrs. Borden was killed, and the last to Lizzie's bedroom. Moody's summary, perhaps unwittingly, evoked the dead-end ambiance of the layout: "When you have got up into this part of the house . . . you can go nowhere except into this clothes closet, into this guest chamber, and into the room occupied by the prisoner." Lizzie's bedroom adjoined Emma's room, a room with no separate access to the hall. (The smaller room had been Lizzie's before her trip to Europe in 1890.)

Moody took special care to note one unusual feature about the upstairs layout. At the rear of Lizzie's bedroom was a door to Andrew and Abby's bedroom. But it might as well have been part of the wall: "It was locked upon the front toward the prisoner's room by a hook. It was locked in the rear toward Mr. and Mrs. Borden's room by a bolt." At the back of the house, separated by that locked door, was a mirror image of Lizzie and Emma's suite. Andrew and Abby shared the larger bedroom. Andrew used the smaller adjoining space as a dressing room. They descended to the first floor and ascended to their bedroom via the back stairs, which also provided access to the servant's quarters and attic storage on the third floor.

Having settled the floor plan, Moody then gave the jurors a minute accounting of the occupants' movements on the morning of August 4. During the recitation, Lizzie

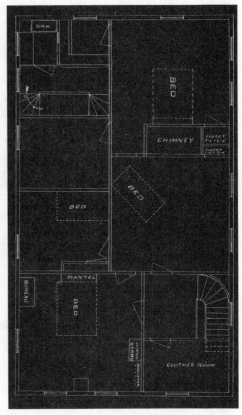

Plan of second floor, *courtesy of Fall River Historical Society*

Borden sat impassively. She might have been listening to a lecture or sermon. Moody's dry remarks gathered power as he held aloft the possible murder weapon, a small hatchet, broken off at the base of its wooden handle. He dismissed two axes found in the basement as "so far out of the question that I need not waste any time on them." He ruled out two hatchets originally thought to have human blood spots. Then he described the hatchet head in his right hand, found by an officer during the original search but then left in the basement. This hatchet, which would become known as the handleless hatchet, "was covered with an adhesion of ashes, not the fine dust which floats about the room where ashes are emptied, but a coarse dust of ashes adhering more or less to all sides of the

Lizzie Borden swoons, *Boston Globe*

hatchet." Moreover, the break in the handle "was a new break and was a fresh break." Calmly, Moody reached for a black bag, announcing "such parts of the mortal remains of the victims as would tend to throw light either in the protection of innocence or the detection of guilt have been preserved and must be presented here." This was an unexpected moment of legal theater: What in heaven's name was in the bag? "Moody made his grand coup," in Howard's words, "by opening very quietly an ordinary hand bag in which reposed side by side the skulls of the late Mr. and Mrs. Borden."

What the jury made of this unexpected exhibition we cannot know. But Lizzie Borden's reaction generated headlines: she swooned! This, finally, was what everyone seemed to have been waiting for. The *Fall River Daily Globe* gleefully announced: "Lizzie Borden, the sphinx of coolness, who has so often been accused of never manifesting a feminine feeling, had fainted." The *Globe* continued, with a hint of schadenfreude: "[P]erhaps it was preliminary to a collapse." Others saw it as proof of her femininity, long masked by her extraordinary nerve, and a natural response. "With the same undemonstrativeness that is her peculiarity she had yielded to more than she could endure," said

Julian Ralph. Describing what he called "the singular and awful misery of her position," Ralph continued: "Whatever she may have done she is a woman, a being who for thirty-two years of her life pursued the quiet and sheltered routine of a maiden of good family." Howard, for his part, offered physical reasons for the episode: "The heat is terrible, the humidity unendurable and the atmosphere sultriness embodied." He added, "Superuncomfortable, then, as she would be were she an ordinary woman, a spectator and listener only, what must she not endure as Lizzie Borden, the target for every eye . . . No wonder she fainted. The only wonder is she ever recovered."

Nonetheless, Lizzie Borden's incapacity was short-lived. Deputy Sheriff Kirby jostled her arm but "he might as well have shaken a pump handle." More effective was Reverend Jubb's timely administration of smelling salts, secreted in Lizzie Borden's own pocket. After resting her head upon the rail in front of her seat and sipping some water, she regained her composure. Her color, however, remained poor and her face glistened with perspiration. Less than five minutes later the trial resumed.

Next came Thomas Kieran, an engineer responsible for the house plans and other diagrams to be used as exhibits in the prosecution's case. A tall man, Kieran stood with perfect posture as he took the oath, the only discordant note in his appearance "a little tuft of coal black hair in the middle of his forehead." Moody questioned him about the distances between the Borden house and the police station—all of 1,300 feet—as well as to other relevant destinations, all measured to help establish timelines. This, however, was a mere appetizer for the twelve men of the jury. They were instructed to go to Fall River and "take the view, not only of the interior and exterior of the Borden house, but of such other points as to which there will be a testimony." The chief judge intoned: "It will not be proper for you to ask questions, or for the counsel to make any statements. You are to keep all together, and all are to see what any of you see." Four policemen swore that they would allow no one except Mr. Moody or Mr. Jennings to speak with them on that trip.

Jury touring crime scene, *Boston Globe*

If they thought it would be a joyful excursion, they underestimated both the weather and the government's "rage for economy." From the courthouse, the jurors assumed what had already become their accustomed formation, trooping under supervision to their hotel "through red-hot streets, beneath the rays of a boiling, blistering sun." After lunch, the jurors and their escorts left New Bedford at 1:15 p.m. on a train that had been held for their arrival. No special transportation awaited them in Fall River. As in New Bedford, jurors again marched from the train station to the Borden house despite the full heat of the midday sun. According to Joe Howard, "The heat was so intense in the city of factories as to make New Bedford's blisterings seem almost bearable." He added, "Even the farmers were unable to bear the oppressive humidity, and gladly availed themselves of palm fans." Robinson was better prepared: he opened an umbrella to shield himself from the full force of the sun. The jurors, said the *Fall River Daily Globe*, resembled "a convict chain gang under guard." The slow-moving procession was, however, a boon to spectators: "It was a kind of holiday in Fall River to the population, to which were added many hundreds from adjacent towns." More than 350 spectators awaited the jury's arrival at the Borden house on Second Street.

After examining the interior of the house and the yard in careful detail, the jurors took an extended tour of the neighborhood. They

looked at all of the neighboring properties, especially Adelaide Churchill's to the north, Dr.
Kelly's to the south, Dr. Chagnon's orchard to
the rear (east), and Dr. Chagnon's house on the
other side of the orchard, kitty-corner with the
Borden barn. Jennings showed them Alice Russell's house on Borden and Third. From there,
they traveled to A. P. Gorman's paint store (the
location of the telephone used to report the
murders) and the A. J. Borden building at
the corner of South Main and Borden. They
continued their procession up South Main
Street, "creating considerable commotion and
causing the greatest excitement." They were
taken to D. R. Smith's (where Lizzie was alleged to have tried to buy prussic acid) and to

Jonathan Clegg's store, near the corner of Spring Street, the last place
visited by Mr. Borden. The jurors retraced Andrew Borden's last walk,
visiting the Union Savings Bank and B.M.C. Durfee Savings Bank.
"The tired and hungry jurors then filed out to the Mellen house,"
where they dined before taking the 6:35 p.m. train back to New Bedford. "So far as this day's experiences are concerned," Howard concluded, "although Lizzie had her bad luck in the morning, the jury
surely suffered in the afternoon."

For the benefit of its readers, the *Boston Globe* printed a map consisting of "a Bird's Eye view of the Borden home and its vicinity . . . for
readers who intend intelligently to follow the Trial of Lizzie Borden."
The heading enjoined the reader: "Cut This Out and Keep It."

While the jury traveled to and from Fall River, the judges enjoyed
a respite and, after dinner, took a carriage ride around the city. According to the *Fall River Daily Herald*, "They were particularly attracted
by the three or four survivors and inanimate representatives of New
Bedford's past industry, the old time whaling vessels, lying abandoned
and slowly decaying at the wharf."

Backyard of Chagnon residence, *courtesy of Fall River Historical Society*

WEDNESDAY, JUNE 7, 1893

Under the heading "Where to Look for Your Wife," the *Fall River Daily Globe* advised: "The New Bedford man who comes home and finds it deserted . . . needn't be alarmed. There has been no elopement; the dear creature is probably in the crowd of morbid females who are storming the door of the county court house, trying to get admission to the Borden trial." For the large number of women on hand, Wednesday, June 7, was the true beginning of the trial. Joe Howard dubbed it "woman's day" in honor of the "multitude of New Bedford's fattest and leanest of the feminine gender" there to partake of the proceedings. The *Fall River Daily Globe* dubbed the female regulars the "Valentines and Daisies." "Taking all the most eligible seats and settling themselves with little black bags containing lunch and fennel seed," these female spectators "prepared for a long and enjoyable session." Julian Ralph commented that "about half of the women were of commanding rank, and the other half were in calico." He added, "A

BIRD'S EYE VIEW OF THE BORDEN HOME
AND ITS VICINITY WHICH THE JURY VISITED YESTERDAY

Reproduced as a Useful Reference for Readers who Intend
Intelligently to Follow the Trial of Lizzie Borden

1 – Borden Home
2 – Borden Barn
3 – The well
4 – Fence with barbed wire on top
5 – Side entrance
6 – Churchill residence
7 – Dr. Bowen's house

8 – Dr. Chagnon's house
9 – Kelly house
10 – Yard from which officers watched
    the Borden house in the days
    following the murders
11 – Kelly's barn
12 – Pear orchard

A bird's-eye view of the neighborhood, *Boston Globe*

little sprinkling of very swarthy Portuguese girls added novelty to the crowd." Lizzie Borden herself seemed in better spirits on Wednesday. Her color had improved and rather than sitting "all but motionless" as she had the prior two days, she followed the proceedings in a more animated way, shifting occasionally in her chair.

The jury selected, the scene of the crime toured, and the opening statement delivered, now, finally, came the witnesses. As Joe Howard observed, "the chief interest in these celebrated cases attaches itself to the personalities involved—some as accessories, some as witnesses." Most important were John Morse, Lizzie Borden's uncle, whose bedroom had been the scene of Abby Borden's murder, and Bridget Sullivan, the Bordens' domestic servant. Aside from Lizzie, they were the only other surviving inhabitants of the household that morning. Joe Howard observed: "Those are three very peculiar people, Bridget, Lizzie, and uncle. Combined they form a suggestive trinity."

But before the members of the household could testify, Knowlton recalled Thomas Kieran to continue his explanation of the plans he had drawn and to which the jurors could refer. Kieran, however, had taken it upon himself to perform "extra work of a curious kind," various "line of sight" experiments about which the animated Jennings questioned him on cross-examination. Jennings, remarked Ralph, was "the smallest of the lawyers in size and the biggest in nervous energy." When Jennings asked Kieran about the exterior views, Knowlton objected, arguing "the jury have seen the exact thing and have the measurements." Chief Justice Mason agreed but let Jennings ask a few questions about the view from Second Street to the Borden barn door and about the various fences on the surrounding properties. Jennings then asked Kieran about those curious experiments that seemed to fall outside the scope of his remit. First, he instructed a man to stand inside the front hall closet. Over the prosecution's objection, he testified that the door was easily shut and, even when ajar, the man might not be seen from assorted points in the front hall. Next, he instructed his assistant to lie down on the floor, mimicking Abby's death pose, to test if he could see a body as he descended and ascended the stairs. He explained that he could see the figure when ascending from "the center of one of the stairs which brought my eye a little above the level of the floor" and could not see the same person from the landing in front of Lizzie Borden's bedroom. Jennings asked, "And that you say was when you were particularly looking to see?"

It was surprising to hear the prosecution's witness give testimony favorable to the defense, and even more surprising that the city engineer decided to perform such experiments. But there was something about the locked-room mystery of the Borden murders that turned everyone into an amateur detective. John Morse had conducted a similar experiment to see if he could have seen Abby's corpse from the staircase. The consensus seemed to be that you could see a body if you were looking for one. Morse and family friend Mary Brigham also tested whether Abby's fall would have reverberated through the house. Jennings, for his part, made a note in his journal: "Get 200 lbs man."

Morse had come to the courthouse the first two days of the trial, waiting to be called as a witness. In the interim, he lingered in the corridor, "entertain[ing] a large number of listeners with tales of his experiences and life in the west." When he took the stand, he again "held the close attention of his listeners." Julian Ralph thought he resembled "Uncle Sam" (as drawn by Conde papers). He testified that he had arrived around 1:30 p.m. on the day before the murders and had seen no one but Andrew, Abby, and Bridget Sullivan. While he and Andrew sat in the sitting room that night, he heard someone come into the house and go directly upstairs. When he went to his room at 10:30 p.m., he noticed that Lizzie's door was shut. The next morning, he ate breakfast with Andrew and Abby and then left at 8:40 a.m. to visit other relatives. According to Howard, "He was asked a multitudinosity of questions about the marriages, first and second, the ages of everybody in any way connected with the household, and a tediosity of apparently irrelevant questions as to what they had had for breakfast, who cooked it, whether the door which was shut was locked, whether the servants whom he didn't see at all slept, and where he passed the day preceding and subsequent to the murder." Robinson's cross-examination returned to the breakfast fare. As Howard explained, "Governor Robinson developed in his confidential way from Mr. Morse that . . . there was nothing mean or stingy about the breakfast." Morse did unintentionally provide a moment of levity. When asked Lizzie Borden's age, he calculated thirty-three. She was, in fact, thirty-two, and "shook her head vigorously at the assertion." As the *New York Times* put it, "There spoke the woman."

To verify the prosecution's timeline of events, a succession of witnesses traced Andrew Borden's last walk the morning of August 4,

1892. Abraham Hart, the treasurer of Union Savings Bank, thought he looked "under the weather" when he saw him at the usual time of 9:30 a.m. John Burrill, the cashier of National Union Bank, observed Andrew speaking to "a colored man" about a loan. Andrew Borden then crossed the street and entered First Union Bank on North Main Street, where, according to Everett Cook, the cashier of First Union Bank, he stayed about ten minutes. From there, he moved on to inspect his commercial properties. He stopped to talk with Jonathan Clegg for about ten minutes about the arrangement for a new store at 92 South Main. Two carpenters, Joseph Shortsleeves and James Mather, working on the windows at Clegg's new store, spotted him at about 10:30 a.m. (though during his cross-examination, Mather admitted that it could have been as late as 10:40 a.m.). The story took an odd turn, suggesting that Andrew Borden might have been preoccupied: He entered and walked to the back of the store. There, he picked up a broken lock and then laid it back down. He was upstairs for a few minutes. He came back downstairs, picked up the broken lock, and left the building, crossing the street. Then he stopped, recrossed the street, and greeted the carpenters. Moody cut off Shortsleeves before he could recount the conversation.

From Julian Ralph's vantage point, he could see Moody's restless hands: "He kept both hands behind him and busied them with his coattails violently and incessantly. He did his coattails up in a bundle, he rolled them up like a scroll, he tied them in a knot, he jiggled them with his fingers, and he pulled them apart." Ralph concluded that each action corresponded to Moody's emotional response to the witness: "Rolling them up indicated plain sailing, doing them up in a bundle meant triumphant success, knotting them up only occurred when the witness was obtuse, and sundering them indicated a failure to get the witness to understand him." Howard fastened on to the one comical interlude in the testimony of Jonathan Clegg, the haberdasher: "Moody yelled himself red in the face that he might make the deaf Clegg hear, while Clegg yelled himself pale in the gills on the supposition that as he couldn't hear himself Moody was in the same condition."

What nugget Shortsleeves might have revealed paled before the excitement caused by the next witness, Bridget Sullivan, the Bordens' twenty-six-year-old housekeeper. She was, in the words of Joe Howard, "a sensation." He explained: "Her disappearance from the Borden premises two days after the tragedy, and her whereabouts since that day, have been a mystery." She had, in fact, been employed by Mrs. Hunt at the New Bedford jail. She would have made a popular suspect but for Lizzie Borden's own account of her movements on the day of the murders. Like Lizzie, she was known to be at the house during the murders; some even wondered if she might have been an accomplice. Others still resented the contrast between the two women's circumstances: Bridget may have lived at a jail, yet, as the *Sun* reported: "Bridget goes shopping and knocks about the streets of New Bedford alone, or in any company she pleases, whenever she likes." She was also suspiciously well-dressed: she wore a dress made of brown serge with lace around the neck and sported a black Van Dyck hat with a large feather. Ralph noticed that "Kid gloves of generous size concealed her hands." Howard divined in the shape of her mouth "a love for the good things in life." But her posture revealed her anxiety, for "she leaned on the left side of the rail, looked straight at Mr. Moody, and spoke so low that he had to tell her to speak louder."

Moody began his examination of Bridget Sullivan with little preamble. He established that her job was "washing, ironing and cooking, with sweeping" in the common areas of the house, but she was only responsible for her own bedroom on the third story over the senior Bordens' bedroom. The Monday before the murders was washing day; therefore, she washed sheets in the cellar. This led Moody to the prosecution's key contention that no outsider could have been in the house during the murders. Bridget was able to confirm that the cellar door, a potential point of entry for an outside assassin, was bolted from the inside between Tuesday and the time of the murders. She also stated that the side door had been securely locked on the night before the murders. This meant that the prosecution could focus on minimizing the small window of opportunity on the morning of August 4.

According to Bridget, she awoke that morning with a "dull

headache," perhaps related to the illness Andrew and Abby experienced the previous day. Nonetheless she was in the kitchen before Abby came down between 6:30 and 6:40 a.m. Andrew followed about five minutes later, bearing a slop pail and the bedroom key. He put the bedroom key on the sitting room mantel and emptied his slop pail outside. When he reentered the house, he brought in a basket of pears, washed his hands, and then joined Abby and John Morse at breakfast. Once they had finished, the men went out to the backyard. Andrew came back inside and retrieved his bedroom key. He then took a bowl of water upstairs. That was the last she saw of him until he came back from his trip downtown. As Bridget was washing the dishes, Lizzie came downstairs with her own slop pail. While Lizzie had coffee and cookies for breakfast, Bridget went outside to vomit. She estimated that she was outside for ten to fifteen minutes at most. When she had recovered, she brought the clean plates into the dining room. There, according to her testimony, she saw Abby Borden for the last time.

Abby interrupted her dusting to ask Bridget to wash the windows inside and outside. Bridget went to the cellar for a bucket and brush to wash the windows. When she was just outside the back door, Lizzie appeared and asked her if she was going to wash the windows. Lizzie then advised: "You needn't lock the door. I will be out around here but you can lock it if you want to." To complete her task, Bridget went in and out of the barn several times for water—the task required six or seven buckets—making it even harder for an intruder to have timed his entry. After washing the outside windows, Bridget came inside and started on the windows inside the sitting room. She heard the sound of someone trying to unlock the door. She went to the door, found it bolted, swore, and unbolted it to admit Andrew Borden. He was carrying a small white parcel. Apparently in response to Bridget's cursing, Lizzie laughed from the upstairs landing. Bridget returned to washing the windows in the sitting room.

Andrew sat down in the dining room. Lizzie came downstairs and asked her father if there was any mail. She volunteered that Abby had received a note and had gone out. Andrew went into the kitchen and then to the sitting room, where he retrieved his bedroom key from the mantel. He then went up to his bedroom. When Bridget had started on the dining room dishes, Andrew returned to the sitting room. Lizzie brought an ironing board into the dining room and ironed handkerchiefs. She asked Bridget if she was going out in the afternoon and told her that if she did go out, she should lock the door, "for Mrs. Borden has gone out on a sick call, and I might go out, too." Later in the kitchen, Lizzie informed her of a "cheap sale of dress goods at Sargent's . . . at eight cents a yard." This was a good deal—Lizzie herself had a cheap Bedford cord dress made from material that had cost between twelve and fifteen cents a yard—and Sargent's was located on North Main Street, less than a ten-minute walk from the house. (It was, in fact, too good of a bargain: Sargent's had already been shuttered for a month by the time Bridget recounted her story in New Bedford.) Bridget, however, was in no condition to go out. Instead, she went upstairs to her bed. It was this midmorning respite that led Julian Ralph to term her "the Queen" of the household.

There was to be no rest for Bridget. Lizzie called for her: "Father's dead. Somebody came in and killed him." Bridget testified that she ran down the stairs and saw Lizzie at the threshold of the screen door at the side of the house. Lizzie told her to get Dr. Bowen, who was not at home. When Bridget asked where she had been, Lizzie replied that she had been out in the backyard and had heard a groan. Lizzie then instructed her to summon Alice Russell. By the time she returned, next-door neighbor Adelaide Churchill and Dr. Bowen had arrived. Adelaide Churchill was in the kitchen with Lizzie as Dr. Bowen emerged from the sitting room, announcing, "He is murdered." When Adelaide asked about Abby, Lizzie volunteered that she thought she had heard her come back. Bridget did not want to look for her but Adelaide Churchill said she would go with her. As they ascended the stairs, Bridget saw Abby's body under the bed.

Her tale told, in Joe Howard's assessment, "straight as a string," Bridget remained standing for Robinson's comprehensive cross-examination. The wily Robinson thrust out his belly, turned his "kindly eye" toward her, and unleashed his insinuating charm. In contrast to the prosecution's careful step-by-step eliciting of Bridget's movements to determine the timeline of events, Robinson probed for background about the household. In his "confidential manner," he asked Bridget if "it was a pleasant family to be in?" Bridget hedged and replied, "I don't know how the family was; I got along all right." Robinson pressed her, moving delicately from a positive description ("pleasant") that she would not confirm to negative descriptions she could firmly disavow. She had not seen anything "out of the way," nor had she seen "conflict" or "quarrelling," for example. She stopped short of agreeing that "they all got along genially," replying "as far as I could see." Bridget had been far less sanguine about Borden family relations in a conversation in late August 1892 with Nellie McHenry, wife and sometime assistant of the detective Edwin McHenry. She had told Nellie that, as a result of the unpleasantness in the house, she had intended to leave on three separate occasions, but "Mrs. Borden had coaxed her to stay and once raised her wages." Robinson, however, suggested that her inquest testimony painted a rosier picture of domestic relations. Julian Ralph described the process as less a dance than a "long duel" in which Bridget Sullivan faced "a learned and cunning man, a man so far her superior that he had been three times Governor of the State." Perhaps, Robinson asked, as a result of her new employment in New Bedford, she had spent more time in the company of prosecutors and police officers? As Howard would put it more bluntly, "During her long stay and virtually confinement in the family of jailer Hunt she has become so permeated with the ideas of the prosecution that she really doesn't know whether she stands on her head or her heels."

Robinson pushed her about other seeming contradictions: earlier she had not been sure she had hooked the screen door at the side of the house and now said she did. If the door was not locked at all times, then it was just possible that an outside assailant could have made fortuitous use of it. Elizabeth Jordan remarked that "one by one [the prosecution] have bolted every door of the house and left every avenue of approach to the house impeded," but Bridget "left that door open." And Bridget admitted—again under pressure from Robinson—that she would not necessarily have seen this hypothetical person enter the house. Robinson inquired: "You were really honestly at work, of course? . . . You were not on the watch looking out for people?" Having gained a theoretical opening for a mystery outsider, Robinson returned to the absence of blood on the defendant, extremity by extremity, and even elicited Bridget's assurance that Lizzie's hair was in order. During this intense phase of the cross-examination, Bridget "mopped the perspiration from her face." Julian Ralph commented: "[Robinson] is very courtly and winning to a woman witness until he lands her where he wants her, and then, if it suits him, he becomes as stern as a pirate. He is as confidential and chatty as a gossip, and his witness becomes very desirous of pleasing him and is easily led into a trap. Then his manner changes, and he makes short work of letting the witness know he has him captive." Robinson's tactics led the *New York Times* to conclude: "He is going to make a more bitter fight against the Commonwealth than he ever engaged in, and every movement of the enemy will be met as far as possible with counter efforts of the most brilliant nature."

On redirect examination, Moody returned to Lizzie's blue dress on the day of the murders. Everyone agreed she had changed into a pink wrapper in the afternoon. The question was her morning attire. Robinson had, after a fashion, muddied the description—one blue dress was much like any other—claiming, "It was a man's mistake." Moody sought to clarify that the dress Lizzie had been wearing that morning was the blue dress made the prior spring with a dark blue figure on a lighter blue background.

At 4:55 p.m., Bridget Sullivan's travail ended. Howard concluded: "The cross-examination of Gov. Robinson was merciless and exhaustive, but as Bridget unquestionably told the truth so far as she told at all, nothing was made against her, nor could it be said that her testimony was especially damaging to the cause of the defense." The *New Bedford Evening Journal* pronounced her an admirable witness: "She was willing to tell what she knew, so far as it was brought out by concrete questions. She was neither eager nor reluctant." She emerged, therefore, from "the whole ordeal unscathed." Lizzie Borden's ordeal, on the other hand, was just beginning.

Chapter 6

UNDER FIRE

Makeshift gate in
front of courthouse,
Boston Globe

Reflecting on the first week, Julian Ralph of the *Sun* praised the Borden trial as "one of the smoothest and fairest" he had attended: "The discipline of the court is almost perfect, and the spectators feel it and keep constant good order. Beyond a buzz of astonishment or a snicker when the general sense of humor is aroused the room is uniformly quiet. The large body of reporters, hard at work, with a troop of boys running with dispatches, conduct the work noiselessly. The people whisper furtively. The public respect for the court is great and marked." Joe Howard lauded the judges and the rest of the courtroom officials for their "urbanity and dignity." In the rest of the building, the atmosphere resembled "the bustle of a mill or the stock exchange": One room housed the busy stenographers who dictated their notes to the pool of "pert and pretty" young women typists. Other rooms served as the waiting area for witnesses. Another was reserved for the district attorneys and also contained the trial exhibits. In the halls, policemen and "under sheriffs in blue coats with brass buttons stand all about the hall, while messenger and newspaper boys dash in and out." Outside, the scene was more chaotic. The police erected a makeshift gate, consisting of rope strung between the courthouse pillars, to block the entrance to the courthouse. By the end of the first week, carpenters were at work on a proper wooden barrier. Elizabeth Jordan took special note of the dogged persistence of female would-be spectators: "Those who were not fortunate enough to gain admission hover about the neighborhood all morning, to be first in line for the opening in the afternoon. They bring cruilers [sic] and cookies and other New England food atrocities in their pockets, and actually camp out and lunch on the scene of battle." Some wandered over to the neighboring houses and had their picnics on the verandas or front stoops. Irritated residents of the neighborhood had little recourse but to post specially printed signs warning the invaders to "keep off the steps."

THURSDAY, JUNE 8, 1893

On Thursday, the heat abated. One paper simply announced, "Prayers have been answered." Another clarified that "the air of the court was not as cool as that of a shady dell . . . but there was a comparative degree of comfort when contrasted with that of the opening." Some speculated that might account for an upsurge in people queueing for seats in the courtroom. A reporter for the *New Bedford Evening Journal*, however, had a different theory: "A great many early breakfasts were taken in New Bedford this morning judging from the time when the people curious to witness the trial begun [*sic*] to arrive on the spot. This was because of the rumors that some of the medical men would be put on the stand today, and that the ghastly exhibits would be brought into view." As it happened, the rumor mill was mistaken. The prosecutors called a series of witnesses who had been on the scene shortly after the murders and could give firsthand observations of Lizzie Borden's actions and demeanor in the immediate aftermath of the crimes. Lizzie Borden herself was viewed as a barometer: there was a "hectic flush upon her face this morning, notably about the eyes, but she had the same calm, unimpassioned look." The same could not be said for the women in the audience. Howard approvingly noted the presence of "two or three very pretty girls" but complained that "a large majority were vinegar faced, sharp-nosed, lean-visaged and extremely spare."

The Bordens' neighbor and physician Dr. Seabury Bowen, "a most unwilling and obviously essential witness," took the stand first. He testified that he saw Andrew Borden's face "badly cut [and] covered with blood" but that his body was lying "apparently at ease, as any one would if they were lying asleep." He asked Lizzie if she had seen any-one. Lizzie told him that she had been in the barn looking for irons. Dr. Bowen reported the death to Officer Allen, by then on the scene, and left to telegraph Emma in Fairhaven. Upon his return, Mrs. Chur-chill, the Bordens' next-door neighbor, informed him that they found Mrs. Borden in the guest room upstairs. Initially he thought she might have fainted, though he denied that he had ever said "she had died of fright." Upon closer examination, he realized she was dead. So far, the testimony was clear and undisputed. Next came sartorial matters at which Dr. Bowen was considerably less adept.

What was Lizzie Borden wearing? All agreed that Lizzie Borden changed her dress after the bodies were discovered and she went up to her room. She answered police questions wearing a pink wrapper. But what had she been wearing earlier in the morning? Some kind of blue dress, everyone agreed. At the inquest, Dr. Bowen described the original dress as a drab calico. Here, under pressure from Moody, who tried fruitlessly to persuade the doctor to amplify the description, he declared, "It was an ordinary, unattractive, common dress that I did not notice specially." He refused to be drawn further. Robinson would later ask for Bridget Sullivan to be recalled. She testified that Lizzie was wearing a blue calico dress with clover-leaf figure and then changed after "the fuss was over" into a gingham dress, plain blue with a white border. So it appeared that there were two blue dresses worn that morning, a point given sinister import by the prosecution.

Melvin Adams, the dapper Boston trial lawyer, rose to question the doctor. He sought to establish that Dr. Bowen did not see Mrs. Borden's body as he climbed the front stairs—an important point, given Lizzie's descent from those stairs. (Both Adelaide Churchill and John Morse had seen the body from that vantage point.) He also foreshadowed a key defense argument about Lizzie's inquest testimony: he asked what Dr. Bowen had given Lizzie for her nerves. Dr. Bowen initially pre-scribed bromo caffeine, an effervescent salt used to alleviate headaches, and, on Friday, added one-eighth of a grain of sulphate of morphine to be taken before bed. (A grain is the standard apothecary measure-ment by weight: Dr. Bowen's initial dose was equivalent to 8 milligrams of morphine.) The next day he doubled the dose, a dose he contin-ued while she was a witness at the inquest. Adams then asked about morphine's mental effects. Bowen agreed that morphine in the higher quarter-grain dosage could affect memory and cause hallucinations, a point only partly undercut by Moody's redirect establishing that Dr. Bowen only personally wit-nessed her taking the bromo caf-feine. Joe Howard asked his readers: "If the administration of morphine tends to produce hallucinations

Adelaide Churchill, *courtesy of Fall River Historical Society*

in persons unused to taking morphine, what must have been Lizzie's mental condition after several days of dosing with the stuff?"

Dr. Seabury Bowen left the stand disgruntled. Adelaide Churchill, by contrast, relished her time in the spotlight. "A middle aged matron of comfortable build and genteel, placid face," Adelaide Churchill was "short, stout, active, and willing." When the police interviewed her on August 8, four days after the murders, she exclaimed: "Must I, am I obliged to tell you all? . . . Well, if I must," she added, "I do not like to tell anything of my neighbor, but this is as it is." Her moment had arrived—she entered the courtroom in a "stylish blue dress and black bonnet"—and she delivered her tale in rounded tones suitable for an elocution lesson. (Elizabeth Jordan, in particular, praised the "enunciation of her English," which she took as a sign of her intelligence.) As Joe Howard put it, "No Mayday queen was ever happier than sister Churchill on the stand."

Adelaide Churchill explained she was the widowed daughter of the former mayor Edward Buffinton and had lived in the house next door to the Bordens for almost all of her life. On the morning of the murders, she watched Andrew Borden leave in the morning before she went out to do her shopping, and on her way back from Hudner's market, she had seen Bridget running back from Dr. Bowen's house. After unloading her purchases in the kitchen, she looked out the window and saw an "excited or agitated" Lizzie leaning against the kitchen door. She asked, "Lizzie, what is the matter?" Lizzie replied, "Oh, Mrs. Churchill, do come over. Someone has killed father." She eventually led the expedition to discover Abby Borden's corpse in the guest bedroom, visible from the front stairs. Unlike Dr. Bowen, Adelaide offered a minute description of Lizzie's dress. She denied it was the dark blue dress shown her by the prosecution. Instead, she said it had a light blue and white mixed groundwork woven together with "a dark navy blue diamond figure on which there was no spot of blood." Adelaide Churchill would later be recalled and asked if she knew what "Bedford cord" was. She said she did not, but said she thought Lizzie had been wearing cotton.

Alice Russell, *courtesy of Fall River Historical Society*

Robinson returned to this point. As with Bridget Sullivan, Robinson led Adelaide Churchill through an exhaustive audit of Lizzie's clothing, hair, and hands to show that there was no blood on her person. He also took the sting out of her original description of Lizzie's manner, inducing her to rephrase her comment that Lizzie seemed "excited" to the more appropriate "appeared and looked distressed . . . and frightened." Alive to the danger a vigilant neighbor—let alone a notorious curtain-twitcher like Mrs. Churchill—might pose to his theory of an outside assassin, he also explored Adelaide Churchill's myriad household duties. Just as he led Bridget Sullivan to agree that an intruder could have slipped into the house while she was busy washing windows, he implied that Adelaide Churchill was far too busy in her own house to notice what might have been going on next door.

Adelaide Churchill provided the trial audience with an amuse-bouche, but the main course of the day was Alice Russell, Lizzie Borden's "turncoat friend." If Adelaide Churchill seemed a stereotypical "merry widow," Alice Russell, "tall, angular, and thin," could have passed as the model for a typical New England spinster. Julian Ralph described her as "a slender, trim woman of precise manners, of spare figure and sallow face." Joe Howard declared: "She held her mouth as though prisms and prunes were its most frequent utterances."

Elizabeth Jordan described her in darker terms, "as though one of the strange women characters in which Wilkie Collins delights, and which flit like ominous specters through deep shadows—through his mysteries—had walked out of the pages of one of the dead novelist's books into real life and real participation in a tragedy more awful and more wrapped in obscurity than any he ever evolved."

A former next-door neighbor for over a decade—she had lived in what was now the Kelly house—Alice Russell had recently moved a short distance but remained an intimate friend of both Borden daughters. Aside from the doctor, she was the first person Lizzie Borden thought to summon for help after discovering the murders. She then stayed in the Borden house until after the funeral. But the friendship ended when Alice Russell decided to tell the grand jury about the dress Lizzie burned the Sunday after the murders. She did not make her choice lightly. She had omitted mention of the incident in her original statement to the police, her inquest testimony, and her first appearance before the grand jury. But after agonizing about the oath she had sworn, an oath to tell "the whole truth," she consulted a lawyer who arranged for Knowlton to recall her to the stand. After she testified at the grand jury about the dress burning, Russell ended her regular visits to Lizzie Borden in jail. It was as if the act of testifying, of unburdening herself of the incriminating details, forced her to recalculate for herself Lizzie Borden's likely culpability. Significantly, Alice Russell's change of position reverberated in their circle: Elizabeth Johnston, who had steadfastly refused to tell the police the contents of Lizzie's letter, also ceased her jail visits.

Despite being certain of her duty, Alice Russell initially seemed a tentative witness. Moody instructed her to speak up twice at the outset of her testimony. From his seat, Robinson even chimed in to ask her to "speak a little louder." Lizzie Borden, too, moved her chair closer to Melvin Adams and whispered something to him. Alice stood at attention as she testified and, according to Julian Ralph, held her handbag "as though it contained her return ticket to Fall River and she did not propose to lose it under any circumstances." Elizabeth Jordan viewed her testimony as a betrayal and characterized her demeanor in unflattering terms: "Today she took the witness stand and not only testified to what will come nearer to putting a rope around her girl friend's neck than anything yet brought out, but she did it with a vicious snap in her voice and a cruel compression of her thin colorless lips, which suggested anything but sorr[ow] for the fact that she was compelled to do this." Whether or not she regretted her felt obligation to testify, Alice Russell had determined her course. She spoke clearly, tapping her black fan as if to underscore her answers.

Moody first asked Alice Russell about Lizzie's visit the night before the murders. She testified that Lizzie told her that she had been depressed: "I feel as if something was hanging over me that I cannot throw off; and it comes over me at times, no matter where I am." As if to puncture the tension in the courtroom, Joe Howard's favorite cow outside the courthouse "gave three tremendous blasts on her accustomed trombone." Most in the courtroom laughed, but Alice Russell did not waver. Instead, she began to testify that Lizzie described her father's enemies, but stopped herself, adding, "Oh, I am a little ahead of the story." Lizzie had first reported the Bordens' illness—she heard them "vomiting" and told her everyone was ill except Bridget Sullivan. She feared the milk could be poisoned. Alice questioned whether such a thing would be possible: "I shouldn't think anybody would dare to come then and tamper with the cans for fear somebody would see them." Lizzie seemed to accept the improbability but spoke of her father's "enemy." She said a man came to see him about renting a property. Her father told him he would not "let his property for such a business." The man responded "sneeringly" as he was ordered out. Lizzie also said she had seen a strange man lurking around the house. More worrying, the barn had been broken into twice. Alice reassured her that thieves were only after pigeons. Lizzie insisted: "I feel as if I wanted to sleep with my eyes half open—with one eye open half the time—for fear they will burn the house down over us." She then revealed a startling daytime break-in: "Father forbad our telling it." She recounted the theft of Abby's keepsakes, Andrew's money and streetcar

Courtroom scene during Alice Russell's testimony, *Boston Globe*

tickets, "and something else I can't remember." She continued, "I am afraid somebody will do something; I don't know but what somebody will do something." Lizzie Borden left about 9:00 p.m.

The next morning just after 11:00 a.m., Bridget Sullivan arrived with the terrible news. Of the sequence of events that Thursday morning, Alice explained: "It is very disconnected. I remember very little of it." But on Thursday night she well recalled visiting the darkened cellar with Lizzie. Lizzie brought her slop pail; Alice brought a light. Lizzie went into the water closet room to rinse out the slop pail. They walked through the room containing the bloodstained clothes taken from the bodies.

On Sunday morning, Alice saw Lizzie by the kitchen stove. Emma asked Lizzie what she was going to do. Lizzie replied, "I am going to burn this old thing up; it is covered in paint." Alice initially left the room, thought the better of it, returned, and said, "I wouldn't let anyone see me do that, Lizzie." She noticed it was a "cheap cotton Bedford cord," light blue with dark figures. The next morning O. M. Hanscom, the Pinkerton detective employed by the family, asked Alice if all of Lizzie's dresses were still in the house. When she saw Emma and Lizzie in the dining room, she declared, "I am afraid, Lizzie, the worst thing you could have done was to burn that dress. I have been asked about your dresses."

Lizzie lamented, "Oh, what made you let me do it?"

Robinson's cross-examination was a masterly attempt at damage control. He tried unsuccessfully to elicit dramatic descriptions of Lizzie Borden's pallor and distress. He had more success with his familiar catalogue of Borden's person, getting Alice to agree that there was no blood visible anywhere on Lizzie. He wanted to be as clear as possible that officers had already searched the house, and that they were present on Sunday when Lizzie burned the dress. Despite his skilled manner, Alice Russell seemed immune to his usually infallible charm. In response to her description of the dress as "Bedford cord," not cambric, Robinson remarked, "No doubt about that, and any woman knows or ought to know the difference between the two, doesn't she." Alice tartly replied, "I don't know as they do." Yet, that rare rebuff did nothing to undermine Julian Ralph's belief that Robinson was "without an equal in New York City as a cross-examiner," observing that "he has not yet found a government witness whom he has not been able to turn more or less to his own account." For Robinson, the critical point had been made: Lizzie Borden burned a cheap Bedford cord dress. For her part, Lizzie, according to Julian Ralph, "was much less interested in the testimony than the most unconcerned among the persons in the court." Instead, she studied her fan, "putting the handle of it in her mouth and out again mechanically."

As if to permit all a change of pace, three witnesses came and went with little fanfare. The local newsdealer John Cunningham recounted his own investigations as he tagged along with reporters from the *Fall River Daily Globe* and *Fall River Daily Herald*. Most significantly, he found the cellar door securely locked. In a report to the police, McHenry had observed spiderwebs across the doorjamb of at least a week's growth. Cunningham also looked for tracks outside in the yard and saw none. Robinson pounced on this point: Did he know that Bridget Sullivan had walked that same area when she went over to the fence to have a chat with the Kellys' "girl"? His powers of observation called into question, he provided a moment of levity describing Adelaide Churchill as running "triangular" toward the house. "Diagonally, you mean?" offered Moody genially.

Officer George Allen, the first policeman at the scene of the crime, and Deputy Sheriff Francis Wixon testified to their searches of the Borden house. Allen said that the front door had been locked and bolted. In response to Moody's question, Allen testified that Lizzie Borden had not been crying. Describing Andrew's body, he offered a poignant detail of his own: he had noticed "how small the ankles was [*sic*]

Assistant Marshal John Fleet, *courtesy of Fall River Historical Society*

for the shoes." His testimony allowed the prosecution to introduce one of "the most horrible exhibits yet seen," the blood-soaked handkerchief Allen had found lying by Abby's feet. Moody held it aloft and it "hung like a scarlet banner before the general gaze." Elizabeth Jordan pronounced it "the sensation of the day." Lizzie averted her eyes and stared at the floor.

Wixon, a long-serving deputy sheriff, had been paying what he termed a "friendly call" to Marshal Hilliard as the alarm sounded. After Allen reported the full horrors of the situation, Wixon went directly over to see for himself. He had seen grievous wounds during his Civil War service and noticed that Andrew's wounds appeared "fresh," while the blood around Abby was coagulated and was "a dark maroon color." Robinson was quick to object before he could state any conclusion about the order of deaths. Robinson, however, was most interested in what Wixon had done outside the Borden house. He had seen a man's hat on the other side of the fence and, after climbing over, saw two other men at work. The men may not have seen anything that day, but the mere fact that Wixon could easily scale the fence provided a theoretical avenue of escape for an outside perpetrator.

Assistant Marshal John Fleet—tall, stalwart, good-looking, and intelligent—was the key police witness of the day. Fleet's story had two key elements: he had heard Lizzie Borden's declaration that Abby was not her mother and he had found the handleless hatchet. He arrived at the Borden house about 11:45 a.m. He viewed the bodies and then went to Lizzie's bedroom. There, he found Reverend Buck and Alice Russell with Lizzie Borden. Lizzie told him that she had advised her father to lie down. She explained that she then went to the barn loft. When she returned, she found her father dead. Lizzie effectively ruled out Morse as a suspect and disavowed any suspicion of Bridget Sullivan. When asked if she had any idea who might have killed her father and her mother, she declared: "She is not my mother, sir; she is my stepmother; my mother died when I was a child." She then volunteered that a man came to the house around nine that morning and, after prompting by Alice Russell, she repeated her story about the angry man who wanted to rent a store.

Fleet then went to the cellar and found Officers Mullaly and Devine looking for a possible murder weapon. They found two axes and two hatchets on the cellar floor. As Moody produced these items for Fleet to identify, they jostled against one another. The noise was jarring, metal against metal, a clanking, according to Julian Ralph, "that sounds terrible to those who sympathize with the prisoner and try to put themselves in her place." Yet Lizzie seemed more intrigued than horrified by the racket: "[s]he raised her head and looked at the weapons with some show of interest."

Fleet testified that he spoke to the other officers on the scene (in the dining room and out in the yard). Then he went to search Lizzie's room himself. This time the door was closed. Dr. Bowen opened the door six to eight inches, asked him what he wanted, and closed the door again. When he reopened the door, Lizzie asked if it was necessary to search the room. Fleet was reluctantly admitted. Lizzie asked him to search as quickly as possible and observed that no one could get into her room so there was really no point in searching. Fleet asked Lizzie about her morning activities. She said she had been in the barn for between twenty minutes to half an hour. She had last seen her stepmother about 9:00 a.m. She also told him that someone had brought a note to Abby.

After searching Lizzie's room, Fleet returned to the cellar. He saw a box containing a hatchet head with other tools, including pieces of iron. He then described what would become known as the handleless hatchet. He observed a new break in the wood close to the head, and where other implements were covered with dust, this blade, oddly, seemed to have ash on both sides. Robinson interrupted to prevent him from sharing how he imagined a hatchet head might have become covered with ash. He confirmed that the cellar door leading to the backyard was bolted from the inside. He also visited the barn and found it "hot and close" in the loft.

Fleet returned to the house on Saturday just after the funeral procession departed for the cemetery. Significantly, he testified about his search of the upstairs clothes closet. He said that he had not seen a dress with any bloodstains, nor had he found a paint-stained dress. In other words, if Lizzie Borden had burned a dress covered with paint, then where was it at the time of the search? Julian Ralph observed: "A hum ran through the court as the minds of the people grasped the fact that if he did not see the paint-soiled dress, it must have been because it was skillfully hidden."

Fleet had done real damage. It was nearly the end of the day and Robinson did not want his testimony to settle in the jury's mind overnight. But Fleet was "the coolest, clearest-headed, shrewdest man the wily lawyer ha[d] yet had to deal with." Robinson assumed a sardonic pose, hoping to rattle the policeman. Gone was the avuncular Robinson who had coaxed Bridget Sullivan into agreeing that the Borden household was "pleasant." "When ex-Gov. Robinson took hold of Assistant Marshal Fleet," pronounced Julian Ralph, "he did so as a terrier takes hold of a rat." Robinson immediately went on the attack: he pressed Fleet about his previous testimony, inquiring, "Do you think you told the same story then that you tell now?" That set the tone for the rest of the day.

Fleet glared and responded "impudently" as Robinson revisited the inconsistencies between his inquest testimony and his testimony of the afternoon. (In fairness, Julian Ralph observed: "Job himself could not have endured his tone and words with patience.") At the inquest, Fleet testified that Lizzie's dresses were covered with a cloth, which he lifted to examine the dresses for any sign of blood. But now, observed Robinson, "you didn't look carefully enough . . . to find whether there was a cloth hung over them."

Robinson quoted so much of Fleet's prior testimony that Moody interjected, "I don't know how much further you are going to read; there should certainly be a limit." Fleet said that he had "just looked in behind the dresses."

Robinson queried, "You were not expecting to find any man behind those women's dresses?"

Fleet insisted: "There was a possibility of a man being in that room."

Robinson sneered, "Really, were you looking for him there . . . You thought you would find him?"

According to Ralph, Robinson "showed his consummate art by simulating irritability, sternness, and impatience." And just before the day's adjournment, Robinson forced Fleet to admit that no one had impeded the search and that Lizzie herself unlocked the clothes closet door. According to Julian Ralph, Fleet "showed evident bias against the prisoner," but, as the *New York Times* observed, "Mr. Fleet's description of the weapon was so minute, and his reputation for veracity and honorable dealing in police and private matters is so well known here, that belief is general that he has really found the weapon with which the deed was committed."

Thursday was the day Lizzie Borden's luck seemed to run out. As one reporter noted, "It is the general belief that the Government brought out its worst to-day." Another put it more simply: "It was a bad day for Lizzie Borden." Knowlton and Moody called a series of witnesses whose testimony revealed Lizzie Borden's odd behavior before and after the murders and, most damaging of all, that she had burned a dress she had worn on the morning of the murders. To Julian Ralph, "The operation could almost be likened to a pigeon-shooting match, in which District Attorney Moody kept flinging up the birds . . . while the ex-Governor as constantly fired, and often, but by no means always, wounded or brought them down." Throughout these exchanges, Lizzie sat motionless. In the words of one observer, "All of her stoicism seemed to have returned to her." Joe Howard wrote: "Lizzie Borden has a remarkable temperament and her control over herself does she lose the strong grasp she has upon the muscles of her entire person . . . It seems that with almost every successive hour of her presence in the courtroom she becomes stronger."

FRIDAY, JUNE 9, 1893

By 7:00 a.m., a crowd of regulars and aspirants was on hand to join the rush for extra seats that Sheriff Wright made available to the public after 8:00 a.m. According to Joe Howard, the would-be spectators composed the most "extraordinary collection of women" he had ever seen, ranging from the refined to the positively unkempt. Depending upon the reporter's vantage point, Lizzie Borden similarly embodied the range of well-being. To Howard, "Lizzie not only looked pale, she felt pale." But Julian Ralph thought she was "as bright as a new dollar." Regardless, the break in the heat held, and the day promised to be temperate.

Friday also saw the return of Assistant Marshal Fleet to the stand, followed by a succession of his police colleagues. Ever on the alert for evidence of police conspiracy, Joe Howard found something unsettling in the parade of blue: "Nearly every one who has taken an active part in the endeavor to fasten this awful crime upon Miss Borden has within the year been promoted, until now captains in Fall River must be as thick as flies in a cow pasture." Knowlton and Moody sought to introduce the possible murder weapon, a hatchet with a handle newly broken close to the eye, and to establish that, despite the police search, no officer had seen the "paint-stained" dress Lizzie had burned.

As police witness after police witness described the searches, the *New York Times* reported, "All the details of the affair were rehearsed with a painful exactness; all the scenes in and about that ill-fated house were presented in clear and almost startling colors."

Before the prosecution could call the rest of the officers, it watched Assistant Marshal Fleet unravel on the stand. He explained that he noticed that one hatchet had its handle broken close to the steel blade, that the break was fresh, and that the handle was nowhere to be seen. He also observed that, unlike the other axes and hatchets in the cellar, ash rather than dust covered the blade and it looked as if someone might have been trying to remove bloodstains from it. Robinson pounced on seeming inconsistencies and omissions in Fleet's testimony. He mocked Fleet for failing to list all the officers and reporters present at the scene so that, as he testified and amended his original list, it seemed as if new people were appearing from thin air. Robinson interrupted to remark: "Oh, he was there, was he? You haven't told me about that." Fleet lost his cool and replied, "There's a good many things I haven't told you." Robinson insisted he list everyone else he could recall: Mr. Sawyer (the painter turned sentry) at the back door, Mr. Manning of the *Fall River Daily Herald* at the front door, Mr. Porter of the *Fall River Daily Globe*, Mr. Stevens of the *Daily News*, Mr. Clarkson at some point, and Mr. Donnelly the hack man. Pressed about how many police officers were in the cellar, he said, "There were so many officers there that I cannot think at the different times that I went into that place who the officers were." Of the now infamous handleless hatchet, Fleet admitted that he had found it on his second trip to the cellar.

Robinson asked, "Why didn't you tell me before?"

Fleet replied, "You didn't ask me." Asked to describe the condition of the handleless hatchet, Fleet insisted that the dust on the broken-handled hatchet looked like ash from the ash pile, not the fine dust on the other items. He noticed ashes on both sides of the blade head but did not recall seeing any on the break. So far, so good for the prosecution. But, the prior day, he had testified that he thought there had been dust or ash on the broken end.

Captain Phillip Harrington, *courtesy of Fall River Historical Society*

Robinson mockingly told him to take the pick of his two statements: "Let us have the one you like best this morning." Then Robinson "dismissed the witness with a wave of his hand, as one might fling away an orange after tasting it and finding it insipid." During this exchange, Lizzie watched like a spectator at a sporting match, leaning forward in her chair to catch every word.

Next came Phillip Harrington, promoted from patrolman to captain since the murders, who was one of the first officers on the scene. Even though he had known Andrew Borden for more than twenty years, he did not recognize the body on the sofa: Andrew Borden's face was covered in blood and the blood was so fresh that "a small drop trickled down the side of the face." Like other witnesses, he had been able to see Abby's body as he ascended the stairs.

While upstairs, Harrington interviewed Lizzie Borden. Over Robinson's objections, he described Borden as "cool" and "steady." And then, most remarkably, he described Lizzie's attire, a pink wrapper, minutely in a manner "creditable to a first class dressmaker." According to Howard, "He gave the colors, the stripes, the cut-bias biz, the flutings of the bosom, the fittings to the figure, the trimming about the bottom, and continued in a blaze of glory about the entire circumference of what he called a bell skirt." As Harrington spoke, Lizzie Borden hid her face in her fan and "her shoulders silently shook." Then she could restrain herself no longer. She "laughed so that her body trembled with the convulsion. Her face was very rosy all over from the strain of her efforts to control herself." Even Moody seemed amused, asking, "That finishes it, does it?" On cross-examination, Robinson peered over his half-spectacles and inquired, "Were you ever in the dressmaking business?" Julian Ralph commented that Harrington "could talk about dresses like an American Worth or a female society reporter." Amazed women in the audience dubbed him "the tailor-made captain." Joseph Howard sneered, "No one would have been surprised if he had drawn a mouchoir from a dainty satchel and deftly dusted the powder from his nose." Of course, there was another, more sinister explanation for his facility with fashion: Harrington may have been reciting prepared remarks from memory.

Harrington had one other nugget to share: he had seen Dr. Bowen with "some scraps of note paper in his hand." Bowen told him it was "nothing." Robinson was out of his seat immediately: "I cannot let this go in unless you give me an assurance that it has nothing whatever to do with it."

Knowlton responded, "It has nothing to do with the case at all."

Robinson pressed, "You claim the paper has no significance."

Knowlton replied, "Well, he said it has no significance."

What worried Robinson? According to Officer Harrington, Dr. Bowen said that the note had something to do with his daughter. Yet, Harrington claimed he saw "Emma" written on the upper-left-hand corner in lead pencil. Did the note contain something damaging to Lizzie's defense? The trial record is silent. But Harrington also said he observed a rolled-up paper "about twelve inches long and no more than two inches in diameter" that had been burned in the stove earlier. The dimensions coincided with the likely length of the missing handle of the handleless hatchet. Robinson appeared concerned that Harrington was implying that the burned paper had been used to cover the hatchet handle.

Patrick Doherty was the next officer on the stand. Moody and Robinson clashed over whether Doherty could repeat Dr. Bowen's exclamation that Mrs. Borden had died of fright. Ultimately, Moody agreed not to pursue it. Doherty was the first officer to examine Abby's body. According to Doherty, Abby was lying facedown, her head to the east, with her hands above her head. Aside from moving one of her hands and lifting her head, he did not move the body. Doherty then left to telephone the marshal. When he returned, he saw Lizzie with Adelaide Churchill and Alice Russell in the kitchen. Lizzie told him that she had been in the barn when the murder had been committed and added that she had heard a peculiar noise, "something like scraping." Thinking about possible suspects, Doherty asked her whether "there was a Portuguese working for your father?" She named her father's two farm employees, Mr. Johnson and Mr. Eddy, but said neither would hurt him.

The next witness, Patrolman Michael Mullaly, a fifteen-year veteran of the Fall River police force, was a disaster for the prosecution. Mullaly, wrote Julian Ralph, "did not look like a powder magazine on the point of exploding, but that is what he proved to be in the metaphorical sense." On the day of the murders, he had searched the attic and, later, it was he who called Fleet's attention to the axes and hatchets in the cellar. He identified the handleless hatchet as the same one Moody proffered but testified that the break had been covered with ashes. On cross-examination, Robinson pursued the exact nature of the material covering the hatchet head. Mullaly then casually disclosed his stunner: he had seen the handle in the box containing the hatchets. He claimed Fleet took it out and then put it back in the box. Elizabeth Jordan wrote that Mullaly seemed "in blissful unconsciousness that he had revealed anything of importance," yet, according to Howard, "if a bomb had fallen in the courtroom more astonishment could not have been caused." Robinson himself exclaimed, "The rest of the handle? The other piece . . . where is it?" Robinson demanded the prosecution produce the handle. Knowlton disclaimed all knowledge of it and offered to send an officer to the Borden house to look for it. Robinson scoffed at that suggestion. Instead, he recalled Fleet to the stand. Meanwhile, Jennings quickly sent his assistant Arthur Phillips and a detective from Cambridge to watch the foot and the head of the courthouse stairs to make sure that Mullaly did not warn Fleet about what he had said.

From then on, Fleet was done for, trapped in Robinson's "merciless and masterful grasp." Fleet agreed Mullaly was present when he found the hatchet but denied that he saw another piece of the handle. As Julian Ralph explained, "The theory of the Commonwealth is that she took the hatchet after murdering her father, broke off the handle, burned it, and then cleansed the blade, rubbed it in ashes, and put it in a box in the cellar." If the handle had been there all along, then the hatchet had no great significance. As the *New York Times* declared, "They nearly destroyed the Government's hope of producing the instrument with which the deed was done." From then on, the prosecution could not claim that it had found the murder weapon without reminding the jurors of the officers' contradictory testimony. As Julian Ralph concluded, "The tattered web which the legal spiders for the Commonwealth have been weaving around her had one of its strongest threads snapped by a sudden and totally unexpected blow." Joe Howard was harsher in his assessment of the police: "Of course he was certain about it; they all are. There hasn't been an officer on the stand who has not been absolutely confident, nor has there been one who has not been flatly contradicted by one of his associates." In the same vein, Elizabeth Jordan declared: "In the minds of those present at the Borden trial a little hatchet will never more be solely emblematical of the father of this country and veracity. It will always bring to their minds the Fall River police force and some of the most extraordinary swearing ever heard on a witness stand."

The rest of the witnesses had little to add. Officer Wilson testified that he heard the conversation between Fleet and Lizzie about the search of her room. Robinson hammered away at the idea of any resistance to the search: "There was no objection made to your search except [to] . . . wait a minute and then you went right in, didn't you?" George Pettey, an acquaintance of Andrew Borden, who had lived in the upper part of the Borden house when it was a two-family tenement, saw Bridget Sullivan washing windows around 10:00 a.m. Like many in Fall River, he went into the house after the murders and viewed the bodies. Remarkably, he testified that he had put his hand on Abby's head, noticing that "the hair was dry, that it was matted." Augustus Gorman owned the paint shop on the corner of Borden and Second Street and did little more than confirm the timeline already established.

Despite the overall defense success, the day still wore on the defendant: Lizzie seemed tired and "looked like a wilted flower." She was not alone. It had been a momentous session inside and out of the courtroom: the ramshackle mill teams "frequently drowned the words of the witness, the birds sang merrily, the old cow gave her punctuating mooings with great deliberation, some stone cutters in an adjacent building chipped in, and a general condition of feverish restlessness dominated the place." When court adjourned at 3:40 p.m., the chief justice cautioned the jury about its responsibilities. Wearing "an expression of paternal solicitude on his intelligently handsome face," he warned the jurors against "allowing their minds to reach any conclusion with reference to the case," adding, "you should not converse about the case until it is finally committed to you." Howard had nothing but sympathy for the jurors, repeatedly lamenting their limited entertainment and enforced temperance. He described their "miserable" lot: "Up at 6 in the morning, breakfast at 7, tramp to the courthouse at 9, sit till 1, tramp through the broiling sun to dinner, back again followed by a gang of hoodlums, hammered till 5 by learned brothers, back to the hotel for supper, and immediately taken to their corridor, where they are locked in without means of amusement, instruction or recreation except their tongues." And nothing to drink except "pure water filtered."

SATURDAY, JUNE 10, 1893

The courthouse was bounded by one of New Bedford's busiest streets, and by the end of the first week Joe Howard was at the end of his patience with the noisy location: "The ingenuity of New Bedford's authorities must have been taxed in their selection of a site for Bristol County's court house, where the greatest possible annoyance in the line of extraneous sounding could be secured." He did not object to the singing of birds or the mooing of the cow, but he complained about the "processional continuity of stone wagons, farmers' carts, coal wagons, mill wagons, loaded with all kinds of material, stone cutters, whistling boys and vociferating crowds, whose combined outputs

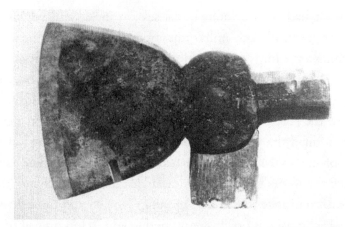

Handleless or "hoodoo" hatchet, *courtesy of Fall River Historical Society*

furnish a bedlamistic hurrahdom, vexatious to the ear and exasperating to the understanding." On a happier note, he observed that the crowd outside the courthouse was enlivened by "a large number of young and rather pretty girls," perhaps schoolgirls on their weekend break. Inside the courtroom, there were fewer women than usual. Those that came earned unflattering descriptions: "In bonnets, yellow was the predominant color and it held its own too, as far as complexions went." It had been a long week; yet, according to the *Fall River Daily Globe*, Lizzie Borden "looks as she would look in church or in any public place where she in common with others, might be observed." "If the strains of the past six days has told on her," the paper continued, "she does not betray it so far as her physical appearance goes."

After the prior day's debacle for the prosecution, the defense was understandably in good humor. But the prosecution doggedly returned to the mystery of the handleless hatchet. As Julian Ralph commented, "The handleless hatchet, now generally known as 'the hoodoo hatchet,' continued its demonish pranks in the trial of Lizzie Borden for her life today. It chopped another great hole in the case." Elizabeth Jordan theorized: "It was upon the three and a half-inch edge of this useful little household tool that the case for the commonwealth would split."

Moody sent an officer to search for the missing piece of the handle.

Lieutenant Francis Edson, seconded later by Officer Mahoney, testified that he went to the Borden house on Friday at 3:40 p.m. and was refused entrance. Charles J. Holmes, president of the Fall River 5 Cents Savings Bank and Lizzie's éminence grise, had apparently been conducting his own fruitless search inside. During the original search, Edson, like the other officers, had been assigned areas to search: he was tasked with the areas in the cellar. He retrieved a small shingle hatchet and two wood axes from the cellar washroom as well as a claw-hammer hatchet from a shelf in the vegetable cellar. He delivered them to Marshal Hilliard on August 5. Robinson questioned him about the thoroughness of the search: "You were there to look, your business, was it not?" In addition to his search of the vegetable cellar, Edson looked in the water closet and saw nothing. But he had seen Officer Medley with the hatchet head, wrapped in paper.

William Medley offered a masculine counterpart to Adelaide Churchill. He was a bit of a chatterbox, delighted to have his moment to shine. Moody repeatedly interrupted him to remind him to stick to the facts and to answer the questions asked of him. Of his conversation with Lizzie in her room, Medley began, "The thought came to me." Forestalling a soliloquy, the lawyer hastily replied, "Well, never mind." At another point, Moody reminded his witness not to repeat conversations with other officers: "I don't ask what was said."

Medley's testimony centered on his search of the barn and his discovery of the handleless hatchet in the cellar of the house. He described the barn loft as undisturbed and "very hot" before his search. Medley looked into the loft from the stairs, where, he said, he had seen no tracks or any sign that someone had been in the loft. But when he put his own hand down on the floor, the dust was so thick that his handprints left distinct impressions. In the cellar of the house, he found a small hatchet head in a box of odds and ends, sitting on a block about a foot and a half above the cellar floor. He noticed that the hatchet head was covered with a coarse substance that looked different than the fine dust he saw on the other items of "old rubbish" in the box. He showed the hatchet head to Captain Desmond and wrapped it up in brown paper to take to the city marshal. When Robinson asked him about the wrapping on cross examination, Medley admitted he was not "very tidy at such things." Alluding to Harrington's closely observed description of Lizzie's dress, Robinson wryly observed, "Well, I am glad to find a man that is not on style."

Captain Dennis Desmond confirmed Medley's description of the handleless hatchet. He saw a small amount of wood in the eye of the hatchet where the handle had been broken off. He agreed that the hatchet head was covered with a coarse material, "a loose, rough matter" rather than ordinary dust found elsewhere in the cellar. Then he testified that he had wrapped the hatchet in a large newspaper, paper that was at hand in the water closet, rather than the brown paper Medley had mentioned. Robinson seized on this point—Medley had just testified that *he* had wrapped up the hatchet head. In Howard's estimation, Robinson was "tremulous with excitement internally, but sweet as a day in June externally" as he let Desmond describe the wrapping "until the unsuspecting captain had cut off all possibility of retreat from his position." By the end, even the officers' descriptions of the package brought to Marshal Hilliard did not match. Not only was the outer covering different, but, as a reporter later explained, one officer described a package the size of a "five cent cut of pie" and the other described a parcel large enough for a "pair of longshoreman's boots."

Robinson tried to pin Desmond down about the purpose of his later searches. But Desmond dodged the question: "I cannot tell you what I was looking for. I was looking for anything that would throw any light." He had already testified that he found no paint-stained dresses. Robinson did win one point: Desmond agreed that everyone in the house cooperated with the searches. In Robinson's words, it was "an absolute, unrestrained, and complete search of everything in the house."

George Seaver was the final police witness. Unlike the others, he was a member of the state district police in Taunton. He, too, went to the Borden house on August 4 and was part of the Saturday search of the house. He searched the garret with Captain Desmond. He also joined in the search of the cellar: he testified that the hatchet was covered with a coarse dust or ashes but that the break was a new one, "a very bright break." He had been a carpenter; he knew about wood. Unfortunately, he could not identify the type of wood of the remaining part of the handle, a fact Robinson repeated with some relish. "Well, look—a carpenter!" remarked Robinson.

According to his testimony, Seaver joined Fleet in examining the dresses in the clothes closet. Seaver took the dresses off the hooks and passed them to Fleet who was positioned near the window so that he could examine them in the light. Fleet had earlier testified that he hardly looked at the dresses, yet it seemed that he had been able to examine them more thoroughly than Seaver. Moody asked if Seaver would have seen a paint-stained dress if it had been there, but Robinson quickly interjected and the question was struck. Seaver opined that he examined twelve to fifteen dresses but could not recall seeing a blue dress—even though Lizzie and Emma together owned ten blue dresses. And he had lost his memorandum about the dresses. Seaver also joined Dr. Dolan in measuring the blood splatter, yet it seemed he had mislaid that memorandum as well.

Unfortunately for the prosecution, its own witnesses contradicted each other about key facts in the discovery of the hatchet and the search of Lizzie's dresses. Most important, it seemed that either Fleet or Mullaly had lied about finding the hatchet handle. Howard declared: "There has never been a trial so full of surprises, with such marvelous contradictions, given by witnesses called for a common purpose." There were other serious discrepancies: First, Medley and Desmond gave vastly different descriptions of the wrapping of the hatchet head. Second, Fleet and Desmond appeared to differ on whether the search of the household was thorough. Finally, there was, in the eyes of some, "a conspicuousity" of Bridget Sullivan in the above events. It was Bridget, according to the officers, who led them to the box containing the hatchet in the basement. According to Mullaly, Bridget handed him the hatchet, though she had testified that she had never touched it. Bridget, too, had blue dresses that were not given the same scrutiny as those of Lizzie Borden's. Howard also wondered about the daytime theft, tantalizingly mentioned but then struck from the record. "What does Bridget Sullivan know about the burglary of the Borden house?" But, for the moment, there would be no answers.

The court adjourned until Monday, June 12, at 9:00 a.m. Lizzie Borden returned to jail in a black coupe. To catch a glimpse of the famous prisoner on her short trip, spectators in carriages and wagons lined both sides of the street. According to Elizabeth Jordan, even "the sidewalks on both sides of the street were packed with people all the way down to the jail, standing as close together as they comfortably could." But the curtains of Lizzie Borden's conveyance were discreetly drawn to frustrate the gawkers. Once back at the jail, Lizzie ate "a New England dinner, with all the trimmings, apparently feeling 100 percent better than she did yesterday." She would spend her weekend in the soothing company of *David Copperfield*. Julian Ralph approved: "The genius of Charles Dickens" served her better than "talking with visitors about the murders which she did or did not do."

Chief Judge Mason and Judge Blodgett left town for the rest of the week, their eyes shining "with the gleam of domestic hope," leaving their colleague Judge Dewey to prepare for the arguments on Monday. That afternoon, however, Judge Dewey took a break. He was spotted relaxing on a rock in nearby Buzzards Bay. By contrast, "The jurors were bundled into an omnibus . . . driven down to the Point and back again in less than an hour, given their suppers, and securely locked in their superheated heated rooms not only without spirituous refreshments, but without any possible enlivenments." As Julian Ralph observed, "Queen Victoria might die, New York could burn up or Boston . . . but the jury would know nothing of it." And in a worrying development, the jurors planned to attend church on Sunday but they disagreed on their preferred minister, "thereby preventing all hands from attending religious service of any kind."

Chapter 7

A SIGNAL VICTORY

The jury in its favorite position, *Boston Globe*

While Lizzie Borden lost herself in Dickens, journalists at the trial discussed the case on their hotel balconies "in an atmosphere like the exhaust from a mighty engine." Elizabeth Jordan later wrote that she and most of her fellow out-of-town reporters believed Lizzie was innocent. Yet, they wondered: "If Miss Borden had not committed the murders, who had?" In the *New York Sun*, Julian Ralph had pointed out the inescapable paradox: it seemed impossible that Lizzie Borden had committed the murders, and equally impossible "to understand how anyone else could have worked such fearful havoc in the house in which she was stirring." His colleagues proposed their own theories: "An escaped maniac?

The crime seemed the work of one." Elizabeth Jordan thought: "A gorilla? A gorilla was indicated, by the appearance of the rooms. *The Murders in the Rue Morgue* came cheerily to mind." That night, Jordan dozed fitfully and woke at three o'clock in the morning to a terrifying sight: "a gorilla standing framed in the open French windows." Her somnolent eyes had deceived her. It was not a murderous beast but rather the night watchman, demonstrating that the balcony was "easily reached from the street below." According to Jordan, "He mentioned maniacs, and the fact that the Borden murderer might still be at large." From then on, despite the heat, Jordan slept with the windows tightly shut.

MONDAY, JUNE 12, 1893

After the short break of the weekend, the crowds surged toward the small fence to the courthouse, impatient to claim any available seats. Even the lawyers had to fight their way "through the perpetual and swollen crowd of women idlers." For those who managed to secure admittance, a grim relic awaited them. Just outside the courtroom itself stood the bloodstained sofa on which Andrew Borden was murdered. It was covered in sackcloth but gawkers lifted the covering to examine it for themselves. After passing that memento mori, Julian Ralph entered the courtroom to find "his favorite seat taken, although it was taken by a much handsomer person, and a woman at that." She was the new illustrator from the *New York World*. Oblivious, she "calmly sketched on." Joe Howard fared better: he had struck up a friendship with a beautiful young woman during the Saturday session and, Monday morning, "they drove up [to the courthouse] in style."

Lizzie was wearing a new black silk dress with a delicate outer layer of black lace, "many times more expensive than the old one." But, despite her new gown, she seemed unwell: "Her color was bad, her manner listless, and it seemed as though the demon of apprehension was dallying with her sensibilities." This was understandable. Before the court adjourned on Saturday, the attorneys filed a stipulation that laid out the agreed facts about Lizzie Borden's inquest testimony. This morning, out of the hearing of the jury, her lawyers would entreat the judges not to permit the prosecution to use that testimony as evidence against her.

THE COORDINATE BRANCHES

Why was the jury removed from the courtroom? Judges and juries have different roles in the legal system: judges explain the law and juries decide the facts. Or, put another way, the judges serve as gatekeepers who decide what evidence the jury can hear. As a general matter, all relevant evidence should be presented to the jury. Relevance, then and now, means the tendency for any piece of evidence to prove or disprove a proposition in the case. It is a broad concept based on reason alone: all facts having rational, probative value are admissible. This general rule comes with an important caveat: judges can exclude relevant evidence for a variety of reasons. There may be statutory or even constitutional prohibitions against admitting certain evidence. An involuntary confession is a classic example of relevant evidence that the jury may not hear. Other common grounds for excluding otherwise relevant evidence are unfair prejudice, confusion, or undue delay. For example, common-law precedent frowns on evidence of bad character on the theory that jurors might unfairly decide that a defendant was likely to act in ways consistent with negative character traits without giving appropriate attention to the actual evidence of guilt. This is often referred to as "propensity" evidence—the idea that a person who has done something in the past has a tendency to repeat the behavior. In such cases, the judges need to balance the importance of the evidence—its probative value—against the risk of unfair prejudice to the defendant who might be judged for who he is rather than what he had actually done. Judges, as legal professionals, are thought to be able to understand the pertinent distinctions involved and to safeguard the legal process from decisions based on bias or emotions.

At the coroner's inquest, Knowlton metaphorically returned Lizzie Borden to the scene of the crime to establish a chronology that made her the only possible killer. She had told different people a range of stories relating to her discovery of her father's body: she told one officer she had heard a "scraping noise"; she told Bridget Sullivan she had heard "a groan." Yet, she had also said she was in the barn looking for iron to make a sinker, or for a piece of iron or tin to fix a screen. The inquest forced her to explain herself under oath. It was not a success. As the *New York Times* observed, "The statements made by her at the inquest were of a contradictory character, extremely damaging to her interests." Even Borden's most fervent supporters acknowledged that her testimony had not gone well. Elizabeth Jordan, for example, wrote sympathetically: "On the confused stories and contradictions in matters for the most part trifling the District-Attorneys have built their strongest hopes of arousing the antagonism of the jury."

In addition to showing her opportunity, Lizzie Borden's inquest testimony also provided evidence of Lizzie's motive for killing her stepmother (the property dispute that divided the family) and Lizzie's "consciousness of guilt." The prosecution was not required to offer a motive for the murders though it was hard to imagine any jury convicting an apparently sane daughter of killing her father and stepmother without some explanation, profound grievance, or dark purpose. By contrast, "consciousness of guilt" was considered strong evidence of underlying guilt of the crime. If Lizzie Borden did something an innocent person would not have done or failed to do something an innocent person would have done in the same circumstances, then that act or omission would demonstrate "consciousness of guilt." More colorfully, a leading authority on evidence argued—in an apt metaphor for the Borden case—"As an axe leaves its mark in the speechless tree, so an evil deed leaves its mark in the evil doer's consciousness."

The prosecution believed that Lizzie Borden's account of her actions that day suggested subterfuge. She had invented a note to her stepmother to prevent her father from looking for Abby, lying dead in the guest bedroom, and to explain why she herself did not think to look for Abby after she found her father's body. Then she had also burned the dress allegedly worn on the day of the murders. The prosecutors believed that "the conduct of the accused after the killing was such that no conceivable hypothesis except that of guilt, will explain the inconsistencies and improbabilities that were asserted by her."

Moody laid out the prosecution's argument for admitting Borden's inquest testimony. First, he reminded the judges of the breadth of legal relevance: "All facts that go either to sustain or impeach a hypothesis logically pertinent are admissible." Acknowledging that there was a separate jurisprudence on the admissibility of confessions, one that might be harder for the prosecution to overcome, he declared that Borden's inquest testimony was "clearly not in the nature of a confession, but rather in the nature of denials." In other words, Lizzie had been trying to exonerate herself; therefore, the case law on compelled confessions was irrelevant. Then, from cases he culled from numerous jurisdictions, Moody derived a clear rule: "Declarations voluntarily given, no matter where or under what circumstances, are competent; declarations obtained by compulsion are never competent." As principal support for these propositions, Moody discussed a series of cases from New York because of its settled law on the question. *People v. Mondon*, 103 N.Y. 211 (1886), the most recent case he cited, offered this bright line rule ostensibly drawn from previous cases: the testimony of a witness before a coroner's inquest may be used against him at trial, regardless of whether he was suspected of being the perpetrator.

According to the prosecution, Lizzie Borden voluntarily testified at the inquest; therefore, her statements should be admitted into evidence. Moody explained that the state was required to hold an inquest about deaths in suspicious circumstances. There was nothing unusual—let alone sinister—in the procedure. Borden was not under arrest or charged with the murders at the time of the inquest, and she had consulted with her attorney before testifying. If Borden wanted to protect herself against the subsequent use of her statements, Moody argued, she should have claimed her privilege against self-incrimination as codified in the Massachusetts Constitution, which contained a correlate to the now familiar Fifth Amendment of the United States Constitution. Because the Constitution did not, at that time, apply to the states, Lizzie Borden could not seek federal constitutional protection—despite her attorneys' reference to the most recent Supreme Court case on the subject.

SHE STOOD ALONE

The defense saw Lizzie's inquest testimony in a different light. Robinson argued that there was a specific prohibition against admitting Lizzie Borden's inquest testimony into evidence. Lizzie's testimony at the inquest was essentially involuntary, a legal term used to characterize coerced confessions, and should not be heard by the jury. She had been subpoenaed to appear and, despite being under suspicion for the murders of her father and stepmother, she was not cautioned about her right not to testify, guaranteed not only by common-law tradition but also by the Massachusetts Constitution.

According to Robinson, Borden was under constructive arrest, as much in custody as if an arrest warrant had actually been served. Marshal Rufus Hilliard, it transpired, had carried an unserved arrest warrant in his pocket during the inquest. And Robinson built upon that small fact to evoke a particular ambiance. Unlike Moody, who immediately launched into the fine points of doctrine, Robinson conjured up an atmosphere of menace in which crowds of men in authority circle a defenseless young woman. He described the police surveillance of the house, the subpoena to appear at the inquest, and the denial of Lizzie's request for representation at the inquest: "She

Juggling with a woman's life, *courtesy of Fall River Historical Society*

alone—a woman unguided by her counsel, confronted with the District Attorney, watched by the City Marshal, at all times surrounded by the police." In Robinson's account, the Fall River authorities were allied in a nefarious official conspiracy to compel Lizzie's testimony, blocking her escape like cats playing with their prey. The arrest warrant proved that they were "keeping her with the hand upon the shoulder—she a woman could not run—covering her at every moment, surrounding her at every instant, empowered to take her at any moment, and under those circumstances taking her to that inquest to testify." How could statements made under those conditions possibly be voluntary?

But, he acknowledged, "I am not talking to the jury." So he pivoted to questions of law. Robinson's line of argument set out two threshold questions: First, was it obvious that there had been a crime? Second, was the defendant then under suspicion? According to Robinson, the inquest was set up to "extort . . . from the defendant something that could be used against her" when she inevitably came to trial. Robinson asked: "What did they want this woman for? To find out if there had been a felonious homicide? No. To find out something, to see if they could not catch her some way." The inquest was little more than a trap. Seventy-three years before the Supreme Court's Miranda decision, Robinson argued that the district attorney or the magistrate should have cautioned her, informing her "that she ought not to testify to anything that would criminate herself." However blistering his critique of the procedure, Robinson presented his argument in his typical "agreeable, confidential manner, pooh-poohing the quotations submitted by Mr. Moody."

It is intriguing that Robinson failed to exploit the powerful rationale of the case law on this point—the psychological insight that involuntary statements are often unreliable. As an earlier case explained, innocent people who know they are suspected may try to conceal damaging facts or concoct stories. "The mind, confused and agitated by the apprehension of danger, cannot reason with coolness," said the court in *State v. Gilman*, "and it resorts to falsehood when the truth would be safer." But Robinson did not need to run the risk of suggesting that Borden might have lied because she felt endangered. Instead he kept the judges focused on the assumption that, as a woman, Lizzie was inherently vulnerable to confusion. He even insisted that the officials had an affirmative duty to protect her and prevent her from testifying. Grief-stricken at the violent death of her father, unsettled by unjust suspicion, and incapacitated by morphine, a woman like Lizzie Borden could not testify clearly. Robinson exclaimed: "Denied counsel . . . she stood alone, a defenseless woman . . . If that is freedom, God save the Commonwealth of Massachusetts!"

In his reply, Moody retorted by paraphrasing a French officer on the Charge of the Light Brigade: "It is magnificent but it is not law." Moody pretended to struggle as he summarized Robinson's argument: "So far as I can understand his position, it is that this testimony is not admissible because it is not." He characterized Robinson's argument as mere "vocal gymnastics and fireworks," an argument unsupported by a single case. Moody insisted that there were no cases in which a person's statements were excluded if that person had not been under arrest at the time of making the statements. He denied that the "absence of the magistrate's caution somehow changed the equation. He reminded the judges that Lizzie's lawyer Andrew Jennings had accompanied her to the inquest. Yes, he was denied permission to be in the room with her, but that was entirely within the commonwealth's discretion. Moody asked, incredulously: "Can your Honors have any doubt, can your Honors have a particle of doubt, that after she had talked with Mr. Jennings . . . that she went in with a full consciousness that she had a right to decline?" Moody could not understand how "an undisclosed warrant, of which she had no suspicion whatever, could bear in any degree upon the exercise of her will."

Joe Howard professed shock that Moody seemed to miss Robinson's larger point that it was "not a question of whether such and such a course was the practice, but whether the practice was right." Moody's "quick intuitions must have told him," Howard continued, "that the learned judges must of necessity decide against him."

While Moody displayed a commanding knowledge of legal doctrine, Robinson's success at depicting an atmosphere of coercion at the inquest depended upon—and exploited—particular notions of late-nineteenth-century femininity. Julian Ralph explained that, at the inquest, Lizzie was "in the hands of Mr. Knowlton, whose manner toward her . . . led her to fear him and to shrink from him as perhaps any woman so placed would fear a powerful man whom she regarded as her enemy and her persecutor." Joe Howard remarked of Lizzie's treatment: "If that is not the equivalent of being under arrest, I do not understand the English language." He continued: "Pushed, examined, cross-questioned, surrounded by hostile officials, she was badgered [and] confused . . . to such an extent that during those long, tedious three days of inquisition she contradicted herself time and time again." For him, Borden's inconsistent testimony was proof she was a woman, not proof she was a murderer. Moreover, there was her "befogged condition as a result of the morphine." As the *New York Times* reported: "Even if Miss Borden had testified without coercion, she was in such a condition that she hardly knew what she was about."

As the judges deliberated in private for over an hour, the tension in the courtroom suggested that the outcome was far from obvious. "Paler than a sheet, her cheeks puffy, her eyes strained, her lips shut tight," Lizzie Borden radiated her distress. When the judges returned, Lizzie Borden "fastened a look upon the chief justice as though she would read his very soul." Chief Justice Mason delivered the court's ruling "in a voice as clear as a bell, with enunciation as distinct as that of [famed actor] Edwin Booth." Though Borden had not been under arrest, he explained, she was "as effectually in custody as if the formal precept had been served." Although he noted that the mere fact of suspicion does not automatically make a defendant's statements under oath involuntary, he concluded: "[B]oth upon principle and authority . . . if the accused was at the time of such testimony under arrest, charged with the crime in question, the statements he made are not voluntary and are inadmissible at the trial." Implying that the investigators strategically held off serving the arrest warrant, the judges issued a firm rebuke: "The common law regards substance more than form. The principle involved cannot be evaded by avoiding the form of arrest if the witness at the time of such testimony is practically in custody."

Lizzie wept. Given the stakes, the reaction was understandable. Howard wrote: "She couldn't help it. She was nervous, upset, tired out, strained with a tension that no man need hope to understand, and when this great, wide horizon of relief was unfolded to her, human nature asserted itself, and of course she broke down and of course she cried." Elizabeth Jordan went beyond mere sympathy, slipping into sentimental caricature: "It would seem that she had become so accustomed to nothing but cruelty from the fates as to be almost callous to all other injuries they have in store for her, but that too much kindness on their part had been quite too much and the spark of relief had quite unstrung her." Meanwhile, the jury returned to the courtroom. Howard wondered what the jury made of the scene: "The agitation of the counsel, the nervous condition of Miss Borden, the cheery look of popular satisfaction on everybody's face, was all Greek to that branch of the court."

All agreed that the defense had won a "signal victory" in excluding Lizzie Borden's inquest testimony. But whether it was the right decision divided experts and laypeople. It was, according to Ralph, "a new point of law in the old Bay State." Public opinion mostly followed the press in commending the judges' ruling. Members of the legal profession took a contrary view. Judge Charles Davis of Boston mildly acknowledged that the question had not been authoritatively decided in Massachusetts, but concluded that "common sense dictated a contrary result." More scathing was a young legal scholar named John Henry Wigmore, who would become the nation's preeminent authority on the law of evidence. Wigmore pointedly inquired: "Is there any lawyer in these United States who has a scintilla of a doubt, not merely that her counsel fully informed the accused on her rights, but that they talked over the expediencies, and that he allowed her to go on the stand because he deliberately concluded that it was the best policy for her, by so doing, to avoid all appearance of concealment or guilt? And yet the ruling of the Court allowed them to blow hot and cold—to go on the stand when there was something to gain and to remain silent when the testimony proved dangerous to use."

For the prosecution, it was a serious blow. Attorney General Pillsbury dropped everything to take the train from Boston to New Bedford on Monday night to discuss this setback with Knowlton and Moody. They met secretly at Knowlton's house on Union Street. The *Fall River Daily Herald* observed, "Very few people knew of his being in town, and his appearance at this time is very significant." Having lost their best evidence about Lizzie's "motive," they would need their medical experts to establish "exclusive opportunity." Across town at the Parker House, the atmosphere among the defense counsel was festive. "It was," according to one correspondent, "impossible to get them to talk seriously." Robinson "retired at once to his room, but Mr. Jennings and Mr. Adams lingered in the corridors." Jennings "puffed at his cigar and grinned."

Having lost the point, the prosecution regrouped as best as possible and proceeded to the medical experts. But first Joseph Hyde, the patrolman assigned to the Borden house until 11:00 p.m. on August 4, took the stand to describe something he witnessed on the night after the murders. While posted on sentry duty outside the house, he looked through the cellar window and saw Alice Russell and Lizzie Borden descend to the cellar about 8:45 p.m.: "Alice Russell was carrying a small hand lamp. Miss Lizzie had a toilet pail." Alice lingered at the foot of the steps while Lizzie went first into the water closet to "empty the slops," then to the sink to rinse the pail and turn on the water. Afterward, they went back upstairs together. Then, ten or fifteen minutes later, Lizzie made a solitary trip to the wash cellar. The cellar also housed the bloodstained clothes from the murder victims. Placing her lamp in the west end of the cellar (closest to the street), she bent down in front of the sink located on the east end of the cellar. Hyde testified: "What she did I don't know."

On cross-examination, Robinson explored the nocturnal visits in some detail, trying to establish the ordinariness of the procedure. Hyde agreed that, on the first visit, the women came down to the cellar "in a perfectly natural way," but that Alice Russell nervously lingered by the stairs with the lamp "as though she would not go." Hyde also agreed that he could see their actions clearly through the windows. As for the later visit, he said he could see Lizzie but could not see the sink or observe what she was doing as she stooped before it. Robinson emphasized that the procedure had taken less than a minute and that the pail containing the bloody towels was near the sink, leaving the jurors to make the obvious inference.

BOWERY CHAMBER OF HORRORS

The prosecution moved on to its medical experts. All would testify, like the local physician Dr. Albert Dedrick, that Andrew and Abby were killed about at least an hour and a half apart and that Abby Borden had died first, her blood being of "a ropy consistency." Julian

Ralph pitied the jury: "Whoever knows how tedious and longwinded the average medical expert is will form an idea of what is in store for the unfortunate jury this week." Most irritating to Ralph, "Their testimony bears little on the vital question" of Lizzie's guilt or innocence, "it being settled that the stepmother was killed first." For the prosecution, the testimony was critical to their case: the order of deaths and the exact interval between the murders established Lizzie's exclusive opportunity.

In an uncanny coincidence, Dr. William Dolan, the medical examiner for Bristol County, happened to be passing the Borden house on August 4 about 11:45 a.m. Dolan examined Andrew Borden's body: Andrew's hands were still warm and bright red blood was still "oozing from the wounds in the head." In his cursory examination, Dolan found eight to ten wounds. He also described Andrew's position: Andrew's head was lying upon a tidy covered sofa cushion. The cushion itself lay on his coat, which had been "doubled up and put under there, and that . . . rested upon an afghan or sofa cover." Dr. Dolan then examined Abby's body. He found her lying on the left side of her face. Dolan touched her head and hand and found them cooler than her husband's corpse. He also noticed that her blood had coagulated and was of a dark color. Indeed, "the blood on the head was matted and practically dry." He found a bloody handkerchief near Abby's head. As Dolan recounted the gory details, Lizzie Borden hid her face under her fan.

After those initial examinations, Dolan arranged for photographs to be taken of the crime scenes and of the bodies. He then set about gathering the medical evidence that would be needed to determine the time and the cause of death. The grisly procedure had a shocking banality in his retelling. He collected samples of the morning's milk and the prior day's milk. He undressed Andrew Borden's body and laid it on an undertaker's board in the same room. He removed Andrew's stomach and put it into a clean jar. He repeated the same procedure for Abby. He packed both stomachs and two jars of milk and sent

Andrew Borden, August 4, 1892, *courtesy of Fall River Historical Society*

them express to Professor Wood at Harvard. Later, he examined the two wood axes and two hatchets found in the cellar. Dolan thought "the heavy claw hammered hatchet . . . looked as though it had been scraped." He also saw spots that looked like rust or blood. Using a microscope, he found two hairs. Those, too, would go to Professor Wood, but he delivered them personally on August 9. Also in that package was a "dress waist, a dress skirt, and an under white skirt" worn by Lizzie on which "there is a minute pin spot of blood."

A more thorough autopsy would wait for a week. He performed that on August 11 at Oak Grove Cemetery. There he cut off the heads and cleaned the skulls. (How and where he rendered off the flesh is not known, but his son later claimed he used lobster pots at the family home for the grisly procedure.) Before testifying, he made plaster casts of the heads to show the positions of the wounds, gruesome exhibits for the trial. Mr. Borden had ten wounds on his head, ranging from two inches to four and a half inches long—all marked in blue ink. Part of the skull by the left ear was crushed. The attack on Mrs. Borden had been even more vicious: there were eighteen head wounds in total,

Abby Borden, August 4, 1892, *courtesy of Fall River Historical Society*

thirteen of which went through the skull. The wounds ranged in size from half an inch to five and a half inches. The right side of her skull also displayed a crushing injury. Abby's last wound (or her first—it was impossible to tell) was of particular interest to Knowlton—a wound at the base of the neck. As Dolan explained the location of the wound, Adams offered Knowlton chalk so that the witness could mark his coat. Knowlton testily refused. Adams, with calculated bonhomie, told the witness: "I have no objection to your marking my coat, and you may do it with a piece of chalk, so that we may see the location and extent of that injury. I hope that I shall not be numbered as an exhibit." When it was his turn to cross-examine Dolan, he did precisely that and turned his back to the jury to display the location of the wound.

As the local physician Albert Dedrick had already testified, Dolan explained that the state of the victims' digestion showed a difference in time of death. Andrew's small intestine was clear and his large intestine was full of solid feces. By contrast, Abby's lower intestine was clear and there was still undigested food in the small intestine. Based on this evidence, Dr. Dolan confirmed that Mrs. Borden died an hour and a half to two hours earlier than her husband. Most critically, Knowlton asked, "Were the wounds that you found upon the skull of Mr. Borden such as could have been inflicted with a hatchet by a woman of ordinary strength?"

"Yes," replied Dr. Dolan.

Adams clearly expected Robinson to challenge Dolan's opinion. Adams said, apparently to Robinson: "Wait a moment. Do you want that?" Knowlton paused politely, then said, "You asked me to wait, so I am waiting." Snapping to attention, Robinson said that he had objected. Knowlton replied that he had not heard him do so. Adams retreated: "We do not insist upon the objection." Knowlton then repeated his question and received another affirmative reply. All in all, it was an odd exchange that underscored the very point most damaging to the defense case.

Adams may not have been able to prevent Dolan from giving his opinion about Lizzie Borden's physical capacity to commit the crime; however, his cross-examination showed the jury that Dr. Dolan had been in less control of the crime scene than he had suggested and that he had perhaps leapt to conclusions about other forensic evidence. Dolan had referred to the state in which he had found the victims as if that were the original state in which they had been found. Adams pointed out one of the policemen (Doherty) "had been there ahead of you and lifted up this woman" and "that Dr. Bowen . . . had pulled out [Abby's] right hand" to check her pulse. Adams also questioned him about the space between the bed and the bureau in which Abby was found. Doherty had also moved the bed—how much? Adams then asked about the hatchets and axes in the cellar. Dolan admitted, reluctantly, after hearing his own preliminary hearing testimony read back to him, that he had originally thought the claw hammer hatchet was the murder weapon. He claimed that, at that time, he had not yet prepared the skulls and therefore did not fully understand the nature of the injuries. He also admitted that he had mistakenly thought there was human hair on the axe. Overall, it was a dispiriting performance by a key prosecution witness.

Summarizing the afternoon's events, Julian Ralph concluded: "The seventh day of the Borden trial did not discredit the reputation the cause has earned as unique and crowded with sensations. Gore and hatchets, axes, plaster casts that might have been borrowed from a Bowery chamber of horrors, bloody garments, bits of bloody carpet and blood-spattered furniture and house fittings—these were the stage properties in this legal drama." Yet he also noticed something interesting about Lizzie Borden herself on the first day of intense medical testimony: "It is said that this woman has no art. That is a mistake . . . Whenever the lawyers who oppose her come to the subject of blood-stains, and the discussion of the gory details of the murders, she hides her face in her hands, but when her own lawyers take up the same subjects of inquiry she keeps her head up and her eyes bright, and tries not to miss a word of what is said. At first it was thought that she could not endure the horrible topic, but enough time has passed to show that it depends upon who discusses it." "Of course," he quickly added, stepping back from the implications of his observation, "this is very natural, and quite feminine, and amounts to nothing one way or the other."

TUESDAY, JUNE 13, 1893

On Tuesday, a light rain in the early morning "seemed only to intensify the discomfort and the irritation of all enveloped by the steaming atmosphere." But this repeat of the prior week's heat wave did nothing to dampen the prospective spectators' enthusiasm for the trial. "Surely," wrote Elizabeth Jordan, "the green grass and the flowers and the waving trees are a prettier sight than the mortuary relics and the awful human misery within, but the women of New Bedford do not seem to think so." The courthouse, according to Joe Howard, "was the scene of universal attraction, the mecca toward which all footsteps tended." Over an hour before the courtroom opened, "the same old crowd was on hand . . . It took four stalwart policemen to hold the three-foot gate, and they were being worsted in the fight when the deputy at the door came to their rescue with a signal to 'let them come,' given ten minutes early." The unexpected arrival of a truant officer "created a panic among the messenger boys. Some of them have been playing 'hookey' to get into the trial and as a purely outside issue earn a few spare quarters." By contrast, the interior of the courthouse was serene: Lizzie Borden arrived at "her usual time, five minutes before 9 o'clock." Though "clad a la mode," she appeared pale, perhaps "anticipating the horrors of the day." For her, the horrors began with the spectators: "the wild-eyed, haggard-featured, thick-skinned women" in the audience "stared at her through their spectacles and opera glasses as though she were a beast." Julian Ralph lamented that the women "create a hostile atmosphere in the courtroom" and "in that cruel environment the prisoner sits every day . . . the loneliest girl of wealth and social position in all America."

Upon arriving, the attorneys immediately went to the judges' room for a private meeting. But whatever the legal teams discussed took no more than five minutes and the proceedings resumed. It was to be a day, in Julian Ralph's words, of "blood, skulls, and bowels."

Dr. Dolan returned to the stand, the first medical expert in a series of witnesses. All were called to establish the estimated times of death, the interval between the murders, and the likely weapon used. The longer the interval between the two murders, the harder it would have been for an outside assailant to lurk in the house undetected. The prosecution also hoped to show that one or more of the hatchets in the house could have been the murder weapon. The identification of the murder weapon cut, as it were, both ways. If the prosecution could not point out the murder weapon, then it needed a theory of its disposal to shore up its case against Lizzie Borden. But the absence of a murder weapon also seemed inconsistent with an outside murderer. It was one thing to imagine a murderer escaping into the midday traffic; it was quite another to imagine his carrying away a bloody hatchet.

Adams resumed Dr. Dolan's cross-examination. He sought to unsettle the timeline, to narrow the interval between the murders and to push Andrew's time of death as late as possible. The defense wanted to give its hypothetical intruder more time to enter and to exit unobserved. To do so, Adams questioned how Dolan arrived at the time of death. The answer was threefold: blood coagulation, body temperature, and state of digestion. But, under pressure, Dolan admitted that blood coagulation was not a reliable indicator of the time of death after fifteen minutes. What about body temperature? Dolan explained that Andrew was still warm, yet Abby felt cool to the touch. Adams affected skepticism: Dolan used no thermometer. How could he be certain? Well, there was always the digestion. Assuming both Abby and Andrew ate their breakfast together, as Bridget Sullivan and John Morse had testified, then the progress of the solids through their respective intestinal tract would provide the answer. Unlike Abby's, Andrew's intestine contained solid feces, suggesting that he died more than an hour later. Unfazed, Adams observed, "Well, the stomach is a rebellious member of the body . . . and often doesn't perform its duty well?" He asked if food sometimes passed through the intestines undigested. Dolan said that would not happen in a normal stomach and neither Abby's nor Andrew's stomach showed any evidence of inflammation that would account for such dysfunction. But, Adams wondered, could Dolan be certain that was not the case here, especially in light of the food poisoning incident? Dolan grudgingly admitted it was possible and, therefore, that the intestinal contents were not sufficient to provide a definitive time of death. By the end of Adams's cross-examination, it was easy to forget that, taken together, the scientific evidence of time of death was clear.

But Adams was not finished. Knowlton had already explored the wounds in detail; the defense wanted its own turn. As Julian Ralph observed, "Horror has been piled upon misery . . . For two days the medical examiner has been going over and over the bloody details of the two murders." It was too much for some listeners. Juror Hodges, the oldest man on the jury, felt woozy and seemed on the verge of fainting, forcing a brief recess until "vigorous fanning, strong salts, and a change of position" restored him and permitted the trial to resume.

The number and size of the wounds gave the defense a useful argument about the murder weapon. Did the prosecution really have a plausible candidate? What sort of a weapon could have produced wounds of varying size and depth? The claw-hammer hatchet, initially thought to be the murder weapon, was about four and a half inches long. The handleless or "hoodoo" hatchet was only three and a half inches long. Yet, one of Abby's deepest wounds was only about two inches wide and others were much longer. At the preliminary hearing, Dr. Dolan had favored the claw hammer as the murder weapon; the day before, he preferred the "hoodoo" hatchet. He agreed with Knowlton that "nothing in the length of wounds . . . is inconsistent with their having been inflicted by a weapon, for example, of three and one half inches in length." Adams suggested an even more basic explanation, asking: "Is there anything unreasonable in a cutting edge four and a half inches in length making a wound on the head or face four and a half inches in length?" The handleless hatchet presented another problem: Was it really sharp enough to have bisected Andrew's eye? Adams asked Dolan if the hatchet had "a good edge, a sharp cutting edge?" Dolan's affirmative prompted a sarcastic follow-up question: "Did you observe that the edge is turned?" When Dolan claimed not to see it, Adams was incredulous and redoubled his attack: "[N]otwithstanding the anatomy of the eye . . . you think a blow which cuts through these three outer coverings and the humor inside—this injury could have been done by a hatchet?"

Flustered by the hatchet question, Dr. Dolan also admitted that blood spatter would have reached the assailant. But he did so reluctantly. Howard observed that Dolan, "an excellent arguer, seemed to have an idea that he must bother the defense as much as possible." Denying he had ever believed that the murderer stood in the dining room, reaching around the doorjamb to kill Andrew, Dolan explained that the assailant likely stood at the head of the sofa and, in Adams's formulation, "rained blow after blow, left and right." He agreed that the murderer would have been spattered with blood on the upper part of the body and also the hands. Dolan believed that, after stunning Abby with an initial blow, the murderer stood astride Abby's body. That position would, of necessity, result in some blood spatter as well.

Professor Edward S. Wood, *courtesy of Fall River Historical Society*

Adams repeatedly attempted to lure Dolan into an opinion that the blows were delivered with great force. The blows that entered Abby's skull had to pass through a mass of hair as well as a thick part of the skull itself. Dolan would not commit to a description of Abby's hair. Howard wrote: "Although this gentleman has cut off Mrs. Borden's head, he could tell nothing about her hair, but he knew all about the wounds, which he had examined and counted, and which he described with such graphic zeal as to send the red blood to the prisoner's face and the hot tears to her eyes, both of which she hid as well as she could with her handkerchief and eyes." Dolan, however, stood firm on the most critical point that the blows required no more than ordinary strength. Indeed, all the medical professionals agreed that a woman could have inflicted the wounds, but the very brutality of the murders favored the defense and was worth emphasizing. Moreover, Howard argued, "thus far the learned brothers have not taken a step to establish the guilt of the accused, nor have they put in one scintilla of testimony which connects her with the case or which does not trend just as certainly in the direction of Bridget Sullivan as in that of Lizzie Borden."

The next witness, Dr. Edward S. Wood, was a professor of chemistry at Harvard Medical School. Wood was the first of a distinguished roster of prosecution medical experts. A "red-faced, gray-haired, stalwart, and handsome man," he looked less like a scientist than "an army officer burned brown by a long life on the plains." He may have been built like "a heavy-weight pugilist," but he was the most distinguished expert at the trial. He alone had years of experience, including investigations of several hundred medicolegal poison and bloodstain cases.

As Howard explained, "Knowlton, in his most gracious way, gently led the professor along a commendatory autobiography, eliciting the fact that he is an expert in medical chemistry and is in every sense on the topmost twig of his branch of a dignified and honorable profession."

Wood testified that he received an express box containing the Borden's stomachs. Later, he received a trunk containing a hatchet, dresses, and carpet and hair samples. Wood began "with a recital of the most repellent, bloody, and altogether unpleasant things that not even a Borden trial could be expected to bring out." Yet, as with the earlier grisly medical testimony, Lizzie seemed transfixed. According to Ralph, "Lizzie Borden's interest in his testimony, bloody and hideous as it was, had no shadow of concealment. It amazed this semi-rustic girl to meet with a man who could extract eloquence from mute, insensate things."

Unlike Dolan, Wood gave his testimony in complete paragraphs "as though lecturing to a class, impressing every hearer with its factualness." First, he examined the stomachs, detailing their contents and concluding that Andrew's digestion was more advanced than Abby's. What he had seen chimed with other estimates of their respective times of death. He calculated that Andrew had lived about an hour and a half longer. He had found no poison in the stomachs, nor had he found any in the milk from August 3 or August 4. To rule out different rates of blood absorption in the upstairs and downstairs carpet samples, he performed a ghoulish experiment: "I opened an artery in the leg of a dog, and let about an ounce or two of blood flow upon both pieces of carpet, and I found they absorbed with equal rapidity."

Wood then turned to the weaponry. He was sent a claw-hammer hatchet with a handle that fit the wounds imperfectly. He subjected the stains on the claw-hammer hatchet "to chemical tests and microscopic tests for the presence of blood, with absolute negative results." Knowlton interrupted him to ask whether the hatchet could have been used and then cleaned. Wood averred that the hatchet "could not have been washed quickly" because of "cavities in between the head and handle . . . in front and behind." With the irritation befitting an eminent professor dealing with a remedial student, he added, "I have already pointed them out." As for the hair found on the hatchet, he found only one in the envelope, not two, and concluded it was animal hair, likely belonging to a cow. Howard gleefully wrote that the neighboring cow then "broke forth into a long and most emphatic wail, just as the expert on the stand testified."

Wood had more to say about the other hatchet he examined, the now infamous handleless hatchet the prosecution believed was the likely murder weapon. He discussed "a white film upon both sides . . . adherent tightly . . . in little cavities here in the rusty surface . . . white dirt, like ashes." As for whether the hatchet could have been cleaned, Wood agreed that it could have been before the handle was broken. These questions prompted repeated objections from Adams. Wood was allowed to answer and further testified that it could not have been broken for long or it would have been "darker and dirtier." On cross-examination, Adams pointed out the "slot on the inner edge of the head" and suggested that "it would be quite a place to clean." Wood agreed. Adams also suggested a plausible explanation for the layer of white dust—it could have fallen into damp ashes.

Wood then moved on to the clothing he had been sent. Except for the white under skirt, he had found no blood. He testified that he found a tiny blood spot—even smaller than the one-sixteenth of an inch estimated—measuring exactly one-thirty-two-forty-third of an inch (1/3243) on the under skirt. It was "thicker upon the outside than upon the inside," leading him to hypothesize that it "probably came on to the skirt from the outside . . . and not from the inside." However, he could not rule out a natural source for the blood spot. On cross-examination, Adams asked if he could exclude menstrual blood. Wood replied that he could not.

The issue of menstruation was a critical point, yet neither the defense nor the prosecution wished to emphasize it. Joe Howard set the tone, writing with uncharacteristic vagueness of the blood spot, "The defense claim, for reasons not necessary to publish . . . that this blood is natural." During Assistant Marshal Fleet's testimony, Robinson introduced the subject of the toilet pail in the cellar and said: "It is agreed that the pail contains the napkins which had been worn within a day or two by the defendant—ordinary monthly sickness—and as to that fact that is all we propose to put in. We do not care to go into the details. It is also agreed that the sickness ended Wednesday night." Robinson was content to let that fact explain the bloody towels soaking in the cellar toilet pail as well as the spot of blood on Lizzie's inner skirt and to move quickly on. But the prosecution's reluctance to explore the issue was surprising. Menstruation, according to medical experts, made women vulnerable to criminal impulses. When Doherty began to describe the pail of bloody towels found during his search of the cellar, Moody curtly interrupted, "Pass from those." Even Borden's suspicious nocturnal visit to the cellar the night after the murders, recounted by Officer Hyde earlier that day, was largely assumed to be related to her "monthly illness." Despite the potential significance of the evidence, the men all let the matter drop; they averted their gaze from the contents of the pail as if it would require staring into the abyss.

Though neither side wished to explore the bloody contents of the pail, they were quite happy to discuss blood spatter. The defense sought to make the crimes as bloody as possible—given the lack of blood found on Lizzie. But Wood was initially unhelpful. He insisted that, given the nature of the blows, blood "might spatter in any direction and might not spatter in every direction." So perhaps the assailant would not have been covered with blood. On cross-examination, Adams methodically worked through the likely scenarios to demonstrate that the murderer could not have avoided blood spatter. Wood agreed that, if Andrew's assailant had been standing behind him, then "I don't see how he could avoid being spattered" above the waist. Also, if one assumed the assailant stood astride Abby, there would have been blood spatter over the lower part of the body. Like Dolan before him, then, Wood finally agreed that the murders were a bloody affair. By the end of the day, Howard expressed his frustration with the medical witnesses: "Witness after witness goes over the same story, describes that with which the jury are nauseatingly familiar, proving again and again facts about which there is no dispute, that the Bordens are dead, that they were brutally murdered, that there was blood all over the place, that they had eaten a mild and moderate breakfast, all of which was found in their several intestinal parts, some digested and some not—and that's all."

The next two witnesses were also Harvard men. Dr. Frank Draper was both a professor of legal medicine (also known as medical jurisprudence) and the medical examiner for Suffolk County (including Boston). Draper had been present at the autopsy performed on August 11. At the time of the Borden murders, he was a former president of the Massachusetts Medico-Legal Society, the organization of medical examiners. By statute, medical examiners were called in "all cases of suspicion." Draper himself had already investigated over 3,500 deaths. By the end of his career, that number would rise to over 8,000 deaths, and, as a capstone, he would publish a *Textbook of Legal Medicine* in 1905. Earlier, he had apparently had some doubts about the times of death. In his correspondence with Attorney General Pillsbury, Knowlton assured his boss that "Dr. Draper is coming round on our side in great shape." Draper himself submitted a memorandum showing "the anatomical proofs of the priority of Mrs. Borden's death," a memorandum that tracked his later testimony. As a pragmatic matter, he recommended avoiding "incidental questions, which are very fascinating in themselves"—such as the "probable first blow in each of the two cases" and "the relative position of Mrs. Borden and her assailant when the first blow was struck"—on the grounds that they would "afford ready opportunity for disagreement among the medical witnesses." Such disagreements, he thought, ran the risk of "interpos[ing] a little dust between the eyes of the jury and the main questions, namely, what was the cause of the deaths and who was the guilty agent?" To that practical consideration, he added a personal note: "Will you kindly put me in communication with a New Bedford host or hostess who will take care

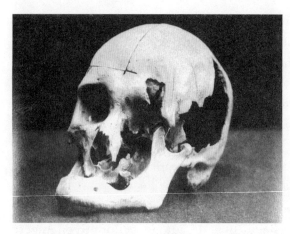

Skull of Andrew Borden,
courtesy of Fall River Histori-
cal Society

of my animal wants as to sleeping and eating during my visit? . . . I am always upset and good for nothing if I am deprived of sleep."

Draper displayed plaster casts of skulls on which he had drawn marks for wounds, and, while holding the one representing Andrew Borden, methodically detailed each blow. Jennings interrupted to ask how many had "penetrate[d] the bone of the skull?" "Four of them," he replied. "The one which cut through the eye, and three . . . above and in front of the left ear." It was almost too much for Lizzie Borden, who put her head down against the back of Robinson's chair. Fortunately, it was time for the midday recess.

The afternoon brought a return of Dr. Draper and his plaster skulls to the stand. But after continuing his meticulous discussion of the injuries, Draper required an additional exhibit. Knowlton asked Dr. Dolan to bring in the actual skull of Andrew Borden. Ralph remarked that the skull was "done up in a white handkerchief and looked like a bouquet, such as a man carries to his sweetheart." By arrangement, Lizzie was spared this display. According to Howard, "District Atty Knowlton, in spite of his forceful manner, has a very tender heart, is a good husband and a considerate father." He, therefore, agreed to let Lizzie Borden wait in "the little adjacency, where although she could neither see nor be seen, she could hear all she chose." Her absence seemed especially fortuitous when Draper unwrapped the skull

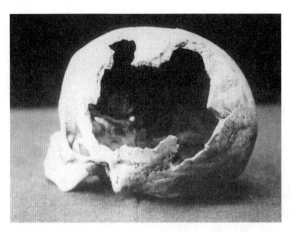

Skull of Abby Borden, *courtesy of Fall River Historical Society*

and the jaw was separated from the rest. Even worse, when Draper put the skull on a makeshift stand of law books, "The old man's jaw sagged back and forth in a grisly suggestion of speech." Recalling that moment, Elizabeth Jordan wrote: "Spectators caught their breath and then exhaled it in a gasp that swept the courtroom like a great sigh." Was he "trying to testify"? Ralph scribbled a question to Jordan: "If the old man, awakened by the first blow, saw his murderer would he tell who it was? If he saw that it was his daughter would he say so?" Jordan replied, "No, not if he was a good man." Howard was struck by the ghastly nature of the exhibits: "The skulls didn't look like the skulls we see in museums, dried and covered with parchment skin. They have been scraped, cleansed, and whitened, the jaws being separated from the general skull." He wondered: "Hideous indeed are they to casual observers, but what would they have been to Miss Lizzie Borden . . . with their eyeless sockets, their toothless gums, their fleshless bones . . . mute witnesses to the brutality of their assassin."

The reporters may have been horrified, but Draper "had a cheery way of fitting the different hatchets into the wounds in the skull." Ralph observed: "Occasionally he would leave one sticking in and then parade it round in front of the jury." Draper initially used a tin plate to demonstrate that the murder weapon had a blade of three and a half inches, the length of the handleless hatchet; at one point,

Dr. Draper fits hatchet into skull, *Boston Globe*

a colleague came forward to hold the skull while Draper fit the plate into a crater. At Knowlton's urging, he used the hatchet itself. Most important, he testified that all the blows could "have been produced by the use of an ordinary hatchet in the hands of a woman of ordinary strength." As a way of helping the jury overcome any lingering doubt that a woman could have inflicted the wounds, Draper also explained that Andrew's skull was very thin, so thin in the temple region that light passed through it.

Draper, like the other medical experts, explained the likely position of the murderer during the crimes. In Abby's murder, "The assailant . . . stood astride the prostrate body of Mrs. Borden, as she was lying face downward on the floor" except when inflicting the wound in the scalp on the left side of her head. That was delivered "while Mrs. Borden was standing and facing her assailant." As for Andrew, he concluded that "he was lying on the sofa on his right side, with the face turned well toward the right." He agreed "that the assailant stood about the head of the sofa, above the head of Mr. Borden, and struck downward upon his head and face." He could not conclusively determine "the direction of the spattering or scattering of the blood."

Adams's cross-examination also covered familiar ground. First, he drew Draper's attention to the wound which "went down through the eyebrow, through the eye, and into the cheek bone." Draper had explained that the bone over the eye "is strong . . . well thickened and buttressed." (Draper clarified: "The thickest point is at the back; the next thickest point is over the top.") In light of that anatomy, asked Adams, "Was it a blow that required considerable force?" Draper agreed, after some wrangling, that it was "the heaviest blow."

Second, Adams drew Draper's attention to the bloodstains at the scene. Draper explained that one of the blows severed Andrew's carotid artery. Surely that plus the injuries to Andrew's temple would also result in a large blood flow? Draper explained that the severed artery would not "cause a spurt"; instead "it would sputter or bubble out through the wound, but would not go beyond the immediate surface of the wound." Adams inquired: Wouldn't "the instrument, whatever it was . . . be naturally covered" with blood such that the "swinging of the weapon and . . . the impact of the weapon" would account for the blood spots on the wall above Andrew and around the sitting room generally? Draper cautiously agreed. As for whether the assailant would have been "spattered," Draper answered, "The part that was exposed, that was not covered either by furniture or by other protecting substances." Draper cautioned that there is no rule of blood spatter. It was impossible for him to rule out or rule in any particular direction of blood spatter. When asked about Abby's murder, Draper made a similar point. Assuming the assailant stood astride the victim, "I should think the front of the dress; possibly the face, possibly the hair." Alive to any assumption that the murderer was female, Adams quickly followed up: "When you say the dress, you speak of the clothing worn by both sexes?"

Third, Adams turned to the weapon that Draper had neatly fit into Andrew's skull. It fit too well for the defense's comfort. He asked: "The handleless hatchet is not an uncommon instrument, is it?" Draper agreed. Adams continued: "It has a very general circulation?" Draper cautiously hedged: "I think so." Adams then produced a hatchet with the same size cutting edge and asked him to fit it in the skull. He seemed to want Draper to note that the typical handle for such a hatchet was about a foot long. Unfortunately for Adams, his new hatchet did not fit as neatly as the one found at the Borden house. Adams's point had been to force Draper to note the length of the foot-long handle standard on such a hatchet, leading him to a discussion of the proximity of the assailant to the victims. Knowlton, however, seized on this apparent miscalculation to show that "not all hatchets with a cutting edge of three and a half inches would fit the wound." He then asked whether the handleless hatchet could have inflicted those wounds.

Adams said, "Wait a moment."

Knowlton explained, "I don't think I asked that question before . . . I had it on my memorandum, but in the numerous details, it escaped me. I did ask whether a hatchet of three and a half inches would. Now I ask whether that hatchet could have done it."

Adams protested that Knowlton had asked "that precise question . . . in the direct examination."

Knowlton turned to him and asked: "What did you understand the answer to be, Mr. Adams?"

The seasoned trial lawyer Adams replied, "I do not propose to tell what the answer was." Draper agreed that the handleless hatchet could indeed have caused all of the wounds.

Adams asked Draper to make a chalk mark showing "the length, location, and direction" of Abby's wound on his own back. Draper described it "as a clean cut wound in the neck, where the neck joins the shoulders, just to the left of the middle line." He explained that the wound could have come from a blow originating "from below upward, from the right toward the left . . . [or] from the left toward the right, downward." He believed the latter description was most likely, but the marks in the skull were all beveled right to left. Draper explained that this meant that the blows came from right to left: "It is a clear indication of the plane at which the edge of the weapon came down upon the plane of the skull." He added: "I found none that would be an exception to the rule."

Finally, Adams did everything possible to make the hatchet hard to clean. No bloody implement had been found in the Borden house: if Lizzie was the killer, then the weapon must still be in the house. How quickly would the blood dry on a hot day "in August, in our climate"? Wouldn't the blood "readily and quickly intermingle with the meshes of clothing and coarse substances like dirt or rust?" Draper thought it would be possible to remove the blood but agreed "that it would not be easily done."

To break the monotony of "a miserable, poky, mind-wearing, physique-exhausting session," the columnists shared their accounts of a curious incident in the courtroom. A young freelance illustrator named de Lipman had permission to attend the trial but could not find a place to sit. He relied upon his colleagues to let him rotate through their assigned seats. But the sheriff had decided that his frequent movements constituted a disturbance and had him ejected "with unnecessary violence." Elizabeth Jordan wrote: "Without a word the Sheriff set upon him a heavy-weight deputy, who seized him by the collar as he was bending over his work, dragged him brutally, and breaking the desk before him and splashing ink all over his clothes, shoving and pushing him as though he were a drunken disturber." Outraged, Howard wrote: "Officials ought to understand that newspaper workers don't attend trials for fun . . . They are present for the transaction of mind-straining, muscle-wearing business in the interests of thousands of individuals who are following intelligently the . . . celebrated case."

The last medical expert was Dr. David W. Cheever, a professor of surgery at Harvard Medical School and former president of the Massachusetts Medical Society. In recommending him to Knowlton, Draper wrote: "To wide knowledge and experience, he adds a peculiarly cool and impressive manner, and is reckoned here a model witness." Cheever had practiced for thirty-five years and had been teaching at

Harvard since the year of Lizzie Borden's birth. "Mild, deliberate, and gracious," Cheever was "very tall, very thin, very methodical and very slow" in his manner. He agreed with his colleagues on the prosecution's most salient points: the order of death, the interval between the two murders, the nature of the wounds, and the likely murder weapon.

Based on his examination of the skulls, Cheever described the murder weapon as "a heavy, metallic weapon with a cutting edge beveled, with a sharp angle, and with the cutting edge not exceeding three and a half inches in length." He agreed that the handleless hatchet could be the culprit, fitting it into the depressions in the skull. Unlike the others, he emphasized that the cutting edge could have been shorter than three and a half inches, but no longer. He had found a notch in one of Andrew's injuries that showed the maximum length of the edge.

But he, like the others, also testified that the assailant would likely have been spattered with blood. Dr. Cheever testified that both arteries in Andrew's head were cut. The temporal artery might spurt a distance of two or three feet, assuming it was exposed. As for the carotid artery wound, whether or not "there would be a good deal of effusion of blood" depended upon whether it was one of the first blows or one of the last. Dr. Cheever said that, for surgeries on the head, he wore protective outer clothing, a "linen jacket or a white linen gown" and "sometimes an India rubber apron." Adams slyly asked why he needed protection.

"Blood," replied Dr. Cheever.

In this as in his prior questions about blood splatter, Adams took care to make the assailant male, asking, for instance, about blood in a beard. Knowlton, however, turned the surgeon's outerwear to the prosecution's advantage.

He asked Cheever: "The garment you speak of, when you put it on in your surgical operations, protects your clothing entirely?"

Cheever not only agreed but also added, to Adams' chagrin, that the garment is "changed between every operation, with rapidity."

Moreover, Cheever testified, like his predecessors, that the wounds could have been inflicted by "a woman of ordinary strength"—"[w]ith a handle of sufficiently long leverage," he added, "I should think not less than twelve or fourteen inches." This length matched the likely handle length of the "handleless" hatchet. Cheever provided a "dramatic illustration" of one of the blows by holding the hatchet "aloft" over his full height, "inclined to the left . . . then [it] flashed through the air, straight as it seemed for the skull of Mr. Adams."

But just before "it seemed as if the crash of bone must be heard," Elizabeth Jordan wrote, "the hatchet stopped and remained steady." The result: a collective gasp, followed by nearly a minute of silence. Adams scored another point when Cheever explained that most of the blows fell from right to left, but that a few might have been left to right. "That is," Adams clarified, "right to left, wood chopping fashion?" Wood chopping, after all, was seen as "male."

The notion that a crime could be clearly gendered was rooted in European models of criminology, but such models of criminality struggled to account for a female criminal. Within the prevailing models of the human mind, women were seen as somewhat less evolved than men and with a corresponding lack of rational control over their actions—barely protected from their underlying degeneracy by male control, especially over their sexuality. Even Lombroso revised his model of the "born criminal" to fit the female counterpart. Though fewer in number than the male "born criminal," the female "born criminal" surpasses him in cruelty and in the exaggerated atavism of her features and sentiment. Because the less civilized woman is really merely impure and not criminal, Lombroso argued that women destined to criminal activity are morally more depraved than their male counterparts. While prostitution is an understandable, even natural atavistic impulse, nonsexual crime represents true depravity for women. "As a double exception," Lombroso wrote, "the criminal woman is a monster." Lombroso, however, noted one exception to his "double exception": "the peculiarity of the female criminal lunatic . . . is that her madness becomes more acute at particular periods." One of those periods was menstruation.

Lizzie Borden's arrest unsettled an ethnically and class-determined model of criminality and, as Jennings had argued at the prelimi-nary hearing, outraged "the natural course of things." As a white, upper-middle-class "lady," Borden fell safely outside the evolutionary framework of degeneration that underlay nineteenth-century crimino-logical discussions. Could the secretary-treasurer of the local Christian Endeavor Society and member of the Ladies' Fruit and Flower Mission be a born criminal? Her combination of good works and an acceptable percentage of noncriminal features—with the exception of her over-sized jaw—seemed to acquit her of that damning charge. Lombroso's model of criminality determined by class, ethnicity, and gender could not reconcile the idea of Lizzie Borden repeatedly wielding a hatchet with the image of the gloved Miss Lizzie who nearly fainted in court. As Howard had pointed out, the medical consensus that a woman of ordinary strength could have directed the blows "trend[ed] just as certainly in the direction of Bridget Sullivan as Lizzie Borden." And Bridget Sullivan was not a lady.

Chapter 8

INTENT, DELIBERATION, AND PREPARATION

Interesting incidents in the Borden trial, *Boston Globe*

I t was widely thought that the prosecution would conclude its case on Wednesday. As he reflected on the developments in the trial, Joe Howard praised the efficiency of the court: "always on time, never loses a second." Julian Ralph, too, commented on the pace of the trial, taking special note of how many witnesses had testified: "The phenomenal feature of this court is still the factorylike facility with which it shucks and shells the witnesses. There is a door behind the witness stand, and it never yet has been closed. It is a great spout that runs witnesses day after day as a faucet emits water." Even the

Witnesses waiting to testify, *Boston Globe*

stenographer, an anonymous figure of apparent continuity, was regularly refreshed: "The court stenographer sits at a desk under the eyes of the witnesses. But the stenographer is in reality a whole troop of short hand men . . . [who] dart in and out." Once cycled out, they handed off their scribblings to the pool of pretty "typewriter girls" who then produced the daily transcript.

WEDNESDAY, JUNE 14, 1893

The previous night's rain did nothing to improve the temperature on Wednesday. Joe Howard described the atmosphere as "more discomfort, heat, and humidity combined, than I had supposed possible in a city so advantageously situated." Even the locals found it oppressive. The *Fall River Daily Globe* declared: "There is no nourishment for the lungs in it. It is like breathing at the bottom of a river." Howard wondered: "How can the jury endure the physical strain?" He continued, "[T]hey are wilting in this torridic atmosphere, subjected as they are to more unusual confinement and seclusion, not alone from their ordinary occupation but from out of door exercise and healthful conditions to which one and all are used." Lizzie Borden, too, appeared "limp and without energy." (No matter how hot the day, she always wore gloves.) By contrast, despite the weather and the reversals in their case to date, the prosecution was eager to continue: "Knowlton rushed up the stairs two steps at a time, quickly and closely followed by his younger and smaller associate, Mr. Moody, both anxious and with determination in every glance."

City Marshal Rufus Hilliard, who had led the Fall River police department for seven years, was the first witness. To Joe Howard, Hilliard was "the deus ex machina of the whole business, having made up his mind in the earliest stage of the game that the Fall River police must have a theory." "A fine, orderly looking man," Hilliard sported "an enormous drooping brown moustache" and was outfitted for the summer heat in a light gray suit.

Hilliard testified about the official police response to the events at the Borden house. First, he recounted the newsdealer John Cunningham's call to him on August 4 to report the trouble on Second Street. After listing the officers he dispatched to the scene, he testified about his own search of the barn and outdoor areas on the morning of the murder (he had found the barn loft "almost suffocating"), on the Saturday after the funeral service (when he had to disperse a crowd of between two and three hundred outside the house), and on Sunday, August 7. Then he provided a window into the atmosphere of the Borden house the weekend after the murders. On the evening of Saturday, August 6, Hilliard and Mayor Coughlin called upon the inmates of the house—Morse, Emma, and Lizzie. In Hilliard's account of the visit, corroborated by others present, the mayor advised the family to stay inside for a few days because of the large crowd outside. Lizzie then asked if anyone in the house was suspected. After some hesitation, the mayor told her that she was suspected. Emma chimed in, "We tried to keep it from her as long as we could."

Robinson's favorite
poses, *Boston Globe*

On cross-examination, the "foxy" Robinson sought to reframe Lizzie's response as a study in innocence. Hilliard testified she had said, "I want to know the truth," and that she was "ready to go at any time."

"Spoke it right out?" Robinson asked.

Hilliard agreed.

"Earnestly?" Robinson wondered.

Hilliard agreed.

Robinson added, "Frankly?"

Hilliard again agreed.

"Sure about that?" asked Robinson.

"Yes," he admitted.

Mayor John Coughlin, the next witness, was less obliging. Howard lauded Mayor Coughlin as a "pleasant-faced, courteous-mannered individual" who was both "a square political and surgeon of repute." After testifying about the conversation on Saturday, August 6, he, unlike Hilliard, resisted Robinson's repeated attempts to present Lizzie's response in a positive light. Robinson asked him if Lizzie "spoke up . . . earnestly."

Coughlin finally answered, "I would not say she did not speak earnestly." Learning of the crowd that threatened John Morse on Friday, August 5, Coughlin accompanied Marshal Hilliard to the Borden house on the evening of Saturday, August 6, to advise the family not to leave the house. Coughlin asked Lizzie "where she went to after leaving her father." Lizzie told him that she had gone to the barn for about twenty minutes to look for lead (to make sinkers). Coughlin assured the family: "If you are disturbed in any way, or if you are annoyed by the crowds upon the street . . . I shall see that you receive all the protection that the police department can afford." Based on "the mayor's manner and words," Howard concluded that, despite his own penchant for conspiracy theories, "nothing occurred at the time of his visit which could in any way reflect against" him or even Hilliard.

Then came two women, as prosecution witnesses, with dark stories about the atmosphere in the Borden house. The Bordens' seamstress, Mrs. Hannah Gifford, was asked to recall an uncomfortable conversation with Lizzie Borden about her stepmother nearly six months before the murders. Robinson objected to her testimony. He described March 1892 as "too remote." But, in a blow for the defense, the judges decided she could answer. Gifford testified that after she casually referred to Abby as Lizzie's mother, Lizzie said, "Don't say that to me, for she is a mean, good-for-nothing thing."

Mrs. Gifford replied, "Oh Lizzie, you don't mean that?"

Lizzie said, "Yes, I don't have much to do with her; I stay in my room most of the time." As if for emphasis, she added, "[W]e don't eat with them if we can help it." Julian Ralph dismissed it as gossip unworthy of a criminal proceeding rather than "the firecracker that the District Attorney had promised."

Veiled Anna Borden posed more trouble for the defense. Anna Borden was, according to Ralph, "the most dainty and charming woman that has thus far appeared in this anything but dainty case." She and

Lizzie Borden shared a cabin on the ship returning from the European trip in 1890. The women had a common great-great-grandfather; however, Anna made a point of denying Lizzie Borden was her cousin. In Fall River, one did not have to claim anyone beyond a second cousin.

Before she could recount a conversation with Lizzie, Robinson again sought to have her story excluded. This time, the judges agreed to let the lawyers make their arguments out of the jury's hearing. In his offer of proof, Moody explained that Lizzie Borden told her repeatedly that she did not want to return to her "unhappy home." "This conversation," Moody said, was not "a mere passing word of resentment" but rather "repeated several times." Robinson distinguished that comment from the one made to the dressmaker in March 1892 on the grounds that the shipboard conversation was too remote in time and was not "an express declaration in regard to one individual." Moody retorted that Hannah Gifford's testimony demonstrated "the continuity of feeling" to spring 1892. The judges, however, sided with Robinson. They determined Lizzie's comments were "too ambiguous, so that aside from its remoteness the evidence is not competent."

Elizabeth Jordan doubted that the story would have damaged Lizzie's defense; yet, as with Alice Russell's testimony about the dress-burning, she considered Anna Borden's revelation a serious betrayal. She painted the scene in mawkish colors: "After this first glimpse of real sunshine Lizzie had had in her narrow, cheerless life, she had lamented the fact that she was coming back to the dreary gloom of her Puritan home. She had confided this much to her cousin on some cosy evening at sea and in the unbosoming intimacy which the close contact of shipboard life breeds, and now, two years later, those words spoken in confidence away off somewhere in the solitude of the North Atlantic, were coming home to her to weigh in the balance against her." Forty years later, Jordan imperfectly recalled the details of testimony but she well remembered her own reaction: "I could have strangled the creature as she sat in the witness chair, feeling important and smugly manufacturing her little strand of the rope that might hang her fellow-voyager."

Moody called a series of minor witnesses who had the distinction of reporting what they did not see on the morning of the murders: no suspicious strangers in the vicinity, no bloodstained maniacs fleeing the scene. They provided the testimonial equivalent of the curious incident of the dog in the Sherlock Holmes story, the dog that didn't bark in the nighttime. Robinson suggested alternative routes of escape in his questions to these witnesses, something they were in no position to dispute. For example, Lucy Collet testified that she had been on the veranda overlooking the Chagnon yard from 11:00 a.m. to 12:00 p.m. on August 4 but had not seen anyone escape over the fence. In response to Robinson's question, however, she admitted she had not seen one of the police officers climb the fence within that window of time. Similarly, the Chagnons' neighbor Aruba Kirby, "a very old lady who wore colored spectacles and who gave various evidences of defective sight," did not see anyone pass by the Chagnon yard at the time of the murders. Robinson's questions demonstrated that, in order to perform her work in the kitchen, she would mostly have been facing away from the window from which one might have spotted a departing murderer.

But Moody would have his revenge: he called Hannah Reagan, the matron of the Fall River police station, who had a tale to unfold. She had overheard a conversation between Lizzie and Emma Borden on August 24. Lizzie had been in her charge for nine or so days and Emma was a frequent visitor. But this time was different. While in an adjoining toilet room, she heard "very loud talk." She looked through the door and saw Lizzie lying on the couch with Emma bending over her.

Lizzie said, "Emma, you have gave me away, haven't you?" Emma denied it. Lizzie said, "You have . . . and I will let you see I won't give in one inch."

According to the matron, "[S]he sat right up and put up her finger" to demonstrate an inch. She then turned onto her left side, faced out the window, and did not speak again until Jennings arrived around 11:00 a.m. The prosecution never explained what Lizzie might have meant by her comment, but it was dynamite nonetheless. If true, Reagan's story undermined the sisters' public show of complete solidarity and revealed an almost preternaturally determined side of Lizzie Borden. Oddly enough, the *New York Times* reported that "Lizzie Borden was unusually cheerful today, and at the conclusion of Mrs. Reagan's testimony laughed and seemed more amused than disturbed by it."

Jennings, however, did not take the matron's story lightly. In his "clean cut, emphatic, and understandable" manner, Jennings attacked her story from every angle. First, he wanted her to admit she had denied the story to Reverend Buck and that she had declared herself willing to sign an affidavit refuting the story. Secondly, he wanted her to agree that Marshal Hilliard had ordered her not to sign the affidavit. Because he himself was present in the marshal's office and instrumental in seeking her signature, Jennings was effectively testifying through his questions. Matron Reagan, however, would not cooperate. She even declared that she could not recall Jennings's presence in the marshal's office that day. Jennings challenged her recollection of the time and day of the alleged conversation, mentioning Lizzie Borden's other regular visitors, Mrs. Charles J. Holmes; her daughter, Miss Annie Holmes; and the ever-attentive Reverend Buck, who visited every day she was held there. And his prompting disclosed an intriguing incident: Mrs. Reagan said that she had bet Lizzie a dollar that she could not break a raw egg by squeezing it in her hand. Lizzie was Andrew Borden's daughter and the apple had not fallen far from the tree: she was up to the challenge but would wager no more than a quarter. After failing the test, she announced, "That is the first thing that I undertook to do that I never could." According to Joe Howard, Jennings "succeeded in working the witness up to a point of defiance," noting Reagan claimed not to recall Lizzie's other visitors but remembered the overheard conversation between Lizzie and Emma verbatim. Even if the cross-examination had not shaken the matron's story, it had all been too much for her. She "staggered" rather than walked out of the room, past the Bordens' bloodstained sofa in the corridor, and collapsed in the next room.

The next witness, Eli Bence, was one the defense was keen to keep from testifying. When Bence took the stand, Lizzie "fairly glared at him, leaned forward and stared him squarely in the eye." Bence had barely begun to detail his service at D. R. Smith's drugstore when Robinson interrupted him to argue that he had a matter "of vital importance . . . to be discussed with the Court alone." Moody happily offered to explain what the prosecution expected to prove. Robinson hastily interjected: "I think you better not state it now." Before Moody could respond, he repeated, "It is nothing that ought to be stated now." Robinson did not want even a whisper of the prosecution's explanation to reach the men of the jury. The judges sent the jury out of the room.

Moody explained that the prosecution sought to offer Bence's testimony that Lizzie Borden had attempted to buy prussic acid on August 3, the day before the murders. Prussic acid, a 2 percent dilution of hydrocyanic acid, was "one of the most deadly poisons that is known to human kind." It was so toxic that, as early as 1837, a physician described it as "commonly used for suicide and is fit for little else." In the latter half of the nineteenth century, physicians prescribed a diluted solution as a sedative or antispasmodic, but it was not the preferred choice. At the normal prescription dilution, less than a teaspoon was a fatal dose.

Bence would also testify that no one had ever asked him for prussic acid before that day—even though, in his account of the conversation, Lizzie insisted that she had bought poison on many occasions—and that she wanted the drug to clean her sealskin cape. Robinson interrupted the presentation to confirm that there was no evidence of any sale at D. R. Smith's or anywhere else. In other words, he wanted to make sure that the prosecution was only proposing to offer evidence of her alleged attempt to buy poison.

Knowlton fielded the question, responding: "It would be fair to say we have evidence to show some attempt to purchase prussic acid in another place, with the same negative results."

Robinson immediately disputed the relevance of such evidence: Lizzie Borden was on trial for "killing these two people with a sharp instrument . . . Nothing else." Even if she did try to buy the substance, where was the connection to the murders? He elaborated: "It is an attempt to buy an article which is used for other purposes . . . [I]t is an article which a person may legitimately buy." He asked rhetorically: "Does it have any tendency at all to show that this defendant killed these two persons with an axe?" Answering his own question, he continued: to the contrary, "It is an attempt to charge her with an act causing death by a wholly different means."

Not at all, claimed Moody. It was not being introduced as evidence of attempted poisoning. Instead it was evidence of intent. Though he readily agreed that the "failure to purchase prussic acid on the 3rd day of August has no tendency whatever to show a killing by an axe on the 4th day of August," he explained that the prosecution needed to demonstrate the defendant's state of mind: "This indictment not only charges that the prisoner killed Mr. and Mrs. Borden, but that she did it with a certain intent and with premeditation." He declared: "[t]here is no purpose of offering this testimony . . . than as bearing upon the state of mind of the defendant prior to the homicide; the intent, the deliberation and the preparation."

Moody reminded the court of the Borden family's gastrointestinal distress the night of Tuesday, August 2. Moody did not claim that Borden poisoned her family; however, he explained that the food poisoning "was an illness suggestive of opportunity to a person desiring to procure the deaths of one or other of those people." In his view, Lizzie seized the moment. On Wednesday morning, she tried to buy poison. That night, Lizzie visited Alice Russell, planting clues about her father's nameless enemies who might harm the family. Thursday morning the hatchet fell. Moody argued that the events leading up to the murders showed her state of mind, specifically her "deliberation and premeditation." The standard for admitting relevant evidence was broad and only required the evidence to be pertinent to that question of intent. Moody asked: Did the attempt to buy prussic acid on Wednesday, August 3, indicate that "this prisoner was in what may be called a murderous state of mind?" Yes, he concluded, because prussic acid "is an article which is not sold except upon the prescription of a physician . . . [I]t is not used for the purpose of cleaning capes, sealskin capes, or capes of any other sort, and has no adaptability to such use."

Ever the master of succinct doctrinal analysis, Moody stated the common-law rule: "Where a given intent is in question . . . any act near in point of time and significant in character is competent, no matter whether it tends to prove the commission of another crime or not." Massachusetts law, as outlined in *Commonwealth v. Bradford,* 126 Mass. 42 (1878), was particularly clear on this point: "When a previous act indicates an existing purpose which, from known rules of human conduct, may be fairly presumed to continue and control the defendant in the doing of the act in question, it is admissible as evidence." Cases from other jurisdictions presented a wide range of factual situations, but each, according to Moody, bore on the central question in the Borden trial: "Was she deliberating mischief towards somebody?" Most important for the prosecution were cases in which the defendant "prepared" to commit a crime with one weapon, but then used a different one. That the defendant in an 1882 New York case, *Walsh v. People of the State of New York,* for example, sharpened a knife on the morning of a stabbing murder posed no great interpretative dilemma. But the court also permitted the state to offer evidence that the defendant asked whether throwing pepper in someone's eyes would cause blindness. Whether the evidence showing intent constituted an independent crime or whether the other acts might be considered innocent in other circumstances did not matter as long as the state offered sufficient evidence of intent in the case at the bar. And, in such cases, the jury should be allowed to draw its own inferences, giving the evidence whatever weight it deserved. To the prosecution, the parallel to the Borden case was indisputable.

Robinson, ignoring Moody's barrage of common-law precedent, disputed the fundamental issue. First and most important, he was not prepared to concede that Lizzie could only have wanted prussic acid for illicit reasons. If the prussic acid had an innocent use, then the attempted purchase did not reveal anything about Lizzie's state of mind. Second, he pointed out that, even assuming she had murder on her mind, "There is nothing to show to whom she meditated the malice." What if she had bought poison to kill Bridget Sullivan? In Robinson's view, the prosecution wanted to introduce the evidence only "to throw some sort of prejudice on the minds of men who are to pass on these facts."

With Lizzie's hostility to her stepmother in mind, Moody coolly responded: "There is a tendency to show to whom the malice is directed." But Robinson argued that the prosecution was bootstrapping, relying upon the murders to give sinister import to earlier inconsequential statements or actions. Taken together, the prosecution's entire showing of malice hinged on Lizzie's comment to the dressmaker in March 1892 and her terse correction of Assistant Marshal Fleet (who had referred to Abby as Lizzie's mother). Robinson pointed out that there was nothing in Lizzie's comment to the dressmaker "that anyone can say manifests a murderous intent, or an intent to injure, to harm physically." And, as for her comment to Assistant Marshal Fleet, Robinson blithely observed: "That was a statement of a truth in either case." He continued: "Now can that statement made by herself to the policeman, which was subsequent to the crime, or the statement made to Mrs. Gifford antecedent to the tragedy, be raised into the force of a declaration indicating any personal violence to Mrs. Borden?" Prior cases, he insisted, involved "an open, absolute, plain declaration of a criminal purpose." "But here," he continued, "there is nothing of that." Without a showing of murderous intent toward the victims, "This evidence ought not to go in so as to operate to the prejudice of this defendant before the jury, unless it is legally, logically and fairly competent to prove the act with which she stands charged."

Perhaps recognizing the weight of authority against his position, Robinson redoubled his efforts to provide innocent explanations for the prussic acid, "an article a person may legitimately buy." Almost in desperation, he asserted that "people buy prussic acid to kill animals— it may be the cat." (There was no cat.) He insisted: "That is innocent. It is not a crime, at any rate." Robinson made several attempts to distinguish the facts in the key cases even though the line of cases seemed uncomfortably on point.

Moody interrupted five times, correcting misstatements of fact. At one point, he simply said, "You mistook my point of illustration." In a rare show of temper, Robinson retorted that, if so, his error came from Moody's reference to something he had heard at a grand jury as one of his examples. Robinson tried again: "Take the Kansas case, which I never saw, but have just read in part." However inelegant his argument, Robinson hewed to his line that "an act which is itself innocent" must be assessed differently from one with "a felonious purpose." He concluded hopefully, "I must say I have said all the Court desires to hear, and I have made my meaning plain."

The judges retired for nearly an hour to consider the matter. Meanwhile, those in the courtroom fanned themselves and waited. "The heat tonight is something fearful," Howard lamented. "I don't see but what a charge of premeditated manslaughter might be suggested in case the jurors melt in their seats or the prisoner goes mad." When the judges returned, Chief Justice Mason asked the prosecution to restate the "purpose for which the testimony is offered." Moody responded that he was offering the testimony as "bearing on the state of mind of the defendant prior to the homicide; the intent, the deliberation and the preparation." The judges then pronounced the evidence competent, assuming "the preliminary evidence comes up to the proffer." In other words, if the actual testimony of the witnesses showed "intent," then the prosecution would have a chance to put Lizzie Borden's alleged attempt to buy poison in front of the jury.

This was a serious setback for the defense. Joe Howard resorted to even more circumlocution than usual to explain the stakes: if "the prosecution is permitted to utilize the prussic acid incident as corroborative proof of premeditation, a new element will have been added which in all candor it must be conceded by the warmest friends of the prisoner tends somewhat to becloud the defense." As Julian Ralph succinctly concluded: "Taken altogether, this was Lizzie Borden's worst day." The poison story also reverberated outside the courtroom. Ralph added: "These occurrences may not prove important in their effect on the jury, but they have had the result of changing many of Miss Borden's friends from enthusiasm to thoughtfulness." Unfortunately for the prosecution, it was time to adjourn.

THURSDAY, JUNE 15, 1893

Because of the poison cliffhanger, Thursday promised thrills for the aspiring spectator. The *New Bedford Evening Standard* reported: "At no time since the trial opened has there been any such rush for seats as there was this morning. At the stockade the officers in charge found it almost impossible to restrain the surging crowd, and several women who had taken up their positions near the entrance . . . were crushed until they screamed with pain." For those fortunate enough to gain admittance, the extreme heat added to the tension in the room. Joe Howard declared: "The atmosphere is supercharged with humidity, and there is not a comfortable individual in town." The judges had decided to allow the prosecution to present the evidence, but they insisted on hearing testimony about the uses of prussic acid out of the hearing of the jury. The jurors—"each armed with a palm leaf fan, and as full of iced water as human corporosities can be"—waited in another room as the prosecution called its witnesses.

The first witness, Charles Lawton, in partnership with his brother, owned two of the largest drugstores in New Bedford, with the "heaviest retail business in the city." He had over thirty years' experience in the trade, so he seemed well placed to know whether prussic acid might be obtained over the counter. Lawton said he kept the drug in stock. But when Knowlton asked him if prussic acid was ever sold in other than a diluted solution, Robinson objected. Knowlton tried another tack, inquiring if Lawton had ever sold prussic acid "other than as a medicine." Robinson objected. "In your experience as a druggist," Knowlton tried again, "Is that drug an article of commerce for any purpose other than as a medicine . . . or upon a prescription of a physician?" Robinson again objected. Knowlton rephrased the question: "Is the drug called prussic acid sold commercially for any other purpose than upon a prescription of a physician?" Robinson rose again to object. Knowlton added, "For medicinal purposes . . . ?" Robinson: "The same objection."

And so it went until Knowlton finally asked, "Do you know of any use to which prussic acid is put other than the purposes of a medicine?" Lawton replied, "Not that I know of." This was a tepid conclusion after all Knowlton's efforts.

Unable to show that druggists did not sell prussic acid except by doctor's prescription, Knowlton called two witnesses with practical and scientific expertise. The first, Henry Tillson, a New Bedford furrier, was prepared to swear that prussic acid was not used to clean furs. When queried on that point by Chief Judge Mason, Knowlton admitted that Tillson was not a scientist but had long practical experience. Knowlton asked: Based on his own experience, did he have "any knowledge of the effects of prussic acid on furs?"

Tillson replied: "Not at all."

Knowlton attempted to follow up and ask whether he had ever heard of anyone using prussic acid on furs. But Robinson quickly objected and Chief Justice Mason disallowed the query. Knowlton reluctantly surrendered and agreed to call his next witness, an analytical chemist named Nathaniel Hathaway.

Knowlton established Hathaway's credentials as an expert and asked, "What will you say of the adaptability or suitability of the drug called prussic acid in connection with furs?" Robinson objected. Knowlton admitted the question was broad, explained his rationale, and then revised his question: "Has prussic acid any suitability or adaptability for use in connection with sealskin furs?" Hathaway answered, "It is unsuitable." Because of its volatility, it could "cause nausea and headache" in evaporated form.

Robinson pursued this point, asking Hathaway whether other volatile gases were in common use, like ether, chloroform, and naphtha. Hathaway warily agreed. Robinson then asked him about a widely available cleaning product called benzene. Hathaway queried what he

meant by benzene. Robinson lightened the mood, asking if he was a
"family man . . . You don't know anything about what we call benzene used for cleansing purposes?" Robinson continued in the same
vein to make the point that volatile compounds—poisons even—
are legitimately used every day in households for purposes ranging
from de-greasing to illumination. And such poisons would work very
well on vermin and insects, like moths in a sealskin cape. Hathaway
thought such volatile poisons unsafe for the person using them and
for any other people nearby. Robinson then brought up the many uses
of another household poison, asking: "Arsenic is a poison, isn't it? . . .
Is it an ingredient of the common article known as 'Rough on Rats'?"
He continued: "Do you know anything about the use of arsenic to
beautify the complexion? What do you kill cats with if you wanted to
do it quietly?" he asked. Worn down by Robinson's salvo, Hathaway
agreed reluctantly—with a caveat about endangering humans in the
vicinity—that prussic acid would kill the moths.

Knowlton attempted to recall Dr. Dolan to testify about prussic acid,
but the court decided the medical examiner was not qualified because
he had not personally investigated a prussic acid poisoning. Knowlton
then tried one last gambit. Perhaps he could at least show that sealskins
were not susceptible to moths, undercutting the argument that Lizzie
might have sought prussic acid to combat an infestation. He recalled
Henry Tillson to ask whether sealskin was sold in its natural state. That
was excluded. He had a final question for Henry Tillson: Were sealskin
capes "subject to the actions of moths or other vermin"? That, too, was
excluded. Knowlton then sought to recall Eli Bence, the Fall River pharmacist, so that he could describe his encounter with the woman who
had asked for prussic acid. But he had come to the end of the line.

To the great relief of the defense, the court excluded the evidence
on the grounds that "the preliminary proceedings have not been sufficient." Robinson's ingenuity in dealing with the poison testimony was
widely credited. He had thwarted Knowlton's every attempt to let his
witnesses offer their opinions, objecting at every level, from the fram-
ing of the questions to the expertise of the witnesses.

According to a later commentator, this decision generated "almost universal surprise by the bar." As the evidence scholar Wigmore later observed, "What a wonderful web of obscurity the legal mind can contrive to weave over the simplest matters! A woman of ordinary knowledge is alleged to have bought prussic acid for cleaning furs; but two men of technical accomplishments are not allowed to say that there is no such use known to their experience!" In his view, the judges should have permitted the evidence and let the defense make its argument about the innocent uses of prussic acid in front of the jury. He asked: "Why was it necessary to exclude all conceivable hypotheses except that of criminal use? If, as the medical man testified, that acid-vapor is the most poisonous known, and there is no ordinary commercial use for it, is not this enough? Admissibility does not require the exclusion of all other conceivable hypotheses but one; it lies on the opponent to demonstrate, after the admission on grounds of fair and ordinary probability, that certain other reasonable hypotheses exist."

Wigmore's rationale juxtaposed the "men of technical accomplishments" and "a woman of ordinary knowledge." One of his students recalled: "He held forth the ideal of the expert, the individual who by mere knowledge would be in demand as an adviser, or an advocate." His confidence in that professionalism was mirrored in the structure of the criminal trial itself. As Wigmore succinctly explained in a later work, "The judge for admissibility, the jury for weight—such is the orthodox and unflinching rule of the common law." Legal professionals—one might call them "men of technical accomplishments"—determined what jurors, men of "ordinary knowledge," could hear as evidence. Some things were thought too dangerous for them to know. Moody blithely insisted that Lizzie Borden's alleged attempts to buy prussic acid merely showed her intent, but the judges knew that it would be difficult for the jury not to conclude that someone who tried to buy poison on Wednesday must have been Thursday's hatchet-wielding assassin. There was another, unstated reason not to let this evidence in. Not only did these efforts to procure a deadly poison show murderous intent, but they also would have offered the jury a plausible explanation for the masculine brutality of the crime. If Lizzie had tried and failed to buy poison, that supremely feminine weapon, then she might well have turned in frustration to a readily available household implement to carry out her murderous design.

All of this assumes that the defense intended to accept the prosecution's claim that Lizzie had indeed attempted to buy prussic acid at D. R. Smith's on August 3. She herself had never acknowledged doing so. Rather, she denied being in the store. Robinson was perfectly capable of arguing in the alternative: that Lizzie had not, in fact, made any attempt to buy prussic acid, and even if she had done so, she would have had an innocent purpose in so doing. Jennings's notebook contains an entry mentioning a pharmacist named Edward Cate who said that "old country people" often bought prussic acid for killing animals. In fact, prussic acid's reputation as a poison for cats—as Robinson himself had pointed out—meant that physicians struggled to convince patients to take it for proper medicinal purposes. But that would have been a risky strategy in front of the jury.

The defense argument about prussic acid's innocent uses also obfuscated a critical point: whoever asked for the prussic acid said she wanted it to clean her sealskin cape and Lizzie Borden owned a sealskin cape. (According to her inquest testimony, there were two sealskin sacks hanging in white bags in the attic.) Sealskin had become a fashionable fur, popular enough to spawn a faux version made out of muskrat, marketed as "Hudson Seal." Owning a sealskin cape may not have been unusual for a woman like Lizzie, but cleaning furs in August was unheard of. Over the summer, furs were stored in homes or at furriers like Henry Tillson's establishment. No one in a well-regulated household would be cleaning a cape in the summer by any method, let alone with prussic acid.

After losing the point, Knowlton formally offered all plans and exhibits. Knowlton had intended the poison evidence as the dramatic finale.

Instead, the prosecution rested at 10:30 a.m. Elizabeth Jordan said: "Knowlton, after another and final parade of the dismal paraphernalia of the crime, sat down in the ruins and rested his case."

It almost seemed as if Knowlton had given up. Not only had he been thwarted by Robinson's nimble lawyering, preventing his expert witnesses from being "qualified" to answer his questions, but he had also seemingly forgotten about his real audience, the jury. The jury, after all, heard no evidence that day. While the lawyers argued about poison, the jury was at loose ends, carefully shielded from the courtroom excitement. The last evidence the jury had heard the prior day was the testimony of the dressmaker Mrs. Gifford, the witnesses that didn't bark, and Matron Reagan. It was a shocking and potentially catastrophic choice. At best, the prosecution went out with "a dull thud."

Howard noted that the judges and the lawyers registered the end of the prosecution's case with professional impassivity. But, he wrote, "I am not so certain about the jury. Every one of them stiffened up in his seat, looked around the courtroom, and seemed pleased that thus far they had proceeded, while Lizzie Borden fairly beamed, the only evidence of unusual excitement being the peculiar rapid motion of her fan, and two or three uneasy shiftings of bodily position." Howard also reported a rumor that the defense "intended to go to the jury without producing a particle of evidence . . . But that was too sensible to be true." More poetically, Julian Ralph observed of the underlying mystery: "It is as if the cause were a deep and pitch dark well, and the commonwealth had said, 'we will rig up a search light and throw its glare into the well and light up the bottom of it.' They took ten months to build the lamp, and on the first day in court set it up with a great flourish in New Bedford. They turned on the blaze, and it seemed very powerful, but the light only deepens the darkness."

Chapter 9

SHORT, BUSY,
AND VERY IMPORTANT

Ladies' corner, *Boston Globe*

Joe Howard used the short recess to survey the crowd: "There were some extraordinary individuals in the room today, some odd developments of human nature, much queer dressing, and one fat old lady, whose bare hands were covered to the knuckles of her fingers with rings and stones, diamonds, rubies and turquoises." Most to his liking were "[a] noticeable number of very pretty girls." But he also lamented the "number of the women experts, who are quite confident that they could prove the guilt of the accused if they had a chance." His colleague Elizabeth Jordan described them as "a sort of self-constituted jury," much less disposed to favor the prisoner. On a happier note, Susan Fessenden, president of the Massachusetts Women's Christian Temperance Union, was in the audience lending moral support to the prisoner, as was the lecturer and suffragist Mary Livermore. But Lizzie drew the most comfort from her chief champion, George Robinson. It was Robinson's jail visits that buoyed her spirits. In the courtroom, she seemed to find emotional support in physical proximity to Robinson, positioning her seat as close behind him as possible. Even then, according to Elizabeth Jordan, she "did not permit him to forget for long that she was there. Her method of calling his attention is by gently and almost timidly touching him on the back or shoulder and leaning forward as he turns his head to her. That is, such is her manner on ordinary occasions, but when some point strikes her suddenly and forcibly the gentle fan touch becomes a quick, sharp poke and she darts her head forward and whispers eagerly, her face slightly flushing with animation." After days "of being under a subdued but terrific tension," Lizzie seemed relieved: "Her eyes were brighter than usual." And her choice of floral bouquet matched her appearance: "In her hand she held the first really gay display of flowers she has had since the trial began."

THURSDAY, JUNE 15, 1893

After a ten-minute break, the defense case officially opened at 10:50 a.m. with Andrew Jennings's opening statement. Using a "low, measured, funereal tone of voice," he spoke for an hour, averring his longstanding connection to the Borden family: Andrew Borden "was for many years my client and my personal friend. I had known him since my boyhood. I had known his oldest daughter for the same length of time, and I want to say right here and now, if I manifest more feeling than perhaps you think necessary in making an opening statement for the defence in this case, you will ascribe it to that cause.

The counsel, Mr. Foreman and gentlemen, does not cease to be a man when he becomes a lawyer."

Jennings emphasized Lizzie Borden's excellent reputation, her good works, and her general demeanor: "We shall show you that this young woman had apparently led an honorable, spotless life; she was a member of the church; she was interested in church matters; she was connected with various organizations for charitable work; she was ever ready to help in any good thing, in any good deed." Having established Lizzie's good character, he turned the police and prosecutors into villains who "for some reason or other" sought "to fasten this crime upon her." Carried away by his own rhetoric, Jennings alluded to the drama of Richelieu, especially "that most dramatic scene . . . when the king in the exercise of absolute authority, without right or justice . . . sends to drag the pure and virtuous ward of Richelieu from his arms, how the old Cardinal draws that circle around her, and no man dares to cross it."

Jennings recovered himself and returned to the flawed legal case against his client. He continued, "Just so, Mr. Foreman and gentlemen, the law of Massachusetts today draws about every person accused of this crime, or any other, the circle of the presumption of his or her innocence, and . . . until it has been proved beyond a reasonable doubt that he or she is the guilty party, they are not allowed to cross the line and take the life of the party who is accused." Reasonable doubt, he explained, was "a doubt for which one could give a reason." For example, he continued, "[i]f you can conceive of any other hypothesis that will exclude the guilt of this prisoner and make it possible or probable that somebody else might have done this deed, then you have got a reasonable doubt in your mind."

Having established this framework, he turned to the evidence against his client. The prosecution's case was "wholly and absolutely circumstantial." He warned: "[T]here is no class of evidence . . . so dangerous and misleading as circumstantial evidence. Our books are filled with cases where the accused has evidently been proven by circumstantial evidence to have committed the crime and subsequent investigations or confessions have shown that he did not." Remember, he told the jury, "your task is not to unravel the mystery." Instead, he said they must ask themselves: "Have they furnished the proof, the proof that the law requires, that Lizzie Andrew Borden did it, and that there is absolutely no opportunity for anybody else?"

Jennings permitted himself a note of triumph as he catalogued the prosecution's deficiencies: "[T]here is not one particle of direct evidence against Lizzie A. Borden." Not a spot of blood. No weapon. Just a parade of unrelated hatchets and axes all rejected as the actual murder weapon.

Howard applauded: "He ridiculed, with neat sarcasm, the futile efforts of the police" to link one weapon after another to the murders. As for Borden's purported exclusive opportunity, Jennings countered that if Andrew Borden had not been seen on part of his morning walk, then surely the assassin could have evaded witnesses as well. And where was the motive? Even if Lizzie had a motive in the case of Abby Borden, would she have killed her "loved and loving father"?

Lizzie Borden wiped her eyes during his oration. According to Julian Ralph, Jennings "championed her cause with an ancient knight's consideration for the sex and herself" and "his belief in her innocence shone in his words like a loving light in the forest." Howard praised his performance as "brushing away the cobwebs of ingenuity, affirming, with emphatic clarity, the duty of the commonwealth to the living, as well as the dead."

The defense case began with a series of witnesses who testified about odd noises and strange characters heard and seen. Marthe Chagnon, the Bordens' neighbor, and her stepmother, Marienne Chagnon, heard a noise about 11:00 p.m. the night before the murders. Prior to the trial, they speculated that someone was climbing over or walking along their fence. According to Marthe, it sounded like "pounding" and came from the direction of the Bordens' house. She said: "I couldn't describe the noise because I didn't see." They did not investigate, nor, they admitted, did their Newfoundland dog. Knowlton suggested, referring to Marthe's testimony at the preliminary hearing, that the noise could have come from ice carts to the south. She doubted it came from the icehouse and denied ever saying that it had. When Knowlton pressed her on the point, quoting her prior statements, Marthe, "a very pretty and rather coquettish young French girl," shrugged with apparent indifference.

After establishing that the windows in the sitting room were shut, he asked, "How could you tell the direction from which the sound came?"

Again the transcript recorded "(No answer)."

Knowlton surrendered: "I won't press it any further if you don't care to answer it."

Knowlton encountered a similar lack of responsiveness in Marthe's stepmother, Marienne Chagnon, but by this time Knowlton should have detected a language barrier. (Both of the Chagnons were born in Francophone Canada.) Their exchange devolved into an unwitting comedic performance. Knowlton asked her if the noise sounded like pounding.

She replied, "What is it?"

Knowlton repeated the question.

She replied, "Like—?"

He repeated, "Pounding?"

"I don't understand the expression," said Marienne. So he tried again in the time-honored Yankee tradition of shouting at foreigners.

"Pounding? . . . Don't you understand what pounding is?"

"Pounding?" she queried.

"Yes," he said.

"No," she said, "I don't understand it."

"Don't know that word? . . . You don't understand the word pounding? . . . To pound."

"Pounding," she said, "No, sir."

The reporters seemed to enjoy the parade of the less critical defense witnesses, a bit of leavening after the high tension of the poison testimony. Joe Howard described Mary Durfee as "a nice looking old lady, in black, rather short, with enormous high bows in her hat." Durfee had been prepared to testify that she had seen a man arguing with Andrew Borden—"You have cheated me and I'll fix you"—sometime before the end of October. But she could not remember exactly when. She explained: "Well, I lost my sister . . . and she died about the 27th of October." The lawyers struggled to get her to pin down the date of the argument. She said: "[W]hat I heard I heard before then, because I went home and told it." It could have been two months before that date. The judges decided it was too remote. She retired "with a graceful bow embracing the court, the jury, and the learned brothers." In contrast, two neighbors were allowed to testify. Charles Gifford and Uriah Kirby, "a venerable white-haired old man of the frontier type," lived just north of the Chagnon house. On the night before the murders, they saw a man on the side steps (on the sidewalk side of the gate). Gifford unsuccessfully attempted to rouse him. Kirby came by a few minutes later. He, too, tried to wake him, shaking him by the straw hat on top of his head.

This was all fairly tame stuff. But Mark Chase, a local hostler, introduced a new character to the mystery with his description of a man, wearing a brown hat and a black coat, sitting in an open buggy in front of the Borden house at about 11:00 a.m. the morning of the murders. The man he described may have been ordinary, but Chase himself made a physically impressive witness. "When he took the oath," the six-foot-six-inch-tall Chase "elevated his arm and hand to their extremest length, as though he would touch the ceiling, sending another ripple of merriment through the audience." Knowlton, however, undercut the impact of his testimony during cross-examination: perhaps the man, visible only from the rear and obscured by a high seat, might not have been a stranger. Wasn't the buggy really parked at the boundary of the Kelly and Borden properties? Couldn't it have been "somebody who was waiting for a call on the Doctor?" Chase also could not say how long the wagon had been parked there, nor how quickly it departed.

Dr. Benjamin Handy, a Fall River physician, testified that he passed by the Borden house at about 10:30 a.m. on August 4 and saw a "medium sized young man of very pale complexion, with his eyes fixed upon the sidewalk, passing slowly towards the south." Over Knowlton's objection, he declared the man "was acting strangely" and walked very slowly. Knowlton pressed him to describe what made the man so noticeable. Dr. Handy replied, "I can't put it into words, sir. He was acting differently than I ever saw any individual on the street in my life. He seemed to be either agitated or extremely weak, staggering, or confused, or something of the kind." In response to Knowlton's repeated prodding about the man's appearance, Handy added: "He didn't see me, his eyes were fixed upon the ground." He ventured that he might have seen him on an earlier occasion, but he was not certain.

Knowlton summarized sarcastically: "And all you can put into words was that he was looking down toward the sidewalk, and didn't notice anything that was going on around [him], and walked slowly?" Pausing for effect, he continued: "You cannot express that agitation any more than that?" In the course of his questioning, Knowlton also reminded the jury that he owned the cottage at Marion at which Lizzie had been expected, marking him as Lizzie Borden's supporter.

Delia Manley may have seen the same man, a stranger also dressed in light clothing. She also lived on Second Street: she knew the Kelly house well because she had often visited her sister-in-law (Alice Russell's mother), who had lived there. She happened to be walking down the street, accompanied by her sister (Mrs. Sarah Hart of Tiverton), when she stopped between the Borden and Churchill houses to see "pond lilies that a young fellow had in a carriage." The man was "standing in the gateway, leaning his left arm on the gatepost." But that was almost an hour earlier, about 9:50 a.m., and, as Knowlton suggested on cross-examination, he was "standing there quietly . . . in full view of everybody . . . where anybody could see him that was on the sidewalk." Sarah Hart would later confirm her sister's testimony. In her telling, the pale young man took on a sinister aspect. He seemed to look at the street "as though he were uneasy, trying to pry into my business." During cross-examination, Knowlton tried to undermine her perspicacity. He pointed out that she had not recognized the man in the carriage, her own nephew, until he spoke to her.

Another set of witnesses demonstrated how easy it was to get into the house after the murders and contradicted the accounts of police witnesses. The day after the murders, Jerome Borden, Andrew Borden's cousin and future pallbearer, stopped by at 2:00 p.m. and walked right in the front door. This suggested that the spring lock on the front door was not secure—an innocent explanation for the bolted front door on the day of the murders.

Walter P. Stevens, reporter for the *Fall River Daily Evening News*, arrived with Officer Mullaly. He also tried to open the rear cellar door, but he found it fastened. Then he went into the house via the kitchen and saw Lizzie Borden and Bridget Sullivan. He also spoke with Mrs. Churchill. After nosing around the house, he walked through the yard, already well trampled, along with John Manning, reporter for the *Fall River Daily Herald*. He then went into the barn, where he saw at least three other people going up the barn stairs, contradicting Fleet's account of a barn loft undisturbed before his visit. Alfred Clarkson, an engineer who happened to be in the neighborhood, said he arrived at the Borden house about 11:30 a.m. He, too, looked around the barn (in the company of Officer Wixon), including the upper story, where he saw three other men. Critically, he, too, had arrived before Fleet. Knowlton worked to undermine his certainty about his arrival time. At the preliminary hearing, he had testified he had arrived closer to 11:40 a.m. Knowlton questioned how many minutes he had spent chatting with Charles Sawyer, the seconded civilian sentry, before going into the barn. He estimated seven or eight minutes. Knowlton inquired: "Would you swear it wasn't nine? . . . ten?"

Hymon Lubinsky, an ice cream peddler, offered significant evidence and unintentional comic relief. Howard saw only the latter, writing that Lubinsky "gave some unimportant testimony at great length, the grain of wheat in the chaff being that . . . when he was on his ice cream route he saw Miss Lizzie Borden coming from the barn toward the house." His account corroborated Lizzie's claim to have been in the barn during her father's murder. Lubinsky knew that the woman he saw was not Bridget Sullivan; he sold her ice cream "two or three weeks" before the murders. Lubinsky said he had been on Second Street in front of the Borden house shortly after 11:00 a.m. Lubinsky might have been sent as a personal trial for the normally even-keeled Knowlton. Trying to pin him down on the exact location, Knowlton fired off an exasperated series of questions: "What part of the street was it on? Don't you understand these questions I put now? Don't you understand all I am saying? Don't you understand I am asking what part of the street your team was on?" As with the Francophone Chagnons, Knowlton seemed to think that Lubinsky might better understand repetition and a raised voice, shouting his questions as he walked back and forth between his desk and the witness stand. Lubinsky, for his part, managed a dignified response, pointing out that he was not "educated in the English language." Knowlton also found Lubinsky maddeningly imprecise about when he had begun his route. Lubinsky said he had looked at his watch because he was running late, but he did not note the exact time. Knowlton asked: "Why could you not tell the time? . . . You did not take notice of the big hand, but you took notice of the little hand?" But Charles Gardner, the owner of the stable where Lubinsky's horses were kept, corroborated Lubinsky's estimate that he had left about ten minutes after 11:00 a.m.

Two boys, Everett Brown and Thomas Barlow, testified that they had also been in the barn, again casting doubt on earlier police testimony. When they arrived on the scene, they tried unsuccessfully to get into the house, guarded by Charles Sawyer. They then dared each other to go into the barn. Hoping to catch the murderer, they looked in the loft, which they said they found cooler than the outdoors. Assistant Marshal Fleet chased them off. But they hung around the street with the other gawkers until their 5:00 p.m. supper hour. After they had eaten, they returned to their spot in front of the Borden house until midnight. Their testimony was a serious attack on the police account of finding the barn undisturbed, an account that had called into question Lizzie's own story about being in the barn before finding her father's body. Knowlton questioned whether they really had been there as early as they testified: "So your usual time for eating dinner was before eleven o'clock?" As for their testimony about the barn loft, he asked, incredulously, "It really struck you as being a cool place, up in the barn?" He continued sarcastically: "A nice, comfortable, cool place?"

The next witness, Joseph Lemay, required a French interpreter to testify. A farmer, he lived about four miles north of City Hall in Steep Brook. He was to testify that, on August 16, he saw a man sitting on a rock, muttering "poor Mrs. Borden." Lemay noticed the man had what seemed to be blood spots on his shirt. He spoke to the man twice in French. The man stood up, lifting a hatchet from the ground by his side, and shook it at him. Lemay brandished his own defensively. After a few minutes, the man "turned, leaped over a wall, and disappeared in the woods."

But before Lemay could tell his story, Knowlton objected to his testimony and the jury left the courtroom. Knowlton said that the memorandum he had prepared was at his house, as he "had not any idea of this matter coming up at this time." Nonetheless, he cogently explained his objection. Given that the prosecution contended that Lizzie Borden had exclusive opportunity, he agreed that the defense could bring in evidence "which would have some tendency to show that some other person was there or that some other person was seen" near the Borden house at the relevant time. But he argued this was different: "This has no relation whatever in time to the occurrence; it has no relation in place to the occurrence; it has no connection with the occurrence excepting some talk had by the person himself." Insofar as the defense wished to use the statements supposedly made by the man Lemay had seen, Knowlton observed that such statements were hearsay and "may well be taken to be the mutterings of some person who had been brooding upon the crime." Hearsay is an out-of-court statement offered for the truth of what it asserts; the rule against admitting hearsay evidence was well established. Indeed, Wigmore called it "that most characteristic rule of the Anglo-American Law of Evidence—a rule which may be esteemed, next to jury trial, the greatest contribution of that eminently practical legal system." Warming to his theme, Knowlton continued, "Four miles away from this town, twelve days afterward" put this incident in the same class as the "wild and imaginative stories" in false confessions that are "either the results of disordered imagination or the creation of some persons undertaking, for reasons unknown, to obstruct the natural and orderly course of justice." There would be no way for the jury to assess whether the mysterious man seen by Lemay was crazy or a crank and no opportunity for the prosecution to cross-examine him about his statement. In short, this was exactly the kind of evidence that sowed confusion and ran the risk of turning "the jury away from the question in hand."

Jennings countered that the site of the encounter was in "easy communication with the centre of the city; the electric cars run every ten minutes to Steep Brook," that the commonwealth took Lemay's report seriously enough to search for the man, and that the man's comments were not hearsay ("in the nature of conversations or in the nature of declarations"). Jennings instead argued that the man's comments were analogous to "exclamations of pain or suffering" and were more like "an act" than a confession, two examples of out-of-court statements that are not considered hearsay and are therefore generally admissible. Jennings argued that Lemay should be able to testify about what he had seen and heard so that the jury could give it "such consideration as they think it deserves." In his later article on the trial, Wigmore agreed with the defense's position, considering it analogous to the prussic acid question. The judges, however, took the matter under advisement to rule on the next day.

The suspense did little to affect the mood among Borden partisans. The day had been "a burst of sunshine for the imprisoned woman." The witnesses who had seen strange men in the neighborhood or contradicted police testimony undermined the prosecution's theory of Lizzie

Borden's exclusive opportunity. But it was the judges' decision to exclude the prussic acid evidence that set the tone for the day. Then came Jennings's opening statement, pointing out the prosecution's weaknesses and averring his client's innocence. As Joe Howard put it, "The entire day has been one of cheer, laughter, good looking witnesses, bright sayings, and general upliftment along the line of defense."

FRIDAY, JUNE 16, 1893

On Thursday afternoon, as the defense was putting on its case in the New Bedford courthouse, a group of boys were playing baseball on Third Street in Fall River. A boy named Potter hauled himself up to the roof of John Crowe's barn, situated to the rear of the Borden property next to the Chagnon orchard, to retrieve a lost baseball. There, he found something far more interesting: he found a weather-beaten shingle hatchet with a three-and-a-half-inch blade—exactly the size thought to have killed the Bordens. "The discovery has created a genuine sensation," reported the *Fall River Daily Herald*. The hatchet

Yard with Crowe's barn, *courtesy of Fall River Historical Society*

retained "a slight coloring of gilt . . . indicat[ing] that the hatchet was at one time used as an ornament or was quite new when lost or discarded." Significantly, Dr. Draper had found such "gilt" in one of Abby's wounds. After conferring with Dr. Cheever before the trial, he told Knowlton he had found "a very small but unmistakable deposit of the gilt metal with which hatchets are ornamented when they leave the factory; this deposit . . . means that the hatchet used in killing Mrs. Borden was a *new* hatchet, not long out of the store." Those unaware of that fact nonetheless considered the location deeply significant: "If the murderer of Andrew J. Borden and his wife escaped from the Borden premises by the rear . . . he could easily have thrown the hatchet to the place where it was found." Others were more skeptical. Even Elizabeth Jordan, by now an avowed Borden partisan, reported: "The general impression is that it was thrown to the place where it was found by the boys for the purpose of creating a sensation." The *Fall River Daily Herald* tracked down a carpenter who had lost a hatchet after working at Dr. Chagnon's house, but nothing definite was proven. The *Fall River Daily Globe* sarcastically suggested that a search of the roof might also reveal "that note which Mrs. Borden is alleged to have received from a sick friend."

Where Thursday had been "a red hot experience" reaching 92 degrees, the weather had cooled on Friday morning to 55 degrees. "The cold east wind," in Howard's view, was "not only a change and a novelty, but a pneumoniac [*sic*] provocation." More seriously, he considered it "a tonic and a bracer" and "everybody in the crowded room, from the black-robed judges on the bench to the last juror in the panel, looked brighter, cheerier and more contented." The judges' bench seemed to bloom in response: "a veritable floral glory . . . a bushel of great golden lilies shining amid a wealth of small white flowers" appeared on their bench. Lizzie Borden also seemed lighter: "The sable-garbed prisoner was at her very best in looks and spirits, and sat wedged in among her lawyers, a bright faced, bright eyed, wide-awake old maid." Overall, Friday was a "gala day" for the defense. Robinson, however, decided to take no chances. He had worn a new pair of trousers on Thursday and "his associates insisted upon his keeping them on until the close of the trial, that the luck might not be changed."

Robinson's new trousers notwithstanding, the judges agreed with the prosecution about Lemay's testimony, handing the defense a rare evidentiary loss. But that small setback did not dampen the defense's momentum. Charles Sawyer, the "ornamental, fancy painter" deputed to guard the side door after the murders, testified about his experience. He had heard "there was a man stabbed," spotted Alice Russell walking to the house, and accompanied her the rest of the short distance to the scene. Officer Allen, arriving around the same time, tasked him with guarding the side door. On cross-examination, he admitted that he locked the interior door leading to the cellar because he feared "somebody might be concealed around there."

Three reporters testified. John Manning, a reporter for the *Fall River Daily Herald* (and the local reporter for the *New York World* and the Associated Press), arrived at the Borden house around 11:25 a.m. He entered the house with Officers Doherty and Wixon. In the guest room, he watched as Officer Doherty moved the bed to permit Dr. Bowen a better look at Abby's body. (Originally, Dr. Bowen barely had room for his foot on that side of Abby's body.) After about ten minutes in the house, Manning walked around the yard and then went into the barn. He, too, saw others there. He also corroborated the *Fall River Daily Evening News*'s Walter Stevens's account of finding the outside cellar door locked. Manning was an excellent witness, in Joe Howard's view, telling his story clearly "without hesitation or zeal, but in a straightforward, businesslike way."

Manning provided key support to the defense argument that Matron Reagan had lied about the Borden sisters' argument. He had interviewed Mrs. Reagan the day the *Boston Globe* published her account of the quarrel between Lizzie and Emma. At that time, Mrs. Reagan denied the story, telling him, "There is nothing in it." Knowlton, on cross-examination, asked where he had conducted the interview. Manning admitted that he had interviewed Reagan at her house that night. With this piece of information, Knowlton implied that Reagan, rather than revealing the truth to Manning, might have been trying to get rid of yet another pesky reporter—there had been "some 30 or 40 in town." But Thomas Hickey, a reporter for the *Fall River Daily Globe* and local reporter for the *Boston Herald*, also testified that, when he asked about the quarrel the next day, Mrs. Reagan had denied the story. Knowlton, however, pointed out that her denial had given Hickey a scoop to match the original one published by the *Globe*: "That was what you were after, to have something to offset the *Globe* scoop, wasn't it?"

Finally, the reporter John R. Caldwell recalled the scene in Marshal Hilliard's office during which Hilliard said to Mrs. Reagan, "If you sign that paper it will be against my express orders." Once Hilliard noticed the reporter, he ordered him out of the office. During his cross-examination, Knowlton pressed Caldwell to describe the crowd that followed her down stairs" to demonstrate the fraught context of Mrs. Reagan's denial.

Lizzie's friends also testified that the story was a hoax. Marianna Holmes, "a nice little old lady with a large face and a large voice," who had known Lizzie Borden since childhood, said Mrs. Reagan had told her, "It isn't so."

When Knowlton insisted that the redoubtable Mrs. Holmes simply answer his questions, she bridled at the implication that she might be embellishing, replying, "I am not used to this business and I expect to overstep." She testified that she heard Mrs. Reagan agree to sign the affidavit, prepared by her husband Charles J. Holmes, denying the quarrel so long as Marshal Hilliard gave his permission.

Knowlton objected on the grounds that the affidavit itself should be produced. Unfortunately, it had been given to reporters. Holmes, in frustration, handed the lawyer his own copy of the paper. He, too, testified that Mrs. Reagan denied the published version of events and was willing to sign the affidavit, which stated: "I expressly and positively deny that any such conversation took place." Thwarted, Knowlton asked a series of questions designed to establish Holmes's partisanship and that of Reverend Buck (who had read the statement to her): "You had been quite actively interested in the case, had you not? . . . You attended the Court as a friend of Miss Borden, did you not? . . . And accompanied her into Court and when she went out? . . . Sat by her side during the trial? . . . All these things are also true of Mr. Buck?"

The Borden sisters' lifelong friend Mary Brigham, "who betrayed much nervousness by her quick, short breathing," nonetheless testified "in a clear, ringing voice" that Mrs. Reagan had told her, "It is a lie from beginning to end." Mrs. Reagan claimed that she had been willing to sign the paper but the marshal would not let her do so.

These witnesses were critical for more than the Reagan story. They humanized Lizzie. Marianna Holmes, for example, listed Lizzie Borden's charitable activities in such detail that Knowlton interjected to ask if it was necessary to present such an extensive résumé of good works. She was also prepared to testify that Lizzie had kissed her father as he lay in his casket. That was not permitted but she did manage to say that Lizzie "shed tears" when viewing her father's body in the sitting room before the funeral began. In an echo of the testimony, Lizzie covered her face with her handkerchief "and when she took it away it was evident she had been crying." Mrs. Holmes also gave an innocent explanation for Lizzie's locked bedroom door, a fact noted and given sinister import by Assistant Marshal Fleet. According to Mrs. Holmes, "The house was full of men, and if we did not have that door locked, as they came up the stairs, they were apt to open it." By then, Lizzie had rebounded, "leaning forward with her face close to ex-Gov. Robinson's shoulder and now and then whispering to him, in an animated way, suggesting questions."

But these witnesses were mere appetizers. Emma Borden was finally to appear. As Elizabeth Jordan put it, Emma's testimony "was the event of the day." Short of Lizzie herself, Emma Borden was the witness the audience craved. When word spread that Emma Borden would take the stand, "Everybody made a rush for the courthouse, but they might as well have rushed to the spire of the nearest church, for the good people already favored with seats knew a good thing when they had it, and not a soul stirred during the entire recess." Within the courtroom, the women spectators "made such a stir," said Julian Ralph, "that the sound of their dresses was like a whiff of wind in an open forest."

Even though, as a witness, she had been absent from the courtroom prior to her testimony, there was no mistaking Emma Borden. To Julian Ralph, Emma looked like the slender "aged double of her sister." Joe Howard amplified the portrait: "She is a little over 40 years of age, and looks it, a prim, little, old-fashioned New England maiden, dressed with an exceeding neatness in plain black with the impress of a Borden in every feature." He hypothesized: "Self-reliance and personal dignity, I should say, are conspicuous factors in her composition." Elizabeth Jordan, as she had throughout, added a plaintive note. "Much older than Lizzie in appearance," Emma had a "curious almost weazened little face; a costume of deep mourning, and a composed melancholy bearing." Jordan also observed that although "the sisters' eyes met as they faced each other, no sign of recognition passed between them."

By any measure, Emma Borden was the key defense witness. Most important, as the unsuspected daughter, she provided the most potent character support for her accused sister. Fortunately, Emma was up to the difficult task: "There was no swaying of her slender form, no dropping of her straight-cut eye, no quivering of her tight-shut mouth." First, Emma repudiated the reported quarrel in Lizzie's jail cell. Jennings took her through Mrs. Reagan's statement sentence by sentence so that she could specifically deny every one. Between her testimony and that of the prior witnesses, most commentators on the trial considered Mrs. Reagan's story "demolished." According to Ralph, "The defense enjoyed perfect and overwhelming success in disposing of all these matters."

The defense then sought to dispel the prosecution's argument about Lizzie's possible motive, her dissatisfaction with her financial circumstances, and her resentment of her father. At Jennings's request, Emma listed all of Lizzie Borden's property and other assets, comprising $2,811 in cash, two shares of the Fall River National Bank (issued in 1883), and nine shares of Merchants Manufacturing Company (two different issues, 1880 and 1881). Many thought if she had enough money to buy the accoutrements of respectable femininity, then she could not have had any motive to commit the murders. A desire for independence apparently did not enter into the calculation. Lizzie herself sounded this theme shortly after the deaths, showing her bankbooks to her friend Mary Brigham and asking why, in light of her healthy balance, she would commit murder. Emma also provided ammunition for the defense's attack on the prosecution's weakest point: the relationship of father and daughter. She testified that Lizzie had given her father a plain gold ring, a ring she had formerly worn and the only piece of jewelry he ever wore. She said he always wore it and it was "upon his finger at the time he was buried."

Emma's next task was to recast her sister's actions after the murders in an innocent light. Regarding the search of the house, Jennings led Emma through each of the police sweeps to show how cooperative she and Lizzie had been. She quoted Dr. Dolan as saying "the search had been as thorough as the search could be made unless the paper was torn from the walls and the carpets taken from the floor." Emma testified that she and Lizzie both helped the officers open a trunk in the attic. Jennings was also able to get his own comment about the search admitted into evidence. Emma testified that he had told her "everything had been examined, every box and bag."

Emma also gave Jennings a comprehensive inventory of the sisters' dresses. Of the eighteen or nineteen they owned, ten were blue. Two of those belonged to Emma; the remaining eight belonged to Lizzie. (One of the dresses in the shared closet was Abby's.) Emma described the Bedford cord dress in detail: "blue cotton Bedford Cord, very light blue ground with a darker figure about an inch long and . . . three quarters of an inch wide." At its creation, it had been a cheap dress, made from eight or nine yards of 12.5- or 15-cent-a-yard fabric, and, at the time of its destruction, "it was very dirty, very much soiled, and badly faded." And it was stained with paint along the front and on one side toward the bottom. Jennings elicited a description of the dress-making intended to evoke cozy domesticity in which all the Borden women participated.

Emma testified that she told Lizzie to destroy her paint-stained dress. She explained the innocuous impetus: on Saturday, when Emma could not find a hook for her own dress, she said, "You have not de-stroyed that old dress yet; why don't you?" When Lizzie announced the next day, the Sunday after the murders, that she planned to burn her dress, Emma told her it was a good idea. She could not remember her exact expression: perhaps she had said "'why don't you,' or 'you had better,' or 'I would if I were you,' or something like that . . . but it meant—Do it!" And she affirmed that the windows were wide open and police were in the yard.

Jennings sought to get the Bordens' "habit" of burning dresses admitted into evidence in order to shore up Emma's account. He tried a number of questions—"Did you or your sister keep a ragbag?"; "What was done with the pieces of cloth . . . that you wanted to dispose of?"; "Do you know of your sister's habit of burning old dresses . . . previous to this time?" but Knowlton objected to each one and the evidence was excluded. In his review of this case, Wigmore questioned this ruling and thought it might have been a reversible error. Not noted, however, was the oddity of thrifty Yankees not keeping a "ragbag" so that they could reuse old fabric.

Emma also put a less ominous gloss on Alice Russell's account. According to Emma, Alice said nothing while Lizzie burned the dress. The next day, however, Alice announced that Hanscom had asked her if all of Lizzie Borden's dresses were in the house. As she herself had testi-fied, Alice Russell lamented she had told a "falsehood" by agreeing that all the dresses were present and accounted for. According to Emma, "it was decided" that Alice should go to Mr. Hanscom and tell him what had happened. A few minutes later, Alice returned to the kitchen and, like a member of a Greek chorus, intoned her grim conclusion that burning the dress was "the worst thing Lizzie could have done."

Knowlton did his best to resurrect the prosecution's theory of consciousness of guilt—shown by the dress burning and the purported conversation in the matron's room. According to the *Fall River Daily Herald*, Knowlton "advanced toward her with something like the impetus of a locomotive and he shook her bits of testimony as a terrier would shake a rat." Elizabeth Jordan viewed the beginning of Knowlton's cross-examination with alarm. Turning the scene into a set piece for a sentimental novel, she reminded readers of Knowlton's "rasping, unrelenting, irritating and not infrequently bullying methods of cross examination" of Lizzie at the inquest and feared for Emma, "now turned over to his tender mercies." According to Jordan, Lizzie "visibly shrank back in her chair, and at the first sound of his voice gave him a startled glance."

Jordan made much of the contrast in the two figures: "She looked very frail and weak compared to the stocky, bulldog build of the lawyer." Contrary to Jordan's imagined fears, Emma held up well under Knowlton's cross-examination, keeping her eyes focused on him and answering his questions clearly and precisely. Julian Ralph reveled in the contest between the "[c]olossus pitted against the slender sister of the prisoner," noting how "she turned a cold, steely eye, a set mouth, and proudly held head" toward Knowlton.

Knowlton brought into focus the tension in the Borden household, forcing Emma to admit that Andrew Borden's gift to Abby's sister caused "trouble" that was not remedied by his gift of the grandfather's house on Ferry Street to his daughters. Knowlton inquired: "Was there some complaint that it was not an equivalent?"

Emma admitted that their grandfather's house was, if anything, more valuable. Yet it did not repair the breach.

Knowlton pressed on: "Were the relations between you and Lizzie and your stepmother as cordial after that occurrence?"

Emma answered carefully: "Between my sister and Mrs. Borden they were." Knowlton read several extracts from her prior testimony that seemed to acknowledge Lizzie's ill will. She admitted that Lizzie began to call Abby "Mrs. Borden" rather than "Mother" at about the time her father intervened to purchase Abby's stepmother's share in the house on Fourth Street. As Ralph observed, "He could not shake her testimony on any main point, so he took to prodding her on the shadings and edgings and lacework of the meanings of words and the smallest details." In frustration after one such exchange, Emma said, "I don't say I didn't say it, if you say I did. I don't remember saying it."

In the afternoon, Knowlton redoubled his attack. The missing note, the dress burning, and the quarrel in the station all pointed to Lizzie's consciousness of guilt. What happened to the note from a sick friend that Lizzie offered as an explanation for Abby's apparent absence on August 4? Had she searched for it? Emma said, "I think I only looked in a little bag that she carried downstreet with her sometimes, and in her work basket." She admitted that they had advertised unsuccessfully for the writer (or messenger) in the *Fall River Daily Evening News*, a newspaper with "a large circulation." Knowlton questioned Emma about the dress burning. Didn't Alice say, "I wouldn't let anybody see me do that, Lizzie"?

Emma replied, "I don't say it was not said. I say that I didn't hear it." He then questioned Emma's description of Alice Russell as a "calling friend" rather than an "intimate friend." The fact that Alice had been such a reluctant witness gave greater weight to her testimony. The closer the friendship, the less likely any untoward suspicion. Hadn't she stayed for four nights at the Borden house after the murders? Knowlton had pointed out that the dress had been stained while the dressmaker was still at the house and "notwithstanding the paint she wore it mornings." What, he implied, was the urgency in destroying it months later? Regarding the matron's story of a quarrel, he tried to pin her down on the physical details. Did she, for example, sit in the chair as Mrs. Reagan had said? These and other details would shore up the matron's story. And, finally, he introduced the subject of "waterproofs," raincoats that might have protected the assassin from blood splatter. Jennings, however, punctured the potential shock: Lizzie's waterproof was still in the closet.

Howard remarked of Emma's performance: "She stood with perfect self-possession on the stand, answered with deliberation and decision every question and met the skillful cross-examination of Mr. Knowlton without defiance, but with an evident determination to have the meaning of her well-weighed words thoroughly understood." Elizabeth Jordan concluded: "Mr. Knowlton's cross-examination was so fruitless that even people who sympathize[d] with the prosecution turned to each other and smiled." Emma, however, was apparently less confident that "she had done her sister's cause . . . any good." She asked Jennings plaintively "why he had called her, when he had more than enough evidence without her."

Jennings still needed confirmation that the dress Lizzie burned had indeed been stained with paint. John Grouard, the housepainter, testified on Thursday that he had painted the Borden house in May 1892. Lizzie had supervised his paint mixing in the barn and then approved his test patch on the house. That explained the source of the paint. The dressmaker Mary Raymond swore that Lizzie's Bedford cord dress did have paint on the hem. She had made it during her three weeks' tenure that May. It was, she said, "light blue with a dark figure, and made of cheap cotton." The dress "had a blouse waist, and a full skirt, straight widths," with "ruffle around the bottom." Jennings managed to sneak in the notion of routine dress burning, asking the dressmaker what Lizzie had done with the old wrapper that the Bedford cord had replaced. Mary Raymond answered: "She cut some pieces out of it and said she would burn the rest." Knowlton objected: the part about burning was not based on her own knowledge. But, of course, the jury had heard the exchange.

With the main event of the day over, the remaining witnesses seemed anticlimactic. So nervous was Dr. Bowen's wife, Phoebe, when she took the stand that her hand shook while she tried to drink a glass of water. She testified that she had gone to the house after the murders. She saw Lizzie "reclining in a chair, with her head resting against Miss Russell." She said: "I thought she had fainted, she was so white, until I saw her lip or chin quiver, and then I knew she hadn't fainted." Significantly, she testified that she saw no blood on Lizzie Borden: she especially noticed how "very white" her hands were "as they laid against her dark dress, in her lap." For Knowlton, "clean and white" hands cast doubt on Lizzie's claim to have been in the barn looking for sinkers. For the defense, all that really mattered was the absence of blood. Like her husband, Phoebe Bowen "noticed nothing unusual about the dress" and insisted she could not describe the dress in much detail. All she could say was that the dress "had a blouse waist, with a white design on it."

The defense also recalled two witnesses, Lizzie's friend Mary Brigham and Annie White, the stenographer who took notes at the inquest. Jennings asked Mary Brigham about the day of the alleged quarrel in the matron's room, which he pinpointed as "the afternoon of the day when some experiments were made with an egg." She testified that the reporter Edwin Porter had been talking with Matron Reagan. Mrs. Reagan had told her: "That reporter has come after me again, and I told him that I had nothing to tell him." She also said Mrs. Reagan said she would have signed the affidavit prepared by Lizzie's friends had the marshal not told her not to do so. Mary also detailed her own amateur sleuthing. After the murders, she experimented with the spring lock on the front door, discovering, as Jerome Borden had testified, that "the spring lock was not sure." Mr. Morse joined in, lying prone on the guest room floor, so that the others could determine if he was visible from the hall. She said that she could not see him from the hall, only when she "advanced a few feet into the room."

Robinson then recalled the stenographer Annie White to confirm something Bridget Sullivan said and something Assistant Marshal Fleet did not. At the inquest, Bridget Sullivan had indeed said that Lizzie "seemed to be more excited than I ever saw her" and that "she was crying" when she first told her that Andrew had been killed. Assistant Marshal Fleet, however, had never testified that Lizzie had told him, as he had claimed during the trial, that "her father was feeble and [she] went to him and advised and assisted him to lie down upon the sofa."

The prosecution had its own slate of rebuttal witnesses. Moody recalled Marshal Hilliard to give his own account of the Reagan imbroglio. After he had heard of the quarrel the morning of Thursday, August 25 (the first day of the hearing), he went to see her at her house that night. The following afternoon, Mr. Buck entered his office, trailed by Mrs. Reagan, and showed Hilliard the affidavit she had apparently agreed to sign. Hilliard testified that he told Mrs. Reagan, "If you sign that paper, you do it in direct violation of my orders. If you have got anything to say about this you will say it on the witness stand in Court." Moody then recalled Officer Mullaly to recount his conversation with Hymon Lubinsky, the ice cream peddler. According to Mullaly, he interviewed Lubinsky on August 8. Lubinsky told him he had seen a woman walking from the barn toward the house at 10:30 a.m. on August 4. Mullaly produced his notebook as corroboration. Robinson questioned whether he had properly investigated the timing or simply learned that Lubinsky's route usually started around that time.

Moody then recalled Annie White to read three significant exchanges from the preliminary hearing. The transcript showed that passerby Alfred Clarkson had originally claimed to have arrived at the murder scene about 11:40 a.m. (and not 11:30, as he had said the day before). Regarding the relations in the Borden household, Emma had been more forthcoming about the tension in the house at the preliminary hearing. When asked whether "the relations between you and your stepmother" were "cordial," she replied, "I don't know how to answer that. We always spoke." She added, "[P]erhaps I should say no then." She also admitted that relations between Abby and Lizzie were not "entirely cordial." When Knowlton inquired about the reason, Emma answered: "Well, we felt she was not interested in us, and at one time father gave her some property, and we felt we ought to have some too; and he afterwards gave us some." But that gift, as Knowlton framed it, "did not entirely heal the feeling." Moody also asked Annie White to read Phoebe Bowen's description of the dress Lizzie Borden wore the morning of the murders. Then she had called it "a blouse waist of blue material, with a white spray . . . running through it."

After a brief consultation, the prosecution decided not to wait for its last witness, then on his way from Fall River. (The tardy witness was a lad who would have contradicted the testimony of Barlow and Brown, the boys who said they had searched the barn for the killer.) Instead came the announcement: "The evidence is closed on both sides."

Chief Justice Mason then admonished the jury that "notwithstanding the evidence is all in, there is much more to be submitted to them, and they should keep their minds open . . . until the last word has been said, and the case finally committed to them." Yet they could not have been unmindful of the fraught atmosphere. As Joe Howard observed: "There has been no communication between the jury and public since they were impaneled two weeks ago . . . Tell me they don't know what popular sentiment is and public feeling? That's nonsense, for they are part of the populace themselves."

SATURDAY, JUNE 17, AND SUNDAY, JUNE 18, 1893

For the jurors, this meant another weekend in the hotel, away from their homes and families, with only each other as company. Elizabeth Jordan lamented: "No convicts at hard labor in Sing Sing prison are under stricter surveillance than the Borden jurors." On Sunday, the jurors agreed to attend church. Howard followed them, observing their military cadence: "Tramp, tramp, tramp, up the street moved the double line." Once seated at the Trinitarian Church, "Sheriffs occupied the end seats in the pews to see that no brother escaped before the benediction was pronounced." Taking 1 Corinthians 1:17 ("For Christ did not send me to baptize, but to preach the gospel") as his text, Reverend Julien told his congregation and their guests: "Clothes did not make the man or the woman; that a black heart could beat beneath a dress suit or a silk dress; that human nature is much the same in all; that moral tendencies and the power of control may differ." The seriousness of the message and its meaning for the duty that still lay ahead of them did not affect their appetites. After a "remarkably hearty dinner at the hotel," the jurors took an excursion to Dartmouth, "packed in like sardines, perspiration taking the place of oil." Whether they enjoyed the trip was not reported.

Unlike his judicial colleagues, Judge Dewey remained in New Bedford for the weekend. He had also attended the church service, sitting a dozen pews behind the jurors. He, too, treated himself to an outing, apparently walking to Clark's Point, more than four miles from the city center. Later that afternoon, he sat by himself on a large rock. "The brisk harbor breeze was dallying with his iron-gray hair and the sunlight was reflected from his shining silk hat," reported Joe Howard. "He looked happy, just and contented."

For the lawyers, it was a busy weekend. Knowlton walked his normal route from home to office and back again. He found time, however, to go to church on Sunday. Robinson, busy crafting his closing argument, took only short breaks for meals. Ralph humorously described him as "working like a beaver, or rather, a lawyer, for lawyers work a good sight harder than beavers." Howard observed Robinson as he "dashed down to breakfast at the hotel, dashed back; hurried down to dinner and hurried back; flitted down at supper time and flitted back." By contrast, "Col. Adams," Howard wrote, "was taking things more moderately, and getting more of the good things of this life to eat and drink. He dallied for some time over the supper table particularly."

The courthouse also enjoyed a respite: "For the past two weeks its windows have been crowded with spectators; its halls and corridors filled with officers and waiting witnesses; its anterooms occupied by attorneys and stenographers; its back yard turned topsy turvy by telegraph operators and newspaper men and its sidewalks lined with unfortunate ones who did not get around in time to enter the portals of the charmed structure." Over the weekend, the windows were wide open and the building vacant. Outside, "The sidewalk [was] frequented by pedestrians who hurried to and fro in attendance on their every day business, while the hive of industry in the back yard looked like a closed-up bar room in a no-license town." Howard reported that the members of the exclusive Wamsutta Club ("nobody admitted under eighty years of age") looked forward to reclaiming their croquet lawn to the rear of the courthouse.

Over the weekend, the reporters were at loose ends. The judges, except for Dewey, were out of town; the lawyers were working and inaccessible; and the jurors were, as always, under guard. The only news of the prisoner, according to Julian Ralph, "was that she has slept well and eaten well and been visited by ex-Gov. Robinson." Elizabeth Jordan took the opportunity of the pause in action to debunk the popular image of Lizzie Borden as a "human sphinx." In an extended profile, entitled "This Is the Real Lizzie Borden," she contrasted the "very real and very wretched woman . . . on trial for her life in the little courthouse at New Bedford, Mass." with the "journalistic creation," which she termed "a thing without heart or soul . . . large, coarse, and heavy." Jordan offered herself as the unbiased observer of the "real" Lizzie. "From the top of her head to the broad sensible soles of her French kid boots," Jordan averred, "she is a gentlewoman . . . a 'lady.'" Far from a "sphinx," Lizzie was a "terrified woman, entirely conscious of the horror of her position, but bearing herself with the dignity which is her own." She was also, warned Jordan, "on the verge of collapse."

While the lawyers polished their closing arguments, nearby, in her cell, Lizzie Borden read. Her long confinement had given her the leisure to work her way through most of the novels of Charles Dickens and Sir Walter Scott. On this last weekend of her trial, she turned to slighter fare, the "summer novels" Robinson had given her. Joe Howard wondered whether the chimes of the church bells prompted "memories of the past . . . or did anxiety for the future prevail?" She had no callers—except Andrew Jennings, who permitted himself only a brief visit, presenting her with a large red rose "with his little boy's compliments." For everyone involved in the trial, Sunday was "a dull day of anxious waiting."

Chapter 10

LAST WORDS
IN THE GREAT TRIAL

Early-morning scene about the New Bedford courthouse, *Boston Globe*

O n its editorial page, the *New York Times* lauded "the conduct
of the Borden trial" as "a model proceeding" and "a credit
alike to the bench and the bar of Massachusetts." Joe Howard singled out the professionalism of the lawyers for special praise:
"Another interesting and striking feature is the cordial courtesy that
obtains among the counsel. There seems to be a perfect understanding
on both sides . . . an interplay of fraternity, most charming to witness.
Sometimes I think it almost too good to be genuine, too millennial, as
it were, but I am convinced by daily observation and some knowledge

of the men that it is honest and truly comradic." To Ralph, accustomed to the rough-and-tumble New York City practice, "The temper of the lawyers is peculiar. They work in almost unbroken harmony, each side treating the other side in a friendly, polite, and respectful manner." Robinson himself made a point of exempting the prosecuting lawyers from his criticism of the underlying case. Knowlton, he declared, "has only one duty . . . and he walks into this Court room only as the representative of the Commonwealth of Massachusetts, that is yours and mine and his . . . He is not here for blood, neither is he helped to such dishonorable work, if it were attempted, by our excellent friend, the District Attorney from the great county of Essex, one of our best and most reliable lawyers. So you will see no small play; you will see no mean tactics on the part of the Commonwealth here."

MONDAY, JUNE 19, 1893

On Monday morning, the police contingent assigned to control the expected spectators was doubled. But it was not enough. Julian Ralph declared: "The mob that besieged the Court house was the greatest that was ever seen around that Ancient Temple of Justice." The crowd was even rowdier than usual, "more like a surging mob trying to gain admittance to some big show, than to a courtroom where a miserable woman is on trial for her life." As on the other days, there were more women than men, a mix of "women in silks, and women in calicoes." Elizabeth Jordan reported: "If the women were frantic to get in before, they were frenzied to-day." They blocked the front and formed an equivalent human barrier at the rear. Joe Howard noted "hundreds standing for hours outside, in the vain hope of making their way to the courtroom, where every available inch of space was utilized." It was, as Ralph observed, "packed as only a clever stevedore knows how to load a ship." Even the corridors were filled. Little wonder, then, that as she entered the courthouse, Lizzie Borden seemed "visibly affected by the great crowd and the great silence that greeted her, and her startled look

Ex-governor Robinson delivering his argument, *Boston Globe*

at the upturned gazing faces indicated how thoroughly her nervous system is strained." She did not look well, her face "swollen and colored slightly purple." Joe Howard struggled to imagine her state of mind as she "was brought a third Monday to confront the commonwealth, listen a while to the pleasurable talk of her senior counsel, endure the impertinent starings of people dressed like women and individuals garbed like men, and lay bare her bosom to the barbed arrows, well aimed and thoroughly poisoned, from the bow in the strong and stalwart hands of the brawny district attorney."

George Robinson rose to her defense. Dressed in his usual plain black suit, he spoke for almost four hours in a "low, earnest voice," his speech "almost bare of eloquence." Julian Ralph would deride it as "commonplace." But Robinson's folksy manner masked a serious purpose, for it was perfectly attuned to "the farmer instinct in the jurymen." Robinson, said Ralph, "twanged his voice, he yaw yawed his last two vowels, he said 'agin' for against, and 'warn't' for was it not." (Elizabeth Jordan observed that he instructed the stenographer to correct his speech for the official record.) While he spoke, Lizzie watched him "intently, now and then fanning herself, occasionally tapping her rather pretty foot on the lower portion of the rail, now and then putting a bouquet to her nose, never taking her eyes from the face of the man upon whom much of her fate, she thinks, depends."

In his opening statement, Jennings had essentially vouched for Lizzie Borden, reminding the jurors that he was a personal friend of the dead; for his part, Adams had done his best to stretch out the timeline in some places and shrink it in others to make it seem just possible that an outsider might have committed the murders; and Robinson had undermined the prosecution's depiction of strained domestic relations in the Borden household and forced the police to contradict each other's testimony. Robinson now sought to weave these threads together, enfolding his client in a cloak of reasonable doubt.

Robinson began by acknowledging the special horror of the crimes. He described the Borden murder case as "one of the most dastardly and diabolical crimes known to the history of Massachusetts." The shock felt by the police led them, Robinson argued, to cast about desperately for someone to arrest: "Policemen are human, made out of men, and nothing else." The police were also under immense public pressure to arrest someone, and Robinson observed, "Suspicion began to fall here and there." But when they had Lizzie in their sights, they became convinced they had their killer. Robinson explained: "Once a theory possesses our minds, you know how tenaciously it holds its place." A policeman is even more susceptible to this bias because "he is possessed and saturated with the thoughts and experiences he has with bad people." "And," as Robinson reminded the jury, "you do not get the greatest ability in the world inside a policeman's coat." (The *New-Bedford Mercury* shared this sentiment: "Not one police officer in a thousand is possessed of acute sensibility or a trained habit of observation." "Success," the paper continued, "is more often a matter of chance, or luck, or the stupidity of the criminal than it is of any well-directed conduct of an investigation.") What else but a fatal combination of overzealousness and ineptitude could explain the police's focus on Lizzie Borden?

Rather than the obvious suspect fingered by the police, Robinson presented Lizzie Borden as the personification of beleaguered innocence. Recalling "a little scene that struck [him] forcibly," Robinson said: "Right at the moment of transition she stood there waiting, between the Court and the jury; and waited, in her quietness and calmness, until it was time for her to properly come forward. It flashed through my mind in a minute. There she stands, protected, watched over, kept in charge by the judges of this court and by the jury who have her in charge. If the little sparrow does not fall unnoticed to the ground, indeed, in God's great providence, this woman has not been alone in this courtroom, but ever shielded by His watchful Providence from above, and by the sympathy and watch[ful] care of those who have her to look after." In his formulation, Lizzie Borden is an orphan in need of paternal guidance and protection, a ward of the court rather than a prisoner in custody. Robinson emphasized her respectful silence and her apparent helplessness, noting she "waited . . . until it was time for her [to] properly come forward." Robinson allied the defense with the protection of God and the legal system, leaving the common-wealth, represented by the prosecution, somehow opposed to justice, both secular and divine. Like Robinson himself, the judges and jury become reassuring paternal figures who take the place of her deceased father. It was a neat rhetorical sleight of hand, considering that Borden was on trial for having created her own orphanhood.

After lulling the jury with that reassuring set piece, he lowered the boom, warning that any mistake would be irreparable. He admonished the jury: "You are trying a capital case, a case that involves her human life, a verdict which against her calls for the imposition of but one penalty, and that is that she shall walk to her death." Against that background, Robinson argued that the prosecution's case was entirely circumstantial and that "the proof must come up in your minds to a moral certainty . . . It must be beyond reasonable doubt." Reasonable doubt, he explained, was the "reasonable doubt of reasonable men, confronted with the greatest crisis you have ever met in the world." Robinson cautioned the jury to put out of mind any rumors or information about the case heard outside the courtroom. And he emphatically reminded jurors that it was not their responsibility "to unravel the mystery."

Robinson then made a bold choice to discuss what was not in evidence. First, he suggested, slyly and without any basis, that Bridget had firsthand knowledge of the note or, at least, provided independent confirmation of Abby's statement. This, Wigmore would later declare, was "the only blot on an otherwise nearly perfectly conducted trial." Robinson did not explain its unaccountable disappearance; he merely remarked that such things happen. Second, he reminded the jury of

Moody's opening statement in which he declared that Lizzie Borden had tried to procure prussic acid the day before the murders. He remarked: "You have not heard any such evidence; it is not proved, the Court did not allow it to be proved and it is not in the case." Third, he also discussed the roll of burned paper in the stove, a roll of paper laden with "dark insinuations." Harrington had seen Dr. Bowen in front of the kitchen stove containing "what he said looked like the embers of a rolled up piece of paper, burned." "That," Robinson insisted, "was all." But, he feared, "There was something in the manner that meanly intimated" that Dr. Bowen had some nefarious purpose in burning the paper. Robinson said he thought the prosecutors were going to argue that the missing hatchet handle had been in the fire, burned up somehow before the fire had finished reducing the paper to ashes. "Did you ever see such a funny fire in the world?" he asked. He professed to have been "troubled about it" himself until Fleet and Mullaly contradicted each other about whether the police found the hatchet handle in the cellar. He gleefully summarized: "Fleet didn't see it and Mullaly did see it. Fleet didn't take it out of the box and Mullaly saw him do it . . . So we rather think that the handle is still flying in the air, a poor orphan handle without a hatchet, flying around somewhere."

After that comic interlude, Robinson turned to the evidence most favorable to the defense. He reminded the jury of the brutality of the crimes, arguing that the Bordens were felled by "well directed blows." "Surely," he continued, "we are prompted to say at the outset the perpetrator of that act knew how to handle the instrument . . . and it was not the careless, sudden, untrained doing of somebody who had been unfamiliar with such implements." Robinson took special care to make the jurors see the murderer as a skilled *male* assassin. After considering the mechanics of the murders, Robinson continued, "You must conclude at the outset that such acts are morally and physically impossible for this young woman defendant." Despite the spatter such blows would have produced, no blood—"[n]ot a spot"—had been noticed on her hair, face, or dress by any of the people who came to lend support in her time of crisis.

After invoking the specter of a mysterious male assassin, Robinson returned to his theme of Lizzie as innocent bystander. He transformed Lizzie into the paradigmatic "angel in the house," her lack of alibi proof of her feminine normality. He argued: "They say she was in the house in the forenoon. Well, that may look to you like a very wrong place to be in. But it is her own home . . . I don't know where I would want my daughter to be . . . than to say that she was at home, attending to the ordinary vocations of life, as a dutiful member of the household." Robinson made a similar point about her account of her actions before and after the murders. She believed her stepmother had received a note and had gone out; therefore, she would have had no reason to look for her. As for the prosecution's contention that "she must have seen . . . the dead body of Mrs. Borden . . . as she went up and down the stairs," Robinson assured the jury, "Now if we had marched you up and down the stairs and told you nothing of what we wanted you to look at, there isn't one of you that would have squinted under the bed, on that particular tread of stairs." He insisted: "Now do not ask her to do things that nobody does." As for her visit to the barn, corroborated by the ice cream peddler Lubinsky, "Is there anything unnatural or improbable in her going to the barn for anything she wanted?" In the same vein, he defended her shifting stories about her whereabouts. He said that variations in witnesses' accounts were often a sign of truthfulness. "Honest people," he claimed, "are not particular about punctuation and prepositions all the time." More important, Robinson provided a belated rejoinder to Knowlton's incredulity about Lizzie's purported inability to recall whether she was upstairs or downstairs or out in the yard or barn at various points in the morning. It was a woman's problem: "Do you suppose that your wives and daughters can tell the number of times they went up and down stairs six months ago on a given day?" Of course, it had not been a typical day, but Robinson emphatically added: "Not at all, or even the day before, unless they were very careful about something."

Next Robinson denied that anything was amiss in the Borden household. He normalized the many locks in the Borden house. Yes, it was a well-secured home, but Robinson dismissed the many locks as "a matter of protection to keep people out." Robinson rejected the notion that Andrew was a miser who deprived his daughters of domestic comforts. Robinson asked the jurors whether they lived as well: "Are all your houses warmed with steam? Do you have carpets on every one of your floors, stairs and all? Do you have pictures and pianos and a library, and all the conveniences of luxury? . . . Well, I congratulate you if you do." Lizzie herself, he reminded the jury, had her own bank account and "property of her own." He asked: "Did she want any more to live in comfort?" For him, this was proof Lizzie had no motive to commit the murders.

Leaving aside the unthinkable notion that Lizzie might have wanted independence rather than mere comfort, Robinson deliberately obscured the source of Lizzie Borden's purported dissatisfaction with her circumstances. It arose from a sense of relative deprivation, not the literal absence of material comfort. She wanted, according to Alice Russell, "to live as others did," and "others," in this context, meant her more socially elevated cousins. Robinson could have revealed that Andrew had been "looking for a nice place for his daughters" in the more fashionable Hill district shortly before his death. But there was a risk in revealing Andrew's apparent change of heart. It might have been seen as the act of a desperate man trying to mollify his disgruntled daughters and buy domestic peace, rather than—as Lizzie had suggested in her pretrial interview with Mrs. McGuirk of the *New York Recorder*—the decision of a considerate father trying to gratify them. That he was apparently contemplating such a significant acquisition also raised the question of whether this was part of a larger plan to put his affairs in order, to finalize a will that may well contain terms to which his daughters might object. Finally, Robinson ignored the most disturbing possibility, that Lizzie would have considered any residence, whatever the size, intolerable if it also housed her stepmother and father.

To the contrary, Robinson trivialized the much-discussed "ill feelings" in the household. He gave a rambling paean to departed mothers, a series of images, in Joe Howard's words, "not fertile in fancy, nor poetic in sentiment, nor particularly felicitous in phrase." Robinson's point, however belabored, was that even a long-departed biological mother held a special place in a child's affections. Therefore, Lizzie's decision to stop calling Abby her mother had no great import because she was not, in biological fact, her mother. As for Lizzie's correction of Assistant Marshal Fleet when he referred to Abby as her mother, Robinson observed: "There is nothing criminal about it . . . nothing that savors of a murderous purpose, is there?" He sarcastically reminded the jurors of Marthe Chagnon's testimony in which she referred to her father's second wife as her stepmother: "I advised the City Marshal to put a cordon around that house, so that there will not be another murder there." More seriously, he agreed that Lizzie's comments to the dressmaker Mrs. Gifford were "not a good way to talk" and admitted that Lizzie was "not a saint." But he contended she was simply a plain speaker. Other people speak hastily, "yet we don't read of murders in those houses." He opined: "It is not the outspoken, blunt and hearty that are to be heard about it that do the injury."

Most tellingly, Robinson made the tension in the Borden household purely feminine. This strategy had two components. First, it reinforced his version of the ill feeling in the household as an inconsequential disagreement among the ladies, an understandable tension between grown daughters and their stepmother. Second, it allowed him to emphasize the undiminished bond between father and daughter. Robinson consistently invoked Andrew Borden's close relationship with Lizzie, presenting a picture of strong paternal attachment, as if her father's love proved her innocence: "No man should be heard to say she murdered the man who so loved her." He emphasized Lizzie and Andrew's special understanding, remarking of Andrew Borden, "He was a man that wore nothing in the way of ornament, of jewelry but one ring, and the ring was Lizzie's . . . and the ring stands as the pledge of plighted faith and love, that typifies and symbolizes the dearest relation that is ever created in life, that ring was the bond of union between the father and the daughter." At the mention of their father's ring, both Borden daughters wept openly . . . and Lizzie dabbed her eyes with a handkerchief. This lachrymose display was, according to

Joe Howard, "but a transient flood: her perfect composure was soon recovered, and, without a glance at any other individuals, she continued her attention to her counsel."

It was fortunate that Lizzie's tears provided a distraction, for Robinson was venturing onto unstable terrain. In theory, he presented the jury with a sentimental fantasy, defusing the tension in the Borden household and creating a portrait of idealized love and harmony particularly attractive to jurors who were fathers themselves. But his suppression of any discord between father and daughter and his decision to depict their relationship as a "union" (symbolized by a ring as "a pledge of plighted faith and love") was unsettling. In his zeal to demonstrate Andrew's undying love, he inflated the significance of the ring, reshuffling the roles of father and daughter into those of husband and wife. Insisting on Lizzie and Andrew's intense attachment raised the possibility that this was, at its heart, a crime of passion. If so, then "periodic insanity"—a form of female temporary insanity in which otherwise respectable women killed husbands or lovers—might provide a way of making sense of the otherwise inexplicable crimes. And, as he pointed out, Lizzie was in the throes of "her monthly illness," a fact he used to explain the bloody towels in the cellar, the tiny spot on the inside of her skirt, her inconsistent stories, her visit to the cellar the night after the murders, and even her premonitions of doom when she visited Alice Russell. He said: "You will recollect that Miss Lizzie's monthly illness was continuing at that time, and we know from sad experience that there is [sic] many a woman at such a time as that is all unbalanced, her disposition disturbed, her mind disabled for a period of time." His choice of language—"unbalanced," "disturbed," "disabled"—was uncomfortably close to the medical-criminological discussions characterizing menstruation as a time in which an otherwise sane woman might be tragically susceptible to an insane impulse.

Whether or not he realized the danger, Robinson pivoted back to safer ground. He had another ready explanation for Lizzie's prescience when she told Alice Russell that she feared "someone would do something." He pointed out "a good many people . . . believe in premonitions, and things will happen sometime for which we see no adequate cause . . . but an event will so happen as to seem to furnish a connection." He said, "I do not say it is one way or another."

As if ticking off events involving Alice Russell, Robinson discussed two incidents that the prosecution believed showed Lizzie's subterfuge after the murders: Lizzie's second visit to the cellar on the night of August 4 and her burning of the dress the next Sunday. Robinson remarked on the ordinariness of the visit, alluding to Lizzie's "monthly sickness" and the location of the pail. He also noted Lizzie's lack of concealment, insisting that "a person who is going to do anything to cover up a crime will not carry an electric light with him." He then turned to the most damning piece of evidence: Lizzie's burning of her dress after the murders. Robinson sowed confusion about what Lizzie was wearing on the morning of the murders: "It was not a time for examining colors and afterwards they recollected as well as they could." "So," he admitted, "there has been a conflict of testimony" about Lizzie's dress. But he reminded the jury: "They had all seen her and every one says there was not a spot of blood on it." As for the burned Bedford cord dress, both the dressmaker and the painter agreed that it had been stained with paint. Moreover, the police had already conducted a comprehensive search of Lizzie's wardrobe. So what if Lizzie burned a paint-stained dress at Emma's suggestion? Ridiculing the prosecution's theory that she used the missing dress as a sort of coverall, he said: "I would not wonder if they are going to claim that this woman denuded herself and did not have any dress on at all when she committed either murder." There was, in fact, a persistent rumor that the prosecution would argue that Lizzie Borden committed the murders in the nude, a suggestion almost as shocking as the killings themselves, but the prosecution never made that argument. (Ralph dismissed the notion as a "peculiarly French" theory.)

Robinson reserved his sharpest humor for the array of hatchets and axes offered into evidence, a collection he described as "all the armory of the Borden house." According to Robinson, "The government has a theory about it, or at least seems to have a theory, and then does not seem to have a theory." Robinson methodically described the hatchets and axes, picking them up and putting them down as he explained they had been "declared innocent." Robinson asked: "Is the Government trying a case of may-have-beens[?] . . . And if they cannot tell you that that is the implement that committed the crimes, where is it?" Echoing the imagery used by the preacher Jonathan Edwards in his most famous and terrifying sermon, "Sinners in the Hands of an Angry God," Robinson warned the jury: "Gentlemen, you walk upon the edge of a precipice. You think you feel the hand of the Common-wealth guiding but . . . [i]t is a fraud, it is a theory, born in an emer-gency at a time of disaster." Had the trial been held any earlier, Lizzie might have been mistakenly convicted on the basis of "cow's hair and the appearance of blood" on the hatchets "now declared to be inno-cent." Relying upon shifting explanations of the medical authorities, they risked "murder at the hands of theorizing experts."

Robinson then turned to the prosecution's most important point: Lizzie Borden's exclusive opportunity. He countered: "Exclusive oppor-tunity is nothing but an anticipation that was not realized." He reminded the jury that the side door was unfastened in the morning: "There is nothing to show that Bridget was in a position so she could control the inside of the house, for she was not." He reminded the jury of the strange man spotted on Second Street the morning of the murders. Rob-inson compared the apparent invisibility of the assassin with the absence of eyewitnesses to parts of Andrew Borden's walk from the house to the bank the last morning of his life: "You cannot see everybody."

Robinson returned to his theme of Lizzie as hapless female victim, again bringing his point literally home to the members of the jury. Comparing Lizzie Borden's story of her activities with one their wives might tell, he cautioned: "I am taking you into the house just as I would go into your house, for instance, and say, What are your wives doing now? Well, doing the ordinary work around the house, get-ting the dinner." His message to the jurors was clear: any respectable woman, perhaps one of their own wives or even daughters, could be sitting in the dock. And he asked them to empathize with her ordeal, his language freighted with innuendo: "How would your wife or mine act if taken by an officer, investigated and crowded and pushed and then bound over to lie in the jail of this county for ten months, being scanned by everybody?"

Warming to his theme, Robinson painted the police investigation as highly improper. He asked them to visualize Assistant Marshal Fleet, "the set of that mustache and the firmness of those lips," interrogating Lizzie Borden in her bedroom: "And there he was, up in this young woman's room in the afternoon, attended with some other officers, plying her with all sorts of questions in a pretty direct and peremptory way." "Is that the way," he asked, "for an officer of the law to deal with a woman in her own house? What would you do with a man . . . that got into your house and was talking to your wife or your daughter in that way?"

After enjoining the jurors to see Lizzie as their own wife or daughter, Robinson advanced the key defense proposition: a woman like Lizzie *could not* have committed these murders. He reminded the jury of the singular brutality of the murders. The murderer stood astride Abby and leaned over Andrew's head to deliver the blows—some of which crushed their skulls—so that "the person of the assailant in both cases must have been thoroughly covered and spattered." "Such acts as those," he insisted, "are morally and physically impossible for this young woman defendant." Though he urged the jury to accept the discredited notion that Lizzie could not physically have committed the murders, he was primarily concerned with the moral impossibility of her having done so. But as if suddenly recalling a weak point in his argument, he urged the jury to suspend judgment about his client's notable composure, even quoting a maudlin song for the proposition that her lack of tears belied a deep reservoir of feeling: "The eyes that cannot weep / Are the saddest eyes of all." (He all but promised the jury that she would have her overdue nervous collapse in private once the trial was over.)

Having dispensed with Lizzie's self-possession, he returned to a variation of his theme that she simply could not have committed the murders. He evoked Lizzie Borden's life before the murders, a life that exemplified respectable feminine virtue. An active church member outside the home and a dutiful daughter within its boundaries, she was a credit to her sex and class. How could such a woman be a murderer? Robinson insisted: "It is not impossible that a good person may go wrong . . . but our human experience teaches us that if a daughter grows up in one of our homes to be 32 years old, educated in our schools, walking in our streets, associating with the best people and devoted to the service of God and man . . . it is not within human experience to find her suddenly come out into the rankest and baldest murderess."

Here, as he had done many times previously, Robinson played upon the incongruity between the image of a raving maniac who perpetrated the murders and the prim embodiment of femininity accused of the crime. He juxtaposed the two contradictory images of Lizzie Borden: "Gentlemen, as you look upon her you will pass your judgment that she is not insane. To find her guilty you must believe she is a fiend. Does she look it? . . . [H]ave you seen anything that shows the lack of human feeling and womanly bearing?" Robinson's formulation left the jury with no rational, scientific explanation for Lizzie Borden's guilt. He had foreclosed a medical diagnosis that would deny Lizzie Borden's responsibility even as it affirmed her guilt. Therefore, she either sanely butchered her stepmother and her father or she was an unjustly accused and persecuted young woman. After presenting the jury with a stark choice—daughter or fiend—he concluded his argument with a warning: "There must be no mistake, gentlemen." Alluding to the mandatory death sentence, he reminded the jury that any error would be "irreparable." This warning morphed into a curse: a guilty verdict in the face of reasonable doubt would be so "deplorable an evil that tongues can never speak of its wickedness." Setting Lizzie free, by contrast, would be "sanctioned and commended." Lizzie, he reminded them—partly as encouragement, partly as a threat—was "not without sympathy in this world." After letting that register, Robinson shifted his tone again, thanking the jurors for their patience and conferring on them, almost as a benediction, the role of paternalistic guardians. He urged them "to take care of her as you have and give us promptly our verdict of not guilty." It was just after 3:00 p.m.

The *Fall River Daily Evening News* declared: It was an "acute and adroit unmasking of the weakness of the case of the prosecution. One by one his sledge hammer seemed to knock the props out from under the case for the prosecution till it hardly seemed as though the state's attorneys had a leg left to stand upon." The *Boston Post* concluded: "As an appeal to the common sense the speech is a mastery." Another reporter explained: "Robinson indulged in no flights, but in a matter of fact way talked to the hardheaded, cool old farmers in the jury." Robinson's simplicity and clarity had already won him "universal admiration." "The argument," another noted, "was worthy of the occasion and of the man."

The New York correspondents were less impressed. Robinson may have been a peerless cross-examiner, an unrivaled "seducer into unwitting admissions," but, in Howard's estimation, his closing argument "fell short of the anticipation in both matter and manner." Ralph went further: "It never reached up to eloquence and it never reached into the heart of the hearer." "Worse yet," he continued, "it was conceived in the wrong spirit . . . There was never a note of triumph in four hours of talking, nor was there one bold declaration of the woman's innocence. Instead of adopting this manner, Mr. Robinson took the defensive."

District Attorney Knowlton for the government, *Boston Globe*

When Hosea Knowlton rose to give his closing argument, he knew he faced a formidable challenge. Knowlton had lost the two most important rulings on evidence, rulings excluding Lizzie's inquest testimony and her alleged attempts to buy prussic acid. He now stood before a jury that had just heard

Robinson's summation, a summation that was as much sentimental narrative as legal argument. And it was so hot in the courtroom that "the crowd inside was one vast fan." But, as Howard put it, "[h]is strong personality, his firm New England temperament, his devotion to duty, but above all his matchless skill in forcible statement, his incisive and logical mind combined with his long experience in prosecuting legal offenders were all at his command."

Knowlton immediately acknowledged the special horror of the crimes: "In the midst of the largest city of this County, in the midst of his household, surrounded by houses and people and teams and civilization in the midst of the day . . . an aged man and an aged woman are suddenly and brutally assassinated. It was a terrible crime. It was an impossible crime. But it was committed." The sense of "impossibility" did not end with the crime. If anything, the identity of the accused increased it. "If you had read the account of these cold and heartless facts in any tale of fiction," Knowlton admitted, "you would have said . . . That will do for a story, but such things never happen." Knowlton acknowledged: "It is no ordinary criminal that we are trying today. It is one of the rank of lady, the equal of your wife and mine . . . of whom such things have never been suspected or dreamed before." This fact, above all others, gave the case its "terrible significance." He explained: "We are trying a crime that would have been deemed impossible but for the fact that it was, and are charging with the commission of it a woman whom we could have believed incapable of doing it but for the evidence that it is my duty, my painful duty, to call to your attention."

Before specifically linking Lizzie Borden to the crimes, Knowlton provided well-known examples of unlikely criminals. First, Knowlton argued that "no station in life is a pledge or security against the commission of crime." Knowlton described ostensibly respectable gentlemen who absconded with funds, particularly those of widows and orphans. For example, in a notorious episode from the 1870s, two socially prominent Fall River businessmen were tried for embezzling bank funds. Knowlton explained: "They were Christian men, they were devout men." Yet, he added, "When the crash came it was found they were rotten to the core." Second, he argued even the "sacred robes of the church are not exempt," for even ministers "have found themselves to be foul as hell inside." Knowlton was referring to the Reverend Ephraim Avery, a Methodist minister tried for the 1832 murder of pregnant factory worker Sarah Cornell, once Fall River's most notorious killing. Third, he argued that youth was no protection against crime, citing the case of Jesse Pomeroy, "a boy of tender years" who was "the most fiendish murderer that the Commonwealth ever knew." Finally, he asked the most important question: "Is sex a protection of crime?" Knowlton reminded the jury of a notorious murder case "within the remembrance of every man I am talking to," involving a woman known as "the Borgia of Somerville." Sarah Jane Robinson's well-insured family died with a suspicious regularity; she was convicted of one poisoning (and suspected of six others) in 1888.

Although he implied that he had intended to theorize a criminal lady, he had not. Instead he separated out the four most disturbing factors—class, religion, youth, and sex—from Lizzie's identity to argue that none of them was, in and of itself, a barrier to criminal behavior. He could easily have ignored youth. But instead of pointing out that Lizzie Borden was, after all, an adult of thirty-two years, Knowlton colluded in the defense's presentation of Borden as a young girl. It seemed that Knowlton could not see past her designated minority as an unmarried daughter living in her father's house. The other factors were even more difficult to dismiss. Class, religion, and sex together formed a potent cocktail. Knowlton's only example of a female murderer was not of Borden's class, nor was she a member of the Christian Endeavor Society. She had also used poison, the quintessential tool of the female murderer.

Knowlton returned to the sex of the accused. He acknowledged that "it is hard . . . to conceive that women can be guilty of crime." But he enjoined the jurors to remember that women "are human like unto us. They are no better than we; they are no worse than we." Despite this nod to equality, Knowlton then drew a picture of the female criminal illustrated by Shakespeare and Dickens (the two "great master[s] of human nature") and supported by prevailing attitudes about women's nature. Contending that "many of the most famous criminals have been women," he alluded to the character of Lady Macbeth, implying that a woman might strike down a sleeping king, the nation's father, when a strong man would, in the same position, lose his nerve. Similarly, he described Tulkinghorn's murder in *Bleak House* as "the most dastardly, the most desperate, the most absolutely brutal crime" in Dickens's oeuvre. Knowlton was a better lawyer than a literary critic: Lady Macbeth, he failed to observe, had not actually delivered any of the blows; and Sikes's bludgeoning of Nancy in *Oliver Twist* was far more brutal than the maid Hortense's shooting of the sinister lawyer Tulkinghorn. After running through these dubious literary examples and failing to produce historical precedents, he fell back upon ancient tropes about female nature: what women "lack in strength and coarseness and vigor," Knowlton contended, "they make up for . . . in cunning, in dispatch, in celerity, in ferocity. If their loves are stronger and more enduring than those of men, am I saying too much that, on the other hand, their hates are more undying, more unyielding, more persistent?" For that reason, he enjoined the jurors to "face this case as men, not as gallants."

As he spoke, Knowlton "time and time again left his place behind the bar, walked around to the jury, stood at their side or immediately in front of them, and spoke with marked earnestness, distinctness, and emphasis." While he moved around the court, Lizzie's gaze never wavered. She craned her head to one side or the other so that her view remained unobscured. According to Howard, "She lost no word, no inflection, no gesture, but looked at him as though with a pitying amazement at the whole procedure."

In a tonal pirouette, Knowlton defended himself and his colleagues. He admitted that he had personally been stung by "slanderous tongues" imputing unworthy motives to his prosecution. Nothing but the sheer weight of evidence could have persuaded him to proceed.

"Gentlemen," he said, "it is the saddest duty of my life." In the same vein, he defended the police, the objects of his opposing counsel's sarcasm: "A blue coat does not make a man any better; it ought not to make him any worse." He admitted the police made mistakes but contended that they did their work "honestly, faithfully." As for the medical experts, whatever cavils they might hear from the defense, the scientific testimony was uncontroverted. He noted: "You will find that their conclusions are accurate because those who could have disputed them have not done so." The most important point of agreement, the evidence that made it seemingly impossible for an outside intruder to have committed the crimes, was the medical judgment that more than an hour separated the two murders, a point to which he would return with great emphasis.

To prepare the jury to understand the cumulative effect of the evidence introduced at trial, he carefully outlined the value of circumstantial evidence. First, he explained the simple distinction between direct and circumstantial evidence: "Direct evidence is the evidence of a man who sees and hears: circumstantial evidence is all other kinds of evidence." He refuted the defense argument that circumstantial evidence was an inferior class of evidence, something calling for special skepticism. If anything, "Men will not tell the truth always: facts cannot tell but one story." "Murder is the work of stealth and craft," he reminded the jury, "in which there are not only no witnesses, but the traces are attempted to be obliterated." Lest anyone still question the reliability of circumstantial evidence, he turned again to classic literature. He alluded to Robinson Crusoe's famous discovery of another set of footprints on his apparently uninhabited island. Knowlton explained: "It was circumstantial: It was nothing but circumstantial evidence but it satisfied him." After all, Knowlton continued, "[H]e had no lawyer to tell him that there was nothing but circumstance." For the nonliterary juror, he provided a natural metaphor: "It is like refuse that floats upon the surface of the stream. You stand upon the banks of the river and you see a chip go by. That is only a circumstance. You see another chip go by. That is another circumstance." Yet, "You would not hesitate," after viewing those chips travel by, "to say you knew which way the current of that river was."

Returning to the case at hand, Knowlton explained that the prosecution's case was based on Lizzie's exclusive opportunity. He explained that the "discovery . . . that these two people did not come to their death at the same time" was the "controlling fact" of the case. The time lapse meant "[i]t was no sudden act of a man coming in and out. It was the act of a person who spent the forenoon in this domestic establishment, killing the woman at her early work and waiting till the man returned for his noon day meal." No one but Lizzie had the opportunity to commit the murders. If no one else could have committed the crimes, then she must have been the perpetrator.

More than that, the very nature of the wounds was feminine. Knowlton remarked of the haphazard injuries to Abby's skull: "What sort of blows were they? Some struck here at an angle, badly aimed; some struck here in the neck, badly directed; some pattered on the top of the head. . . . weak, puttering, badly aimed, nerveless blows." He concluded: "The hand that held that weapon was not the hand of masculine strength . . . It was the hand of a person strong only in hate and the desire to kill." Leaving that aside for the moment, he wondered how Lizzie, assuming she was innocently in the house, could not have heard her stepmother fall. Knowlton reminded the jury: "This poor woman was standing when she was struck, and fell with all the force of that 200 pounds of flesh, flat and prone and dead on the floor. That jar could not have failed to have been heard all over that house . . . Nothing happened in one part of that house that wasn't heard in the other."

To match Lizzie's opportunity was her enmity toward her stepmother: "It was . . . malice against Mrs. Borden that inspired the assassin. It was Mrs. Borden whose life this wicked person sought; and all the motive that we have to consider . . . bears on her." Knowlton reminded the jury that Lizzie was the only person known to wish Abby ill. He chastised Lizzie for slighting the woman who raised her, for denying her the honorific of "Mother" in favor of Mrs. Borden: "It was a living insult to that woman, a living expression of contempt." But he reserved his greatest condemnation for what he described as her ingratitude to her father. Commenting on the property transfer that sparked the tension in the household, he remonstrated: "How wicked to have found fault with it. How petty to have found fault with it." Andrew was well within his rights to give anything he wanted to Abby, "his faithful wife who has served him thirty years for her board and clothes."

Knowlton's diction reduced Abby to the status of servant in her own household. Whether or not that was strictly accurate, it was metaphorically apt, capturing the consistent treatment of her death as the lesser tragedy. According to the prosecution's theory, Abby was the intended murder victim, yet nearly a month elapsed before her murder was added to the charges against Lizzie Borden. Abby herself remains a cipher. She might as well be a domestic ghost, materializing only as the unwitting precipitant of the Bordens' slow-burning conflagration. Yet, at times, she looms much larger, cast as the stepmother of fairy tales, the usurper who comes between father and daughter, who siphons off family wealth to her own impecunious line, and whose physical size instantiates her greed. As for clues to her actual personality, according to Bridget Sullivan, Abby was "always very kind and good to her." Mrs. Southard Miller, Dr. Bowen's mother-in-law, who also lived across the street from the Bordens, said that "she had lost in Mrs. Borden, the best and most intimate neighbor she had ever met." And before the property dispute, Lizzie said that she would ask her stepmother to intervene with her father on the rare occasions he denied her something she really wanted. Though that perceived influence was recast as betrayal, Abby's single monetary demand on the Borden fisc was for the benefit of her half sister (and her own stepmother), not for herself.

Knowlton depicted the Borden house as one beset by festering tensions, literalized in the family's elaborate locking rituals. Knowlton expounded: "It is said that there is a skeleton in the household of every man, but the Borden skeleton . . . was fairly well locked up from view." The external and internal system of locks and hooks made it impossible, he claimed, for anyone else to be hiding in the house before the murders. But, more than that, the myriad locks showed the nature of the household. When you have a dispute with an outsider, "He goes his way and you go yours." "But," Knowlton explained, "these people day in and day out, year in and year out under the same roof, compelled to eat the same bread, compelled to sleep in the same house, compelled to meet each other morning, noon and night yet maintain this strained, unnatural hostility." Finally, at a loss to convey the psychological damage wrought by such an existence, he said, "This was a cancer."

Despite his evident distaste for her behavior before the murders and his belief in her guilt of the crimes, Knowlton found himself in verbal knots at the thought of calling Lizzie Borden a liar. The missing note Lizzie claimed Abby had received was a key part of the prosecution case. It prevented Andrew from looking for Abby upon his return. Had he done so, he would have found her already murdered, perhaps preventing his own death. The purported note also gave Lizzie a convenient rationale for not seeking out Abby immediately after discovering her father's body. Knowlton, however, prefaced one of his strongest pieces of evidence with a caveat: "Conscious as I am . . . that any unjust or harsh word of mine might do injury that I never could recover my peace of mind for, I reaffirm that serious charge." Putting aside the absurdity of someone seeking to lure an old, frail woman out of the house while leaving two younger, heartier women inside, Knowlton asked why, if a note existed, its author had never come forward: "Little did it occur to Lizzie Borden when she told that lie to her father that there would be 80,000 witnesses to the falsity of it." He then oddly asserted that he had "hoped somebody would come forward . . . and relieve this case of that falsehood" as if the lie were more shocking to contemplate than the murders. Recovering himself, he concluded simply: "No note came; no note was written; nobody brought a note; nobody was sick; Mrs. Borden had not had a note."

It seemed as though Knowlton was "warming up . . . to a white heat of intense mental activity and physical development, walking to and fro, gesticulating with violence, and looking with comprehensive sweep . . . from the bench to the jury, from the prisoner to the counsel, and thence about the audience." But, realizing that the afternoon session was drawing to a close, Knowlton gave the jury a précis of his argument thus far: "God forbid that anybody should have committed this murder, but somebody did." Abby Borden, he insisted, "was killed, not by the strong hand of a man, but by the weak and ineffectual blows of a woman . . . the only person in the universe who could be benefitted by her taking away." As Knowlton walked up and down in front of the jury, everyone in the courtroom leaned forward so as not to miss a moment of his oration—including Lizzie, who "looked at him fixedly and steadily with a curious, set expression upon her features." Reaching deep into his rhetorical quiver, he then delivered a biblically inspired rhetorical coup de grâce, causing a sensation in the courtroom: "There was coming a stern and just man who knew the feelings between them and would say to her, as the Almighty said to Cain, 'Where is Abel, thy brother?'"

The assumption had been that Knowlton would finish his closing argument that evening, but after a short recess the judges decided "that a late session would be an intolerable burden in this day of excessive heat." The court adjourned until the following morning. As Joe Howard wryly observed, "The judges are in no hurry; they are on the bench for life."

TUESDAY, JUNE 20, 1893

On the last day of the trial, interested citizens redoubled their efforts and laid siege to the courthouse. The *Fall River Daily Globe* reported: "Over an hour before the time of opening, the doors were besieged by people, mostly ladies in holiday attire, all hoping for seats. But there were too few of them for accommodation for the tenth part of the claimants." The *Fall River Daily Herald* also drew attention to the feminine element: "The intensity of the crush this afternoon is abominable. The pushing and struggling New Bedford women are a disgrace to femininity. Every foot within the bar enclosure is filled, and every seat without is occupied." They flowed out into the anterooms, the stairways, and the halls. Outside, the approach to the courthouse resembled a human wall as people vainly attempted to secure admittance. All wished to be present for what one newspaper termed "The Last Scene in the Great Borden Trial."

Lizzie Borden herself arrived early, bearing a bouquet of pond lilies and white carnations. She had "an animated conversation" with former governor Robinson before the start of the court proceedings. The *New Bedford Evening Standard* noticed that "there was a restless activity about her which betrayed itself in an unusual nervousness, and it is plain to see that despite her wonderful self-control that she is full of internal excitement." When Knowlton began speaking, she watched him intensely, and "blood ebbed and flowed to her face."

Knowlton resumed his argument with a reminder that the commonwealth did not have to prove motive: "We are called upon to prove that the thing was done, and our duty stops there." No motive, he acknowledged, could ever be adequate to explain the murders. But he directed the jury to focus on Lizzie Borden's hatred of her stepmother: "The malice was all before the fact. The wickedness was all before the fourth day of August." He speculated that Andrew may have been planning to make a new will. But, he admitted, "We cannot tell . . . what new fuel was added to the fire of discontent . . . We do not know what occurred in that family that kept that young woman from the delightful shore of Marion, where all her friends are; and kept her by her father and mother during those hot days of that hot summer." He may have sensed the gravitational force of intense family feuds, but he faltered as he tried to explain the intensity of the hatred, concluding that "there was a jealousy which was unworthy of that woman." Then he asked the jury to leave "the dead body of that aged woman upon the guest-chamber floor . . . and . . . come down with me to a far sadder tragedy, to the most horrible word that the English language knows, to a parricide."

At this point, Knowlton stumbled over the corpse of Andrew

Borden. Even he could not bring himself to accuse Lizzie Borden of premeditation in the "far sadder" murder of her father. Knowlton assured the jury that "it is a grateful relief to our conceptions of human nature to be able to find reasons to believe that the murder of Andrew Borden was not planned by his younger daughter, but was done as a wicked and dreadful necessity." In his telling, Lizzie Borden plotted the demise of her loathed stepmother, but Andrew Borden's unexpected return interrupted her in her plan to establish an alibi, and she was forced to kill him as well. Alluding to the earlier daylight theft hushed up by Andrew, Knowlton contended that Lizzie must have suddenly realized that this was too horrible an act for her father to keep in the family: "When the deed was done she was coming down stairs to face Nemesis." But in suppressing any motive but that of hatred of her stepmother, Knowlton was forced to argue that Lizzie Borden killed her father because whoever killed one victim murdered the other, a weakness Robinson was able to exploit. Significantly, Knowlton ignored the most straightforward reason for the order of the murders: if Andrew Borden had been killed first, his daughters would have shared the estate with their stepmother's beneficiaries. Even Knowlton could not bring himself to raise the crime to this level of cold-blooded calculation. When he suggested that Andrew might have been about to make a will, he considered it only as adding "new fuel" to Lizzie's malice against Abby, not as a motive for Andrew's murder. Whether he himself could not contemplate this eminently practical scenario or he believed that the jury would find it as unthinkable as the crime itself, he sacrificed a coherent narrative in favor of a more palatable motive: feminine frenzy erupting out of a stepdaughter's smoldering resentment. By refusing the more probable plot, he was left with a chain of circumstantial evidence, a chain with one very weak link—the apparent normality of Lizzie Borden.

Just as the defense had earlier argued that only a fiend could have committed the murders, Knowlton seized upon this metaphor as a compromise that held Lizzie Borden responsible for the crime, yet ultimately not responsible for her father's death. According to Knowlton,

"It was not Lizzie Andrew Borden, the daughter of Andrew J. Borden, that came down those stairs, but a murderess, transformed from all the thirty-three years of an honest life, transformed from the daughter, transformed from the ties of affection, to the most consummate criminal we have read of in all our history or works of fiction." Lizzie Borden's imagined transformation solved the problem of her apparent normality. Knowlton envisioned a kind of temporary insanity reminiscent of Dr. Jekyll's metamorphosis into Mr. Hyde. If she committed the murders in an altered state, then she could be found guilty without being morally responsible for her actions. But even if Knowlton's explanation seemed momentarily reassuring, such an argument still left the jury in an uncomfortable quandary. How could one tell if a dutiful daughter harbored an inner fiend?

Knowlton simply evaded that essential dilemma. He reminded the jury: "The Commonwealth is charged with a duty of satisfying you that she killed her mother and father; not why." Instead, he returned to comfortable ground, a methodical discussion of the timeline of events. Andrew returned; Lizzie told him that Abby was out. Here the staunch Universalist Knowlton indulged in the most inflammatory New Testament metaphor possible: Lizzie "suggests to him, with the spirit in which Judas kissed his master, that, as he is weary with his day's work, it would be well for him to lie down upon the sofa and rest." Knowlton pointed out that Lizzie said she returned to the dining room to iron handkerchiefs, a task left undone in the morning. Yet again, despite the need to reheat the iron every time, she did not finish that simple chore. As Knowlton explained, "She had begun her work before Bridget went upstairs; she was engaged in it when Bridget left her; it was a job that could not have taken her more than ten minutes at the outside." But, in her account, she left that work and decided to look for a piece of iron in the barn, variously, to fix a screen or make a sinker. Knowlton described Lizzie Borden's account of her actions as "simply incredible." He reminded the jurors: "We must judge all facts, all circumstances, as they appeal to our common sense." Reviewing Lizzie's account of her morning, in particular, her decision to visit the stifling barn loft to get fishing sinkers, he asked the jury the questions Lizzie had left unanswered at the inquest. Where, for example, was the fishing line? In that light, he concluded, Lizzie Borden's story about being in the barn loft was "not within the bounds of reasonable possibilities." It only made sense as a concocted alibi for murder, for "it was not only the hottest place in all this hot . . . city . . . it was the only place where she could put herself and not have known what took place." In a similar vein, he pointed out her "presentiments" of doom, arguing that she went to see Alice Russell and "prepared her for something dreadful." Knowlton dismissed the defense's notion that "presentiments" are common: "All the disasters of your life, Mr. Foreman, all the things that ever came with crushing weight upon the happiness of your life, came like a flash of lightning out of the clear sky. Today you are happy; tomorrow you are plunged in grief."

Knowlton then abandoned his prior gallantry. In an attempt to destroy this image of the bereaved daughter, Knowlton focused upon Lizzie Borden's conduct after the murders, in particular her transgressions of femininity. He described her as "cool to a degree of coolness that . . . has challenged the amazement of the world." He acknowledged "that the absence of tears, that the icy demeanor, may have either meant consciousness of guilt or consciousness of loss"; however, he quickly dismissed the latter explanation. Lizzie Borden's behavior at the scene of the murder suggested a masculine courage highly suspicious in a woman. Knowlton contrasted her "calm and quiet demeanor" at the scene of the crime with the "agitation of a man in the same position fifteen minutes afterwards." Knowlton also emphasized her willingness to go into the room containing her late parents' bloodstained clothing the night after the murders, commenting, "All I propose to make of that incident is to emphasize from it the almost stoical nerve of a woman, who, when her friend, not the daughter or the stepdaughter of these murdered people, but her friend, could not bear to go into the room where those clothes were, should have the nerve to go down there alone, alone, and calmly enter the room for some purpose that had I know not what connection with this case." He reminded the jury of Lizzie's comments after failing the egg experiment reported by Matron Reagan, that it was the only thing she had ever put her mind to that she could not do.

Knowlton then turned to the defense's trump card: Where was the blood? As he put it, "How could she have avoided the spattering of her dress with blood if she was the author of these crimes?" Acknowledging this weakness, he suggested that she might have taken advantage of the "solitude of the house with ample fire on the stove." Perhaps Lizzie used a roll of paper to protect her dress or, more likely, she hid the bloodstained dress until she burned it in the kitchen the next Sunday. But he admitted: "I cannot answer it. You cannot answer it . . . You have neither the craft of the assassin nor the cunning and deftness of the sex."

Speaking of dresses, he pointed to the disputed blue dress Lizzie wore on the morning of the murders. He argued that the dress handed over to the police was not the dress she had been wearing. Adelaide Churchill, "clear eyed, intelligent, honest daughter of one of Fall River's most honored citizens," described the dress as some kind of cheap cotton, a calico or cambric. He reminded the jurors that she had first seen Lizzie Borden that morning before she knew the full horror of the scene and did not think the trial exhibit was the same dress. Compare her forthrightness, he advised the jury, to Phoebe Bowen's evasiveness. "When Mrs. Bowen raised her hand to take her oath," he said, "it shook like an aspen leaf." Nonetheless, she described it as a "cheap morning dress."

Where was the paint-stained dress before Alice Russell saw Lizzie destroy it? None of the officers had encountered a paint-stained dress during their searches—"It was not where the officers could find it"— proof, according to Knowlton, "it was concealed." And, to make sure it would never be examined, Lizzie burned it the morning after the officers conducted their inventory of her dresses. "That dress," he said, "had been good enough to keep through May, through June, through July, through the first weeks in August. It was a singular thing that of all times in the world it should be selected on the Lord's day to destroy a dress which had been concealed from the search of the officers made the afternoon before and within twelve hours of the time that Lizzie was told that formal accusation was being made against her." What could that demonstrate but consciousness of guilt? Knowlton paused to wonder aloud what might have been Bridget Sullivan's fate had she behaved in the same way: "Supposing she had told wrong stories; supposing she had put up an impossible alibi; supposing she had put up a dress that never was worn that morning at all, and when the coils were tightening around her had burned a dress up that it should not be seen, what would you think of Bridget? Is there one law for Bridget and another for Lizzie? God forbid."

As if to emphasize that point, the court stood in recess for five minutes. When Knowlton resumed his argument, he stepped back from the specifics of the case to laud the Anglo-American tradition of the jury trial. He explained: "It is absolutely necessary . . . that the witnesses that are to give their evidence shall be brought before you for you to look at them, for you to look in their faces, for you to hear them answer the questions that are put to them, for you to hear them sustain the test of cross examination." "There is," he insisted, "no better test." This paean revealed itself as Knowlton's rehabilitation of Matron Reagan's testimony. Mrs. Reagan claimed to have overheard a quarrel between the sisters during which Lizzie told Emma, "You've given me away!" Knowlton said: "I am not quite so willing to dismiss the conduct of Miss Lizzie Borden in the guard room of the police station in so supercilious and satirical a manner as my distinguished friend." In spite of (or perhaps even because of) the efforts of Lizzie's allies to suppress the story, Knowlton considered it "extremely significant." Much like the tale of the dress burning wrenched from the "Puritan conscience" of Alice Russell, the story of the quarrel came from someone who liked Lizzie and who was even willing to retract it so long as it was not under oath.

One other mystery remained: the murder weapon. Knowlton observed: "My distinguished friend has seen fit to make some humorous comments upon the various hatchets that have been produced in this case." He offered a more straightforward explanation for the initial mistake in identifying the claw-hammer hatchet as the murder weapon. When the police found a hatchet stained with blood and with a hair on it, they naturally assumed that was the weapon. As it happens, they were wrong. They then turned their attention to the handleless hatchet head, a hatchet head that was covered in ashes rather than dust. He reminded the jury that the hatchet head with the broken handle fit Mr. Borden's wounds precisely. (Out of deference to the sensibilities of Lizzie Borden, whom he called "this unfortunate woman," Knowlton did not ask for the skulls to be brought into the courtroom for another demonstration.) Most tellingly, the "handle was broken off not as axe handles are splintered . . . broken off not as accidental, but as by design, that no part of the wood of that handle should be exposed to view." Nonetheless, he continued, "We do not say that was the hatchet. It may well have been." Lizzie could have an inaccessible hiding space: "The recesses and mysteries of that house are all within her twenty years [sic] acquaintance of it. How little can any one else know of it?" Most significantly, the apparent absence of a murder weapon at the scene contradicted the idea of an outside assassin: "The very fact that no hatchet was found there is a piece of evidence, is one of those chips that float right with the stream, which points directly to the inmates of the house as authors of this awful crime." The killer "never would have gone into the streets, armed and loaded and fated with the evidence that would convict him."

Knowlton returned to the overwhelming circumstantial evidence in his summary of the prosecution case, arguing that every piece of the puzzle made sense if Lizzie was the killer. He said: "We find a woman murdered by blows which were struck with a weak and indecisive hand . . . We find that woman had no enemies in all this world except the daughter that had repudiated her. We find that the woman was killed at half past nine when it passes the bound of human credulity to believe it could have been done without her knowledge, her presence, her sight, her hearing. We find a house guarded by night and by day so that no assassin could find lodgment in it for a moment . . . We say these things float down on the great current of our thoughts and tell us where the stream leads to." Knowlton concluded: "We get down now to the elements of ordinary crime. We get hatred, we get malice . . . we get absurd and impossible alibis. We get contradictory stories . . . we get fraud upon the officers by the substitution of an afternoon silk dress as the one she was wearing that morning ironing, and . . . a guilty destruction of the dress that she feared the eye of the microscope might find blood upon." Ending his closing with a burst of eloquence, Knowlton thundered: "What's the defense? Nothing. Nothing. I stop and think, and I say again, nothing." He enjoined the jury: "I submit these facts to you with the confidence that you are men of courage and truth . . . Rise, gentlemen, rise to the altitude of your duty. Act as you would like to think of having acted when you stand before the Great White Throne at the last day." Knowlton sermonized, "What shall be your reward? The ineffable consciousness of duty done . . . Only he who hears the voice of his inner consciousness—it is the voice of God himself, saying to him, 'Well done, good and faithful servant'—can enter into the reward and lay hold of eternal life."

Most commentators applauded Knowlton's efforts. Julian Ralph and Joe Howard, two of Borden's most fervent supporters, agreed that it was a great speech. Howard, for his part, believed Knowlton "rank[ed] with the ablest advocates of the day." In Knowlton, a "big burly man with a square, earnest face, a tremendous physique, a powerful voice and a bearing indicative of great courage," Howard saw "the same pride of bearing, the same earnestness of purpose, the same tremendous potentiality which we find displayed in the engine No. 999 on its 20 hour trip from New York to Chicago." Ralph agreed: "The magnificent figure of the speaker helped him. His powerful voice was seldom raised, but, impressively subdued, kept the people silent and still." But would such eloquence be enough? "Down to the opening of Gov. Robinson," Howard reported, "the bets were 2 to 1 in favor of an acquittal; now they were 2 to 1 in favor of a disagreement."

After a recess for lunch, the court resumed proceedings. Chief Judge Mason informed Lizzie Borden, "It is your privilege to add any word which you may desire to say in person to the jury." Lizzie stood erect and responded in a clear voice: "I am innocent. I leave it to my counsel to speak for me." Ralph thought that, in speaking those words, "she added to her extraordinary gracefulness a surprising dignity."

Judge Dewey delivered the charge to the jury, the formal instructions on the law meant to guide their deliberation. Dewey looked like "a college professor" and was reputed to be both a "clear-headed logician" and "a tender-hearted man." Here, he favored the latter. First, he explained: "Your decision can properly rest only on the law and the evidence given you, together with those matters of common knowledge and experience relating to the ordinary affairs of life, and the common qualities of human nature and motive of action . . . which, as jurors, you are expected to bring with you." But the jury must not consider any of the prior proceedings—the inquest, the preliminary hearing, or the grand jury—as evidence. The jury must weigh all the evidence presented at this trial and decide if there was reasonable doubt. Dewey defined the concept: "Proof beyond reasonable doubt . . . is proof to a moral certainty, as distinguished from absolute certainty."

Turning to the specifics of the case, he reminded the jurors that "the defendant's character has been good . . . one of positive, of active benevolence in religious and charitable work." "You are not," he warned the jury, "inquiring into the action of some imaginary being, but into the action of a real person, the defendant, with her character, with her habits, with her education, with her ways of life." He also explained that the government need not prove a motive. But what he seemed to give to the prosecution, he took away with his subsequent observation that "imputing a motive to the defendant does not prove she had it." He asked: "Unless the child be destitute of natural affection, will the desire to come into possession of the inheritance be likely to constitute an active, efficient inducement for the child to take the parent's life?" Judge Dewey then characterized Borden's notorious comment to the dressmaker Mrs. Gifford as merely the "intense expression" of a "young woman, not of a philosopher or a jurist." He instructed jurors to "[C]onsider whether or not they do not often use words, which, strictly taken, go far beyond their real meaning. Would it be a just mode of reasoning to make use of the alleged subsequent murder to put enmity into the words and then use the words, thus charged with hostile meaning, as evidence the defendant committed the murder?" Of Borden's predictions of doom, which Robinson dismissed as a side effect of her "monthly illness," Judge Dewey offered another rationale for disregarding them: "Suppose some person in New Bedford contemplated the perpetration of a great crime . . . [and] contemplated doing it soon. Would he naturally, probably, predict, a day or two beforehand, that anything of the nature of that crime would occur?"

As for the note, Dewey rebutted the prosecution's claim that Lizzie lied about the note. "What motive," he asked, "had she to invent a story like this? What motive? Would it not have been more natural for her to say simply, that her step-mother had gone out?" She need not have pointed to something tangible. Instead, he suggested that, if we "contemplate the possibility of there being another assassin than herself," it could have been part of his plan to write the note and then remove it himself.

He then turned to the biggest stumbling block for the prosecution: the gruesome nature of the hatchet blows. "Is there anything in the way and manner of doing the acts of killing, the weapon used, whatever it was, or the force applied, which is significant as to the sex and strength of the doer of the acts?" he asked. He reminded the jurors of how the medical experts had testified "as to the way in which they think the blows were inflicted on Mrs. Borden" (wood-chopping-style), and "as to the position of the assailant" (astride her body). Dewey asked a series of questions that seemed rhetorical: "Are these views correct? If so, are they favorable to the contention that a person of the defendant's sex and size was the assailant? Is it reasonable and credible that she could have killed Mrs. Borden at or about the time claimed by the Government, and then, with the purpose in her mind to kill her father at a later hour, have gone about her household affairs with no change of manner to excite attention?" He reminded the jury: "You have a right to reason and judge from what you know of the laws and property of human nature and action; and if it is suggested to you that the killing of Mr. Borden was not part of the original plan . . . it will be for you to consider . . . whether that suggestion to you seems to be reasonable."

Judge Dewey explained the law in Massachusetts about defendants testifying at their own trials. He drew their attention to "the guarded language of the statute," providing that a person charged with commission of a crime "shall, at his own request, but not otherwise, be deemed a competent witness; and his neglect or refusal to testify shall not create any presumption against him." The law derived from the common-law practice of not permitting defendants to testify on their own behalf and from the Massachusetts Bill of Rights protecting against self-incrimination. In plain language, unless she herself decided to testify, it was as if she had no right to testify. No negative inference could be drawn about her failure to testify. But Dewey went further. He offered reasons she might not wish to testify: "If she were required to explain, others might think the explanation insufficient"; she would also be subject to cross-examination like any other witness. He explained: "She may be asked questions that are legally competent which she is not able to answer, or she may answer questions truly and yet it may be argued against her that her answers were untrue, and her neglect to answer perverse."

Warning the jurors not to consider any information from any prior accounts of the case they might have read, he urged them to deliberate "with impartial and thoughtful minds, seeking only for truth" so that they would "lift the case above the range of passion and prejudice and excited feeling, into the clear atmosphere of reason and law." Yet, like Robinson and Knowlton before him, Dewey invoked a higher law and omniscient power to guide the jury's deliberations, expressing his hope that Providence "may express in its results somewhat of that justice with which God governs the world."

Judge Dewey's charge buoyed Lizzie Borden's friends. Indeed, Joe Howard called it "a plea for the innocent." "Had he been the senior counsel for the defense," Howard continued, "he could not have more absolutely pointed out the folly of depending upon circumstantial evidence alone." As they waited for a verdict, Judges Blodgett and Dewey went for a walk, leaving Chief Judge Mason alone in the judges' room. The reporters melted into the crowd, interviewing spectators or simply eavesdropping. Lizzie remained in the dock, chatting with friends sitting around her. Eventually she, too, went out for a short break. Suddenly the festive atmosphere ended. Less than an hour and a half into their deliberations, the jury was ready with its verdict. "The silence became impressive and fearful" as Lizzie Borden returned to her seat. She did not falter. As one commentator declared: "At no time during the trial has the prisoner's almost supernatural courage so appalled the spectators as at this sublime moment of her entry into the court room to hear her doom."

The jurors were no less somber: they entered with a "look of fixed determination on their countenances as of men who had done a trying duty faithfully to their consciences." Even the clerk shook perceptibly. When asked for the verdict, the foreman could no longer contain his excitement, interrupting the question and declaring Lizzie Borden "Not guilty." As the courtroom erupted in what seemed to be a single yell, joined, after a momentary delay, by an answering cheer from the spectators outside "which might have been heard half a mile away," Lizzie Borden sank back into her chair "as if she was shot," placed her face on the rail in front of her seat, and sobbed. Even her supporters were startled: "Every man of them was as pale as a corpse, as they looked toward her." The clerk continued: "Gentlemen of the jury, you, upon your oaths, do say that Lizzie Andrew Borden, the prisoner at the bar, is not guilty?"

"We do!" replied the jurors.

"Say you, Mr. Foreman, so say all of you?"

A unanimous "We do" followed.

The court adjourned at 4:38 p.m. The trial was over.

Different stories of the jury deliberations later surfaced. In one account, the jurors argued, nearly coming to blows. Another declared that a juror bought the verdict by promising liquor to the others if

Last scene in the Great Borden Trial, *Boston Globe*

they voted for acquittal on the first ballot. In yet another, the first ballot found one juror committed to convict; the second found them unanimous for acquittal. But the truth was less dramatic. An informal ballot was taken once they were in the room. Finding themselves already unanimous, they discussed the evidence to seem "reasonably deliberative," out of courtesy to the district attorney. They then voted unanimously for acquittal, remaining in the room, again "as a matter of courtesy," for an additional half hour.

Lizzie's friends had been "warned by the counsel that, in the event of a verdict of acquittal, they should make no demonstration that would mar the dignity of the court." As Howard put it, "He might as well have given directions for stopping the flow of the tides." In any event, Sheriff Wright "never saw the people rising in their seats and waving their handkerchiefs in unison with their voices, because his eyes were full of tears and were completely blinded." He was not alone: "Tears gushed from hundreds of eyes" and "It was whispered that two of the three judges had cried." Knowlton and Moody congratulated the defense counsel. Jennings assisted his client to her feet and Robinson "put his arm around the now strengthened girl, and he pressed close down to her cheek as though a loving father was caressing a much loved daughter." Joe Howard declared: "The extraordinary and visible affection between these two persons will always remain as one of the refreshing memories of the trial." Lizzie extended her hand to Melvin Adams but "one wasn't enough . . . and he took both."

Robinson watched "with a fatherly interest in his kindly eyes" as the jurors, "still moving like a lot of convicts out for exercise, gathered themselves in a bunch, and then, in Indian file, marched down to shake hands with the woman for whom they had done so very much." Lizzie greeted "each of them with a fresh sparkle of her eyes, a warm grasp of the hand and a look so grateful and kindly that the heart of every man among them must have been touched." Once liberated, the jurors rushed to the bar of the Parker House for a long-overdue drink. Robinson then led his client out of the court while Jennings held the door. Lizzie herself said very little to most of the reporters, "her warmest greetings being given to Julian Ralph, the man who, from the first, portrayed her actions with unerring skill and judgment."

What were her plans? Where would she go? The reporters asked, and the crowds waited. And with the wide world before her, she chose Fall River.

Part 3

VERDICT

Chapter 11

THE OLD PLACE

Lizzie Borden on piazza
in Newport, circa 1893,
*courtesy of Fall River Histor-
ical Society*

L izzie Borden's acquittal on June 20, 1893, was heralded
throughout the country as confirmation of her obvious innocence. Invoking the Salem witch trials two hundred years
earlier, Julian Ralph wrote: "The suspected witch was in the dock, the
fagots had been piled all around her . . . and the hard-headed District
Attorney was flourishing an unlighted torch before the audience. But it
took only an hour for the jury to decide that witches are out of fashion
in Massachusetts and no one is to be executed there on suspicion and
on parrot-like police testimony." Less dramatically but with similar

The Borden jury, *courtesy of Fall River Historical Society*

passion, the *New York Times* declared: "The acquittal of the most unfortunate and cruelly persecuted woman was, by this promptness . . .
a condemnation of the police authorities and of the legal officers who
secured the indictment and have conducted the trial. It was a declaration, not only that the prisoner was guiltless, but that there never was
any serious reason to suppose that she was guilty . . . Her acquittal is
only a partial atonement for the wrong that she has suffered."

Lizzie Borden's own first thoughts were of home. Joe Howard
heard her declare to her sister: "I want to go home; take me straight
home tonight . . . I want to see the old place and settle down at once."
After leaving the courtroom, Lizzie packed up her belongings from her
cell before beginning the hour-long trip to Fall River by carriage. A
crowd gathered in front of the Second Street house. By nightfall, two
thousand people waited to welcome the former prisoner home. But
Lizzie was instead taken to spend a quiet night at the home of Charles
and Marianna Holmes on Pine Street. There, the former prisoner answered letters from well-wishers far and wide: "Telegrams of congratulation are also arriving, and for some days at least Lizzie Borden will be
a very busy correspondent." One of the jurors brought Lizzie Borden

a photograph of the group, for which they had posed after the verdict. Contrary to the press rumors of "crankiness" among the men, they were, in the words of one of their number, "a jolly crowd" and met annually for at least a decade after the trial. Lizzie wrote each a personal letter, lauding them as her "faithful friends and deliver[ers]."

Some speculated that Lizzie and her sister would move to New York City or somewhere in Europe, change their names, and live out their lives in comfortable anonymity. Those closer to her rejected that notion. Robinson told reporters: "She said she had no other place she cared to go but to Fall River." Besides, as Mary Livermore, one of her most prominent defenders, argued: "No matter where she goes, the news of the tragedies will precede or follow her. If she remains in Fall River, people must be persuaded eventually by her own conduct and character that she is one of the most estimable and most unjustly suspected women in the world."

But in Fall River public sympathy for Lizzie Borden quickly plummeted. The working classes were never on her side. People gathered on street corners to discuss the verdict, expressing "surprise, bordering on indignation." "The line," Julian Ralph observed, was "drawn between rich and poor over her case." But the members of the elite who had protected her during the ordeal cooled in their enthusiasm after her acquittal and eventually shut her out. Her circle of acquaintances shrank. She discovered she was no longer welcome at the Central Congregational Church, in whose good works she had spent so much of her time. When she attended the service on Sunday, July 23, she sat surrounded by empty pews. The next month saw the publication of *The Fall River Tragedy: A History of the Borden Murders* by Edwin Porter, the reporter for the *Fall River Daily Globe* who first published Matron Reagan's story about the sisters' jailhouse quarrel. It was mostly a compilation of Porter's articles for the *Globe*, but it included an unwelcome amount of detail about the official case against Lizzie Borden from the preliminary hearing to the grand jury. Andrew Jennings had promised that "Lizzie and her sister will leave no stone unturned to discover . . . who the real murderer is." Porter's book was a reminder that there were still no other suspects. Much later, Lizzie told a friend that she had her own suspicion about the murderer, but, as she knew well what it was like to be falsely accused, she would not state her opinion.

Lizzie was expected to live down her notoriety. Joe Howard confidently predicted: "She will lead her old life." Instead, she moved on and up. At the end of an impassioned plea for his client, former governor Robinson had asked the court to acquit her so "that she may go and be Lizzie Andrew Borden of Fall River in that bloodstained and wrecked home where she has passed her life so many years." She and Emma promptly vacated the "bloodstained and wrecked home" on Second Street and moved to a larger and more expensive home on French Street, at the top of the Hill district, the city's elite residential area. (They did not sell the old house; they were Andrew Borden's daughters and understood the value of a good investment property.) Lizzie named the new house "Maplecroft" and, as if that were not sufficiently tactless, had the name chiseled onto the granite steps she added during a renovation. There was something grasping and a little vulgar about the gesture. Naming houses in Fall River was unusual, and generally reserved for the mansions of Fall River's most august residents like the

Maplecroft, Lizzie Borden's house on French Street, *courtesy of Fall River Historical Society*

philanthropist Sarah Brayton, who owned a brick Gothic pile named Broadview, or Colonel Spencer Borden, whose estate on North Watuppa Pond, some distance from the city, was known as Interlachen. Neither required a sign or other marker to announce the name.

Lizzie practiced her aspirational nomenclature on herself, changing her own girlish name to the grander-sounding Lizbeth. Lizbeth of Maplecroft, unlike Miss Lizzie Borden of Second Street, went to the theater in Boston and dropped her Christian charities. (One could argue that they dropped her. She supported Central Congregational Church, maintaining a pew where she herself was unwelcome, until 1905.) About this time, Emma consulted Reverend Buck about "happenings at the French Street house" of which she strongly disapproved. There were rumors about "a fine looking young" man named Joseph Tetrault who worked as the Bordens' coachman. Perhaps even more significantly, Lizzie developed a close if short-lived friendship with the actress Nance O'Neil, then "the greatest tragedienne . . . on the stage [outside of New York]," that purportedly scandalized her more retiring sister. Indeed it may well have been O'Neil's influence that led Lizzie to recast herself as "Lizbeth." O'Neil inscribed a copy of *The Poems of Thomas Bailey Aldrich*—Aldrich was the author of the play *Judith of Bethulia*, in which O'Neil appeared as the eponymous heroine—to "Lizbeth" and signed herself "Daphne." Lizzie invited the entire cast of one of O'Neil's productions for a lavish party that featured a full orchestra and champagne, belying her previous temperance work. In the midst of litigation with her manager, Nance

Nance O'Neil as Judith of Bethulia, *courtesy of Fall River Historical Society*

O'Neil borrowed money from Lizzie (who was also touched for a $50 loan by a supporting actress in O'Neil's company). Finding the atmosphere "unbearable," Emma belatedly followed Reverend Buck's advice to make her home elsewhere. In 1905, she moved out and never spoke to her sister again. The rest of their circle followed Emma's example.

Lizzie Borden may have been shunned, but she was not ignored. To mark the anniversary of the murders, her journalistic nemesis, the Irish-Catholic *Fall River Daily Globe*, published an annual reminder of the town's most infamous crime. Its 1904 article included, in the headline, the following disingenuous afterthought: "Perhaps the Murderer or Murderess May Be in the City. Who Can Tell?" The following year, under the headline, "Great Wrong Is Righted," the *Globe* provocatively declared: "There were no Borden murders! Both the victims of 13 years ago died as the result of excessive heat!" This taunting continued for more than two decades.

Lizzie Borden was also dogged by less veiled innuendo. Schoolchildren began to sing an insistent little rhyme:

> *Lizzie Borden took an ax,*
> *Gave her mother forty whacks,*
> *When she saw what she had done,*
> *She gave her father forty-one.*

Papers printed improbable reports of engagements, including a betrothal to one of her former jurors. It was said that salespeople would find items missing after Borden's visits, itemize the loss, and report the figure to the manager, who would, in turn, send the bill to Borden's French Street address. At one point, her alleged transgressions became newsworthy. A woman brought a painted Meissen porcelain plaque to the Tilden-Thurber gallery in Providence for restoration, stating that Lizzie Borden had given it to her. The saleswoman, apparently recognizing the piece, informed the manager that a stolen item had been brought into the store. He notified Borden that she would have to pay for it and had the police issue a warrant for her arrest. She was

Lizzie Borden on piazza with dog Laddie, circa 1926, *courtesy of Fall River Historical Society*

not arrested but the story was featured in the local papers under the headline "Lizzie Borden Again."

Despite her isolation, Lizzie Borden remained in Fall River for the rest of her life. She took comfort in her Boston terriers, for whom she built a special raised seat in her black Packard; she befriended the children of her domestic staff, treating them to ice cream in Tiverton and special-delivery birthday wishes from Auntie Borden. She died quietly at Maplecroft on June 1, 1927. She left instructions "to be laid at my Father's feet" in the Borden family plot at Fall River's Oak Grove Cemetery, less than a mile from her home. The mourners were few, the interment "strictly private," her grave bricked to prevent disturbance. There, she also joined Abby; her mother, Sarah; and her infant sister, Alice. Emma died ten days later, thus reuniting the family in death. They lie together, in perpetual rest, less than two miles from the house on Second Street.

It is tempting to speculate about Lizzie Borden's motivation for remaining in Fall River and enduring the ostracism of the community whose good opinion she had so assiduously sought. But perhaps, half a century earlier, Nathaniel Hawthorne penned the most convincing explanation for his fictional outcast in *The Scarlet Letter*:

> It may seem marvellous, that, with the world before her . . . this woman should still call that place her home, where, and where only, she must needs be the type of shame. But

there is a fatality, a feeling so irresistible and inevitable that it has the force of doom, which almost invariably compels human beings to linger around and haunt, ghost-like, the spot where some great and marked event has given color to their lifetime; and still the more irresistibly, the darker the tinge that saddens it.

Lizzie Borden herself never publicly commented about the case that altered the course of her otherwise drab life. Like the town that bred her and then ostracized her, as she aged, Lizzie Borden turned inward, reclusive, and, above all, silent.

Chapter 12

THE ENDURING ENIGMA

Borden monument, Oak Grove Cemetery, *courtesy of Fall River Historical Society*

The popular fascination with the Borden mystery and its central enigmatic character has endured for over 125 years. Three years before Lizzie Borden died, the celebrated true crime writer Edmund Lester Pearson opined: "The Borden case is without parallel in the criminal history of America. It is the most interesting and perhaps the most puzzling murder which has occurred in this country." Despite having written what was then the definitive account of the case in his 1924 compendium *Studies in Murder*, Pearson returned again and again to the Borden story. In the course of his correspondence with Hosea Knowlton's son (whom he had met, years earlier, in Memorial Hall at Harvard), Pearson even reported his own failed attempt to set eyes upon the "famous citizen of Fall River." After lurking in front of Lizzie's home on French Street, he described being "more disappointed than I was many years ago when I waited one and one-half hours in Hyde Park but failed in the end to see the Queen of England." Seeking to explain the story's continuing allure, he argued:

> There are in it all the elements which make such an event worth reading about, since, in the first place, it was a mysterious crime in a class of society where such deeds are not only foreign, but usually wildly impossible . . . The evidence was wholly circumstantial. The perpetrator of the double murder was protected by a series of chances which might not happen again in a thousand years. And, finally, the case attracted national attention, and divided public opinion, as no criminal prosecution has done since, nor, to the best of my belief, as any murder trial in the United States had ever done before.

Immortalized in rhyme, told and retold in every conceivable genre, the Borden murders and the subsequent trial reveal, in Pearson's words, "the extraordinary fascination of this case as a problem in human character and human relations." Combining the enduring emotional force of myth and the more prosaic intellectual challenge of a detective story, it is a "locked room" mystery written by Sophocles. Even as the murders themselves seemed summoned from a mythic reservoir of human darkness, the trial of the alleged perpetrator occurred in a specific time and place: America in the Gilded Age, its most deeply held convictions and its most troubling anxieties inscribed in every moment of the legal process. Lizzie Borden was a devout young woman "of good family"—a lady—and an accused axe-wielding parricide. It should not have been possible.

Throughout the trial, Lizzie Borden remained a sphinxlike cipher. Reporters "found texts for columns in her looks, her bearing, her method of speech, her personal habits, her ability to sleep, her fattening process . . . and everything connected with her." Yet, for all the scrutiny, she remained elusive. As the *New York Times* correctly predicted, "The verdict, if there shall be a verdict, will make little difference."

In the last 125 years, the Borden mystery and its central enigmatic figure have been explored in fiction, reimagined in ballet and opera, and dramatized in films, plays, and even musicals. When writers of fiction train their gaze on the events, most find the basic plot lacking romance and have generally invented a mystery lover—much like the unscrupulous private detective McHenry—to provide Lizzie Borden with a more conventional motive and, occasionally, with an accomplice or coconspirator. Lizzie's dance card was not replete with potential gentlemen callers; however, recent authors (including the screenwriter of the 2018 film *Lizzie*) have found Lizzie's paramour hiding in plain sight, suggesting that Lizzie and Bridget shared an illicit passion that precipitated the murders.

Others have tried to solve the case without a romantic subplot, instead finding new reasons to suspect nearly everyone associated with the family. Edward Radin's *Lizzie Borden: The Untold Story*, for example, argues that the Bordens' maid Bridget Sullivan was the real culprit. It is a gripping read—Radin was a two-time winner of the Edgar Award for Fact Crime—and he devotes an entire chapter to refuting Edmund Pearson's classic account of the case, characterizing it, more in sorrow than in anger, as "a literary hoax." In Radin's telling, Abby's demand that Bridget wash the windows outside, after "a difficult work week in all the heat," was the final straw and she snapped. For Pearson, Knowlton was a dedicated public servant who did his best to bring a murderess to justice; for Radin, Hosea Knowlton is the villain of the story, a ruthless district attorney who "was willing to blight her life with nothing more than a belief that she might be guilty." Other authors imagine Emma as the murderer. After all, by her own admission, she was supplanted as Lizzie's substitute mother by her father's remarriage and she testified that she, not Lizzie, held the strongest grudge about Abby's role in the property dispute. For his part, Radin also considered her a possible suspect: she could have returned from Fairhaven, killed Abby, secreted herself in the house until her father's return, killed him, and then disposed of the weapon somewhere far from the scene. For aficionados of detective fiction, John V. Morse's alibi is so perfect that it must have been concocted. One writer suggested that he realized Abby was dead and rushed out to give himself a plausible story. Still others see conspiracies of Harvard men or town grandees pulling the strings in the investigation, trial, and ultimate acquittal of Lizzie Borden. Perhaps Dr. Handy's wild-eyed man was Andrew Borden's illegitimate son intent on killing the father who would not acknowledge him. Even sports statistician Bill James, the father of sabermetrics, has weighed in, using the Borden case to illustrate a mathematical system that could be used to determine guilt. His conclusion: not guilty. But he contends that such a system should not have been necessary in Lizzie Borden's case. Modern forensics would have quickly ruled her out as a suspect.

Most interpretations tell us more about the preoccupations of its chroniclers than any essential truth about the mystery. Just as Lizzie Borden's contemporaries saw their own worst fears refracted through the prism of her trial, later commentators have seized upon whatever aspect of the mystery speaks most eloquently to their time. For example, an early-1950s solution imagined Lizzie Borden as a nightmarish "feminist" heroine, concluding: "If today woman has come out of the kitchen, she is only following Lizzie, who came out of it with a bloody ax and helped start the rights-for-women bandwagon." Equally telling is the widely held speculation, which gained currency in the early 1990s, that Lizzie Borden committed the murders after enduring years of sexual abuse by her father. The bedrooms that opened onto each other, the dead mother, the powerless stepmother, the special understanding between father and daughter symbolized by the "thin gold band"—all crystalized into a suddenly obvious solution, a solution that seemed to explain not only the identity of the killer but also the very brutality of the crimes. In such examples, the Borden case serves as a cultural Rorschach test, in which Lizzie Borden's guilt is assumed and her imagined acts are wrenched out of their time and place. In this way, every generation reinvents the case.

While most "whodunits" largely ignore the specific Fall River context,

Victoria Lincoln's *A Private Disgrace: Lizzie Borden by Daylight* makes the case that it could only have happened there. Lincoln, a novelist and Fall River native, provides a richly textured insider's account of the setting. She argues that Lizzie committed the murders but did so, echoing the prosecutor Hosea Knowlton, in an altered state. In her telling, Lizzie was planning to poison her stepmother and killed both stepmother and father during an ambulatory epileptic seizure. Criminologists of Lizzie Borden's day would have applauded the diagnosis. For them, epilepsy, an extreme form of periodicity, went hand in hand with crime. What Lincoln captures better than any other chronicler, however, is the Fall River elite's complicity, its closing of ranks against outsiders and the collective unspoken vow of silence on the part of those who had firsthand knowledge of the murders. For Fall River native Lincoln, Lizzie Borden was "the skeleton in our cupboard, the black sheep in our family, a disgrace, but a private disgrace."

This local reticence has been abandoned in favor of a desire to cash in on the legend. The long-serving former curator of the Fall River Historical Society, Florence Brigham, a diminutive lady of impeccable Fall River pedigree, was given to lament that tourists trooped through the restored mansion (which houses the society), ignoring displays highlighting Fall River's belle epoque in search of some Borden relic. Her successors, Michael Martins and Dennis Binette, have put this unseemly interest in Fall River's most notorious citizen in the service of preserving and promoting the city's rich history. Their nearly thousand-page prosopography, *Parallel Lives: A Social History of Lizzie A. Borden and Her Fall River*, traces the arc of Fall River over the course of Lizzie Borden's life. The murders and trial feature in only 35 of the 998 pages, yet their epic effort restores Lizzie Borden to her own world.

Less circumspect is the Lizzie Borden Bed & Breakfast Museum, operated out of the family's house on Second Street, opposite the looming posterior of Fall River's five-story Justice Center, home to the criminal division of the Bristol County Superior Court. The present owners, Donald Woods and Lee-ann Wilber, have cultivated the occult aspects of the legend, employing a house psychic and encouraging paranormal investigations. But it still caters to those drawn by the siren call of the underlying mystery. On the anniversary of the murders, the bed-and-breakfast offers a special tour, repeated on the hour, featuring actors in period costume portraying key figures in the case. One year, guests were greeted as reporters by an agitated Bridget and encouraged to ask questions of the family members; another year, patrons were deputized to assist the police in their investigations, viewing the bodies along with their police tour guide. Dead Andrew had a cameo, his hand dropping with a comic thud from under a bloodstained sheet. Woods and Wilber purchased Maplecroft in 2018, consolidating their status as guardians of Lizzie Borden's residential real estate. There, they plan to showcase the second part of Lizzie Borden's story. Woods remarked, "She really was a complex character. She's not just an alleged ax murderer."

This desire to see Lizzie Borden as a whole person rather than "a Halloween tchotchke," as Sarah Miller puts it in her elegant 2016 young adult study of the Borden murders, informs recent imaginings of the story. In *See What I Have Done*, novelist Sarah Schmidt unspools the madness of her protagonist in the context of the Borden household's claustrophobic interiority. But the Lizzie of the post-#MeToo moment may well be Chloë Sevigny's portrayal in the 2018 film *Lizzie*. A longtime passion project, informed by visits to the Lizzie Borden Bed & Breakfast Museum, *Lizzie* was originally envisioned by Sevigny and screenwriter Bryce Kass as a "rousing, smash-the-patriarchy piece." Sevigny was reportedly disappointed with the final version, which "features more than a few shots of Lizzie's backside" but is "a little more vague" about Lizzie's desire for freedom as a motivation for the murders. The film, like Schmidt's novel, is a speculative solution grounded in extensive research. Absent (so far) from the Borden canon is an extended documentary series in the vein of *The Staircase* or *Making a Murderer*, carefully crafted and paced narratives that upend official accounts of notorious crimes.

More than ninety years ago, Pearson wondered, "Will the whole truth ever come out?" One untapped source remains but is stubbornly out of reach, shielded by an ancient Anglo-American legal privilege that survives the grave.

THE DEFENSE FILE

Lizzie Borden's grave, Oak Grove Cemetery, *courtesy of Fall River Historical Society*

Lizzie Borden did not take all her secrets to her final resting place; some repose in an unlikely location. On the sixteenth floor of an unremarkable office building on Main Street in Springfield, Massachusetts, sits a file on Lizzie Borden, guarded by the law firm Governor George Robinson founded in 1866. Robinson died in 1896, yet he protects Lizzie still.

Robinson likely had no such master plan. He died unexpectedly, "stricken with paralysis" on his way home from the courthouse. His office and its files were intact. Andrew Jennings, by contrast, lived well into retirement and, for reasons of his own, deposited his Lizzie Borden files and memorabilia in an old hip bath, a small, shallow basin used to immerse the hips and the buttocks. His stash included the trial exhibits, books of clippings, and Jennings's own handwritten trial notebooks. When he died in 1923, his family inherited the hip bath and its contents. In 1967, they donated part of the collection to the Fall River Historical Society; the remainder, including the trial journals, followed in 2012. Or so it was thought. The hip bath was not entirely drained. The power of attorney executed by Lizzie Borden at the time of her arrest in Fall River was auctioned off in 2016 (by a Jennings descendent) and it, too, is now on display at the Fall River Historical Society.

What is the distinction between the two caches—one locked away, the other open to public view? What is in the Robinson file on Lizzie Borden? Perhaps the lawyer's trial diary or clippings akin to notebooks Jennings left in the hip bath, perhaps something even more tantalizing to the amateur sleuth. But the rationale for shielding Robinson's file from scrutiny has nothing to do with any potential revelations in its contents. Robinson's firm has concluded that it may not release any of its Lizzie Borden material—a position, it says, that was dictated by the Massachusetts Board of Bar Overseers.

The attorney-client privilege has a long history in Anglo-American jurisprudence. Originally, it ensured that a lawyer could not be called to testify against his client or to provide information that would assist in his client's prosecution. As the preeminent evidence scholar (and Borden trial legal commentator) John Henry Wigmore explained: "In order to promote freedom of consultation of legal advisers by clients, the apprehension of compelled disclosure by the legal advisors must be removed; and hence the law must prohibit such disclosure except on the client's consent." But the attorney-client privilege has expanded to prevent not only the disclosure of any communications between lawyer and client, but also of any "work product" created in anticipation of litigation. It was feared that opposing counsel could use that "work product" against the client, a prosecution with "wits borrowed from the adversary." Together, these components protect clients by preventing lawyers from being "called as a witness or otherwise required to

produce evidence concerning a client." But, irrespective of any antici-
pated or threatened litigation, professional ethics impose a broad duty
of confidentiality, a duty that survives the client's death. There is no
expiration date.

Jennings took no special pains to secure his papers—his grandson later recalled that he had broken with Lizzie Borden over the alleged shoplifting at the Tilden-Thurber gallery—and his children were
under no professional or ethical obligation to prevent their disclosure.
Robinson's Borden file, by contrast, has been lodged continuously in
the possession of the law firm he founded, bound by the original attorney's duty of confidentiality—even though both the original attorney
and client are long past care.

Given that the law firm believes it can never disclose the contents
of the file—the only one preserved from Robinson's era—why keep
it? Why not, as befits a Victorian murder mystery, consign the last
documents to the flames or, less dramatically, to the office shredder?
Current Robinson Donovan senior partner Jeffrey McCormick, who
learned about the file when he arrived at the firm in 1977, said it
would be "abhorrent" to dispose of something that has such historic
value. So there, in Springfield, Massachusetts, locked in a five-drawer
filing cabinet, the file languishes, more than 125 years after Lizzie Borden, gloved hand on Robinson's arm, walked out of the New Bedford
courtroom a free woman.

Acknowledgments

As I bring this long project to a close, I am struck by my good fortune. A full accounting would require another book-length work.

First and foremost, I thank my agent, Tina Bennett, for her peerless advocacy, keen eye, and inexhaustible patience (which I tested). In addition to being my first and best reader, she has been a partner in this project for more than fifteen years. Tina's assistant, Svetlana Katz, has been a helpful presence during all that time. Sally Willcox put me in touch with Tina. Leslie Teicholz would have done so. I thank them both!

I am especially grateful to Jonathan Karp for believing in this project—twice—and for expanding my vision of what might be possible to write. I was also lucky to find in Emily Simonson someone who calmly and kindly shepherded me through the publishing process. Many thanks also to my copy editor, David Courtright, who saved me from countless errors and infelicities, and to production editor Kayley Hoffman, production manager Lisa Erwin, and managing editor Kristen Lemire. The designers Lewelin Polanco and Pete Garceau made it beautiful inside and out.

An unanticipated pleasure of working on this particular case was my time in the basement of the Fall River Historical Society in the company of the omni-talented duo of Michael Martins and Dennis Binette. I am indebted to them and their monumental endeavor, *Parallel Lives*. Had I spent less time laughing with Dennis, I might have been more productive, but it would have been much less fun. Other local friends, Betsy Denning and Tim Belt, added to the merriment. Thanks also to James Smith for the photo of Lizzie's grave. I am honored to have known the late Frank Knowlton Jr., whom I met at my college graduation (and his fifty-fifth reunion), and who invited me to a reenactment of the Borden trial in 1992.

In the course of my research, I met many Bordenologists who shared their time and their thoughts on the case. In particular I am grateful to Shelley Dziedzic, Stefani Koorey, Kat Koorey, Faye Musselman, William Pavao, Len Rebello, and Lee-ann Wilbur. I also appreciate Jeffrey McCormick's willingness to let me ask him questions about the Borden file that he could not answer.

I am grateful for the research assistance of several graduate students who helped me as I struggled to move from the microfilm era to the modern age: Darby Copeland, Chris Brick, Joshua Clough, Claire Payton, and Jessica Malitoris.

This project began its life at Harvard as a senior thesis and was launched with a Pforzheimer Summer Research Grant from the Schlesinger Library. I am especially grateful to Marc Dolan and Alexandra Owen, my faculty advisers, and to all my teachers, at every stage of education. A number deserve special mention for their enduring influence: Barbara Babcock, Christine Bruner, Catherine Clinton, George Fisher, Ellen Fitzpatrick, Joyce Flynn, Lawrence Friedman, Thomas Gray, Anne Harrington, Robert Lamb, Peter Mancall, Nancy Ruttenburg, King Schofield, Thomas Siegel, Eva Sikora, Robert Weisberg, and the incomparable Dame Olwen Hufton. I was similarly fortunate in my mentors in the law: James Browning, Theodor Meron, Harry Pregerson, Byron White, and John Paul Stevens.

The National Humanities Center provided an intellectual home and a community of scholars for which I am profoundly grateful. I benefited from comments on earlier work from a contingent of that convivial bunch: Karen Halttunen, Deborah Harkness, Cynthia Herrup, Lisa Lindsay, Gregg Mittman, Jocelyn Olcott, John Sweet, and Timothy Tyson. I am also grateful to the staff of the center, especially two directors of the fellowships program—Kent Mullikin and Elizabeth Mansfield—and the fellowship coordinator Lois Whittington.

Friends have helped move this project along in myriad ways. Deborah Cohen, Ann Haskell, Sherry Kramer, Patrick Pacheco, and Sarah Tilton were enthusiastic proponents when I first thought this might be a book and each taught me important lessons about how to tell a story. Alison Aubrejaun, Susan Cleveland-Knowles, Gail Mosse, and Lisa Sitkin joined me for a memorable performance of *Lizzie! A Rock Musical* in San Jose in 2017 and have been stalwart supporters through the years. Ticky Kennedy and Nick Raposo debriefed me after my Fall River excursions and shared their comprehensive knowledge of southern Massachusetts folkways. Elijah Leed demonstrated the finer points of wood chopping. Josh Bond consistently nudged me in the right direction when I was at risk of faltering.

Other friends read and improved the manuscript: Janet Alexander, Joshua Bond, Scott Casper, Deborah Cohen, Kit Fine, Nikolas Gisborne, Jill Horwitz, Jennifer Kennedy, James Lesher, Caroline Lewis, Quentin Pell, Eleanor Rutledge, Adam Samaha, Eva Sikora, and Ruth Chang (who generously read several iterations). Any errors are my own.

I am more grateful than I can say to my brother, Chip. I could not have completed this book without his support. Finally, I dedicate this book to my parents, to whom I owe my greatest debt and who have my abiding love.

Notes

Some passages of this book were previously published in the *Yale Journal of Law and the Humanities*. See Cara W. Robertson, "Representing 'Miss Lizzie': Cultural Convictions in the Trial of Lizzie Borden," *Yale Law and the Humanities* 8 (1996): 351–416.

Abbreviations

FRHS: Fall River Historical Society

Hilliard Papers: Rufus Bassett Hilliard Collection, Fall River Historical Society

Inquest: Inquest upon the Deaths of Andrew J. Borden and Abby D. Borden. Annie M. White, stenographer. August 9–11, 1892. Collection of the Fall River Historical Society.

Jennings Notebooks: The Hip Bath Collection, Fall River Historical Society

Kent: David Kent, *The Lizzie Borden Sourcebook*. Boston: Branden Publishing, 1992.

Knowlton Papers: M. Martins and D. A. Binette, *The Commonwealth of Massachusetts v. Lizzie A. Borden: The Knowlton Papers 1892–93*. Fall River: Fall River Historical Society, 1994.

Preliminary Hearing: *Preliminary Hearing: Commonwealth of Massachusetts v. Lizzie A Borden, August 25, 1892–September 1, 1892*, Second District Court, Fall River, MA. Annie M. White, Stenographer.

Trial Transcript: *Trial of Lizzie Andrew Borden upon an Indictment Charging Her with the Murder of Abby Durfee Borden and Andrew Jackson Borden Before the Superior Court for the County of Bristol; Mason, C.J., and Blodgett and Dewey, J.J., Presiding*. Official Stenographic Report by Frank H. Burt, 1893.

WS: Witness Statements, August 4–October 6, 1892. Collection of Fall River Historical Society.

Newspapers

Boston Globe: Boston Daily Globe
FRDG: Fall River Daily Globe
FRDH: Fall River Daily Herald
FREN: Fall River Daily Evening News
NBDM: New Bedford Mercury
NBEJ: New Bedford Evening Journal
NBES: New Bedford Evening Standard
NY Sun: [New York] Sun
NYT: New York Times
NY World: [New York] World
Providence Journal: Providence Daily Journal

Part 1
MURDER

Chapter 1: Somebody Will Do Something

3   *If a person wished to kill and avoid detection . . . hydrocyanic acid would be the first choice among all deadly drugs*: "Fall River's Tragedy," *NBES*, August 5, 1893, 2.

3   *to put on the edge of a sealskin cape*: Testimony of Eli Bence, Inquest, in Knowlton Papers, 160; Interview with Eli Bence, Officers Doherty and Harrington, WS, 8.

4   *Miss Borden*: Testimony of Eli Bence, Inquest, 160.

4   *This is Andrew J. Borden's daughter*: Testimony of Eli Bence, Inquest, 160.

4   *more closely*: Testimony of Eli Bence, Inquest, 160.

4   *her peculiar expression around the eyes*: Testimony of Eli Bence, Inquest, 162.

4   *did not parade their difficulties*: Trial Transcript, in Knowlton Papers, 1774.

4   *things were not as pleasant at the Borden house as they might be*: Jane Gray, Interview with Harrington, August 17, 1892, WS, 17.

5   *He was a plain-living man with rigid ideas, and very set*: Testimony of Alice Russell, Inquest, 151.

5   *He was too hard for me*: "No Clearer," *FRDH*, August 6, 1892, 4.

5   *He was what is called close-fisted, but square and just in his dealings*: "Mr. Borden's Life," *Boston Daily Advertiser*, August 4, 1892, in Kent, 5.

5   *Keep constantly on hand, Burial Cases and Coffins, Ready-made of all kinds*

now in use in this section of the country: Advertisement, *FREN*, May 5, 1859, FRHS.

5   *he never made a purchase of land for which he was not ready to pay cash down*: "Reminiscences of the late Andrew J. Borden," *FRDG*, August 19, 1892, 7.

6   *one of the finest business blocks in the city located at the corner of South Main and Anawan streets*: E. H. Porter, *The Fall River Tragedy: A History of the Borden Murders* (Fall River, MA: Geo. Buffington, 1893), 22.

6   *was his or her own chambermaid*: "Lizzie Borden at the Bar," *NY Sun*, June 5, 1893, 2.

7   *uterine congestion*: Death Record #706, March 26, 1893, Fall River Vital Statistics, Office of the City Clerk, Government Center, Fall River, MA. Andrew married Abby D. Gray on June 6, 1865. Massachusetts: Vital Records, 1841–1910. (From original records held by the Massachusetts Archives. Online datatbase: AmericanAncestors.org, New England Historic Genealogical Society, 2004.)

7   *had never ceased to regard Abby D. Borden . . . with jealous regard the sweet memories of a sanctified mother*: "Mrs. Livermore Talks," *NBDM*, June 19, 1893, 1.

7   *When my darling mother was on her deathbed . . . watch over "Baby Lizzie"*: "Guilty?—No! No!", *Boston Sunday Herald*, April 13, 1913, 25.

8   *always went to Emma*: Lizzie Borden's Inquest Testimony, *NBES*, August 12, 1893.

8   *a monument of straightforwardness*: "Firm in Faith," *FRDG*, August 15, 1892, 8. ("I never shall believe, even if she were convicted of the deed, that she committed it unless she were to confess to it herself, and then the marvel would be greater to me that she had concealed her act than that she did it.")

8   *close in money matters . . . had to ask two or three times*: "Lizzie Borden," *Boston Post*, May 18, 1893, 2; "A Talk with Lizzie Borden," *Woman's Journal*, May 27, 1893, 163.

8   *Mrs. Borden did not control the house; the whole summing up of it, was that*: Testimony of Alice Russell, Inquest, 151.

8   *was to select the color, and . . . not go on with it until the color was determined*: Trial Transcript, 1349.

8   *dark drab*: Trial Transcript, 1349.

9   *closed-mouth woman . . . bear a great deal and say nothing*: Jane Gray, Interview with Harrington, August 17, 1892, in WS, 17.

9   *We always spoke*: Testimony of Emma Borden, Inquest, 113.

9   *Don't say that to me, for she is a mean good-for-nothing thing*: Testimony of Hannah Gifford, Inquest, 158.

10   *Lizzie told me she thought her stepmother . . . and another to her back*: Testimony of Augusta Tripp, Inquest, 144.

10   *I told Mrs. Borden I would not change places with her for all her money*: Jane Gray, Interview with Harrington, August 17, 1892, WS, 17.

10   *He was a very plain living man . . . why they should care for anything different*: Testimony of Alice Russell, Inquest, 151–52.

10   *They had quite refined ideas, and they would like to have been cultured girls*: Testimony of Alice Russell, Inquest, 151–52.

10   *She thought she should entertain . . . lavishly angered her*: "No Clearer," *FRDH*, August 6, 1892, 4.

11   *6 or 8 penny nail*: Report of Capt. Desmond, June 24, 1891, in Knowlton Papers, 74–75.

11   *Someone might have come in that way*: Report of Capt. Desmond, June 24, 1891, in Knowlton Papers, 75.

11   *I am afraid the police will not be able to find the real thief*: Report of Capt. Desmond, June 24, 1891, in Knowlton Papers, 75.

12   *was an illness suggestive . . . deaths of one or other of those people*: Trial Transcript, 1246.

12   *I feel as if something . . . no matter where I am*: Trial Transcript, 375.

12   *I don't know but somebody will do something*: Trial Transcript, 379.

Chapter 2: An Incredible Crime

13   *What is the matter?*: Testimony of Adelaide Churchill, Inquest, 128.

13   *Oh, Mrs. Churchill, do come over. Someone has killed father*: Testimony of Adelaide Churchill, Inquest, 128.

14   *hacked to pieces*: "Shocking!" *FRDG*, August 4, 1892, 1.

16   *Where were you?*: Interview with Adelaide Churchill, August 8, 1892, WS, 11.

17   *to clear [her] eyes above the second floor*: Interview with Adelaide Churchill, August 8, 1892, WS, 11.

17   *Is there another?*: Interview with Adelaide Churchill, August 8, 1892, WS, 11.

17   *O, I shall have to go to the cemetery myself*: Interview with Adelaide Churchill, August 8, 1892, WS, 11.

18   *Physician that I am and accustomed to all sorts of horrible sights, it sickened me*: E. H. Porter, *The Fall River Tragedy*, 18.

18   *the cry of murder swept through the city of Fall River like a typhoon*: Porter, *The Fall River Tragedy*, 13.

18 *a dyed-in-the-wool policeman*: "Dark for Lizzie Borden," *NY Sun*, June 9, 1893, 2.

19 *Did He Have a Presentiment?*: "No Arrest Yet," *FRDH*, August 11, 1892, 4.

20 *must have jarred the house*: "Done with Theories," *NBES*, August 9, 1892, 2.

21 *much too dressy for Fall River*: Michael Martins and Dennis A. Binette, *Parallel Lives: A Social History of Lizzie A. Borden and Her Fall River* (Fall River: Fall River Historical Society, 2011), 355.

24 *No true Borden has ever placed a stumbling block*: "Lizzie Borden's Arrest," *NBES*, August 12, 1892, 6.

24 *the Golden Horseshoe*: Martins and Binette, *Parallel Lives*, 159. M. C. D. Borden shared Box 8 with Cornelius Bliss, William Harkness, and John Clafin. Mrs. William B. Astor Jr. was their neighbor in Box 7. Among Borden's possessions was a 251-foot yacht and a formidable art collection, including Rembrandt's *Lucretia Stabbing Herself*. Martins and Binette, *Parallel Lives*, 163.

25 *piling up dollars*: "Lizzie Borden at the Bar," *NY Sun*, June 5, 1893, 2.

26 *a peculiar phase of life in New England—a wretched phase*: "Lizzie Borden at the Bar," *NY Sun*, June 5, 1893, 2.

26 *the daughters of a class of well-to-do New England men . . . born to these fortunes*: "Lizzie Borden at the Bar," *NY Sun*, June 5, 1893, 2.

26 *Crime . . . seems to attend that phase*: "Lizzie Borden at the Bar," *NY Sun*, June 5, 1893, 2.

26 *The true criminal has something . . . who has remained animalized*: Arthur MacDonald, "Criminological," *American Journal of Psychology* 3 (January 1890): 114. MacDonald reviewed European criminology, including works by Lombroso and French socialist and criminologist Gabriel Tarde.

26 Juke: Lawrence Friedman, *Crime and Punishment in American History* (New York: Basic Books, 1993), 141. "Juke" was a pseudonym coined by Richard Dugdale.

27 The Dangerous Classes: Charles Loring Brace, *The Dangerous Classes of New York and Twenty Years' Work Among Them*, Third Ed. (New York: Wynkoop and Hallenbeck, 1880), 42–43.

27 *An invasion of migrating peoples, outnumbering the Goths and Vandals*: Mary A. Livermore, "The Boy of Today," in *The Story of My Life: The Sunshine and Shadow of Seventy Years* (Hartford, CT: A. D. Worthington and Company, 1897), 634.

27 *a Swede or a Portuguese*: "Police Baffled," *NBES*, August 5, 1892, 8.

27 *dirty dresses on, which were caked with blood*: Notes of Officer Harrington, August 9, 1892, WS, 13.

28 *very subject to the nose bleed*: Notes of Officer Harrington, August 9, 1892, WS, 13.

28 *old, dull, and . . . worn*: Notes of Officer Harrington, August 9, 1892, WS, 13.

28 *a Portuguese . . . a satisfactory account of himself*: Notes of Officer Harrington, August 4, 1892, WS, 6.

28 *effeminate . . . Chinaman*: Anonymous Letter, September 1, 1892, in Knowlton Papers, 59.

28 *What must have been the person . . . he must have been a maniac*: "Minister Jubb," *FRDH*, August 8, 1892, 4.

28 *a mass of raw meat*: Diary of Charles Henry Wells, August 4, 1892. Collection of FRHS.

28 *Look for the maniac*: "Legal Aspects," *FRDH*, August 17, 1892, 4.

28 *We who have had some experience with criminals . . . dogged brutality of the insane*: "Legal Aspects," *FRDH*, August 17, 1892, 4.

29 *Dr. Handy's wild-eyed man*: Porter, *The Fall River Tragedy*, 50.

29 *Mike the Soldier*: Porter, *The Fall River Tragedy*, 60–61.

29 *readily pronounced him not the man . . . his face was very much shaded*: Notes of Officer Doherty, August 10, 1892, WS, 13.

29 *multitude of crank communications*: Letter from Albert Pillsbury to Hosea Knowlton, May 27, 1893, in Knowlton Papers, 203.

29 *Dark mysteries have been brought to light in this manner by means of photography*: Hilliard Papers 32, *FRHS*.

29 *I have devoted attention to many stories that were foolish*: "A Motive for the Murders," *NBES*, August 18, 1892, 2.

30 *come at once . . . arrest Morse, Lizzie and the man at West Port*: Letter from J. Burns Strand, August 10, 1892, in Knowlton Papers, 8.

30 *there was a diversity of opinion in the spirit world*: "More from the Spirits," *FRDH*, August 17, 1892, 4.

30 *Spirits don't know everything . . . they couldn't be expected to know about it*: "More from the Spirits," *FRDH*, August 14, 1892, 129.

30 *The Suspected Man*: "The Suspected Man," *NBES*, August 5, 1892, 4. For another discussion of Morse's alibi, see "Fall River's Tragedy," *NBES*, August 6, 1892, 2.

30 *long, lanky, hard-featured fellow, who dressed like a scarecrow and ate like a cormorant*: "The Fall River Murders," *NBES*, August 19, 1892, 1.

30 *regarded by his neighbors as a very eccentric and peculiar man*: "The Fall River Murders," *NBES*, August 19, 1892, 1. He was considered suspicious because of his reported connection to a group of itinerant horse traders

camped in the nearby town of Westport. "To the Grave," *FRDG*, August 6, 1892, 7.

30 *close, almost to the point of penuriousness*: "The Fall River Murders," *NBES*, August 19, 1892, 1.

30 *regarded Mr. Morse with more tenderness than most nieces feel for their uncles*: "A Strange Story," *FRDH*, August 19, 1892, 4. This rumor sounds very different to modern ears. For a discussion of incest in this period based on the records of Massachusetts Society for Prevention of Cruelty to Children, see Linda Gordon, *Heroes of Their Own Lives: The Politics and History of Family Violence, Boston 1880–1960* (New York: Viking Press, 1988), 204–249.

30 *he was constantly on the alert to see the breath of scandal did not reach his home*: "A Strange Story," *FRDH*, August 19, 1892, 4.

31 *Some remarked how courageous . . . perhaps she has acceptable company*: Jane Gray, Interview by Harrington and Doherty, September 25, 1892, WS, 21.

31 *covered with blood*: Notes of Officer Medley, August 4, 1892, WS, 28.

31 *it had been explained to him, and was alright*: Notes of Officer Medley, August 4, 1892, WS, 28.

31 *she had not noticed the pail . . . and put the contents in the wash*: Notes of Officer Medley, August 4, 1892, WS, 28.

32 *It does not amount to anything*: Notes of Officer Harrington, August 4, 1892, WS, 6.

32 *carried out the orders of her priest . . . true Americans will learn in time never to imploy [sic] a catholic*: Anonymous Letter, Hilliard Papers 004, *FRHS*.

32 *a sly and lying class*: Anonymous Letter, August 18, 1892, Hilliard Papers 82, FRHS.

33 *In the natural course of things who would be the party to be suspected?*: Preliminary Hearing, 508.

33 *Lizzie stood by the foot of the bed . . . she knew more than she wished to tell*: Officer Harrington, August 4, 1892, WS, 5–6.

33 *I don't like that girl*: Officer Harrington, August 4, 1892, WS, 6.

33 *If any girl can show you or me . . . I would like to have her do it*: Officer Harrington, August 4, 1892, WS, 6.

34 *strange . . . that the boy who delivered the note has not made himself known*: "Done with Theories," *NBES*, August 9, 1892, 2.

34 *When the perpetrator of this foul deed is found, it will be one of the household*: Hiram Harrington, Interviewed by Doherty and Harrington, August 6, 1892, WS, 11.

34 *I had a long talk with Lizzie yesterday, Thursday, the day of the murder, and I am not at all satisfied with [her] . . . demeanor*: Hiram Harrington, Interviewed by Doherty and Harrington, August 6, 1892, WS, 11.

34 *She is very strong-willed, and will fight for what she considers her rights*: Hiram Harrington, Interviewed by Doherty and Harrington, August 6, 1892, WS, 11. Harrington gave variations of this description to assorted reporters. In an interview with Porter, he characterized Lizzie as "haughty and domineering with the stubborn will of her father and bound to contest for her right." Porter, *The Fall River Tragedy*, 26.

34 *simply to get them out of the way*: "A Hired Assassin," *NBES*, August 9, 1892, 8.

34 *to any one who may secure the arrest . . . the death of Andrew J. Borden and his wife*: "$5000 Reward," *NBES*, August 5, 1892, 1.

34 *disappeared as mysteriously as he came*: Porter, *The Fall River Tragedy*, 41. Hanscom's given name was either Orrinton or Orrington.

34 *it must clear up the mystery or go insane*: Porter, *The Fall River Tragedy*, 53.

Chapter 3: Done with Theories

35 *There was no singing and no remarks*: "The Murder Mystery," *NBES*, August 6, 1892, 6.

36 *leaning on the undertaker's arm*: "The Murder Mystery," *NBES*, August 6, 1892, 6.

36 *As the procession wended its way along North Main Street . . . to raise their hats*: "The Murder Mystery," *NBES*, August 6, 1892, 6.

36 *their first chance to work undisturbed by the presence of the Borden girls . . . They ransacked the house from attic to cellar*: "No Motive Yet Found for the Borden Murder," *New York Herald*, August 6, 1892, in Kent, 17.

36 *an elderly lady in plain dress*: Porter, *The Fall River Tragedy*, 33.

36 *employed long ago by the Bordens*: Porter, *The Fall River Tragedy*, 33.

36 *discreet pause of perhaps five minutes*: Porter, *The Fall River Tragedy*, 32.

37 *the intense excitement in Fall River . . . fever heat*: Porter, *The Fall River Tragedy*, 52.

37 *remarkable vitality*: Porter, *The Fall River Tragedy*, 81.

37 *a hack, containing Marshal Hilliard . . . to convey Miss Lizzie and a friend*: Porter, *The Fall River Tragedy*, 52.

37 *business was partially suspended . . . the tragedy was first made known*: Porter, *The Fall River Tragedy*, 52.

37 *a lovely woman*: Porter, *The Fall River Tragedy*, 54.

38 *deep distress*: Porter, *The Fall River Tragedy*, 54.

38 *a head as hard as iron . . . and he snorts like a war horse*: "Emma Borden Testifies," *NY Sun*, June 17, 1893, 1.

38 *no trace of anything artificial, either in his manner, his language, or his nature*: Attorney General Parker's Address, Tribute of the Bristol County Bar to the Memory of the late Hon. Hosea Morrill Knowlton, Taunton, April 21, 1903 (New Bedford: E. Anthony and Sons), 29.

39 *mostly sentimental*: Hosea Knowlton, *Annual Report of the Attorney General for the Year Ending January 17, 1900* (Boston, 1900), xv.

39 *The punishment of murder by death . . . the whipping post, and the stake*: Hosea Knowlton, *Annual Report of the Attorney General for the Year Ending January 16, 1901* (Boston, 1901), xviii–xix.

40 *a hard fighter*: "Her Father's Murder Charged Against Her," *NY Herald*, August 13, 1892, in Kent, 109.

40 *a splendid dancer*: Martins and Binette, *Parallel Lives*, 957. For Jennings's leadership of the Brown Varsity Nine, see "Prisoner's Counsel," *NBES*, August 27, 1892, 2.

40 *His eyes . . . fairly snap when he is in motion*: "The Borden Jury Chosen," *NY Sun*, June 6, 1893, 1.

40 *ability to be everywhere and see everything at once*: "The Borden Jury Chosen," *NY Sun*, June 6, 1893, 1.

40 *admirable voice, which he use[d] to great effect*: "One Side," *Boston Globe*, June 16, 1893, 1.

41 *Do you know of anybody that your father was on bad terms with?*: Lizzie Borden's Inquest Testimony, *NBES*, June 12, 1893. The rest of the colloquy is from the same source.

44 *very sharp hatchet*: Officer Harrington drew Knowlton's attention to the newspaper stories about Lizzie's letter. Letter from Phil Harrington to Hosea Knowlton, September 8, 1892, in Knowlton Papers, 73.

44 *If this is so, it means insanity*: Letter from Hosea Knowlton to Albert Pillsbury, September 12, 1892, in Knowlton Papers, 76.

44 *I have said all I think I should about that letter*: Elizabeth M. Johnston, Interview with Doherty and Harrington, September 25, 1892, WS, 20.

44 *who told her that she need not tell the contents of the letter if she did not want to; and she did not want to*: Elizabeth M. Johnston, Interview with Medley, September 12, 1892, WS, 33.

45 *I sprinkled my handkerchiefs . . . Then I went in the sitting room and got the* Providence Journal *and took that into the kitchen*: Lizzie Borden's Inquest Testimony, *NBES*, June 12, 1893. The remaining questions and answers are taken from that source.

51   *did not entirely heal the feelings*: Testimony of Emma Borden, Inquest, 112.

51   *a very dear uncle of ours, of mine*: Testimony of Emma Borden, Inquest, 113.

51   *an unfriendly way*: Hiram C. Harrington, Inquest, 113.

51   *She said she wished . . . she had heard her come in*: Testimony of Adelaide Churchill Inquest, 129.

51   *on account of my position . . . when this thing is settled*: Charles C. Cook, Notes of Officer Medley, August 7, 1892, WS, 30.

51   *an expert operator under police surveillance*: "The Borden Safe Opened," *NBES*, August 12, 1892, 6.

52   *quite a sum of money and many valuable papers*: "The Borden Safe Opened," *NBES*, August 12, 1892, 6.

52   *Inquest continued at 10 to-day . . . Nothing developed for publication*: Porter, *The Fall River Tragedy*, 59.

52   *Your attention has already been called . . . on the day before the tragedy?*: Lizzie Borden's Inquest Testimony, *NBES*, June 12, 1893. The rest of the questions and answers are from the same source.

53   *wrangling*: Testimony of Alice Russell, Inquest, 152.

53   *their tastes differed in every way*: Testimony of Alice Russell, Inquest, 150.

54   *a woman who kept everything to herself*: Testimony of Sarah Whitehead, Inquest, 156.

54   *a mean old thing*: Testimony of Hannah Gifford, Inquest, 158.

55   *found her reclining upon a lounge in the matron's room*: "Arrested at Last," *NBES*, August 11, 1892, 2.

55   *She took the announcement of her arrest with surprising calmness*: "Miss Borden Arrested," *NYT*, August 12, 1892, 2.

55   *she fell into a fit of abject and pitiable terror*: "Lizzie Borden Under Arrest," *NY Herald*, August 12, 1892, in Kent, 51.

55   *Height: 5'4"; Complexion: Light; Hair: Light; Eyes: Gray*: Arrest Records of the Fall River Police Department.

55   *took the form of a public ceremonial*: "Behind the Bars," *Boston Daily Advertiser*, August 13, 1892.

55   *an affecting scene*: "Her Father's Murder Charged Against Her," *NY Herald*, August 13, 1892, in Kent, 110.

56   *some bright bits of color and other things*: "Divided Opinion," *FRDH*, August 13, 1892, 4.

56   *sincere sympathy . . . and confident belief that she will soon be restored to her former place of usefulness among us*: "Divided Opinion," *FRDH*, August 13, 1892, 4.

56   *thirty years of virtuous living should count for much in such a doubtful case*:

Susan Fessenden, Petition to the Governor of Massachusetts, adopted at the Massachusetts WCTU meeting on September 4, 1892, quoted in "Tremont Temple Petition," *Boston Globe*, September 6, 1892, 2. Lizzie Borden herself asked: "Is my character of thirty years to count for nothing—nothing?" See "Lizzie Borden Speaks," *NBES*, May 18, 1893; "A Talk with Lizzie Borden," *Woman's Journal*, May 27, 1893, 163.

56 *Should Miss Borden . . . It would be a legal murder:* "Justice to Lizzie Borden," *FRDG*, October 20, 1892, 7.

56 *She talked to me freely of the whole case, but very calmly and sadly . . . You can see that the girl feels her position keenly:* "Lizzie Borden," *Boston Post*, May 18, 1893, 2; "A Talk with Lizzie Borden," *Woman's Journal*, May 27, 1893, 162.

56 *I Believe Her Innocent:* "I Believe Her Innocent," *NBES*, August 22, 1892, 2.

56 *I think the whole lot . . . He has had time to get to California:* Hilliard Papers 29, FRHS.

57 *It is high time some one should inform you . . . would be your just desserts [sic]:* Hilliard Papers 98, FRHS.

57 *I have chased down more than 100 outside clews:* "Lizzie Borden's Arrest," *NBES*, August 15, 1892, 6. According to the *Boston Globe*, Hilliard continued his investigations after the preliminary hearing. "Borden Clews Run Down," *Boston Globe*, September 6, 1892, 2.

57 *You do not show much energy . . . you would not stand on ceremony with them:* Hilliard Papers 003, FRHS.

57 *A remark that is going the rounds is that if the parties at present suspected were poor people they would have been locked up before now:* "Inquest Begun," *FRDH*, August 9, 1892, 4.

57 *wearing a mask of stoical indifference that fit her like a glove:* "On Trial," *NBES*, June 5, 1892, 1.

Chapter 4: A Most Remarkable Woman

59 *awake nights forming plans:* "Borden Murder Trial," *NBES*, December 17, 1892, 1.

59 *Dear Sir . . . who can and will supply his place:* Letter from Andrew Jennings to Curtis Piece, Hilliard Papers 140. Lizzie, in fact, "could hardly tolerate him." Notes of Officer George Seaver, WS, 34.

60 *The difference between this proceeding and the inquest:* "Her Father's Murder Charged Against Her," *NY Herald*, August 13, 1892, 109.

61 *cool, metallic voice:* "Her Father's Murder Charged Against Her," *NY Herald*, August 13, 1892, in Kent, 109.

61 *There is nothing extraordinary in these proceedings . . . an exact parallel*: "Her Father's Murder Charged Against Her," *NY Herald*, August 13, 1892, 109; Porter, *The Fall River Tragedy*, 73.

61 *This is a splendid time to take a vacation*: "Awaiting Monday," *FRDH*, August 20, 1892, 4.

61 *they are worth it*: "The Borden Jury Chosen," *NY Sun*, June 6, 1893, 1.

61 *great, handsome brown eyes*: "The Borden Jury Chosen," *NY Sun*, June 6, 1893, 1.

61 *the generous full mouth of an orator and the strong nose that usually goes with it*: "The Borden Jury Chosen," *NY Sun*, June 6, 1893, 1.

62 *Never in the history of this section has a criminal trial*: "Lizzie Borden's Hearing," *NYT*, August 26, 1892, 1.

62 *crowds commenced to gather in Court Square*: Porter, *The Fall River Tragedy*, 83.

62 *an immense delegation of mill women*: Porter, *The Fall River Tragedy*, 83.

62 *It was worth one's life to attempt to enter or leave the building*: Porter, *The Fall River Tragedy*, 83.

62 *like sardines in a box*: "Adjourned to Thursday," *Boston Globe*, August 23, 1892, 3.

62 *a confused murmur of voices on all sides, and the one theme of debate was the fair prisoner's guilt or innocence*: "Adjourned to Thursday," *Boston Globe*, August 23, 1892, 3.

62 *the buzz of conversation that had been going on in the courtroom ceased, and every eye was riveted on the door*: "Awaiting Her Fate!" *FRDH*, August 25, 1892, 4.

62 *blue bonnet trimmed with ribbon and [a] small flower . . . bodice of this season's pattern*: "The Arraignment," in Kent, 113.

62 *a condition of apparent abstraction*: "Adjourned to Thursday," *Boston Globe*, August 23, 1892, 1.

62 *glanced impatiently at his watch*: Porter, *The Fall River Tragedy*, 84.

63 *Suspense . . . individual past middle age*: "Adjourned to Thursday," *Boston Globe*, August 23, 1892, 3.

63 *dressed in a steel gray suit with frock coat and white tie*: "Adjourned to Thursday," *Boston Globe*, August 23, 1892, 3.

63 *a pepper and salt suit*: "Adjourned to Thursday," *Boston Globe*, August 23, 1892, 3.

63 *jaunty white straw hat*: "Adjourned to Thursday," *Boston Globe*, August 23, 1892, 3.

63 *killed with the Bordens*: Letter from Knowlton to Pillsbury, August 26, 1892, in Knowlton Papers, 35.

63 *Dressed in a suit of navy blue*: "Adjourned to Thursday," *Boston Globe*, August 23, 1892, 3.

63 *despite the heat, looked as cool and placid . . . mercury was at freezing*: "Adjourned to Thursday," *Boston Globe*, August 23, 1892, 3.

63 *The air was stale, the heat very oppressive, and those within were almost as anxious to get out as those outside were to get in*: "Adjourned to Thursday," *Boston Globe*, August 23, 1892, 3.

63 *Emma, You've given me away*: Porter, *The Fall River Tragedy*, 85; "You Gave Me Away, Emma," *NBES*, August 25, 1892, 8.

64 *remain silent until she was called upon to testify to what she had heard*: Porter, *The Fall River Tragedy*, 86.

64 *An excited scene followed in which there was much animated talk*: Porter, *The Fall River Tragedy*, 86.

64 *some other jealous papers, exasperated . . . doubt on the* Globe's *exclusive*: "You Gave Me Away, Emma," *Boston Globe*, August 31, 1892, 7.

64 *touched elbows all around as they wrote*: "A Day of Sparring," *Providence Journal*, August 25, 1892, 1.

64 *The entrance of Bridget Sullivan . . . selling the stuff*: Porter, *The Fall River Tragedy*, 87.

64 *calm and self possessed, with less apparent agitation than the throng of men and women who were watching her*: "Miss Lizzie Borden in Court," *Boston Globe*, August 26, 1892, 1.

64 *If the prisoner had been a spectator idly drawn by curiosity to the scene, she could not have been more self-controlled*: "Miss Lizzie Borden in Court," *Boston Globe*, August 26, 1892, 1.

64 *As she came in from the outer corridor . . . came before the throng*: "Miss Lizzie Borden in Court," *Boston Globe*, August 26, 1892, 1.

65 *a majority of whom were women . . . dressed in holiday attire*: "Miss Lizzie Borden in Court," *Boston Globe*, August 26, 1892, 1.

65 *almost unbearable*: "Lizzie Borden's Hearing," *NYT*, August 26, 1892, 2.

65 *somewhat inclined to be stout*: "Miss Lizzie Borden in Court," *Boston Globe*, August 26, 1892, 1.

65 *ghastly*: "Still Circumstantial," *Providence Journal*, August 27, 1892, 1.

65 *Possessing a very gentlemanly manner . . . examination with confidence and distinctness*: "Miss Lizzie Borden in Court," *Boston Globe*, August 26, 1892, 1.

65 *There were a number of bad habits the District Attorney had acquired . . . Mr. Knowlton's hitting him over Mr. Jennings' shoulder*: Porter, *The Fall River Tragedy*, 91.

66 *Frequent wrangles took place . . . than at any time during the day*: "Miss Lizzie Borden in Court," *Boston Globe*, August 26, 1892, 1.

66 *scathing attack*: "Miss Lizzie Borden in Court," *Boston Globe*, August 26, 1892, 6.

66 *bungling*: "Miss Lizzie Borden in Court," *Boston Globe*, August 26, 1892, 6.

66 *Mr. Adams was at times very severe*: "Miss Lizzie Borden in Court," *Boston Globe*, August 26, 1892, 6.

66 *This announcement created a mild sensation*: "Headless Trunks," *FRDH*, August 26, 1892, 4.

67 *Mr. Borden said the milk might have been poisoned*: "Bridget Tells Her Story," *NYT*, August 27, 1892, 1.

67 *Her face was very white and her eyes downcast*: Boston Globe, "Lizzie Borden's Ordeal," *NYT*, August 28, 1892, 8.

67 *inaudible at the distance of ten feet from the witness stand*: "Lizzie Borden's Ordeal," *NYT*, August 28, 1892, 8.

67 *The crowd in the court room began to show a decided interest, which increased in her testimony*: "Link by Link," *Boston Globe*, August 27, 1892, 1.

67 *Emma Borden sat with her gloved hand shading her eyes*: "Lizzie Borden's Ordeal," *NYT*, August 28, 1892, 8.

67 *flush . . . she carefully listened to every sentence as it was presented*: "Lizzie Borden's Ordeal," *NYT*, August 28, 1892, 8.

68 *habit to notify you when she went out*: Porter, *The Fall River Tragedy*, 104.

68 *Then the only thing you know about her going out was what Lizzie told you?*: Porter, *The Fall River Tragedy*, 104.

68 *directing the questions at the young woman with unprecedented rapidity*: "Lizzie Borden's Ordeal," *NYT*, August 28, 1892, 8.

68 *stood the ordeal very well and her stereotyped answers were "Yes, Sir." And "No, Sir"*: "Lizzie Borden's Ordeal," *NYT*, August 28, 1892, 8.

68 *hearty laugh*: "Lizzie Borden's Ordeal," *NYT*, August 28, 1892, 1.

68 *She was decidedly nervous, shifting about in her seat and keeping her fan going*: "Link by Link," *Boston Globe*, August 27, 1892, 1.

68 *These officers say that the story of the servant . . . first her mother and then her father*: "Lizzie Borden's Ordeal," *NYT*, August 28, 1892, 8.

69 *He has also given it as his opinion . . . in holding Lizzie Borden for the Grand Jury*: "Lizzie Borden's Ordeal," *NYT*, August 28, 1892, 8.

69 *There has been, up to the present . . . stands absolutely without a motive*: "Lizzie Borden's Ordeal," *NYT*, August 28, 1892, 8.

69 *It was the first time I was ever asked for prussic acid in that manner*: "Bad Day for Lizzie Borden," *NYT*, August 30, 1892, 1.

69   *a purse or bag*: Preliminary Hearing, 310.

69   *Do you make any pretensions to vocal culture?*: Preliminary Hearing, 315.

69   *Do you claim to have a particularly sensitive or educated ear for sounds?*: Preliminary Hearing, 315.

69   *What was the peculiarity about this voice?*: Preliminary Hearing, 315.

69   *She spoke in a tremulous voice*: Preliminary Hearing, 315. See also "Bad Day for Lizzie Borden," *NYT*, August 30, 1892, 1.

69 · *I suppose you are reasonably sure . . . you had made a mistake in identification?*: Preliminary Hearing, 316.

70   *a matter of common experience*: Preliminary Hearing, 317.

70   *Bence once made a bet that*: Notebooks of Andrew Jennings, FRHS.

70   *A woman also called at Corneau & Latourneau's*: "Story of a Drug Clerk," *FRDH*, August 6, 1892, 4. Mrs. McCaffrey, a state police inspector's wife, visited that store and was said to resemble Lizzie Borden "very closely in build." "He Wore Russet Shoes," *NY Recorder*, August 7, 1892, 1.

70   *loud tone*: Preliminary Hearing, 319.

70   *tremulous tones*: Preliminary Hearing, 319.

70   *The prisoner herself has been more uneasy . . . self-control which she seems to possess*: "Bad Day for Lizzie Borden," *NYT*, August 30, 1892, 1.

71   *it was very painful . . . to hear the recital she had given of her visit to the barn and her purpose in going*: "No Trace of Poison Found," *NYT*, August 31, 1892, 1.

71   *to keep cool when other people are warm or excited*: "Last Day of Testimony," *NBES*, September 1, 1892, 3.

71   *adorned with a few red berries*: "Said Not Guilty," *NBES*, August 12, 1892, 1.

71   *drew his pathetic pictures . . . sitting with her hands in her eyes*: "Bound Over," *Boston Globe*, September 2, 1892, 6.

71   *on the rack*: "Lizzie on the Rack," *NBES*, August 10, 1892, 1.

71   *In the natural course of things . . . Is there nothing in the ties of love and affection?*: Preliminary Hearing, 508.

72   *Every blow showed that . . . not a powerful wrist and experience in handling a hatchet*: Preliminary Hearing, 507.

72   *Who could have done it?*: Preliminary Hearing, 513.

72   *[N]o man could have struck them . . . imperfect feminine hand*: Preliminary Hearing, 513.

72   *The first obvious inquiry is who is benefitted by that removal?*: Preliminary Hearing, 513.

72   *[T]he crime was done as a matter of deliberate preparation*: Preliminary Hearing, 515.

72 *singular*: Preliminary Hearing, 515.

72 *While everyone is dazed, there is but one person, who . . . has not been seen to express emotion*: Preliminary Hearing, 515.

72 *[S]he has been dealing in poisonous things; . . . hers alone has been the opportunity for commission of the crime*: Preliminary Hearing, 515.

72 *a deathly silence*: "Lizzie Borden Held," *Providence Journal*, September 2, 1892, 1.

72 *the sun, which had been . . . moment came in at the open window*: "Bound Over to the Grand Jury," *Boston Globe*, September 2, 1892, 1.

72 *Paler than usual*: "Bound Over to the Grand Jury," *Boston Globe*, September 1, 1892, 1.

72 *allowed his keen eyes to wander about the courtroom*: "Bound Over to the Grand Jury," *Boston Globe*, September 2, 1892, 1.

72 *the large piece of legal paper which the officers . . . could see was the murder complaint*: "Bound Over to the Grand Jury," *Boston Globe*, September 2, 1892, 1.

72 *in a husky voice, almost inaudible*: "Bound Over to the Grand Jury," *Boston Globe*, September 2, 1892, 1.

72 *its impressiveness enhanced by the palpable reluctance with which it was uttered*: "Bound Over to the Grand Jury," *Boston Globe*, September 2, 1892, 1.

72 *Suppose for a single moment that . . . what should be done with such a man?*: Preliminary Hearing, 517.

73 *almost a whisper*: "Bound Over to the Grand Jury," *Boston Globe*, September 2, 1892, 1.

73 *So there is only one thing . . . the Superior Court*: Preliminary Hearing, 517.

73 *sat calm and apparently unmoved*: "Bound Over to the Grand Jury," *Boston Globe*, September 2, 1892, 1.

73 *strong men lowered their heads . . . Every woman in the courtroom sobbed and wept except one*: "Bound Over to the Grand Jury," *Boston Globe*, September 2, 1892, 1.

73 *she was as resolute, as composed, and as self-possessed as at any time during the entire hearing*: "Bound Over to the Grand Jury," *Boston Globe*, September 1, 1892, 1. Porter wrote: "She sat like a statue of stone, totally unmoved, and without the slightest evidence of emotion or interest in the proceedings." Porter, *The Fall River Tragedy*, 140.

73 *Don't be afraid. I am all right. I feel quite composed*: "Bound Over to the Grand Jury," *Boston Globe*, September 2, 1892, 6.

73 *It is for the best, I think. It is better that I get my exoneration in a higher court,*

for then it will be complete: "Bound Over to the Grand Jury," *Boston Globe*, September 2, 1892, 6.

73   *I am all tired out and want to go home*: "Bound Over to the Grand Jury," *Boston Globe*, September 2, 1892, 6.

73   *[T]he government has not the slightest . . . committed by some one outside the family*: "Bound Over to the Grand Jury," *Boston Globe*, September 2, 1892, 1.

73   *Lizzie Borden's Secret*: *Boston Globe*, October 10, 1892, 1.

74   *the most gigantic "fake" ever laid before the reading public*: Porter, *The Fall River Tragedy*, 145.

75   *After Mr. Trickey had made the proposition . . . three o'clock in the morning*: Porter, *The Fall River Tragedy*, 151.

75   *heartfelt apology . . . inflicted upon her*: *Boston Globe*, October 12, 1892, 1; "The Borden 'Fake,'" *NBES*, October 13, 1892, 4.

75   *funeral in Providence if he ever laid his eyes*: Porter, *The Fall River Tragedy*, 153.

75   *that it is actually Trickey who was killed*: Letter from Albert Pillsbury to F. W. Hurd, December 5, 1892, in Knowlton Papers, 119; "Reporter Trickey Killed," *NY Sun*, December 5, 1892, 2.

75   *pretty well . . . to be capable of a number of things*: Letter from Albert Pillsbury to F. W. Hurd, December 5, 1892, in Knowlton Papers, 119.

75   *moving spirit*: Porter, *The Fall River Tragedy*, 145.

75   *found McHenry a capable, reliable, and trustworthy officer*: Porter, *The Fall River Tragedy*, 145.

76   *practicing in a gymnasium for a long*: Notes of Edwin D. McHenry, WS, 46.

76   *that there was one thing she saw in the house the day of the murder*: Notes of Edwin D. McHenry, WS, 46.

76   *one George Wiley, a clerk in the Troy Mill*: Notes of Edwin D. McHenry, WS, 46.

76   *I plodded through in silence, and where is my reward?*: Porter, *The Fall River Tragedy*, 150.

76   *So delicate in fact has the matter become*: Porter, *The Fall River Tragedy*, 144.

76   *In Massachusetts the grand jury . . . does not determine guilt or innocence*: Robert Sullivan, *Goodbye Lizzie Borden* (Brattleboro, VT: Stephen Greene Press, 1974), 53.

77   *substantial but not unanimous*: Letter from Knowlton to Pillsbury, December 3, 1892, in Knowlton Papers, 118.

77   *not even know how any man voted*: Letter from Knowlton to Pillsbury, December 3, 1892, in Knowlton Papers, 118.

77   *is almost a household word . . . men in the state*: "Life and Honor at Stake,"

Boston Globe, June 5, 1893, 5; "Robinson Dead," *Boston Sunday Herald*, February 23, 1896, 7.

77 *an old fashioned type*: "The Borden Jury Chosen," *NY Sun*, June 6, 1893, 1.

77 *His build shows that he loves the good things of life*: "The Borden Jury Chosen," *NY Sun*, June 6, 1893, 1.

78 *calm cheerfulness*: Henry Cabot Lodge, *An Address Commemorative of the Life and Services of George D. Robinson, Governor of the Commonwealth, 1884–86* (Boston: Geo. H. Ellis, Printer, 1896), 26.

78 *an extended knowledge of human nature possessed by but few professional men*: "Robinson Dead," *Boston Sunday Herald*, February 23, 1896, 7.

78 *He was the plain, blunt man . . . never been able to express quite so well*: Henry Cabot Lodge, *An Address Commemorative of the Life and Services of George D. Robinson, Governor of the Commonwealth, 1884–86*, 26.

78 *gave her no hope of anything* soon, or ever of an acquittal: Letter from Lizzie Borden to Annie Lindsey, October 1892, quoted in *Parallel Lives*, 480.

78 *the quietest boy I ever saw but is lots of company for me*: Letter from Lizzie Borden to Annie Lindsey, October 1892, quoted in *Parallel Lives*, 480.

79 *My spirits are at ebb tide. I see no ray of light amid the gloom . . . seems greater than I can bear*: Letter from Lizzie Borden to Annie Lindsey, May 11, 1893, quoted in *Parallel Lives*, 487.

79 *An Asylum May Be Her Lot*: "Insanity Indicated," *NBES*, September 3, 1892, 2.

79 *an average scholar, neither being exceptionally smart, nor noticeably dull*: Horace Benson, quoted in *Parallel Lives*, 59. See also "Lizzie Borden: Her School, and Later Life," *Boston Herald*, August 7, 1892, 6.

79 *rather blue*: Diary of Louisa Holmes Stilwell, quoted in *Parallel Lives*, 94.

79 *When I was at the table . . . "Lizzie, why don't you talk"*: Trial Transcript, 378.

79 *the murder[s] looked like the work of a lunatic*: "Visited the Tomb," *FRDH*, August 8, 1892, 4.

79 *No jury will believe that woman*: "Borden Jury Chosen," *NY World*, June 6, 1893, 8. Other observers found her to have a "peculiar expression of the eyes": "Strange Look in Her Eyes," *Boston Globe*, August 30, 1892, 7.

79 *impassive coolness*: "The Borden Tragedy," *Boston Herald*, quoted in *FRDH*, August 27, 1892, 4.

79 *There is nothing that tends more to induce the belief in insanity in this case than this most extraordinary exhibition*: "The Borden Tragedy," *Boston Herald*, quoted in *FRDH*, August 27, 1892, 4. The *Boston Globe* also quoted an anonymous official who made a similar point about her affectless demeanor. See "Strange Look in Her Eyes," *Boston Globe*, August 30, 1892, 7.

79   *It is a well-known fact that one may be comparatively sound on all matters but one. That is the way I think it is with Lizzie*: "Insanity Indicated," *NBES*, September 3, 1892, 2.

80   *It is an open secret in police circles . . . at the time of the murders*: "Miss Borden's Side," *Boston Advertiser*, August 15, 1892. See also "Insanity Indicated," *NBES*, September 3, 1892, 2, and "Indicted!," *NBES*, December 2, 1892, 1.

80   *mechanical aspects . . . that it was the work of a maniac*: Letter from Albert Pillsbury to Dr. Edward Cowles, September 22, 1892, in Knowlton Papers, 86.

80   *inferences have been* against . . . her conduct *before or after the event*: Letter from Dr. Edward Cowles to Albert Pillsbury, September 24, 1892, in Knowlton Papers, 86–87.

80   *I could do nothing whatever . . . if he consented to anything*: Letter from Hosea Knowlton to Pillsbury, November 22, 1892, in Knowlton Papers, 96.

80   *went away saying that he must see Adams*: Letter from Albert Pillsbury to Hosea Knowlton, November 22, 1892, in Knowlton Papers, 100.

80   *We could not do anything which suggested a doubt of her innocence*: Letter from Andrew Jennings to Pillsbury, November 22, 1892, in Knowlton Papers, 96.

80   *We can make some investigations into family matters without him . . . if we had his assistance*: Letter from Hosea Knowlton to Pillsbury, November 22, 1892, in Knowlton Papers, 96.

81   *a peculiar woman. She had a* very bad temper: Captain James C. Stafford, Report of Moulton Batchelder, November 24, 1892, in Knowlton Papers, 102.

81   *I always heard that they were somewhat peculiar and odd*: Mrs. Holland, Report of Moulton Batchelder, November 24, 1892, in Knowlton Papers, 102. This seems to be a misspelling of "Howland." Anna Howland was a contemporary of Lizzie Borden who likely knew the family through an aunt who had been a neighbor of the Bordens when they lived on Ferry Street. See Knowlton Papers, 442.

81   *We never heard that any one of them is or ever was insane but* I think some of them are worse then [*sic*] insane: Rescom Case, Report of Moulton Batchelder, November 24, 1892, in Knowlton Papers, 105.

81   *woman of bad disposition if they tell all what they know*: D. S. Brigham, Report of Moulton Batchelder, November 24, 1892, in Knowlton Papers, 105.

81   *ugly*: George A. Pettey, Report of Moulton Batchelder, November 24, 1892, in Knowlton Papers, 105.

81   *She was a girl of very even temper*: "Awaiting Monday," *FRDH*, August 20, 1892, 4.

81   *Although hysteria is common to that sex . . . she never showed any signs of it*: "Lizzie on the Rack," *NBES*, August 10, 1892, 1.

82   *Women warp morally if long nervously ill*: G. S. Weir Mitchell, "Doctor and Patient," *American Journal of Psychology* 5 (October 1892): 93.

82   *Menstruation may bring women to the most terrible crimes*: Hans Gross, *Criminal Psychology: A Manual for Judges, Practitioners and Students*, trans. Horace M. Kallen, Modern Criminal Science Series (Boston: Little, Brown and Co., 1915), 316. There were dissenting views about the link between menstruation and mental disorders. Mary Putnam Jacobi concluded that menstruation need not be debilitating, winning Harvard's Boylston Medical Prize in 1876 for her essay "The Question of Rest for Women During Menstruation." In a similar vein, Dr. Mary Dixon Jones questioned the dire warnings of T. S. Clouston, an eminent English gynecologist, about the mental risks of menstruation, asking, "Can any normal function give rise to abnormal impulses?" Mary Dixon Jones, "Insanity, Its Causes: Is There in Woman a Correlation of the Sexual Function with Insanity and Crime?," *Medical Record* (December 15, 1900): 926. Dixon Jones underwent her own legal trials, culminating in a libel trial against the *Brooklyn Daily Eagle* in 1892. See Regina Morantz-Sanchez, *Conduct Unbecoming a Woman: Medicine on Trial in Turn-of-the-Century Brooklyn* (New York: OUP, 1999).

82   *the relation of . . . a disorder of menstruation*: H. L. MacNaughton-Jones, "A Discussion on the Correlation Between Sexual Function, Insanity, and Crime," *British Medical Journal* (September 1900): 791.

82   *fleas*: Inquest, August 10, 1892.

83   *There was no evidence . . . any unusual mental condition*: Arthur S. Phillips, *The Borden Murder Mystery: In Defense of Lizzie Borden* (Portland, ME: King Publishing Co., 1986), 13–14. This is taken from Arthur S. Phillips's three-volume history of Fall River.

83   *Ask Emma if she took cat out which scratched her, put it on chopping block & cut head off*: Jennings Notebooks, FRHS.

83   *to look up the cat story in which Lizzie Borden killed some time ago*: Hilliard Papers 167, FRHS.

83   *knew for a* fact *that Miss Lizzie decapitated a kitten which belonged to her step-mother*: Anonymous Letter to Knowlton, June 14, 1893, in Knowlton Papers, 241.

83   *which Professor Wood said looked like a cow's hair, may have come from this*

cat: Letter from Mrs. Apthorp to Knowlton, June 14, 1893, in Knowlton Papers, 242.

83 *Nobody would be authority for this story*: "This Is the Real Lizzie Borden," *NY World*, June 18, 1893, 15.

83 *I cannot for the life of me see how you . . . full of hope over the case*: Letter from Lizzie Borden to Annie Lindsey, January 18, 1893, quoted in *Parallel Lives*, 483.

83 *the tangled threads would* never *be smoothed out*: Letter from Lizzie Borden to Annie Lindsey, May 11, 1893, quoted in *Parallel Lives*, 487.

84 *neither of us can escape the conclusion that she must have had some knowledge of the occurrence*: Letter from Hosea Knowlton to Albert Pillsbury, April 24, 1893, in Knowlton Papers, 159.

84 *Personally I would like very much to get rid of the trial of the case*: Letter from Hosea Knowlton to Albert Pillsbury, April 24, 1893, in Knowlton Papers, 158.

84 *however, I cannot see my way clear to any disposition of the case other than a trial*: Letter from Hosea Knowlton to Albert Pillsbury, April 24, 1893, in Knowlton Papers, 158.

84 *The case . . . has proceeded so far and an indictment*: Letter from Hosea Knowlton to Albert Pillsbury, April 24, 1893, in Knowlton Papers, 158–59.

84 *I do not feel sure that we shall . . . nor anything of an unusually trying character*: Letter from Albert Pillsbury to William Moody, May 3, 1893, in Knowlton Papers, 172.

84 *I will of course heed your injunction as to silence, knowing as I do the uncertainty of the course you may adopt, and remembering your caution*: Letter from William Moody to Albert Pillsbury, May 2, 1893, in Knowlton Papers, 168.

85 *as high a reputation as any public prosecutor in the state*: "Selecting the Jury," *Boston Globe*, June 6, 1893, 5.

85 *as bright and alert as he is handsome*: "The Borden Jury Chosen," *NY Sun*, June 6, 1893, 1.

85 *Chief Judge Mason says they conclude . . . Miss Borden should be arraigned and plead*: Letter from Albert Pillsbury to Hosea Knowlton, May 2, 1893, in Knowlton Papers, 168.

85 *not in sight more than two seconds*: "Arraigned," *NBES*, May 9, 1893, 8.

85 *she faltered*: "Arraigned," *NBES*, May 9, 1893, 8.

85 *It was but an instant, however, for she seemed to brace herself and then walked steadily to the dock*: "Arraigned," *NBES*, May 9, 1893, 8.

86 *nervous and agitated*: "Arraigned," *NBES*, May 9, 1893, 8.

86 *In a voice firm, clear, and resonant, she replied, "I am not guilty"*: "Arraigned," *NBES*, May 9, 1893, 8.

86 *spectators paced anxiously*: "Arraigned," *NBES*, May 9, 1893, 8.

86 *prepare the case thoroughly . . . He is going into the case* con amore: Letter from Hosea Knowlton to Albert Pillsbury, May 14, 1893, in Knowlton Papers, 179.

86 *I regret more than I can express . . . relieve us from criticism, more or less offensive*: Letter from Hosea Knowlton to Albert Pillsbury, May 14, 1893, in Knowlton Papers, 179.

86 *The preliminaries are completed, and this morning . . . the opening of the act, and the ending of the suspense*: "Strange Sunday Scenes," June 4, 1893, 1. See also "The Borden Murders," *Providence Journal*, June 5, 1893, 1.

Part 2

TRIAL

Chapter 5: The Curtain Ascends

89 *twenty-three distinct and separate axe wounds*: "Jose Correiro Held for the Murder of Bertha Manchester," *Boston Globe*, June 5, 1893, 1.

89 *The Man with the Axe*: "The Man with the Axe," *Providence Journal*, June 2, 1893, 1.

89 *So it seems there is in Fall River some Jack the Chopper*: "The Case of Lizzie Borden," *NY World*, June 4, 1893, 1.

90 *Everything about the Borden mystery*: "A Clew," *NBES*, June 1, 1893, 1.

90 *modest, retiring, self-sacrificing*: "Horrible Crime," *NBES*, May 31, 1892, 1.

90 *convenience and expense*: "The Borden Trial," *FREN*, May 1, 1893, 4.

91 *My client is very anxious*: Letter from Jennings to Knowlton, December 12, 1892, in Knowlton Papers, 122. See also "Mr. Jennings Talks," *FRDH*, May 4, 1893, 7.

91 *blubber artistocracy*: "Rather Rough," *FRDG*, June 7, 1893, 4. New Bedford itself was derisively called "Whaleopolis."

91 *one of the most beautiful towns in New England*: "Plans in the Borden Case," *NY Sun*, June 12, 1893, 1.

91 *one of the most picturesque buildings*: "Lizzie Borden at the Bar," *NY Sun*, June 5, 1893, 2.

91 *one of the greatest murder trials*: "One Trial for Her Life," *Providence Journal*, June 6, 1893, 1.

91 *the trial of the most extraordinary criminal case*: "Borden Jury Chosen," *NY World*, June 6, 1893.

91 *It will be impossible to exaggerate the interest*: "Selected," *Boston Globe*, June 6, 1893, 1.

91 *there are at this moment 100,000 persons*: "Life and Honor at Stake," *Boston Globe*, June 5, 1893, 1. As the *New Bedford Daily Mercury* observed, "The turning of millions of eyes to the courthouse on County Street . . . is a remarkable piece of testimony to the efficiency of the newspaper as a diffuser of information." *NBDM*, June 5, 1893, 4.

93 *you could hang all the washings*: "Pen and Eye," *Boston Globe*, June 12, 1893, 5.

93 *narrat[ing] the news with an eye toward character*: Karen Roggenkamp, *Narrating the News: New Journalism and Literary Genre in Late Nineteenth-Century American Newspapers and Fiction* (Kent: Ohio State University Press, 2005), xiii.

93 *know[ing] what to write*: Julian Ralph, *The Making of a Journalist* (New York: Harper & Brothers, 1903), 14.

94 *unconquerable persistence*: Julian Ralph, *The Making of a Journalist*, 99.

94 *The life of every journalist is as hard as nails*: Ralph, *The Making of a Journalist*, 26.

94 *It was a case of pitting cold logic against detective stupidity*: Ralph, *The Making of a Journalist*, 54.

94 *according to an age-old superstition*: Ralph, *The Making of a Journalist*, 61–62.

95 *a haphazard, unmethodical business*: Ralph, *The Making of a Journalist*, 26–27.

95 *a most demonstrative cow*: "Selected," *Boston Globe*, June 6, 1893, 1.

96 *The irreverent cow that moos beneath the windows*: "Editorial Points," *Boston Globe*, June 10, 1893, 4. The cow was "famous the land over." "Pen and Eye," *Boston Globe*, June 12, 1893, 5.

96 *888 in 1890 to 2,193*: Karen Roggenkamp, *Sympathy, Madness, and Crime: How Four Nineteenth-Century Journalists Made the Newspaper Women's Business* (Kent: Ohio State University Press, 2016), 4.

96 *more numerous, and they are further in*: Elizabeth Jordan, "The Newspaper Woman's Story," *Lippincott's Monthly Magazine* 51 (March 1893): 340.

97 *fresh white linen tailor made suit*: Elizabeth Jordan, *Three Rousing Cheers* (New York: Appleton-Century, 1938), 33.

97 *This was the simple tale of a sick baby*: Jordan, *Three Rousing Cheers*, 37.

97 *to drop the damned formality*: Jordan, *Three Rousing Cheers*, 39.

97 *warmer emotion than a pleasant friendship*: Jordan, *Three Rousing Cheers*, 216.

97   *the strange power of Henry James's eyes*: Jordan, *Three Rousing Cheers*, 210.

97   *Ruth Herrick's Assignment*: "Ruth Herrick's Assignment," *Cosmopolitan Magazine*, vol. XVII, May 1894–October 1894: 365–72.

98   *The reporters around me were for Miss Borden as one man*: Jordan, *Three Rousing Cheers*, 119–20.

Monday, June 5, 1893

98   *modest little carryall*: "Selected," *Boston Globe*, June 6, 1893, 1.

98   *fitted her as perfectly as if she had been measured for it in Paris*: "The Borden Jury Chosen," *NY Sun*, June 6, 1893, 2.

98   *a model for theatregoers*: "Selected," *Boston Globe*, June 6, 1893, 1.

98   *She is, in truth, a very plain-looking old maid*: "The Borden Jury Chosen," *NY Sun*, June 6, 1893, 1.

99   *Every picture which has been made of this woman*: "Borden Jury Chosen," *NY World*, June 6, 1893, 8.

99   *Viewed fully in the face Lizzie Borden is plain*: "Borden Jury Chosen," *NY World*, June 6, 1893, 8.

99   *a brawny, big, muscular, hard-faced, coarse-looking girl*: "With Skulls and Hatchets," *NY Sun*, June 14, 1893, 3.

99   *She is, in fact, neither large nor small*: "With Skulls and Hatchets," *NY Sun*, June 14, 1893, 3.

99   *about her that indefinable quality which we call ladyhood*: "With Skulls and Hatchets," *NY Sun*, June 14, 1893, 3.

99   *lower part of her countenance . . . greatly overweighted*: "The Borden Jury Chosen," *NY Sun*, June 6, 1893, 1.

99   *beautiful, fine, nut-brown hair, soft and glossy to a degree*: "The Borden Jury Chosen," *NY Sun*, June 6, 1893, 1.

99   *I could not be sure, but I strongly suspect*: Boston journalist Mildred Aldrich quoted in *Parallel Lives*, 509.

99   *A most interesting study is this young lady from Fall River*: "Selected," *Boston Globe*, June 6, 1893, 1.

99   *She behaved like a self-possessed girl*: "The Borden Jury Chosen," *NY Sun*, June 6, 1893, 1.

100   *sheer force of an iron resolution*: "Borden Jury Chosen," *NY World*, June 6, 1893, 8.

100   *aloof as a Buddha in a temple*: Jordan, *Three Rousing Cheers*, 118.

100   *I never did reveal my feelings*: "In a New Light," *New York Recorder*, September 20, 1892.

100 *more energy than all the rest of the people*: "The Borden Jury Chosen," *NY Sun*, June 6, 1893, 1.

100 *a powerful triumvirate*: "The Borden Murders," *Providence Journal*, June 5, 1893, 1.

100 *If he were a witch burner*: "Emma Borden Testifies," *NY Sun*, June 17, 1893, 1.

100 *a veritable Cromwell*: "The Borden Jury Chosen," *NY Sun*, June 6, 1893, 1.

101 *imposing bench . . . to his very marrow*: "Borden Jury Chosen," *NY World*, June 6, 1893, 8.

101 *a dignified old gentleman*: "Selected," *Boston Globe*, June 6, 1893, 1.

101 *large brown eyes . . . searching melancholy*: "Borden Jury Chosen," *NY World*, June 6, 1893, 8.

101 *a scholarly looking man with a large head*: "Guilty or Not?," *Boston Sunday Globe*, June 18, 1893, 1.

101 *reputation for wisdom and impartiality*: "Attorney General Withdraws," *FRDH*, May 26, 1893, 7.

101 *a younger and of a more modern type*: "Guilty or Not?," *Boston Sunday Globe*, June 18, 1893, 1.

101 *too merciful, even lenient*: "Attorney General Withdraws," *FRDH*, May 26, 1893, 7.

101 *precisely the kind of trio*: "Under Fire," *Boston Globe*, June 8, 1893, 1.

102 *[t]o enter a trial of this character*: Letter from Judge Albert Mason to Albert Pillsbury, May 2, 1893, Knowlton Papers, 167.

102 *the objections to attempting legislation*: Letter from Judge Albert Mason to Albert Pillsbury, May 3, 1893, Knowlton Papers, 171.

102 *a preacher of intense vitality and great aplomb*: "Selected," *Boston Globe*, June 6, 1893, 1.

102 *the intense prejudice for and against the prisoner*: "Guilty or Not," *Boston Globe*, June 19, 1893, 1.

103 *The examination of jurors in a Massachusetts court*: "Selected," *Boston Globe*, June 6, 1893, 5.

103 *He spoke very carefully, firmly, and distinctly*: "The Borden Jury Chosen," *NY Sun*, June 6, 1893, 2.

103 *incisive, yet there is something so suave*: "On Trial," *NBES*, June 5, 1893, 4.

104 *this sentiment is spreading with noticeable strength*: "Selected," *Boston Globe*, June 6, 1893, 1.

104 *possesses the faculty of making a rapid and accurate judgment*: "The Prosecuting Attorney," *FRDH*, June 5, 1893, 7.

104 *It is said that so thorough . . . every man summoned*: "Their Opinions Known," *FRDH*, June 6, 1893, 7; *NBES*, June 5, 1893, 4.

104   *American . . . Good practical man*: Knowlton Papers, 221.

104   *schoolgirls holding a pantomime conversation*: "The Borden Jury Chosen," *NY Sun*, June 6, 1893, 2.

104   *Japanese fan*: "Borden Jury Chosen," *NY World*, June 6, 1893, 8.

105   *good man: a very Intelligent Irishman*: Knowlton Papers, 219.

105   *Every one of them wears a mustache*: "Selected," *Boston Globe*, June 6, 1893, 5.

105   *a kindly featured man with a full head of hair*: "Borden Jury," *NBES*, June 6, 1893, 8.

105   Doubtful: Knowlton Papers, 218.

105   *under the legal guidance . . . Borden's fate*: "The Case of Lizzie Borden," *NY World*, June 4, 1893, 1.

105   *as could be desired or obtained*: "The Progress of the Trial," *NBEJ*, June 6, 1893, 4.

105   *their strong and typical New England faces*: "The Progress of the Trial," *NBEJ*, June 6, 1893, 4.

105   *unaccustomed . . . any nature*: "Selected," *Boston Globe*, June 6, 1893, 5.

106   *It is not considered to be decent*: "Moved at Last!," *FRDH*, May 1, 1893, 8.

Tuesday, June 6, 1893

106   *Every word seeming to fall like an additional weight*: "Miss Borden Faints," *NY World*, June 7, 1893.

106   *the rare gift of common sense*: "On Trial," *Boston Globe*, June 7, 1893, 1.

106   *Upon the fourth day of August . . . these crimes*: Trial Transcript, 47.

107   *a narrow scale*: Trial Transcript, 48.

107   *Some controversy had arisen about some property*: Trial Transcript, 49.

107   *an unkindly feeling*: Trial Transcript, 49.

107   *[I]t will be impossible for us*: Trial Transcript, 49.

107   *I know of nothing that will appear in this case more significant*: Trial Transcript, 50.

107   *Although they occupied the same household . . . impassable wall*: Trial Transcript, 51.

108   *It may fairly be called a thoroughfare*: Trial Transcript, 55.

109   *When you have got up . . . room occupied by the prisoner*: Trial Transcript, 58.

109   *It was locked . . . by a bolt*: Trial Transcript, 59.

110   *so far out of the question*: Trial Transcript, 82.

110   *was covered with an adhesion of ashes*: Trial Transcript, 83.

111   *was a new break and was a fresh break*: Trial Transcript, 84.

111 *such parts of the mortal remains of the victims . . . presented here*: Trial Transcript, 84.

111 *Moody made his grand coup*: "On Trial," *Boston Globe*, June 7, 1893, 1.

111 *Lizzie Borden, the sphinx of coolness*: FRDG, June 7, 1893, 7.

111 *With the same undemonstrativeness*: "Lizzie Borden Swooned," *NY Sun*, June 7, 1893, 3.

112 *the singular and awful misery of her position . . . of a maiden of good family*: "Lizzie Borden Swooned," *NY Sun*, June 7, 1893, 3.

112 *The heat is terrible*: "On Trial," *Boston Globe*, June 7, 1893, 1.

112 *he might as well have shaken a pump handle*: "Lizzie Borden Swooned," *NY Sun*, June 7, 1893, 3.

112 *a little tuft of coal black hair*: "On Trial," *Boston Globe*, June 7, 1893, 1.

112 *take the view . . . testimony*: Trial Transcript, 96.

112 *It will not be proper for you to ask questions*: Trial Transcript, 97.

113 *rage for economy*: "Visit to Fall River," *Boston Globe*, June 7, 1893, 5.

113 *through red-hot streets*: "On Trial," *Boston Globe*, June 7, 1893, 5.

113 *The heat was so intense*: "On Trial," *Boston Globe*, June 7, 1893, 5.

113 *a convict chain gang under guard*: "Somewhat Inconsiderate," FRDG, June 7, 1893, 4.

113 *It was a kind of holiday in Fall River*: "On Trial," *Boston Globe*, June 7, 1893, 5.

114 *creating considerable commotion*: "Visit of the Jury," FRDH, June 7, 1893, 7.

114 *The tired and hungry jurors*: "On Trial," *Boston Globe*, June 7, 1893, 5.

114 *a Bird's Eye view*: "On Trial," *Boston Globe*, June 7, 1893, 5. The next day, the editorial section of the *Boston Globe* pronounced the map "the best help to an intelligent understanding of the testimony . . . Thousands of people have cut it out for reference all through the trial." "Editorial Points," *Boston Globe*, June 8, 1893, 4.

114 *They were particularly attracted . . . decaying at the wharf*: "Judges See the Town," FRDH, June 7, 1893, 7.

Wednesday, June 7, 1893

115 *Where to Look for Your Wife*: FRDG, quoted in *NBES*, June 7, 1893, 4.

115 *Valentines and Daisies*: "Lizzie's Testimony Excluded," FRDG, June 12, 1893, 8.

115 *Taking all the most eligible seats*: "Under Fire," *Boston Globe*, June 8, 1893, 1.

115 *about half of the women were of commanding rank*: "Lizzie Borden Was Cheery," *NY Sun*, June 8, 1893, 1.

116 *all but motionless*: "Lizzie Borden was Cheery," *NY Sun*, June 8, 1893, 1.

117 *the chief interest in these celebrated cases*: "Under Fire," *Boston Globe*, June 8, 1893, 1.

117 *Those are three very peculiar people*: "Under Fire," *Boston Globe*, June 8, 1893, 1.

117 *extra work of a curious kind*: "Lizzie Borden Was Cheery," *NY Sun*, June 8, 1893, 1.

117 *the smallest of the lawyers in size and the biggest in nervous energy*: "Lizzie Borden Was Cheery," *NY Sun*, June 8, 1893, 1.

117 *the jury have seen the exact thing and have the measurements*: Trial Transcript, 99.

117 *And that you say was when you were particularly looking to see?*: Trial Transcript, 110.

118 *Get 200 lbs man*: Jennings Notebooks, FRHS.

118 *entertain[ing] a large number of listeners*: "Borden Jury," *NBES*, June 6, 1893, 8.

118 *He was asked a multitudinosity of questions*: "Under Fire," *Boston Globe*, June 8, 1893, 1.

118 *Governor Robinson developed in his confidential way*: "Under Fire," *Boston Globe*, June 8, 1893, 1.

118 *shook her head vigorously at the assertion*: *NYT*, quoted in *FRDH*, June 8, 1893, 6.

119 *under the weather*: Trial Transcript, 106.

119 *He kept both hands behind him*: "Lizzie Borden Was Cheery," *NY Sun*, June 8, 1893, 2.

119 *Moody yelled himself red in the face*: "Under Fire," *Boston Globe*, June 8, 1893, 2.

120 *a sensation*: "Under Fire," *Boston Globe*, June 8, 1893, 2.

120 *Bridget goes shopping*: "The Borden Jury Chosen," *NY Sun*, June 6, 1893, 2.

120 *Kid gloves of generous size concealed her hands*: "Lizzie Borden Was Cheery," *NY Sun*, June 8, 1893, 1.

120 *a love for the good things in life*: "Under Fire," *Boston Globe*, June 8, 1893, 2.

120 *she leaned on the left side of the rail*: "Bridget Sullivan a Witness," *NYT*, June 8, 1893, 2.

120 *washing, ironing, and cooking, with sweeping*: Trial Transcript, 195.

120 *dull headache*: Trial Transcript, 204.

121 *You needn't lock the door*: Trial Transcript, 229.

122 *for Mrs. Borden has gone out*: Trial Transcript, 237.

122 *cheap sale of dress goods*: Trial Transcript, 238.

122 *Father's dead*: Trial Transcript, 240.

122 *straight as a string*: "Under Fire," *Boston Globe*, June 8, 1893, 2.

122 *kindly eye*: "Under Fire," *Boston Globe*, June 8, 1893, 1.

123 *confidential manner*: "Under Fire," *Boston Globe*, June 8, 1893, 1.

123 *I don't know how the family was*: Trial Transcript, 255.

123 *out of the way . . . quarreling*: Trial Transcript, 255.

123 *they all got along genially*: Trial Transcript, 257.

123 *Mrs. Borden had coaxed her to stay and once raised her wages*: Statement of Bridget Sullivan to Nellie S. McHenry, August 25, 1892, in Knowlton Papers, 35.

123 *long duel*: "Lizzie Borden Was Cheery," *NY Sun*, June 8, 1893, 2.

123 *a learned and cunning man*: "Lizzie Borden Was Cheery," *NY Sun*, June 8, 1893, 2.

123 *During her long stay . . . her heels*: "Under Fire," *Boston Globe*, June 8, 1893, 1.

123 *one by one . . . the house impeded*: "Borden Boomerangs," *NY World*, June 8, 1893, 1.

124 *You were really honestly at work*: Trial Transcript, 279.

124 *mopped the perspiration from her face*: "Lizzie Borden Was Cheery," *NY Sun*, June 8, 1893, 2.

124 *is very courtly and winning to a woman witness*: "Dark for Lizzie Borden," *NY Sun*, June 9, 1893, 1.

124 *He is going to make a more bitter fight*: "Two Important Witnesses," *NYT*, June 9, 1893, 2.

124 *It was a man's mistake*: Trial Transcript, 293.

124 *The cross-examination . . . cause of the defense*: "Under Fire," *Boston Globe*, June 8, 1893, 2.

124 *She was willing to tell what she knew*: "Carroll's Horoscope," *NBEJ*, June 8, 1893, 4.

124 *the whole ordeal unscathed*: "Carroll's Horoscope," *NBEJ*, June 8, 1893, 4.

Chapter 6: Under Fire

125 *one of the smoothest and fairest*: "The State's Case Tangled," *NY Sun*, June 10, 1893, 2.

125 *The discipline of the court is almost perfect . . . for the court is great and marked*: "The State's Case Tangled," *NY Sun*, June 10, 1893, 2.

126 *urbanity and dignity*: "Under Fire," *Boston Globe*, June 8, 1893, 1.

126 *the bustle of a mill or the stock exchange*: "The State's Case Tangled," *NY Sun*, June 10, 1893, 2.

126 *pert and pretty*: "Pen and Eye," *Boston Globe*, June 12, 1893, 5.

126 *under sheriffs in blue coats . . . in and out*: "The State's Case Tangled," *NY Sun*, June 10, 1893, 2.

126 *Those who were not fortunate enough to gain admission . . . scene of battle*: "Lizzie's Dark Day," *NY World*, June 9, 1893, 2.

Thursday, June 8, 1893

126 *Prayers have been answered*: "Carroll's Horoscope," *NBEJ*, June 8, 1893, 4.

126 *the air of the court was not as cool as that of a shady dell*: "New Facts," *NBES*, June 8, 1893, 1.

126 *A great many early breakfasts . . . brought into view*: "Carroll's Horoscope," *NBEJ*, June 8, 1893, 4.

127 *hectic flush upon her face this morning*: "Face Flushed," *NBES*, June 9, 1893, 8.

127 *two or three very pretty girls . . . and extremely spare*: "Even Fight," *Boston Globe*, June 9, 1893, 1.

127 *a most unwilling and obviously essential witness*: "Even Fight," *Boston Globe*, June 9, 1893, 1.

127 *badly cut and covered with blood*: Trial Transcript, 301.

127 *apparently at ease*: Trial Transcript, 302.

127 *she had died of fright*: Trial Transcript, 308.

128 *It was an ordinary, unattractive, common dress*: Trial Transcript, 311.

128 *If the administration of morphine . . . dosing with the stuff?*: "Lizzie's Mind Clouded," *Boston Globe*, June 8, 1893, 1.

129 *A middle aged matron of comfortable build*: "Dark for Lizzie Borden," *NY Sun*, June 9, 1893, 1.

129 *short, stout, active, and willing*: "Lizzie's Mind Clouded," *Boston Globe*, June 8, 1893, 1.

129 *Must I, am I obliged to tell you all?*: WS, August 8, 1892, 11.

129 *stylish blue dress and black bonnet*: "Lizzie's Dark Day," *NY World*, June 9, 1893, 2.

129 *enunciation of her English*: "Lizzie's Dark Day," *NY World*, June 9, 1893, 2.

129 *No Mayday queen was ever happier*: "Even Fight," *Boston Globe*, June 9, 1893, 1.

129 *excited or agitated*: Trial Transcript, 347.

129 *a dark navy blue diamond figure*: Trial Transcript, 352.

130 *appeared and looked distressed . . . and frightened*: Trial Transcript, 358.

130 *turncoat friend*: "Defense in Good Humor," *Boston Sunday Globe*, June 11, 1893, 1.

130 *tall, angular, and thin*: "Even Fight," *Boston Globe*, June 9, 1893, 1.

130 *a slender, trim woman of precise manners*: "Dark for Lizzie Borden," *NY Sun*, June 9, 1893, 2.

130 *She held her mouth . . . most frequent utterances*: "Even Fight," *Boston Globe*, June 9, 1893, 1.

131 *as though one of the strange women characters . . . than any he ever evolved*: "Lizzie's Dark Day," *NY World*, June 9, 1893, 1.

131 *speak a little louder*: Trial Transcript, 373.

131 *as though it contained her return ticket*: "Dark for Lizzie Borden," *NY Sun*, June 9, 1893, 1.

132 *Today she took the witness stand . . . she was compelled to do this*: "Lizzie's Dark Day," *NY World*, June 9, 1893, 1.

132 *I feel as if something was hanging over me*: Trial Transcript, 375.

132 *gave three tremendous blasts on her accustomed trombone*: "Even Fight," *Boston Globe*, June 9, 1893, 1.

132 *Oh, I am a little ahead of the story*: Trial Transcript, 376.

132 *let his property for such a business*: Trial Transcript, 377.

132 *I feel as if I wanted to sleep*: Trial Transcript, 378.

132 *Father forbad our telling it*: Trial Transcript, 378.

133 *It is very disconnected*: Trial Transcript, 380–81.

133 *I am going to burn this old thing up*: Trial Transcript, 391.

133 *cheap cotton Bedford cord*: Trial Transcript, 394.

134 *I am afraid, Lizzie, the worst thing you could have done*: Trial Transcript, 393.

134 *No doubt about that*: Trial Transcript, 408.

134 *without an equal in New York City as a cross-examiner*: "Dark for Lizzie Borden," *NY Sun*, June 9, 1893, 1.

134 *was much less interested in the testimony . . . in her mouth and out again mechanically*: "Dark for Lizzie Borden," *NY Sun*, June 9, 1893, 2.

135 *how small the ankles was [sic] for the shoes*: Trial Transcript, 438.

135 *the most horrible exhibits yet seen*: "Dark for Lizzie Borden," *NY Sun*, June 9, 1893, 2.

135 *hung like a scarlet banner*: "Dark for Lizzie Borden," *NY Sun*, June 9, 1893, 2.

135 *friendly call*: Trial Transcript, 445.

135 *"a dark maroon color"*: Trial Transcript, 449.

136 *She is not my mother*: Trial Transcript, 464.

136 *that sounds terrible to those who sympathize*: "Dark for Lizzie Borden," *NY Sun*, June 9, 1893, 2.

136 *[s]he raised her head . . . some show of interest*: "Dark for Lizzie Borden," *NY Sun*, June 9, 1893, 2.

137 *hot and close*: Trial Transcript, 482.

137   *A hum ran through the court*: "Dark for Lizzie Borden," *NY Sun*, June 9, 1893, 2.

137   *the coolest, clearest-headed, shrewdest man*: "Dark for Lizzie Borden," *NY Sun*, June 9, 1893, 1.

137   *When ex-Gov. Robinson took hold of Assistant Marshal Fleet*: "Dark for Lizzie Borden," *NY Sun*, June 9, 1893, 2.

137   *Do you think you told the same story then that you tell now?*: Trial Transcript, 484.

138   *Job himself could not have endured*: "Dark for Lizzie Borden," *NY Sun*, June 9, 1893, 2.

138   *you didn't look carefully enough*: Trial Transcript, 495.

138   *I don't know how much further you are going to read*: Trial Transcript, 495.

138   *You were not expecting to find any man*: Trial Transcript, 498.

138   *showed his consummate art by simulating irritability, sternness, and impatience*: "Dark for Lizzie Borden," *NY Sun*, June 9, 1893, 2.

138   *showed evident bias against the prisoner*: "Break in the State's Case," *NYT*, June 10, 1893, 1.

138   *Mr. Fleet's description of the weapon . . . the deed was committed*: "Two Important Witnesses," *NYT*, June 9, 1893, 2.

138   *It is the general belief that the Government brought out its worst to-day*: "Dark for Lizzie Borden," *NY Sun*, June 9, 1893, 1.

138   *It was a bad day for Lizzie Borden*: "Dark for Lizzie Borden," *NY Sun*, June 9, 1893, 1.

139   *The operation could almost be likened . . . brought them down*: "Dark for Lizzie Borden," *NY Sun*, June 9, 1893, 1.

139   *All of her stoicism seemed to have returned to her*: "Dark for Lizzie Borden," *NY Sun*, June 9, 1893, 1.

139   *Lizzie Borden has a remarkable temperament . . . she becomes stronger*: "Lizzie's Mind Was Cheery," *Boston Globe*, June 8, 1893, 1.

Friday, June 9, 1893

139   *extraordinary collection of women*: "New Light," *Boston Globe*, June 10, 1893, 1.

139   *Lizzie not only looked pale, she felt pale*: "New Light," *Boston Globe*, June 10, 1893, 1.

139   *as bright as a new dollar*: "The State's Case Tangled," *NY Sun*, June 10, 1893, 1.

139   *Nearly every one who has taken an active part*: "Defense in Good Humor," *Boston Sunday Globe*, June 11, 1893, 1.

140 *All the details of the affair were rehearsed*: "Break in the State's Case," *NYT*, June 10, 1893, 8.

140 *Oh, he was there*: Trial Transcript, 515.

140 *There's a good many things I haven't told you*: Trial Transcript, 512.

140 *There were so many officers there*: Trial Transcript, 527.

140 *Why didn't you tell me before*: Trial Transcript, 529.

141 *Let us have the one you like best this morning*: Trial Transcript, 541.

141 *dismissed the witness with a wave of his hand*: "The State's Case Tangled," *NY Sun*, June 10, 1893, 2.

141 *a small drop trickled down the side of the face*: Trial Transcript, 559.

141 *creditable to a first class dressmaker*: "New Light," *Boston Globe*, June 10, 1893, 2.

141 *He gave the colors, the stripes*: "New Light," *Boston Globe*, June 10, 1893, 12. For Harrington's full description: see Trial Transcript, 565–66.

141 *laughed so that her body trembled*: "The State's Case Tangled," *NY Sun*, June 10, 1893, 2.

141 *That finishes it, does it?*: Trial Transcript, 566.

142 *Were you ever in the dressmaking business?*: Trial Transcript, 582.

142 *could talk about dresses like an American Worth or a female society reporter*: "The State's Case Tangled," *NY Sun*, June 10, 1893, 2.

142 *the tailor-made captain*: "Break in the State's Case," *NYT*, June 10, 1893, 2.

142 *No one would have been surprised if he had drawn a mouchoir*: "New Light," *Boston Globe*, June 10, 1893, 2.

142 *some scraps of note paper in his hand*: Trial Transcript, 566.

142 *I cannot let this go in . . . no significance*: Trial Transcript, 567.

142 *about twelve inches long and no more than two inches in diameter*: Trial Transcript, 568.

143 *something like scraping*: Trial Transcript, 595.

143 *did not look like a powder magazine*: "The State's Case Tangled," *NY Sun*, June 10, 1893, 1.

143 *in blissful unconsciousness that he had revealed*: "Miss Borden's Hope," *NY World*, June 10, 1893, 14.

143 *if a bomb had fallen in the courtroom*: "New Light," *Boston Globe*, June 10, 1893, 2.

143 *The rest of the handle?*: Trial Transcript, 631.

143 *merciless and masterful grasp*: "The State's Case Tangled," *NY Sun*, June 10, 1893, 1.

143 *The theory of the Commonwealth . . . in the cellar*: "The State's Case Tangled," *NY Sun*, June 10, 1893, 2.

144 *They nearly destroyed the Government's hope*: "Break in the State's Case," *NYT*, June 10, 1893, 8.

144 *The tattered web . . . totally unexpected blow*: "The State's Case Tangled," *NY Sun*, June 10, 1893, 1.

144 *Of course he was certain*: "Defense in Good Humor," *Boston Sunday Globe*, June 11, 1893, 7.

144 *In the minds of those present . . . on a witness stand*: "In Favor of Lizzie," *NY World*, June 11, 1893, 1.

144 *There was no objection made to your search*: Trial Transcript, 638.

144 *the hair was dry, that it was matted*: Trial Transcript, 646.

144 *looked like a wilted flower*: "New Light," *Boston Globe*, June 10, 1893, 1.

145 *frequently drowned the words . . . dominated the place*: "New Light," *Boston Globe*, June 10, 1893, 2.

145 *an expression of paternal solicitude*: "New Light," *Boston Globe*, June 10, 1893, 1.

145 *allowing their minds to reach any conclusion*: Trial Transcript, 651.

145 *Up at 6 in the morning . . . except their tongues*: "New Light," *Boston Globe*, June 10, 1893, 2.

145 *pure water filtered*: "Pen and Eye," *Boston Globe*, June 12, 1893, 5.

Saturday, June 10, 1893

145 *The ingenuity of New Bedford's authorities*: "Defense in Good Humor," *Boston Sunday Globe*, June 11, 1893, 1.

146 *a large number of young and rather pretty girls*: "Defense in Good Humor," *Boston Sunday Globe*, June 11, 1893, 1.

146 *In bonnets . . . as far as complexions went*: "Sixth Day," *FRDG*, June 10, 1893, 9.

146 *looks as she would look in church*: "Sixth Day," *FRDG*, June 10, 1893, 9.

146 *If the strains of the past six days has told on her*: "Sixth Day," *FRDG*, June 10, 1893, 9.

146 *The handleless hatchet . . . another great hole in the case*: "Borden Case in Tatters," *NY Sun*, June 11, 1893, 1.

146 *It was upon the three and a half-inch edge*: "In Favor of Lizzie," *NY World*, June 11, 1893, 1.

147 *You were there to look*: Trial Transcript, 659.

147 *The thought came to me*: Trial Transcript, 690.

147 *I don't ask what was said*: Trial Transcript, 697.

147 *Very truly at such things*: Trial Transcript, 715.

147 *Well, I am glad to find a man that is not on style*: Trial Transcript, 716.

148 *a loose, rough matter*: Trial Transcript, 720.

148 *tremulous with excitement internally*: "Day of Days," *Boston Globe*, June 12, 1893, 1.

148 *five cent cut of pie*: "State's Case in Tatters," *NY Sun*, June 11, 1893, 2.

148 *I cannot tell you what I was looking for*: Trial Transcript, 726.

148 *an absolute, unrestrained, and complete search*: Trial Transcript, 735.

149 *a very bright break*: Trial Transcript, 744.

149 *Well, look—a carpenter!*: Trial Transcript, 758.

149 *There has never been a trial so full of surprises*: "Day of Days," *Boston Globe*, June 12, 1893, 1.

149 *a conspicuousity*: "New Light," *Boston Globe*, June 10, 1893, 1.

150 *What does Bridget Sullivan know about the burglary*: "Day of Days," *Boston Globe*, June 12, 1893, 1.

150 *the sidewalks on both sides of the street*: "Lizzie's Dark Day," *NY World*, June 9, 1893, 2.

150 *a New England dinner*: "Defense in Good Humor," *Boston Globe*, June 11, 1893, 7.

150 *The genius of Charles Dickens*: "Plans in the Borden Case," *NY Sun*, June 12, 1893.

150 *with the gleam of domestic hope*: "Day of Days," *Boston Globe*, June 12, 1893, 1.

150 *The jurors were bundled into an omnibus . . . any possible enlivenments*: "Day of Days," *Boston Globe*, June 12, 1893, 5.

150 *Queen Victoria might die*: "Day of Days," *Boston Globe*, June 12, 1893, 5.

150 *thereby preventing all hands from attending religious service of any kind*: "Mr. Swift Backed Out," *FRDG*, June 12, 1893, 7.

Chapter 7: A Signal Victory

151 *in an atmosphere like . . . a mighty engine*: Elizabeth Jordan, *Three Rousing Cheers* (New York: D. Appleton-Century Co., 1938), 119.

151 *If Miss Borden had not committed the murders*: Jordan, *Three Rousing Cheers*, 119.

151 *to understand how anyone else . . . in the house in which she was stirring*: "Lizzie Borden at the Bar," *NY Sun*, June 5, 1893, 2.

151 *An escaped maniac? . . . came cheerily to mind*: Jordan, *Three Rousing Cheers*, 119.

152 *a gorilla standing framed*: Jordan, *Three Rousing Cheers*, 120.

152 *He mentioned maniacs*: Jordan, *Three Rousing Cheers*, 120.

Monday, June 12, 1893

152 *through the perpetual and swollen crowd*: "A Point for Lizzie Borden," *NY Sun*, June 13, 1893, 1.

152 *his favorite seat taken*: "Scenes and Incidents," *FREN*, June 12, 1893, 1.

152 *many times more expensive than the old one*: "A Point for Lizzie Borden," *NY Sun*, June 13, 1893, 1.

152 *Her color was bad*: "Lizzie Wept," *Boston Globe*, June 13, 1893, 1.

154 *The statements made by her . . . her interests*: "Big Gain for Lizzie Borden," *NY Times*, June 13, 1893, 1.

154 *On the confused stories . . . antagonism of the jury*: "Going Lizzie's Way," *NY Sun*, June 12, 1893, 1.

155 *As an axe leaves its mark*: John Henry Wigmore, *A Treatise on the System of Evidence in Trials at Common Law Including the Statutes and Judicial Decisions of All Jurisdictions of the United States*, 4 vols. (2nd ed., Boston: Little, Brown, and Co., 1923), I:544.

155 *the conduct of the accused after the killing*: John Henry Wigmore, "The Borden Case," *American Law Review* 27 (November–December 1893): 819–45.

155 *All facts that go either to sustain or impeach a hypothesis*: Trial Transcript, 1247.

155 *clearly not in the nature of a confession, but rather in the nature of denials*: Trial Transcript, 777.

155 *Declarations voluntarily given*: People v. Mondon, 103 N.Y. 211 (1886): "When a coroner's inquest is held . . . before any person has been arrested or charged with the crime, and a witness is called and sworn before the coroner's jury, the testimony of that witness, should he afterward be charged with the crime, may be used against him on his trial, and the mere fact that at the time of his examination he was aware that a crime was suspected and that he was suspected of being the criminal, will not prevent his being regarded as a mere witness whose testimony may be afterwards given in evidence against himself."

156 *She alone . . . surrounded by the police*: Trial Transcript, 795–96.

157 *keeping her with the hand upon the shoulder*: Trial Transcript, 798.

157 *I am not talking to the jury*: Trial Transcript, 800.

157 *What did they want this woman for?*: Trial Transcript, 811.

158 *that she ought not to testify*: Trial Transcript, 798.

158 *agreeable, confidential manner*: "Lizzie Wept," *Boston Globe*, June 13, 1893, 2.

158 *The mind, confused and agitated*: State v. Gilman, 51 Maine 206, 207

(1862): "If innocent, and yet conscious of the existence of circumstances tending to show guilt, there is the strongest temptation to make such statements, without regard to their truth, as will serve to conceal . . . these circumstances . . . The mind, confused and agitated by the apprehension of danger, cannot reason with coolness; and it resorts to falsehood when the truth would be safer, and is hurried into acknowledgments which the facts do not warrant."

158 *Denied counsel*: Trial Transcript, 798.

158 *It is magnificent but it is not law*: Trial Transcript, 819.

158 *So far as I can understand his position*: Trial Transcript, 819–20.

158 *vocal gymnastics and fireworks*: Trial Transcript, 820.

159 *Can your Honors have any doubt*: Trial Transcript, 824.

159 *an undisclosed warrant*: Trial Transcript, 827.

159 *not a question of whether such and such a course*: "Lizzie Wept," *Boston Globe*, June 13, 1893, 2.

159 *in the hands of Mr. Knowlton . . . her enemy and her persecutor*: "A Point for Lizzie Borden," *NY Sun*, June 13, 1893, 1.

159 *If that is not the equivalent of being under arrest*: "Defense in Good Humor," *Boston Globe*, June 11, 1893, 7.

159 *Pushed, examined, cross-questioned . . . time and time again*: "Lizzie Wept," *Boston Globe*, June 13, 1893, 1.

159 *befogged condition*: "A Point for Lizzie Borden," *NY Sun*, June 13, 1893, 1.

159 *Even if Miss Borden had testified without coercion*: "Break in the State's Case," *NYT*, June 10, 1893, 8.

160 *Paler than a sheet*: "Lizzie Wept," *Boston Globe*, June 13, 1893, 2.

160 *fastened a look upon the chief justice*: "Lizzie Wept," *Boston Globe*, June 13, 1893, 2.

160 *in a voice as clear as a bell*: "Lizzie Wept," *Boston Globe*, June 13, 1893, 2. Edwin Booth, the great Shakespearean actor, had died the preceding week. "Edwin Booth Is Dead," *NYT*, June 7, 1893, 1.

160 *as effectually in custody*: Trial Transcript, 831.

160 *The common law regards substance*: Trial Transcript, 830.

160 *She couldn't help it*: "Lizzie Wept," *Boston Globe*, June 13, 1893, 2.

160 *It would seem . . . spark of relief had quite unstrung her*: "Going Lizzie's Way," *NY World*, June 13, 1893, 1.

160 *The agitation of the counsel*: "Lizzie Wept," *Boston Globe*, June 13, 1893, 2.

160 *signal victory*: "Lizzie Wept," *Boston Globe*, June 13, 1893, 1.

161 *a new point of law in the old Bay State*: "A Point for Lizzie Borden," *NY*

Sun, June 13, 1893, 1. By the end of the nineteenth century, the laws of evidence seemed to be unfolding haphazardly to the chagrin of those who believed in a unified theory of law. Arriving at Northwestern University as an expert in comparative law, John Henry Wigmore set himself the daunting task of rationalizing the law of evidence, culminating, a decade later, in his monumental *Treatise on Evidence*. In it, he sought to "expound the Anglo-American law of Evidence as a system of reasoned principles and rules . . . and . . . to deal with the apparently warring mass of judicial precedents as the consistent product of those principles and rules." John Henry Wigmore, *A Treatise on the System of Evidence in Trials at Common Law Including the Statutes and Judicial Decisions of All Jurisdictions of the United States*, 4 vols. (Boston: Little, Brown and Co., 1904), I, vi. In a review of its third edition published in 1940, Professor George James remarked: "What can the critic say, except here is the authoritative text—perhaps the greatest modern legal treatise—bigger and better than ever." George F. James, "The Contribution of Wigmore to the Law of Evidence," *University of Chicago Law Review* 78 (1940), 78.

161   *common sense dictated a contrary result*: Charles G. Davis, "The Conduct of the Law in the Borden Case," *A Collection of Articles Concerning the Borden Case* (Boston: Boston Daily Advertiser, 1894), 9.

161   *Is there any lawyer . . . proved dangerous to use*: Wigmore, "The Borden Case," *American Law Review* (November–December 1893), 843.

161   *Very few people . . . this time is very significant*: "The Attorney General," *FRDH*, June 12, 1893.

161   *It was . . . impossible to get them to talk seriously*: "New Bedford Women," *FREN*, June 13, 1893, 5.

162   *Alice Russell was carrying a small hand lamp*: Trial Transcript, 834.

162   *empty the slops*: Trial Transcript, 840.

162   *What she did I don't know*: Trial Transcript, 835.

162   *in a perfectly natural way*: Trial Transcript, 839.

162   *a ropy consistency*: Trial Transcript, 833.

163   *Whoever knows how tedious and longwinded*: "A Point for Lizzie Borden," *NY Sun*, June 13, 1893, 1.

163   *oozing from the wounds in the head*: Trial Transcript, 854.

163   *the blood on the head was matted*: Trial Transcript, 862.

164   *the heavy claw hammered hatchet . . . looked as though it had been scraped*: Trial Transcript, 867.

164   *there is a minute pin spot of blood*: Trial Transcript, 885.

165   *I have no objection to your marking my coat*: Trial Transcript, 921.

166 *Were the wounds . . . a woman of ordinary strength?*: Trial Transcript, 905.

166 *Wait a moment*: Trial Transcript, 905.

166 *had been there ahead of you and lifted up this woman*: Trial Transcript, 911.

167 *The seventh day of the Borden . . . this legal drama*: "A Point for Lizzie Borden," *NY Sun*, June 13, 1893, 1.

167 *It is said that this woman has no art*: "A Point for Lizzie Borden," *NY Sun*, June 13, 1893, 1–2.

Tuesday, June 13, 1893

167 *seemed only to intensify . . . steaming atmosphere*: "No Blood," *Boston Globe*, June 14, 1893, 1.

167 *Surely . . . the women of New Bedford do not seem to think so*: "Murders Re-Enacted," *NY World*, June 14, 1893, 8.

167 *was the scene of universal attraction*: "No Blood," *Boston Globe*, June 14, 1893, 1.

167 *the same old crowd . . . given ten minutes early*: *FREN*, June 13, 1893, 5.

168 *created a panic among the messenger boys*: "New Bedford Women," *FREN*, June 13, 1893, 5.

168 *her usual time*: "New Bedford Women," *FREN*, June 13, 1893, 5.

168 *clad a la mode*: "No Blood," *Boston Globe*, June 14, 1893, 1.

168 *anticipating the horrors of the day*: "No Blood," *Boston Globe*, June 14, 1893, 1.

168 *the wild-eyed, haggard-featured, thick-skinned women*: "No Blood," *Boston Globe*, June 14, 1893, 1.

168 *create a hostile atmosphere*: "With Skulls and Hatchets," *NY Sun*, June 14, 1893, 3.

168 *blood, skulls, and bowels*: "With Skulls and Hatchets," *NY Sun*, June 14, 1893, 3.

169 *Well, the stomach is a rebellious member*: Trial Transcript, 970.

169 *Horror has been piled upon misery*: "With Skulls and Hatchets," *NY Sun*, June 14, 1893, 3.

169 *vigorous fanning*: "Taken Sick," *NBES*, June 13, 1893, 3.

170 *nothing in the length of wounds*: Trial Transcript, 977.

170 *Is there anything unreasonable . . . four and a half inches in length?*: Trial Transcript, 986.

170 *a good edge*: Trial Transcript, 987.

170 *Did you observe that the edge is turned?*: Trial Transcript, 938.

170 *[N]otwithstanding the anatomy of the eye . . . by a hatchet?*: Trial Transcript, 988.

170 *an excellent arguer*: "No Blood," *Boston Globe*, June 14, 1893, 2.

170 *rained blow after blow, left and right*: "No Blood," *Boston Globe*, June 14, 1893, 1.

171 *Although this gentleman has cut off Mrs. Borden's head*: "No Blood," *Boston Globe*, June 14, 1893, 2.

171 *thus far the learned brothers*: "No Blood," *Boston Globe*, June 14, 1893, 2.

171 *red-faced, gray-haired, stalwart, and handsome man*: "With Skulls and Hatchets," *NY Sun*, June 14, 1893, 3.

171 *an army officer*: "With Skulls and Hatchets," *NY Sun*, June 14, 1893, 3.

171 *a heavy-weight pugilist*: "With Skulls and Hatchets," *NY Sun*, June 14, 1893, 3.

172 *Knowlton, in his most gracious way, gently led the professor*: "No Blood," *Boston Globe*, June 14, 1893, 2.

172 *with a recital of the most repellent*: "With Skulls and Hatchets," *NY Sun*, June 14, 1893, 3.

172 *Lizzie Borden's interest in his testimony . . . insensate things*: "With Skulls and Hatchets," *NY Sun*, June 14, 1893, 3.

172 *as though lecturing to a class*: "No Blood," *Boston Globe*, June 14, 1893, 2.

172 *I opened an artery in the leg of a dog*: Trial Transcript, 1006.

172 *to chemical tests and microscopic tests*: Trial Transcript, 1000.

172 *could not have been washed quickly*: Trial Transcript, 1001.

173 *I have already pointed them out*: Trial Transcript, 1001.

173 *broke forth into a long and most emphatic wail*: "No Blood," *Boston Globe*, June 14, 1893, 2.

173 *a white film upon both sides*: Trial Transcript, 1014.

173 *darker and dirtier*: Trial Transcript, 1026.

173 *slot on the inner edge of the head*: Trial Transcript, 1024.

173 *thicker upon the outside than upon the inside*: Trial Transcript, 1005.

173 *The defense claim, for reasons not necessary to publish*: "No Blood," *Boston Globe*, June 14, 1893, 1.

174 *It is agreed that the pail*: Trial Transcript, 550.

174 *Pass from those*: Trial Transcript, 596.

174 *might spatter in any direction and might not spatter in every direction*: Trial Transcript, 1028.

174 *I don't see how he could avoid being spattered*: Trial Transcript, 1029.

175 *Witness after witness . . . that's all*: "No Blood," *Boston Globe*, June 14, 1893, 2.

175 *Dr. Draper is coming round on our side in great shape*: Letter from Knowlton to Pillsbury, May 27, 1893, in Knowlton Papers, 204.

175 *the anatomical proofs of the priority of Mrs. Borden's death*: Letter from Draper to Knowlton, May 28, 1893, in Knowlton Papers, 205.

175 *incidental questions, which are very fascinating in themselves*: Letter from Draper to Knowlton, May 28, 1893, in Knowlton Papers, 205.

175 *Will you kindly put me in communication*: Letter from Draper to Knowlton, May 28, 1893, in Knowlton Papers, 206–7.

176 *penetrate[d] the bone of the skull?*: Trial Transcript, 1037.

176 *done up in a white handkerchief*: "With Skulls and Hatchets," *NY Sun*, June 14, 1893, 3.

176 *District Atty Knowlton . . . a considerate father*: "No Blood," *Boston Globe*, June 14, 1893, 1.

176 *the little adjacency . . . hear all she chose*: "No Blood," *Boston Globe*, June 14, 1893, 1.

177 *the old man's jaw sagged back and forth*: Jordan, *Three Rousing Cheers*, 120.

177 *Spectators caught their breath*: Jordan, *Three Rousing Cheers*, 120.

177 *If the old man, awakened by the first blow*: "With Skulls and Hatchets," *NY Sun*, June 14, 1893, 2.

177 *The skulls didn't look like the skulls we see in museums*: "No Blood," *Boston Globe*, June 14, 1893, 1.

177 *had a cheery way of fitting the different hatchets*: "With Skulls and Hatchets," *NY Sun*, June 14, 1893, 3.

178 *have been produced by the use of an ordinary hatchet in the hands of a woman of ordinary strength*: Trial Transcript, 1055.

178 *the assailant . . . downward on the floor*: Trial Transcript, 1056.

178 *he was lying on the sofa on his right side*: Trial Transcript, 1058.

179 *went down through the eyebrow*: Trial Transcript, 1060.

179 *it would sputter or bubble*: Trial Transcript, 1084.

179 *The part that was exposed*: Trial Transcript, 1065.

179 *I should think the front of the dress*: Trial Transcript, 1075.

179 *The handleless hatchet is not an uncommon instrument*: Trial Transcript, 1067.

180 *not all hatchets with a cutting edge of three and a half inches*: Trial Transcript, 1082.

180 *I don't think I asked that question*: Trial Transcript, 1084.

180 *that precise question*: Trial Transcript, 1085.

180 *What did you understand the answer to be*: Trial Transcript, 1085.

180 *the length, location, and direction*: Trial Transcript, 1070.

180 *from below upward from the right toward the left*: Trial Transcript, 1070.

180 *It is a clear indication of the plane*: Trial Transcript, 1080.

180 *I found none that would be an exception to the rule*: Trial Transcript, 1075.

181 *in August, in our climate*: Trial Transcript, 1076.

181 *readily and quickly intermingle*: Trial Transcript, 1076.

181 *a miserable, poky, mind-wearing, physique-exhausting session*: "No Blood," *Boston Globe*, June 14, 1893, 1.

181 *Without a word the Sheriff set upon him*: "Murders Re-Enacted," *NY World*, June 14, 1893, 8.

181 *Officials ought to understand*: "Hatred," *NBES*, June 14, 1893, 3.

181 *To wide knowledge and experience*: Letter from Draper to Knowlton, May 28, 1893, Knowlton Papers, 206.

182 *Mild, deliberate, and gracious*: "No Blood," *Boston Globe*, June 14, 1893, 2.

182 *very tall, very thin, very methodical and very slow*: "No Blood," *Boston Globe*, June 14, 1893, 2.

182 *a heavy, metallic weapon . . . three and a half inches in length*: Trial Transcript, 1090.

182 *there would be a good deal of effusion of blood*: Trial Transcript, 1098.

182 *a linen jacket or a white linen gown*: Trial Transcript, 1099.

182 *changed between every operation, with rapidity*: Trial Transcript, 1108.

183 *[w]ith a handle of sufficiently long leverage*: Trial Transcript, 1094.

183 *dramatic illustration*: "Murders Re-Enacted," *NY World*, June 14, 1893, 8.

183 *it seemed as if the crash of bone must be heard*: "Murders Re-Enacted," *NY World*, June 14, 1893, 8.

183 *That is . . . right to left, wood chopping fashion?*: Trial Transcript, 1106.

183 *As a double exception . . . the criminal woman is a monster*: Cesare Lombroso and William Ferrero, *The Female Offender* (London: T. Fisher Unwin, 1895), 152. As Joe Howard put it, "History shows us that murder, when committed by women . . . is invariably attended by circumstances most atrocious and revolting:" "Life and Honor at Stake," *Boston Globe*, June 5, 1893, 1.

184 *the peculiarity of the female criminal lunatic*: Lombroso, quoted in MacNaughton-Jones, 791.

184 *trend[ed] just as certainly in the direction*: "No Blood," *Boston Globe*, June 14, 1893, 2.

Chapter 8: Intent, Deliberation, and Preparation

185 *always on time, never loses a second*: "One Side," *Boston Globe*, June 16, 1893, 1.

185 *The phenomenal feature of this court . . . as a faucet emits water*: "Lizzie Borden's Defence," *NY Sun*, June 16, 1893, 2.

186 *The court stenographer . . . dart in and out*: "Lizzie Borden's Defence," *NY Sun*, June 16, 1893, 2.

186 *typewriter girls*: "Lizzie Borden's Defence," *NY Sun*, June 16, 1893, 2. He added: "When business is slack . . . the typewriter girls picnic in the doorway."

Wednesday, June 14, 1893

186 *more discomfort, heat, and humidity*: "Even So!," *Boston Globe*, June 15, 1893, 1.

186 *How can the jury endure the physical strain?*: "Even So!," *Boston Globe*, June 15, 1893, 1.

187 *limp and without energy*: "Lizzie Borden's Worst Day," *NY Sun*, June 15, 1893, 1.

187 *Knowlton rushed up the stairs . . . both anxious and with determination in every glance*: "Even So!," *Boston Globe*, June 15, 1893, 1.

187 *the deus ex machina*: "Even So!," *Boston Globe*, June 15, 1893, 1.

187 *A fine, orderly looking man*: "Even So!," *Boston Globe*, June 15, 1893, 1.

187 *an enormous drooping brown moustache*: "You Gave Me Away!," *Boston Globe*, June 15, 1893, 3.

187 *almost suffocating*: Trial Transcript, 1112.

187 *We tried to keep it from her*: Trial Transcript, 1118.

188 *foxy*: "Borden Boomerangs," *NY World*, June 8, 1893, 3.

188 *I want to know the truth*: Trial Transcript, 1152.

188 *Spoke it right out?*: Trial Transcript, 1153.

188 *pleasant-faced, courteous-mannered individual*: "Even So!," *Boston Globe*, June 15, 1893, 1.

188 *a square political and surgeon of repute*: "Even So!," *Boston Globe*, June 15, 1893, 1.

189 *spoke up . . . earnestly*: Trial Transcript, 1165.

189 *I would not say she did not speak earnestly*: Trial Transcript, 1166.

189 *If you are disturbed in any way*: Trial Transcript, 1163.

189 *the mayor's manner and words . . . which could in any way reflect against*: "Even So!," *Boston Globe*, June 15, 1893, 1.

189 *Don't say that to me*: Trial Transcript, 1169.

189 *Oh Lizzie . . . if we can help it*: Trial Transcript, 1169.

189 *the firecracker that the District Attorney had promised*: "Lizzie Borden's Worst Day," *NY Sun*, June 15, 1893, 1.

189 *the most dainty and charming woman*: "Lizzie Borden's Worst Day," *NY Sun*, June 15, 1893, 2.

190 *unhappy home*: Trial Transcript, 1173.

190 *an express declaration in regard to one individual*: Trial Transcript, 1175.

190   *the continuity of feeling*: Trial Transcript, 1176.

190   *too ambiguous*: Trial Transcript, 1177.

190   *After this first glimpse of real sunshine . . . balance against her*: "You Gave Me Away!," *NY World*, June 15, 1893, 3.

190   *I could have strangled the creature*: Elizabeth Jordan, *Three Rousing Cheers*, 119.

191   *a very old lady who wore colored spectacles*: "You Gave Me Away!," *NY World*, June 15, 1893, 3.

191   *very loud talk . . . put up her finger*: Trial Transcript, 1214.

192   *Lizzie Borden was unusually cheerful today*: "Prussic Acid in the Case," *NYT*, June 15, 1893.

192   *clean cut, emphatic, and understandable*: "Even So!," *Boston Globe*, June 15, 1893, 1.

192   *That is the first thing*: "Even So!," *Boston Globe*, June 15, 1893, 1.

192   *succeeded in working the witness up*: "Even So!," *Boston Globe*, June 15, 1893, 1.

192   *staggered*: "Even So!," *Boston Globe*, June 15, 1893, 2.

192   *fairly glared at him*: "Even So!," *Boston Globe*, June 15, 1893, 2.

193   *of vital importance . . . the Court alone*: Trial Transcript, 1239.

193   *I think you better not state it now*: Trial Transcript, 1239.

193   *one of the most deadly poisons that is known to human kind*: Trial Transcript, 1263.

193   *commonly used for suicide*: M. P. Earles, "The Introduction of Hydrocyanic Acid into Medicine: A Study in the History of Pharmacology," *Medical History* 11.3 (1967): 311–12.

193   *It would be fair to say . . . negative results*: Trial Transcript, 1242.

193   *killing these two people*: Trial Transcript, 1242.

193   *It is an attempt . . . legitimately buy*: Trial Transcript, 1244.

194   *Does it have any tendency . . . an axe?*: Trial Transcript, 1244.

194   *It is an attempt . . . wholly different means*: Trial Transcript, 1243.

194   *failure to purchase . . . August*: Trial Transcript, 1244.

194   *This indictment . . . with premeditation*: Trial Transcript, 1244.

194   *[t]here is no purpose of offering this testimony*: Trial Transcript, 1273.

194   *was an illness suggestive of opportunity*: Trial Transcript, 1246.

194   *this prisoner . . . murderous state of mind?*: Trial Transcript, 1247.

194   *is an article . . . no adaptability to such use*: Trial Transcript, 1240.

195   *Where a given intent . . . commission of another crime or not*: Trial Transcript, 1253.

195   *When a previous act indicates . . . it is admissible as evidence*: *Commonwealth v. Bradford*, 126 Mass. 42 (1878).

195   *Was she deliberating mischief towards somebody?*: Trial Transcript, 1247.

196   *There is nothing to show*: Trial Transcript, 1266.

196   *to throw some sort of prejudice*: Trial Transcript, 1267.

196   *There is a tendency to show*: Trial Transcript, 1267.

196   *that anyone can say manifests a murderous intent*: Trial Transcript, 1264.

196   *That was a statement of a truth*: Trial Transcript, 1264.

196   *Now can that statement made by herself*: Trial Transcript, 1264.

196   *an open, absolute, plain declaration*: Trial Transcript, 1265.

196   *This evidence ought not to go in*: Trial Transcript, 1265.

196   *an article a person may legitimately buy*: Trial Transcript, 1266.

196   *people buy prussic acid to kill animals*: Trial Transcript, 1267. Prussic acid was used for killing cats. John Epps, "Hydrocyanic Acid Prescription," *Lancet* 20, no. 521 (August 24, 1833): 699.

197   *You mistook my point of illustration*: Trial Transcript, 1270.

197   *Take the Kansas case*: Trial Transcript, 1272.

197   *an act which is itself innocent*: Trial Transcript, 1272.

197   *I must say I have said all the Court desires to hear*: Trial Transcript, 1272.

197   *The heat tonight*: "Even So!," *Boston Globe*, June 14, 1893, 2.

197   *purpose for which the testimony is offered*: Trial Transcript, 1273.

197   *bearing on the state of mind of the defendant*: Trial Transcript, 1273.

197   *the prosecution is permitted to utilize the prussic acid . . . becloud the defense*: "Even So!," *Boston Globe*, June 15, 1893, 1.

197   *Taken altogether, this was Lizzie Borden's worst day*: "Lizzie Borden's Worst Day," *NY Sun*, June 15, 1893, 1.

198   *These occurrences may not prove important . . . enthusiasm to thoughtfulness*: "Lizzie Borden's Worst Day," *NY Sun*, June 15, 1893, 1.

Thursday, June 15, 1893

198   *At no time since the trial opened . . . screamed with pain*: "Defense!," *NBES*, June 15, 1893, 1.

198   *The atmosphere is supercharged with humidity*: "One Side," *Boston Globe*, June 16, 1893, 1.

198   *each armed with a palm leaf fan*: "One Side," *Boston Globe*, June 16, 1893, 1.

198   *heaviest retail business in the city*: Trial Transcript, 1277.

198   *other than as a medicine*: Trial Transcript, 1279.

198   *In your experience as a druggist*: Trial Transcript, 1279.

198   *Is that drug an article of commerce*: Trial Transcript, 1280.

199   *Do you know of any use to which prussic acid is put*: Trial Transcript, 1281.

199 *any knowledge of the effects of prussic acid on furs?*: Trial Transcript, 1284.

199 *Has prussic acid any suitability or adaptability . . . sealskin furs?*: Trial Transcript, 1285. Robinson objected that it was beyond the prosecution's offer of proof and then asked for an exception when the objection was overruled.

199 *It is unsuitable*: Trial Transcript, 1287.

199 *cause nausea and headache*: Trial Transcript, 1288.

200 *family man . . . benzene used for cleaning purposes?*: Trial Transcript, 1290.

200 *Arsenic is a poison*: Trial Transcript, 1293.

200 *Do you know anything . . . if you wanted to do it quietly?*: Trial Transcript, 1294.

200 *subject to the actions of moths or other vermin?*: Trial Transcript, 1303.

200 *the preliminary proceedings have not been sufficient*: Trial Transcript, 1304.

201 *almost universal surprise by the bar*: Davis, "The Conduct of the Law in the Borden Case," 8.

201 *What a wonderful web of obscurity*: Wigmore, "The Borden Case," 839.

201 *[W]hy was it necessary . . . other reasonable hypotheses exist*: Wigmore, "The Borden Case," 843.

201 *He held forth the ideal of the expert*: Quoted in Andrew Porwancher, *John Henry Wigmore and the Rules of Evidence: The Hidden Origins of Modern Law* (Columbia: University of Missouri Press, 2016), 19.

201 *The judge for admissibility, the jury for weight*: John Henry Wigmore, *A Supplement to A Treatise on the System of Evidence in Trials at Common Law, Containing the Statutes and Judicial Decisions, 1904–7* (Boston: Little, Brown, and Co., 1908), vi.

203 *Knowlton, after another and final parade . . . rested his case*: "Lizzie's Side Heard," *NY World*, June 16, 1893, 14.

203 *a dull thud*: *Springfield Union*, quoted in Kent, *The Lizzie Borden Sourcebook*, 286.

203 *I am not so certain about the jury . . . two or three uneasy shiftings of bodily position*: "One Side," *Boston Globe*, June 16, 1893, 1.

203 *intended to go to the jury . . . too sensible to be true*: "One Side," *Boston Globe*, June 16, 1893, 1.

203 *It is as if the cause were a deep and pitch dark well*: "Borden Case in Tatters," *NY Sun*, June 11, 1893, 1.

Chapter 9: Short, Busy, and Very Important

205 *There were some extraordinary individuals*: "One Side," *Boston Globe*, June 16, 1893, 1.

205 *a sort of self-constituted jury*: "This Is the Real Lizzie Borden," *NY World*, June 18, 1893, 15. The *Fall River Daily Globe* declared: "The real jury of her peers, which is trying Lizzie Borden, is the job lot of femininity which fill the jury box on the south side of the New Bedford courthouse." "Not My Mother," *FRDG*, June 9, 1893, 7.

206 *did not permit him to forget . . . flushing with animation*: "You Gave Me Away!," *NY World*, June 15, 1893, 3.

206 *of being under a subdued but terrific tension*: "Lizzie's Side Heard," *NY World*, June 16, 1893, 14.

206 *Her eyes were brighter than usual*: "Lizzie's Side Heard," *NY World*, June 16, 1893, 14.

206 *In her hand she held the first really gay display*: "Lizzie's Side Heard," *NY World*, June 16, 1893, 14.

Thursday, June 15, 1893

206 *low, measured, funereal tone of voice*: "Lizzie Borden's Turn Now," *NY Sun*, June 15, 1893, 2.

206 *was for many years my client*: Trial Transcript, 1305.

207 *We shall show you that this young woman had apparently led*: Trial Transcript, 1306.

207 *for some reason or other . . . to fasten this crime upon her*: Trial Transcript, 1306.

207 *that most dramatic scene . . . no man dares to cross it*: Trial Transcript, 1308.

207 *Just so . . . party who is accused*: Trial Transcript, 1308.

207 *a doubt for which one could give a reason*: Trial Transcript, 1309.

207 *[i]f you can conceive of any other hypothesis*: Trial Transcript, 1309.

207 *wholly and absolutely circumstantial*: Trial Transcript, 1310.

207 *[T]here is no class of evidence*: Trial Transcript, 1311.

208 *your task is not to unravel the mystery*: Trial Transcript, 1315.

208 *Have they furnished the proof*: Trial Transcript, 1315.

208 *[T]here is not one particle of direct evidence*: Trial Transcript, 1310.

208 *He ridiculed, with neat sarcasm*: "One Side," *Boston Globe*, June 16, 1893, 1.

208 *loved and loving father?*: Trial Transcript, 1323.

208 *championed her cause with an ancient knight's*: "Lizzie Borden's Turn Now," *NY Sun*, June 15, 1893, 2.

208 *his belief in her innocence shone*: "Lizzie Borden's Turn Now," *NY Sun*, June 15, 1893, 2.

208 *brushing away the cobwebs of ingenuity*: "One Side," *Boston Globe*, June 16, 1893, 1.

208 *I couldn't describe the noise*: Trial Transcript, 1325.

209 *a very pretty and rather coquettish young French girl*: "Lizzie's Side Heard," *NY World*, June 15, 1893, 14.

209 *How could you tell the direction*: Trial Transcript, 1331.

209 *What is it?*: Trial Transcript, 1343.

210 *a nice looking old lady*: "One Side," *Boston Globe*, June 16, 1893, 1.

210 *Well, I lost my sister*: Trial Transcript, 1353.

210 *with a graceful bow embracing the court*: "One Side," *Boston Globe*, June 16, 1893, 1.

210 *a venerable white-haired old man of the frontier type*: "One Side," *Boston Globe*, June 16, 1893, 1.

210 *When he took the oath . . . through the audience*: "One Side," *Boston Globe*, June 16, 1893, 1.

211 *medium sized young man of very pale complexion*: Trial Transcript, 1369.

211 *I can't put it into words . . . something of the kind*: Trial Transcript, 1372.

211 *He didn't see me*: Trial Transcript, 1373.

211 *And all you can put into words . . . walked slowly?*: Trial Transcript, 1375.

211 *You cannot express that agitation any more than that?*: Trial Transcript, 1375.

211 *pond lilies that a young fellow*: Trial Transcript, 1379.

211 *standing in the gateway*: Trial Transcript, 1379.

211 *standing there quietly*: Trial Transcript, 1381.

211 *as though he were uneasy*: Trial Transcript, 1462.

212 *Would you swear it wasn't nine?*: Trial Transcript, 1403.

212 *gave some unimportant testimony*: "One Side," *Boston Globe*, June 16, 1893, 1.

213 *What part of the street . . . your team was on?*: Trial Transcript, 1414.

213 *Why could you not tell the time?*: Trial Transcript, 1418.

214 *So your usual time for eating dinner*: Trial Transcript, 1447.

214 *It really struck you as being a cool place*: Trial Transcript, 1449.

214 *poor Mrs. Borden*: Trial Transcript, 1455.

214 *had not any idea of this matter coming up at this time*: Trial Transcript, 1455.

214 *This has no relation . . . some talk had by the person himself*: Trial Transcript, 1456.

214 *may well be taken to be the mutterings*: Trial Transcript, 1456.

215 *that most characteristic rule*: Wigmore, *A Treatise on the System of Evidence in Trials at Common Law* (1904), vol. 2, § 1364, 1695.

215 *Four miles away . . . twelve days afterward*: Trial Transcript, 1456.

215 *wild and imaginative stories*: Trial Transcript, 1457.

215 *either the results of disordered imagination*: Trial Transcript, 1457.

215 *easy communication with the centre of the city*: Trial Transcript, 1457–58.

215 *in the nature of conversations . . . exclamations of pain or suffering*: Trial Transcript, 1458.

215 *such considerations as they think it deserves*: Trial Transcript, 1459.

215 *a burst of sunshine*: "Lizzie Borden's Turn Now," *NY Sun*, June 15, 1893, 1.

216 *The entire day has been one of cheer*: "Lizzie Borden's Turn Now," *Boston Globe*, June 15, 1893, 1.

Friday, June 16, 1893

216 *The discovery has created a genuine sensation*: "Another Hatchet!," *FRDH*, June 15, 1893.

216 *a slight coloring of gilt*: "Defense," *NBES*, June 15, 1893, 3.

217 *a very small but unmistakable . . . not long out of the store*: Letter from Dr. Draper to Hosea Knowlton, May 31, 1893, in Knowlton Papers, 212.

217 *If the murderer . . . the place where it was found*: *NBEJ*, June 16, 1893, 7.

217 *The general impression is that it was thrown . . . for the purpose of creating a sensation*: "Lizzie's Side Heard," *NY World*, June 16, 1893, 14.

217 *that note which Mrs. Borden is alleged to have received from a sick friend*: *FRDG*, June 15, 1893, 4.

217 *a red hot experience*: "Hopeful," *Boston Globe*, June 17, 1893, 1.

217 *The cold east wind . . . provocation*: "Hopeful," *Boston Globe*, June 17, 1893, 1.

217 *a tonic . . . more contented*: "Hopeful," *Boston Globe*, June 17, 1893, 1.

217 *a veritable floral glory*: "Emma Borden Testifies," *NY Sun*, June 17, 1893, 1.

217 *The sable-garbed prisoner . . . wide-awake old maid*: "Emma Borden Testifies," *NY Sun*, June 17, 1893, 1.

217 *gala day*: "Emma Borden Testifies," *NY Sun*, June 17, 1893, 1.

218 *his associates . . . might not be changed*: "Hopeful," *Boston Globe*, June 17, 1893, 1.

218 *ornamental, fancy painter*: Trial Transcript, 1468.

218 *there was a man stabbed*: Trial Transcript, 1469.

218 *somebody might be concealed*: Trial Transcript, 1478.

218 *without hesitation or zeal*: "Hopeful," *Boston Globe*, June 17, 1893, 1.

218 *There is nothing in it*: Trial Transcript, 1485.

219 *some 30 or 40 in town*: Trial Transcript, 1491.

219 *That was what you were after*: Trial Transcript, 1495.

219 *If you sign that paper*: Trial Transcript, 1523.

219 *a nice little old lady*: "Hopeful," *Boston Globe*, June 17, 1893, 1.

219 *It isn't so*: Trial Transcript, 1507.

219 *I am not used to this business*: Trial Transcript, 1498.

219 *I expressly and positively deny*: Trial Transcript, 1516.

220 *You had been quite actively interested*: Trial Transcript, 1520.

220 *who betrayed much nervousness by her quick, short breathing*: "All the Evidence In," *NY World*, June 17, 1893, 3.

220 *It is a lie from beginning to end*: Trial Transcript, 1528.

220 *and when she took it away . . . crying*: "All the Evidence In," *NY World*, June 17, 1893, 3.

220 *The house was full of men*: Trial Transcript, 1505.

220 *leaning forward with her face close to ex-Gov. Robinson's shoulder*: *What was done with the pieces of cloth*: Trial Transcript, 1544.

220 *was the event of the day*: "All the Evidence In," *NY World*, June 17, 1893, 3.

220 *Everybody made a rush . . . entire recess*: "Hopeful," *Boston Globe*, June 17, 1893, 1.

221 *made such a stir*: "Emma Borden Testifies," *NY Sun*, June 17, 1893, 2.

221 *aged double of her sister*: "Emma Borden Testifies," *NY Sun*, June 17, 1893, 1.

221 *She is a little over 40 years of age*: "Hopeful," *Boston Globe*, June 17, 1893, 2.

221 *Self-reliance and personal dignity*: "Hopeful," *Boston Globe*, June 17, 1893, 2.

221 *Much older than Lizzie in appearance*: "Emma Borden Testifies," *NY World*, June 17, 1893, 3.

221 *There was no swaying of her slender form*: "Hopeful," *Boston Globe*, June 17, 1893, 1.

221 *The defense enjoyed perfect and overwhelming success*: "Emma Borden Testifies, *NY Sun*, June 17, 1893, 1.

222 *upon his finger*: Trial Transcript, 1530.

222 *the search . . . taken from the floor*: Trial Transcript, 1533.

222 *everything had been examined*: Trial Transcript, 1536.

222 *blue cotton Bedford Cord*: Trial Transcript, 1537.

222 *it was very dirty*: Trial Transcript, 1540.

223 *You have not destroyed that old dress yet*: Trial Transcript, 1540.

223 *'why don't you' . . . 'Do it!'*: Trial Transcript, 1542–43.

223 *Did you or your sister keep a ragbag?*: Trial Transcript, 1544.

223 *it was decided*: Trial Transcript, 1545.

223 *the worst thing Lizzie could have done*: Trial Transcript, 1545.

224 *advanced toward her . . . as a terrier would shake a rat*: "Emma Borden Testifies," *NY Sun*, June 17, 1893, 1.

224 *rasping, unrelenting . . . cross examination*: "All the Evidence In," *NY World*, June 17, 1893, 3.

224 *visibly shrank back in her chair*: "All the Evidence In," *NY World*, June 17, 1893, 3.

224 *She looked very frail*: "All the Evidence In," *NY World*, June 17, 1893, 3.

224 *[c]olossus pitted against the slender sister*: "Emma Borden Testifies," *NY Sun*, June 17, 1893, 1.

224 *Was there some complaint*: Trial Transcript, 1557.

224 *Were the relations between you and Lizzie and your stepmother*: Trial Transcript, 1557.

224 *Between my sister and Mrs. Borden they were*: Trial Transcript, 1557.

225 *He could not shake her testimony*: "Emma Borden Testifies," *NY Sun*, June 17, 1893, 1.

225 *I don't say I didn't say it*: Trial Transcript, 1561.

225 *I think I only looked in a little bag*: Trial Transcript, 1566.

225 *I don't say it was not said*: Trial Transcript, 1575.

225 *calling friend*: Trial Transcript, 1570.

225 *She stood with perfect self-possession*: "Hopeful," *Boston Globe*, June 17, 1893, 2.

226 *Mr. Knowlton's cross-examination . . . and smiled*: "All the Evidence In," *NY World*, June 17, 1893, 3.

226 *she had done her sister's cause . . . evidence without her*: "Emma Borden Testifies," *NY Sun*, June 17, 1893, 1.

226 *light blue with a dark figure*: Trial Transcript, 1578.

226 *She cut some pieces out of it*: Trial Transcript, 1580.

226 *reclining in a chair*: Trial Transcript, 1584.

226 *I thought she had fainted*: Trial Transcript, 1584.

226 *very white . . . in her lap*: Trial Transcript, 1585.

227 *noticed nothing unusual about the dress*: Trial Transcript, 1586.

227 *the afternoon of the day*: Trial Transcript, 1590.

227 *That reporter has come after me again*: Trial Transcript, 1590.

227 *the spring lock was not sure*: Trial Transcript, 1592.

227 *advanced a few feet into the room*: Trial Transcript, 1592.

227 *seemed to be more excited*: Trial Transcript, 1594.

228 *If you sign that paper*: Trial Transcript, 1598.

228 *the relations between you and your stepmother*: Trial Transcript, 1604.

228 *Well, we felt she was not interested in us*: Trial Transcript, 1605.

228 *a blouse waist of blue material*: Trial Transcript, 1605.

229 *The evidence is closed on both sides*: Trial Transcript, 1608.

229 *notwithstanding the evidence . . . the case finally committed to them*: Trial Transcript, 1608.

229 *There has been no communication . . . the populace themselves*: "Guilty or Not?," *Boston Globe*, June 18, 1893, 7.

Saturday, June 17, and Sunday, June 18, 1893

229   *No convicts at hard labor*: "Borden Jurors Wrangle," *NY World*, June 18, 1893.

229   *Tramp, tramp, tramp*: "Sang Hymns," *Boston Globe*, June 19, 1893, 1.

229   *Clothes did not make the man*: "Sang Hymns," *Boston Globe*, June 19, 1893, 1.

229   *remarkably hearty dinner . . . place of oil*: "Sang Hymns," *Boston Globe*, June 19, 1893, 1.

230   *The brisk harbor breeze*: "Sang Hymns," *Boston Globe*, June 19, 1893, 1.

230   *working like a beaver*: "Turning Now to the Jury," *NY Sun*, June 19, 1893, 3.

230   *For the past two weeks . . . charmed structure*: "With Light Heart," *NY Sun*, June 18, 1893.

230   *nobody admitted under eighty years of age*: "Sang Hymns," *Boston Globe*, June 19, 1893, 1.

231   *was that she has slept well*: "Turning Now to the Jury," *NY Sun*, June 19, 1893, 3.

231   *human sphinx*: "This Is the Real Lizzie Borden," *NY World*, June 18, 1893, 15.

231   *memories of the past*: "Sang Hymns," *Boston Globe*, June 19, 1893, 1.

231   *with his little boy's compliments*: "Lizzie Not Over-Anxious," *NY World*, June 18, 1893.

231   a *dull day of anxious waiting*: "With a Light Heart," *Sunday Herald*, in Kent, 295.

Chapter 10: Last Words in the Great Trial

233   *the conduct of the Borden trial*: "The Conduct of the Borden Trial," *NYT*, June 19, 1893, 4.

233   *Another interesting . . . truly comradic*: "One Side," *Boston Globe*, June 16, 1893, 1.

234   *The temper of the lawyers . . . respectful manner*: "The State's Case Tangled," *NY Sun*, June 10, 1893, 2.

234   *has only one duty . . . no mean tactics on the part of the Commonwealth here*: Trial Transcript, 1616–17.

Monday, June 19, 1893

234   *The mob that besieged the Court . . . Ancient Temple of Justice*: "Pleas in the Borden Case," *NY Sun*, June 20, 1893, 1.

234 *more like a surging mob*: "Seen from Without," *NBEJ*, June 19, 1893, 2.

234 *women in silks*: "Pleas in the Borden Case," *NY Sun*, June 20, 1893, 1.

234 *If the women were frantic to get in before, they were frenzied to-day*: "A Plea for Life," *NY World*, June 20, 1893, 7.

234 *hundreds standing for hours outside*: "Last Words in the Great Trial," *Boston Globe*, June 20, 1893, 1.

234 *packed as only a clever stevedore*: "Pleas in the Borden Case," *NY Sun*, June 20, 1893, 1.

234 *visibly affected . . . nervous system is strained*: "Arguments," *FRDH*, June 19, 1893, 7.

235 *swollen and colored slightly purple*: "Pleas in the Borden Case," *NY Sun*, June 20, 1893, 1.

235 *was brought a third Monday . . . brawny district attorney*: "Last Words in the Great Trial," *Boston Globe*, June 20, 1893, 1.

235 *low, earnest voice*: "Last Words in the Great Trial," *Boston Globe*, June 20, 1893, 1.

235 *almost bare of eloquence*: *NYT*, June 20, 1893, 9.

235 *commonplace*: "Pleas in the Borden Case," *NY Sun*, June 20, 1893, 1. Both Jordan and Howard pronounced his closing plea a "disappointment." "A Plea for Life," *NY World*, June 20, 1893, 7; "Last Words in the Great Trial," *Boston Globe*, June 20, 1893, 1.

235 *twanged his voice . . . for was it not*: "Pleas in the Borden Case," *NY Sun*, June 20, 1893, 1.

235 *intently, now and then fanning herself*: "Last Words in the Great Trial," *Boston Globe*, June 20, 1893, 2.

236 *one of the most dastardly and diabolical crimes*: Trial Transcript, 1610.

236 *Policemen are human*: Trial Transcript, 1618.

236 *Suspicion began to fall here and there*: Trial Transcript, 1613.

236 *Once a theory possesses our minds*: Trial Transcript, 1613.

236 *he is possessed and saturated*: Trial Transcript, 1618.

236 *you do not get the greatest ability*: Trial Transcript, 1618.

236 *Not one police officer . . . well-directed conduct of an investigation*: New-Bedford *Mercury*, June 19, 1893, 4. In a similar vein, the *Providence Journal* pronounced the proceedings less a trial of Lizzie Borden and more like "an exposition of the incompetency of the Dogberrys of the Fall River police force." Quoted in "What Others are Saying," *FREN*, June 20, 1893, 4.

236 *a little scene . . . to look after*: Trial Transcript, 1621.

237 *waited . . . until it was time*: Trial Transcript, 1621.

237 *You are trying a capital case*: Trial Transcript, 1621.

237   *the proof must come up . . . in the world*: Trial Transcript, 1628–29.

237   *to unravel the mystery*: Trial Transcript, 1621.

237   *the only blot*: Wigmore, "The Borden Case," 830.

238   *You have not heard . . . it is not in the case*: Trial Transcript, 1634.

238   *dark insinuations*: Trial Transcript, 1643.

238   *what he said looked like . . . meanly intimated*: Trial Transcript, 1643.

238   *Did you ever see such a funny fire*: Trial Transcript, 1643.

238   *troubled about it*: Trial Transcript, 1644.

238   *Fleet didn't see it . . . flying around somewhere*: Trial Transcript, 1644.

238   *well-directed blows*: Trial Transcript, 1612.

238   *Surely . . . such implements*: Trial Transcript, 1612.

238   *You must conclude . . . this young woman defendant*: Trial Transcript, 1615.

238   *[n]ot a spot*: Trial Transcript, 1641.

239   *They say she was in the house . . . a dutiful member of the household*: Trial
        Transcript, 1645–46.

239   *Now if we had marched*: Trial Transcript, 1647.

239   *Now do not ask her to do things*: Trial Transcript, 1649.

239   *Is there anything unnatural or improbable*: Trial Transcript, 1665.

239   *Honest people*: Trial Transcript,1667.

239   *Do you suppose that your wives and daughters*: Trial Transcript, 1661–62.

239   *Not at all . . . careful about something*: Trial Transcript, 1662.

240   *a matter of protection*: Trial Transcript, 1691.

240   *Are all your houses warmed with steam?*: Trial Transcript, 1679.

240   *Did she want any more to live in comfort?*: Trial Transcript, 1680. In a simi-
        lar vein, after her interview with Lizzie Borden in jail, Mrs. McGuirk sim-
        ilarly wrote that Lizzie "made more money than they knew how to spend."
        "In a New Light," *New York Recorder*, September 20, 1892.

240   *to live as others did*: Testimony of Alice Russell, Inquest, 151.

240   *looking for a nice place for his daughters*: Jennings notebooks, FRHS. Ac-
        cording to Wm. Chace, a real estate broker, Andrew "wanted the first show
        at the Wm Mason estate if it came to market." The property was not tech-
        nically on the Hill but it was in the good part of North Main Street, also
        home to his cousin Colonel Richard Borden. Another entry reports that
        Alexander Milne said that he had talked with Andrew about "buying a
        house for them up north."

240   *not fertile in fancy*: "Last Words in the Great Trial," *Boston Globe*, June 20,
        1893, 1.

241   *There is nothing criminal about it*: Trial Transcript, 1683.

241   *I advised the City Marshal*: Trial Transcript, 1683.

241   *not a good way to talk . . . not a saint*: Trial Transcript, 1685.

241   *yet we don't read of murders in those houses*: Trial Transcript, 1686.

241   *It is not the outspoken*: Trial Transcript, 1684.

241   *No man should be heard to say she murdered the man who so loved her*: Trial Transcript, 1689. Jennings had made a similar point in his opening statement, challenging the jury "whether the government have satisfied you beyond a reasonable doubt that she did not only kill her stepmother, Abby Durfee Borden, but her loved and loving father, Andrew Jackson Borden, on the fourth of August last." Trial Transcript, 1322–23.

241   *He was a man . . . between the father and the daughter*: Trial Transcript, 1689.

242   *but a transient flood*: "Last Words in the Great Borden Trial," *Boston Globe*, June 20, 1893, 1.

242   *her monthly illness . . . her mind disabled for a period of time*: Trial Transcript, 1694.

242   *a good many people*: Trial Transcript, 1694.

243   *I do not say it is one way or another*: Trial Transcript, 1694.

243   *A person who is going*: Trial Transcript, 1695.

243   *It was not a time for examining colors*: Trial Transcript, 1697.

243   *So . . . there has been a conflict of testimony*: Trial Transcript, 1697.

243   *I would not wonder . . . committed either murder*: Trial Transcript, 1703.

243   *peculiarly French*: "Lizzie Borden at the Bar," *NY Sun*, June 5, 1893, 2.

243   *all the armory of the Borden house*: Trial Transcript, 1708.

244   *Is the Government trying a case*: Trial Transcript, 1716.

244   *Gentlemen, you walk upon the edge of a precipice*: Trial Transcript, 1717.

244   *cow's hair and the appearance of blood*: Trial Transcript, 1716.

244   *now declared to be innocent*: Trial Transcript, 1716.

244   *murder at the hands of theorizing experts*: Trial Transcript, 1718.

244   *Exclusive opportunity is nothing*: Trial Transcript, 1719.

244   *There is nothing to show . . . for she was not*: Trial Transcript, 1726.

244   *You cannot see everybody*: Trial Transcript, 1725.

244   *I am taking you into the house*: Trial Transcript, 1722.

245   *How would your wife . . . scanned by everybody?*: Trial Transcript, 1745.

245   *the set of that mustache and the firmness of those lips*: Trial Transcript, 1660.

245   *And there he was . . . peremptory way*: Trial Transcript, 1660.

245   *Is that the way . . . daughter in that way?*: Trial Transcript, 1660.

245   *the person of the assailant in both cases*: Trial Transcript, 1707.

245   *Such acts as those . . . are morally and physically impossible*: Trial Transcript, 1615.

245 *The eyes that cannot weep*: Trial Transcript, 1746.

246 *It is not impossible . . . rankest and baldest murderess*: Trial Transcript, 1743.

246 *Gentlemen, as you look upon her*: Trial Transcript, 1748.

246 *to say whether the Government . . . fourth of August last*: Trial Transcript, 1749.

246 *to take care of her*: Trial Transcript, 1750.

247 *acute and adroit unmasking . . . One by one*: "Gov. Robinson's Plea," *FREN*, June 20, 1893, 4.

247 *As an appeal . . . speech is a mastery*: *Boston Post* quoted in "Lizzie Borden's Trial," *FREN*, June 20, 1893, 4.

247 *Robinson indulged in no flights*: "Lizzie Borden's Trial," *FREN*, June 20, 1893, 4.

247 *The argument . . . was worthy of the occasion and of the man*: "Gov. Robinson's Plea," *FREN*, June 20, 1893, 4.

247 *seducer into unwitting admissions*: "Under Fire," *Boston Globe*, June 8, 1893, 1.

247 *fell short of the anticipation*: "Last Words in the Great Trial," *Boston Globe*, June 20, 1893, 1.

247 *It never reached up to eloquence . . . took the defensive*: "Pleas in the Borden Case," *NY Sun*, June 20, 1893, 1.

248 *the crowd inside was one vast fan*: "Last Words in the Great Trial," *Boston Globe*, June 20, 1893, 1.

248 *[h]is strong personality . . . were all at his command*: "Last Words in the Great Trial," *Boston Globe*, June 20, 1893, 2.

248 *In the midst . . . it was committed*: Trial Transcript, 1753.

248 *If you had read the account . . . such things never happen*: Trial Transcript, 1752.

248 *It is no ordinary criminal . . . dreamed before*: Trial Transcript, 1753.

248 *terrible significance*: Trial Transcript, 1753.

248 *We are trying a crime . . . to call to your attention*: Trial Transcript, 1754.

248 *no station in life*: Trial Transcript, 1754.

248 *They were Christian men . . . rotten to the core*: Trial Transcript, 1754.

249 *sacred robes of the church . . . foul as hell inside*: Trial Transcript, 1754.

249 *a boy of tender years*: Trial Transcript, 1754.

249 *the most fiendish murderer*: Trial Transcript, 1755.

249 *within the remembrance of every man I am talking to*: Trial Transcript, 1755.

249 *it is hard . . . guilty of crime*: Trial Transcript, 1756.

249 *are human like unto us . . . no worse than we*: Trial Transcript, 1756.

250 *great master[s] of human nature*: Trial Transcript, 1757.

250 *many of the most famous criminals*: Trial Transcript, 1757.

250 *the most dastardly*: Trial Transcript, 1757.

250 *lack in strength . . . more persistent?*: Trial Transcript, 1756–57.

250 *face this case as men, not as gallants*: Trial Transcript, 1757.

250 *time and time again*: "Last Words in the Great Borden Trial," *Boston Globe*, June 20, 1893, 1.

250 *She lost no word . . . the whole procedure*: "Last Words in the Great Borden Trial," *Boston Globe*, June 20, 1893, 1.

250 *slanderous tongues*: Trial Transcript, 1758.

251 *Gentlemen . . . the saddest duty of my life*: Trial Transcript, 1758.

251 *A blue coat does not make a man any better*: Trial Transcript, 1763.

251 *honestly, faithfully*: Trial Transcript, 1762.

251 *You will find that their conclusions are accurate*: Trial Transcript, 1764.

251 *Direct evidence is the evidence of a man who sees and hears*: Trial Transcript, 1765.

251 *Men will not tell the truth always*: Trial Transcript, 1768.

251 *Murder is the work of stealth and craft . . . obliterated*: Trial Transcript, 1766.

251 *It was circumstantial . . . but it satisfied him*: Trial Transcript, 1766.

251 *[H]e had no lawyer to tell him*: Trial Transcript, 1766.

251 *It is like refuse . . . another circumstance*: Trial Transcript, 1767.

251 *You would not hesitate . . . that river was*: Trial Transcript, 1767.

252 *discovery . . . same time*: Trial Transcript, 1769.

252 *controlling fact*: Trial Transcript, 1773.

252 *[i]t was no sudden act . . . noon day meal*: Trial Transcript, 1773.

252 *What sort of blows were they? . . . nerveless blows*: Trial Transcript, 1783.

252 *The hand that held the weapon . . . desire to kill*: Trial Transcript, 1783.

252 *This poor woman . . . heard in the other*: Trial Transcript, 1790.

252 *It was . . . malice against Mrs. Borden*: Trial Transcript, 1773.

252 *It was a living insult*: Trial Transcript, 1777.

253 *How wicked to have found fault with it*: Trial Transcript, 1776.

253 *his faithful wife*: Trial Transcript, 1776.

253 *always very kind and good to her*: Statement of Bridget Sullivan to Nellie S. McHenry, August 25, 1892, in Knowlton Papers, 34. Bridget also revealed Abby's only known instance of pique. Abby apparently complained about Morse's visit, remarking "now he is here I suppose we will have him on our hands all summer, I don't see why he don't [*sic*] get married and go away."

253 *she had lost in Mrs. Borden, the best and most intimate neighbor she had ever met*: "Thursday's Affray," *FRDH*, August 5, 1892, 1.

253 *It is said that there is a skeleton*: Trial Transcript, 1774.

254 *He goes his way . . . these people day in and day out*: Trial Transcript, 1778.

254 *This was a cancer*: Trial Transcript, 1780.

254 *Conscious as I am*: Trial Transcript, 1795.

254 *Little did it occur to Lizzie Borden*: Trial Transcript, 1797.

254 *No note came*: Trial Transcript, 1795.

254 *warming up . . . the audience*: "Last Words in the Great Trial," *Boston Globe*, June 20, 1893, 2.

255 *God forbid that anybody*: Trial Transcript, 1799.

255 *was killed . . . benefitted by her taking away*: Trial Transcript, 1799.

255 *looked at him fixedly and steadily with a curious, set expression upon her features*: "A Plea for Life," *NY World*, June 20, 1893, 7.

255 *There was coming a stern and just man*: Trial Transcript, 1793.

255 *that a late session would be an intolerable burden*: "Last Words in the Great Borden Trial," *Boston Globe*, June 20, 1893, 1.

255 *The judges are in no hurry*: "Last Words in the Great Borden Trial," *Boston Globe*, June 20, 1893, 1.

Tuesday, June 20, 1893

255 *Over an hour before the time of opening*: FRDG, June 20, 1893, 1.

255 *The intensity of the crush this afternoon*: "For the State," FRDH, June 20, 1893, 1.

256 *The Last Scene in the Great Borden Trial*: "Not Guilty," *Boston Globe*, June 21, 1893, 1.

256 *an animated conversation*: "For the State," NBES, June 20, 1893, 1.

256 *there was a restless activity about her*: "For the State," NBES, June 20, 1893, 1.

256 *blood ebbed and flowed to her face*: "For the State," FRDH, June 20, 1893, 7.

256 *We are called upon to prove that the thing was done*: Trial Transcript, 1801.

256 *The malice was all before the fact*: Trial Transcript, 1805.

256 *[W]e cannot tell . . . that hot summer*: Trial Transcript, 1805.

256 *there was a jealousy which was unworthy of that woman*: Trial Transcript, 1805.

256 *the dead body . . . to a parricide*: Trial Transcript, 1806.

257 *it is a grateful relief*: Trial Transcript, 1808.

257 *When the deed was done*: Trial Transcript, 1807.

258 *It was not Lizzie Andrew Borden*: Trial Transcript, 1807.

258 *The Commonwealth is charged . . . not why*: Trial Transcript, 1808.

258 *suggests to him . . . lie down upon the sofa and rest*: Trial Transcript, 1811.

258 *She had begun her work . . . at the outside*: Trial Transcript, 1813.

258   *simply incredible*: Trial Transcript, 1820.

258   *We must judge all facts*: Trial Transcript, 1820.

259   *not within the bounds of reasonable possibilities*: Trial Transcript, 1820.

259   *it was not only the hottest place . . . not have known what took place*: Trial Transcript, 1824.

259   *All the disasters of your life*: Trial Transcript, 1834.

259   *cool to a degree of coolness*: Trial Transcript, 1818.

259   *that the absence of tears . . . consciousness of loss*: Trial Transcript, 1833.

259   *agitation of a man*: Trial Transcript, 1836.

259   *All I propose to make of that incident*: Trial Transcript, 1836.

260   *How could she have avoided the spattering*: Trial Transcript, 1838.

260   *solitude of the house with ample fire on the stove*: Trial Transcript, 1838.

260   *I cannot answer it*: Trial Transcript, 1838.

260   *clear eyed, intelligent, honest daughter*: Trial Transcript, 1839.

260   *When Mrs. Bowen raised her hand*: Trial Transcript, 1843.

260   *It was not where the officers could find it*: Trial Transcript, 1848.

260   *That dress . . . made against her*: Trial Transcript, 1854.

261   *Supposing she had told wrong stories*: Trial Transcript, 1857.

261   *It is absolutely necessary . . . cross examination*: Trial Transcript, 1858.

261   *There is . . . no better test*: Trial Transcript, 1858.

261   *I am not quite so willing to dismiss*: Trial Transcript, 1858.

261   *Puritan conscience*: Trial Transcript, 1855.

261   *My distinguished friend . . . various hatchets that have been produced in this case*: Trial Transcript, 1862.

262   *this unfortunate woman*: Trial Transcript, 1871.

262   *handle was broken off not as axe handles*: Trial Transcript, 1873.

262   *We do not say that was the hatchet*: Trial Transcript, 1874.

262   *The recesses and mysteries of that house*: Trial Transcript, 1863.

262   *The very fact that no hatchet was found*: Trial Transcript, 1875.

262   *never would have gone into the streets*: Trial Transcript, 1875.

262   *We find a woman murdered by blows*: Trial Transcript, 1879.

263   *We get down now to the elements of ordinary crime*: Trial Transcript, 1881.

263   *What's the defense*: Trial Transcript, 1881.

263   *I submit these facts to you*: Trial Transcript, 1883.

263   *What shall be your reward?*: Trial Transcript, 1884.

263   *rank[ed] with the ablest advocates of the day*: "Not Guilty," *Boston Globe*, June 21, 1893, 1.

263   *big burly man*: "Last Words in the Great Borden Trial," *Boston Globe*, June 20, 1893, 2.

263   *the same pride of bearing . . . from New York to Chicago*: "Not Guilty," *Boston Globe*, June 21, 1893, 1.

263   *The magnificent figure of the speaker . . . people silent and still*: "Pleas in the Borden Case," *NY Sun*, June 20, 1893, 2.

263   *Down to the opening . . . in favor of a disagreement*: "Last Words in the Great Trial," *Boston Globe*, June 20, 1893, 2.

263   *It is your privilege to add any word*: Trial Transcript, 1885.

264   *I am innocent*: Trial Transcript, 1885.

264   *she added to her extraordinary gracefulness a surprising dignity*: "Lizzie Borden Free," *NY Sun*, 1893, 1.

264   *Your decision can properly rest only on the law*: Trial Transcript, 1887.

264   *Proof beyond reasonable doubt*: Trial Transcript, 1887.

264   *the defendant's character has been good*: Trial Transcript, 1891.

264   *You are not . . . ways of life*: Trial Transcript, 1891.

264   *imputing a motive to the defendant*: Trial Transcript, 1893.

264   *Unless the child be destitute of natural affection*: Trial Transcript, 1892.

264   *intense expression*: Trial Transcript, 1894.

264   *[C]onsider whether or not they do not often use words*: Trial Transcript, 1893.

265   *Suppose some person in New Bedford*: Trial Transcript, 1923.

265   *What motive . . . had she to invent a story like this?*: Trial Transcript, 1903.

265   *contemplate the possibility*: Trial Transcript, 1903.

265   *Is there anything in the way and manner of doing the acts*: Trial Transcript, 1908.

265   *as to the way in which they think the blows were inflicted*: Trial Transcript, 1908.

265   *Are these views correct?*: Trial Transcript, 1908.

265   *You have a right to reason and judge . . . seems to be reasonable*: Trial Transcript, 1908.

266   *the guarded language of the statute*: Trial Transcript, 1916. Prior to 1866, criminal defendants were not permitted to testify at their own trials in Massachusetts. For a discussion of the background to this reform, see Alan Rogers, *Murder and the Death Penalty in Massachusetts* (Amherst: University of Massachusetts Press, 2008), 116–17.

266   *If she were required to explain*: Trial Transcript, 1917.

266   *She may be asked questions*: Trial Transcript, 1917.

266   *with impartial and thoughtful minds . . . reason and law*: Trial Transcript, 1926.

266   *may express in its results somewhat of that justice*: Trial Transcript, 1927.

266 *a plea for the innocent . . . circumstantial evidence alone*: "Not Guilty," *Boston Globe*, June 21, 1893, 1.

267 *The silence became impressive and fearful*: "Free Woman!," *FRDH*, June 21, 1893, 3.

267 *At no time . . . hear her doom*: *FRDH*, June 21, 1893, 3.

267 *which might have been heard half a mile away*: "Lizzie Borden Acquitted," *NYT*, June 21, 1893, 1.

267 *as if she was shot*: "Lizzie Borden Free," *NY Sun*, 1893, 1.

267 *Every man of them was as pale as a corpse*: "Not Guilty!," *FRDH*, June 21, 1893, 1.

268 *reasonably deliberative*: *FREN*, June 20, 1893, 4. This was reported in multiple newspapers.

268 *as a matter of courtesy*: "Lizzie Borden Free," *NY Sun*, June 21, 1893, 7.

268 *warned by the counsel . . . dignity of the court*: "Free Woman!," *FRDH*, June 21, 1893, 3.

268 *He might as well have given directions*: "Free Woman!," *FRDH*, June 21, 1893, 3.

268 *never saw the people rising in their seats*: "Lizzie Borden Is Acquitted," *NYT*, June 21, 1893, 1.

268 *Tears gushed from hundreds of eyes*: "Lizzie Borden Free," *NY Sun*, June 21, 1893, 1.

268 *put his arm around the now strengthened girl . . . much loved daughter*: "Free Woman!," *FRDH*, June 21, 1893, 1. Elizabeth Jordan similarly described the scene in familiar terms: "Presently his left arm slipped round her waist and, like the father he has been to her, he raised her up." "Lizzie Borden Free," *NY Sun*, 1893, 2.

269 *The extraordinary and visible affection*: "Free Woman!," *FRDH*, June 21, 1893, 1.

269 *one wasn't enough*: "Lizzie Borden Free," *NY Sun*, June 21, 1893, 2.

269 *with a fatherly interest in his kindly eyes*: "Lizzie Borden Is Acquitted," *NYT*, June 21, 1893, 1.

269 *still moving like a lot of convicts out for exercise*: "Free Woman!," *FRDH*, June 21, 1893, 1.

269 *her warmest greetings being given to Julian Ralph*: "Free Woman!," *FRDH*, June 21, 1893, 1.

Part 3
VERDICT
Chapter 11: The Old Place

273   *The suspected witch was in the dock . . . parrot-like police testimony*: "Lizzie Borden Free," *NY Sun*, June 21, 1893, 1. Ralph's articles on the case frequently alluded to the Salem witch trials. For a discussion of this trope, see Roggenkamp, *Narrating the News*, 68–70.

274   *The acquittal of the most unfortunate and cruelly persecuted woman*: Editorial, *NYT*, June 21, 1893, 4.

274   *I want to go home*: "Not Guilty," *Boston Globe*, June 21, 1893, 1. Lizzie turned to her sister and said: "Now take me home. I want to go to the old place and go at once tonight."

274   *Telegrams of congratulation are also arriving*: "Lizzie Borden Arrives in the City," *FRDG*, June 21, 1893, 7.

275   *a jolly crowd*: "Twelve Jolly Jurors Freed Lizzie Borden," *New Bedford Sunday Standard*, June 8, 1919, quoted in *Parallel Lives*, 513.

275   *faithful friends and deliver[ers]*: Letter from Lizzie Borden to Frederick Wilbur, July 14, 1893, quoted in *Parallel Lives*, 514.

275   *She said she had no other place she cared to go*: "Verdict Was Righteous," *Boston Globe*, June 22, 1893, 5.

275   *No matter where she goes*: "Miss Borden's Chaperone," *FRDH*, June 20, 1893, 7.

275   *surprise, bordering on indignation*: "The News at Fall River," *NBES*, June 21, 1893, 3.

275   *The line . . . case*: "Lizzie Borden Free," *NY Sun*, June 21, 1893, 2.

275   *Lizzie and her sister will leave no stone unturned*: "In Their Own Home," *Boston Globe*, June 22, 1893, 5. Similarly the *New York Sun* reported that the Borden sisters would devote their energies to "ferreting out the murderers of the old couple." "Lizzie Borden Free," *NY Sun*, June 21, 1893, 2. The following month, the *Fall River Daily Globe* noted acidly, "It has always seemed singular . . . that so little apparent effort was made by the Borden sisters or their friends to locate the real murderer." "Little Effort," *FRDG*, July 11, 1893, 7.

276   *She will lead her old life*: "Her Old Home," *Boston Globe*, June 22, 1893, 1.

276   *that she may go and be Lizzie Andrew Borden . . . so many years*: Trial Transcript, 1750.

277   *happenings at the French Street house*: "Guilty?—No! No!," *Boston Sunday Herald*, April 13, 1913, 25.

277 *a fine looking young*: "Lizzie Borden Left by Sister," *Boston Sunday Herald*, June 4, 1905, 11.

277 *the greatest tragedienne*: FREN, October 21, 1904, quoted in *Parallel Lives*, 723.

278 *unbearable*: "Guilty?—No! No!," *Boston Sunday Herald*, April 13, 1913, 25.

278 *Great Wrong Is Righted*: "Great Wrong," FRDG, August 4, 1905, 1.

279 *to be laid at my Father's feet*: Funeral Instructions of Lizzie Borden, quoted in *Parallel Lives*, 980.

279 *It may seem marvellous . . . the tinge that saddens it*: Nathaniel Hawthorne, *The Scarlet Letter* (Cambridge, MA: Harvard University Press, 2009), 77–78.

Chapter 12: The Enduring Enigma

281 *The Borden case is without parallel*: Edmund Lester Pearson, "The Borden Case," *Studies in Murder* (New York: Macmillan, 1924), 3.

281 *famous citizen of Fall River*: Edmund Lester Pearson, letter to Frank Knowlton, November 22, 1923, FRHS.

282 *There are in it all the elements*: Pearson, "The Borden Case," 3–4.

282 *the extraordinary fascination of this case*: Pearson, "The Borden Case," 4.

282 *found texts for columns in her looks . . . and everything connected with her*: "Not Guilty," *Boston Globe*, June 21, 1893, 1.

283 *a literary hoax*: Edwin D. Radin, *Lizzie Borden: The Untold Story* (New York: Simon & Schuster, 1961), 175.

283 *was willing to blight her life*: Radin, *Lizzie Borden*, 254.

284 *If today woman has come out of the kitchen*: Charles Samuels and Louise Samuels, *The Girl in the House of Hate* (New York: Aeonian Press, 1953), 143.

285 *the skeleton in our cupboard*: Victoria Lincoln, *A Private Disgrace: Lizzie Borden by Daylight* (New York: G. P. Putnam's Sons, 1967), 23.

286 *She really was a complex character*: "Maplecroft Officially Sold to Owners of Lizzie Borden Bed and Breakfast," *Fall River Herald News*, February 2, 2018.

286 *a Halloween tchotchke*: Sarah Miller, *The Borden Murders: Lizzie Borden and the Trial of the Century* (New York: Schwartz & Wade Books, 2016), 253.

286 *rousing smash-the-patriarchy piece*: "Chloë Sevigny's Lizzie Borden Biopic Isn't the Ax Murderer Movie She Originally Imagined," *Huffington Post*, January 22, 2018.

286 *Will the whole truth ever come out?*: Pearson, "The Borden Case," 129.

Coda: The Defense File

287 *stricken with paralysis*: "Ex-Gov. Robinson Dead," *NYT*, February 23, 1896, 9. Other newspapers described it as "apoplexy," most likely a stroke. "Robinson Dead," *Boston Herald*, February 23, 1896, 1.

288 *In order to promote freedom of consultation . . . client's consent*: Wigmore, *A Treatise on the System of Evidence in Trials at Common Law* (1904), vol. 4, § 2291, 3196.

288 *work product . . . wits borrowed from the adversary*: *Hickman v. Taylor*, 329 U.S. 495, 516 (1947).

289 *abhorrent*: Telephone interview with Jeffrey McCormick, March 4, 2018. McCormick did not share any details about the contents of the file or its storage. All of the information cited came from a published interview with the firm's former office manager. Paul Edward Parker, "Lizzy [*sic*] Borden's Legal Papers Found," *South Coast Today*, April 14, 1998.

Selected Bibliography

LEGAL PROCEEDINGS

Inquest upon the Deaths of Andrew J. Borden and Abby D. Borden. Annie M. White, stenographer. Fall River, MA, August 9–11. Collection of Fall River Historical Society.

Preliminary Hearing: Commonwealth of Massachusetts v. Lizzie A. Borden, August 25–September 1, 1892. Judge Josiah C. Blaisdell, presiding. District Court, Fall River, MA. Annie White, stenographer. Collection of Fall River Historical Society.

Trial of Lizzie Andrew Borden upon an Indictment Charging Her with the Murder of Abby Durfee Borden and Andrew Jackson Borden Before the Superior Court for the County of Bristol; Mason, C.J., Blodgett, J., and Dewey, J., presiding. Official Stenographic Report by Frank H. Burt, 1893.

Witness Statements for the Lizzie Borden Murder Case, August 4–October 6, 1892. Collection of Fall River Historical Society.

Abelson, Elaine. *When Ladies Go A-Thieving: Middle-Class Shoplifters in the Victorian Department Store.* New York: Oxford University Press, 1989.

Adler, Gabriela Schalow. "Our Beloved Lizzie: Reconstructing an American Legend." PhD diss., University of Rhode Island, 1995.

Blewitt, Mary. *Constant Turmoil: The Politics of Industrial Life in Nineteenth-Century New England.* Amherst: University of Massachusetts Press, 2000.

Boyer, Paul S. "Borden, Lizzie Andrew." In *Notable American Women: 1607–1950: A Biographical Dictionary*, edited by Edward T. James. Cambridge, MA: Harvard University Press, 1971, pp. 210–12.

Brace, Charles Loring. *The Dangerous Classes of New York and Twenty Years' Work Among Them*. 3rd ed. New York: Wynkoop and Hallenbeck, 1880.

Brown, Arnold R. *Lizzie Borden: The Legend, the Truth, the Final Chapter*. New York: Dell Publishers, 1991.

Carlisle, Marcia R. "What Made Lizzie Borden Kill?" *American Heritage* 43, no. 4 (June–July 1992): 66–72.

Carter, Angela. "The Fall River Axe Murders." In Angela Carter, *Saints and Strangers*. New York: Penguin Books, 1987.

Chapman, Sherry. *Lizzie Borden: Resurrections*. Fall River, MA: PearTree Press, 2014.

Cohen, Adam. *Imbeciles: The Supreme Court, American Eugenics, and the Sterilization of Carrie Buck*. NY: Penguin Press, 2016.

Cole, Simon A. *Suspect Identities: A History of Fingerprinting and Criminal Identification*. Cambridge, MA: Harvard University Press, 2001.

Conforti, Joseph A. *Lizzie Borden on Trial: Murder, Ethnicity, and Gender*. Lawrence: University of Kansas Press, 2015.

Cumbler, John T. *Working-Class Community in Industrial America: Work, Leisure, and Struggle in Two Industrial Cities, 1880–1930*. Westport, CT: Greenwood Press, 1979.

Davis, Charles Gideon. *The Conduct of the Law in the Borden Case, with Suggestions of Changes in Criminal Law and Practice*. Boston: *Boston Daily Advertiser*, 1894.

de la Torre, Lillian. *Goodbye, Miss Lizzie Borden: A Sinister Play in One Act*. Boston: Baker's Plays, 1947.

De Mille, Agnes. *Lizzie Borden: A Dance of Death*. Boston: Little, Brown and Co., 1968.

Evening Standard, New Bedford, MA. *Lizzie Borden: Did She? Or Didn't She?* Verplank, New York: Historical Briefs, 1992.

Fenner, Henry M. *History of Fall River, Massachusetts*. Fall River, MA: Munroe Press, 1911.

Ferguson, Robert A. *The Trial in American Life*. Chicago: University of Chicago Press, 2007.

Fowler, Orin. *History of Fall River with Notices of Freetown and Tiverton*. Fall River, MA: Almy & Milne, Printers, 1862.

Freeman, Mary E. Wilkins. "The Long Arm." In *The Long Arm and Other Stories*. London: Chapman and Hall, 1895.

Friedman, Lawrence M. *The Big Trial: Law as Public Spectacle.* Lawrence: University of Kansas Press, 2015.

————. *Crime and Punishment in American History.* New York: Basic Books, 1993.

Gordon, Linda. *Heroes of Their Own Lives: The Politics and History of Family Violence, Boston 1880–1960.* New York: Viking Press, 1988.

Gross, Hans. *Criminal Investigation: A Practical Handbook for Magistrates, Police Officers, and Lawyers.* 1907.

————. *Criminal Psychology: A Manual for Judges, Practitioners and Students.* 1911.

Halttunen, Karen. *Murder Most Foul: The Killer and the American Gothic Imagination.* Cambridge, MA: Harvard University Press, 1998.

Hawthorne, Nathaniel. *The Scarlet Letter.* Cambridge, MA: Harvard University Press, 2009.

Hixson, Walter L. "Gendered Justice: Lizzie Borden and Victorian America." In *Murder, Culture, and Injustice: Four Sensational Cases in American History.* Akron, OH: University of Akron Press, 2001.

Hoffman, Paul Dennis. *Yesterday in Old Fall River: A Lizzie Borden Companion.* Durham, NC: Carolina Academic Press, 2000.

Holba, Annette M. *Lizzie Borden Took an Axe, or Did She?: A Rhetorical Inquiry.* Youngstown, NY: Teneo Press, 2008.

Hunter, Evan. *Lizzie: A Novel.* New York: Dell Publishers, 1985.

Jacob, Kathryn Allamong. "She Couldn't Have Done It, Even if She Did: Why Lizzie Borden Went Free." *American Heritage* 29, no. 2 (February–March 1978): 42–53.

James, Bill. *Popular Crime: Reflections on the Celebration of Violence.* New York: Scribner, 2011.

Jones, Ann. *The Lizzie Borden Sourcebook.* Boston: Branden Publishing Company, 1992.

————. *Women Who Kill.* Boston: Beacon Press, 1996.

Jordan, Elizabeth. "The Newspaper Woman's Story." *Lippincott's Monthly Magazine* 51 (March 1893).

————. "Ruth Herrick's Assignment." *Cosmopolitan Magazine,* Vol. XVII (May 1894–October 1894): 365–72.

————. *Three Rousing Cheers.* New York: D. Appleton-Century Co., 1938.

Kent, David. *Forty Whacks: New Evidence in the Life and Legend of Lizzie Borden.* Emmaus, PA: Yankee Books, 1992.

Knowlton, Frank W., and Edmund Lester Pearson. *The Knowlton/Pearson Correspondence: 1923–1930.* Fall River, MA: Fall River Historical Society, 1997.

Lancaster, Paul. *Gentleman of the Press: The Life and Times of an Early Reporter, Julian Ralph of the* Sun. Syracuse, NY: Syracuse University Press, 1992.

Lane, Roger. *Murder in America: A History.* Columbus, OH: Ohio State University Press, 1997.

Lincoln, Victoria. *A Private Disgrace: Lizzie Borden by Daylight.* New York: G. P. Putnam's Sons, 1967.

Livermore, Mary A. *The Story of My Life: The Sunshine and Shadow of Seventy Years.* Hartford, CT: A. D. Worthington and Co., 1897.

Lombroso, Cesare, and William Ferrero. *Criminal Woman, the Prostitute, and the Normal Woman.* Trans. by Nicole Hahn Rafter and Mary Gibson. Durham, NC: Duke University Press, 2004.

———. *The Female Offender.* New York: D. Appleton and Company, 1915.

Lombroso-Ferrero, Gina. *Criminal Man According to the Classification of Cesare Lombroso.* 1911. Reprint, Montclair, NJ: Patterson Smith, 1972.

Lowndes, Marie Belloc. *Lizzie Borden: A Study in Conjecture.* New York: Longmans, Green and Co., 1939.

Lunday, Todd. *The Mystery Unveiled: The Truth About the Borden Tragedy.* 1893. Reprint, Portland, ME: King Phillip Publishing Company, 1990.

Martins, Michael, and Dennis A. Binette. *Parallel Lives: A Social History of Lizzie A. Borden and Her Fall River.* Fall River, MA: Fall River Historical Society, 2010.

Martins, Michael, and Dennis A. Binette, eds. *The Commonwealth of Massachusetts vs. Lizzie A. Borden: The Knowlton Papers, 1892–1893: A Collection of Previously Unpublished Letters and Documents from the Files of Prosecuting Attorney Hosea Morrill Knowlton.* Fall River, MA: Fall River Historical Society, 1994.

McAdam, Roger Williams. *The Old Fall River Line.* New York: Stephen Daye Press, 1937.

Miller, Sarah. *The Borden Murders: Lizzie Borden and the Trial of the Century.* New York: Schwartz & Wade, 2014.

Morantz-Sanchez, Regina. *Conduct Unbecoming a Woman: Medicine on Trial in Turn-of-the-Century Brooklyn.* New York: Oxford University Press, 1999.

Nickerson, Catherine Ross. "The Deftness of Her Sex: Innocence, Guilt, and Gender in the Trial of Lizzie Borden." In *Lethal Imagination: Violence and Brutality in American History.* Ed. Michael A. Bellesiles. New York: New York University Press, 1999.

Pearson, Edmund Lester. "The Borden Case." In *Studies in Murder.* Garden City, New York: Garden City Publishing Company, 1924, 3–120.

———. "The Bordens: A Postscript." In *Murder at Smutty Nose and Other*

Murders. Garden City, New York: Doubleday, Page & Company, 1927, 291–302.

———. "The End of the Borden Case." In *Five Murders: With a Final Note on the Borden Case*. Garden City, NY: Doubleday, Doran & Company, Inc., 1928, 263–94.

———."Legends of Lizzie." In *More Studies in Murder*. New York: Harrison Smith & Robert Haas, 1936, 121–31.

Pearson, Edmund Lester, ed. *The Trial of Lizzie Borden*. New York: Doubleday, Doran & Company, 1937.

Phillips, Arthur S. *The Borden Murder Mystery: In Defence of Lizzie Borden*. Portland, ME: King Phillip Publishing Company, 1986.

———. *The Phillips History of Fall River*. 3 vols. Fall River, MA: Dover Press, 1944.

Porter, Edwin H. *The Fall River Tragedy. A History of the Borden Murders*. Fall River, MA: George R. H. Buffinton, 1893.

Porwancher, Andrew. *John Henry Wigmore and the Rules of Evidence: The Hidden Origins of Modern Law*. Columbia: University of Missouri, 2016.

Radin, Edward D. *Lizzie Borden: The Untold Story*. New York: Simon & Schuster, 1961.

Ralph, Julian. *The Making of a Journalist*. New York: Harper & Brothers, 1903.

Rebello, Leonard. *Lizzie Borden, Past & Present*. Fall River, MA: Al-Zach Press, 1999.

Robertson, Cara W. "Representing 'Miss Lizzie': Cultural Convictions in the Trial of Lizzie Borden." *Yale Journal of Law and the Humanities* 8, no. 2 (1996): 351–416.

Rogers, Alan. *Murder and the Death Penalty in Massachusetts*. Amherst: University of Massachusetts Press, 2008.

Roggenkamp, Karen. *Narrating the News: New Journalism and Literary Genre in Late Nineteenth-Century American Newspapers and Fiction*. Kent, OH: Kent State University Press, 2005.

———. *Sympathy, Madness, and Crime: How Four Nineteenth-Century Journalists Made the Newspaper Women's Business*. Kent, OH: Kent State University Press, 2016.

Russett, Cynthia Eagle. *Sexual Science: The Victorian Construction of Womanhood*. Cambridge, MA: Harvard University Press, 1989.

Ryckebusch, Jules R., ed. *Proceedings, Lizzie Borden Conference: Bristol Community College, Fall River, Massachusetts, August 3–5, 1992*. Portland, ME: King Phillip Publishing Company, 1993.

Samuels, Charles, and Louise Samuels. *The Girl in the House of Hate: The Story and All the Facts of the Lizzie Borden Murders*. New York: Fawcett Publications, 1953.

Schmidt, Sarah. *See What I Have Done*. New York: Atlantic Monthly Press, 2017.

Schofield, Ann. "Lizzie Borden Took an Axe: History, Feminism, and American Culture." *American Studies* 34, no. 1 (1993): 91–103.

Shteir, Rachel. *The Steal: A Cultural History of Shoplifting*. New York: Penguin, 2011.

Silvia, Phillip, Jr., ed. *Victorian Vistas: Fall River, 1886–1900*. Fall River, MA: R. E. Smith Printing Co., 1988.

Smith, Thomas Russell. *The Cotton Textile Industry of Fall River, Massachusetts: A Study of Industrial Localization*. New York: King's Crown Press, 1944.

Snow, Edward Rowe. "The Lizzie Borden Murder Case." In Snow, Edward Rowe, *Piracy, Mutiny, and Murder*. New York: Dodd, Mead & Company, 1959, 248–90.

Spiering, Frank. *Lizzie*. New York: Random House, 1984.

Starr, Paul. *The Creation of the Media: Political Origins of Modern Communication*. New York: Basic Books, 2004.

Sullivan, Robert. *Goodbye Lizzie Borden*. Brattleboro, VT: Stephen Greene Press, 1974.

Venet, Wendy Hammond. *A Strong-Minded Woman: The Life of Mary A. Livermore*. Amherst: University of Massachusetts Press, 2005.

White, Richard. *The Republic for Which It Stands: The United States During Reconstruction and the Gilded Age, 1865–1896*. Oxford History of the United States. New York: Oxford University Press, 2017.

Whitman, Ruth. *The Passion of Lizzie Borden: New and Selected Poems*. New York: October House, 1973.

Wigmore, John H. "The Borden Case." *American Law Review* (November–December 1893): 819–45.

————. *A Pocket Code of the Rules of Evidence in Trials at Law*. Boston: Little, Brown and Company, 1910.

————. *A Supplement to a Treatise on the System of Evidence in Trials at Common Law*. Boston: Little, Brown and Company, 1907.

————. *A Treatise on the System of Evidence in Trials at Common Law*. 4 vols. Boston: Little, Brown and Company, 1904.

Williams, Joyce G., J. Eric Smithburn, and M. Jeanne Peterson, eds. *Lizzie Borden: A Case Book of Family and Crime in the 1890s*. Bloomington, IN: T. I. S. Publications Division, 1980.

Wilson, Colin. "Lizzie Borden, the New Solution." In *The Mammoth Book of True Crime*. New York: Robinson Publishing Company & Graf Publishers, 1990, 310–20.

Index

About the Author

Cara Robertson began researching the Borden case in 1990 and has been captivated ever since. She holds a BA from Harvard, a PhD in English from Oxford, and a JD from Stanford Law School. She clerked at the Supreme Court of the United States, served as a legal adviser to the International Criminal Tribunal for the former Yugoslavia in The Hague, and has written for various publications. Her scholarship has been supported by the National Endowment for the Humanities and the National Humanities Center, of which she is a Trustee. *The Trial of Lizzie Borden* is her first book.